Sat Chit Anand

Truth Consciousness Bliss

Extemporaneous talks given by Osho at OSHO International Meditation Resort, Pune, India

OSHO

Sat Chit Anand

Truth Consciousness Bliss

MACMILLAN

First published in the Indian subcontinent 2015 by Macmillan
This updated edition published 2024 by Macmillan
an imprint of Pan Macmillan Publishing India Private Limited
707 Kailash Building
26 K. G. Marg, New Delhi 110001
www.panmacmillan.co.in

Pan Macmillan, The Smithson, 6 Briset Street, Farringdon, London EC1M 5NR
Associated companies throughout the world
www.panmacmillan.com

ISBN 978-93-82616-56-6

The material in this book is a transcript of a series of original OSHO Talks, Satyam Shivam Sundaram, given to a live audience. All of Osho's talks have been published in full as books, and are also available as original audio recordings. Audio recordings and the complete text archive can be found via the online OSHO Library at www.osho.com/library

1 3 5 7 9 8 6 4 2

Typeset in Adobe Garamond Pro by R. Ajith Kumar, New Delhi
Printed and bound in India by Gopsons Papers Pvt. Ltd., Noida

Contents

A Note about Language

Spoken Words: Osho's books are not "written" but rather are transcribed from recordings of his talks. These talks are extemporaneous, without reference to notes other than copies of questions, stories or scriptures he has been asked to comment upon, or jokes he might use to drive home a particular point. He has asked his editors to preserve that quality of the spoken word in his printed books.

Pronouns: When hearing him speak, it is quite clear to the listener that generally when Osho talks about "man" he is referring to "human beings." His use of "he" as a default pronoun simply serves an ease and flow of speaking – in no way does it imply that "she" (or "they") is being dismissed or disregarded.

Osho's unique vantage point is good to keep in mind:

A meditator is neither a man nor a woman,
because meditation has nothing to do with your body;
neither does it have anything to do with your mind.
In meditation you are simply and purely consciousness.
And consciousness is neither male nor female.

– Osho

A Note about Languages

1

Everybody Can Be a Mystic

Osho,
Is there any definition of the ultimate experience other than satyam shivam sundaram: truth, godliness, beauty?

The experience of the ultimate is always the same, but the expression can be different. The expression depends on the mystic; the experience does not depend on him.

The first definition I gave you is the definition by the poetic, aesthetic, sensitive individual for whom *satya* – truth – can come only as beauty; truth and beauty create the ultimate peak of godliness. The poet cannot imagine that beauty will not be a part of the ultimate unity. His eyes are receptive to beauty. In his expression, truth comes to him and is transformed as beauty. Beauty is the god of the poet, of the painter, of all creative artists.

So the first definition was the definition from the artistic soul. Most of the mystics have been poets – not ordinary poets, concerned with the mundane, but poets of the sacred. This sensitivity of the poet is essential to arrive at the definition of the ultimate experience as truth, godliness, and beauty.

But there are also other mystics, who are not poetic because to be a poet takes a certain talent. Everybody can be a mystic – the mystic is our very being, the unfolding of the mystic rose within us – but not everybody can be a poet. Poetry is a talent, though it comes very close to mysticism. So either the poet becomes the mystic – then comes the definition *satyam shivam sundaram* – or the mystic suddenly finds himself filled with tremendous beauty and out of his spontaneity starts singing and dancing. He may not be linguistically right, but that is not his concern.

Meera, Kabir, Farid were not poets from the very beginning. They became poets when the experience happened. As they opened their hearts to the universe, perhaps a talent that was dormant in them suddenly became active; everything opened. An immense poetry started flowing through them, a poetry no poet can write, because the poems are not compositions but their heartbeats, their very life.

There are other people who have attained the ultimate, for example, Gautam Buddha or Socrates or Pythagoras or Lao Tzu. They were not poets. They didn't have the talent of being a poet, either at the beginning or at the end of their experience. Their definition is bound to be different. The experience, remember, is always the same, but the expression will depend on the individual.

The second most important definition, which is in the same category as *satyam shivam sundaram*, is *sat-chit-anand. Sat* means truth; *chit* means consciousness; *anand* means bliss. Certainly, in any definition, truth is going to be the essential part that cannot be dropped. It is the experience of ultimate truth. In the second definition – just as in the first definition – *sat* remains the most prominent. But two new things have come in: consciousness and blissfulness.

Although the first definition is beautiful – tremendously beautiful – it will not be many people's experience because the talent to be a poet is rare. The second definition is going to be the experience of many more.

Meditation brings you to the final peak of consciousness – that is *chit*, exactly in the middle. On one side is truth; on the other side is bliss. As meditation flowers, you will find that on the one hand truth has revealed to you all its mysteries and on the other that blissfulness is showering all its treasures on you. It is as significant a definition as the first, but you can see the difference: there is no place for *sundaram*, beauty. The person has no sensitivity toward beauty, but the person is absolutely alert and conscious of great blissfulness overflowing in him and a feeling, an indubitable feeling, that he has arrived home. That is his truth.

In Sanskrit, unlike other languages, words can be joined together. Sanskrit has an approach, and perhaps this approach has come from the enlightened ones. So many people have become enlightened in this country and they have left their impact on Sanskrit, on the language. They will not say *sat-chit-anand* the way I have explained it to you. I have cut one word into three, just to explain it to you, because in English there cannot be one word for all three. You cannot join truth, consciousness, blissfulness into a single word. The Sanskrit word is *sachchidanand*. All three words are joined together. *Sat* is there, *chit* is there, *anand* is there, but they are not separate and there is no gap: *sachchidanand*.

It is significant to remember that the experience is one orgasmic, organic, unitary experience. It does not come in parts as *sat*, as *chit*, as *anand*. It comes into existence in totality, and that totality is *sachchidanand*. To denote, to emphasize, the unity – neither *sat* can exist without *chit*, nor can *chit* exist without *anand* – they have used a joined word: *sachchidanand*. It is not only a question of language. Deep down it is an experience that they all come together. In fact there is no way to create demarcations: this is truth, this is consciousness, this is bliss. Suddenly they are all within you. In other words, truth is consciousness and bliss; or vice versa, bliss is consciousness and truth.

The division I made was just to make you understand. Now I want you to be aware that in the experience itself there is no division. It has the fragrance of blissfulness, it has the light of consciousness, it has the revelation of truth – all simultaneously and together.

They are not steps to each other. It is not possible to drop one of them and experience the other two; they are an intrinsic unity, an organic unity.

This is also a very beautiful definition, and is applicable to more mystics than the first definition. Gautam Buddha would never have defined the ultimate experience in terms of beauty. Beauty somehow carries a sense of our ordinary life. You may say it is a much higher beauty but still something of the ordinary remains. The moment you say 'beauty,' you come down to the body, you come down to the flowers, you come down to the sunset. The beauty the mystics are talking about is not the beauty of these small experiences but the beauty of the whole – a beauty of which we have no idea, of which we have not even dreamed.

The second definition I am giving to you today is absolutely a unity. Nothing of it connects with our unconsciousness and its world – neither truth, nor consciousness, nor bliss. In a way, it is purer; in a way, it simply makes it clear that you have gone beyond the mundane and entered the sacred. The whole vision has changed, not even a trace of the mundane is left. It can be said to be a more authentic definition than the first, and more mystics have defined their experience with the second definition.

Naturally, most probably, if you ever experience the ultimate, you will come to the second definition. Very few of you may experience beauty as that is a minority definition. But I respect minorities, so I took it first.

This is the majority definition: more logical, more perfect, but less sensitive, less human. The first was more human – at least there was a connecting link between our ordinary world and the extraordinary experience. In this definition, all bridges are broken. You are no longer part of the ordinary. You have simply transported your consciousness to the extraordinary which is not visible to the eyes, which is not tangible: you cannot hear it, you cannot see it, you cannot taste it.

But in the first definition, the word *sundaram*, beauty, gives a sense that your eyes are capable of seeing it; perhaps your hands can feel it, perhaps your ears can hear the beautiful music in it. The word *beauty* functions almost as a bridge. In the second definition there is no bridge but a quantum leap. You simply jump from mind to no-mind. Only no-mind can be aware of truth; only no-mind can be filled with consciousness; only no-mind can be showered with thousands of flowers of bliss. Nothing relates to your ordinary world, so in this way it is purer.

Both have their pros and cons, and I want you to be aware of them. But remember: don't choose the definition. First choose the experience, then the definition will come on its own accord. If you choose the definition first, it may not fit your individuality and the definition itself may become a hindrance.

Go deeper into meditation. Experience is the thing that matters. Then how you express it is dependent on you. Most probably you will define it as *sat-chit-anand*: truth, consciousness, bliss. It is more universal; very few people are poets.

I am reminded of Rabindranath Tagore. He absolutely insisted that there is only one definition of the ultimate experience, and that is *satyam shivam sundaram*. He could not conceive of the ultimate experience not having beauty in it. He could drop anything but beauty. His poetic soul was even ready to say that you can drop truth, you can drop godliness, but please save beauty.

It happened that Mahatma Gandhi wanted the temples of Khajuraho ... These are some of the most beautiful creations of man; there is nothing comparable on the whole earth. The temples of Puri and Konark, which are similar, have not achieved the perfection of Khajuraho. There must have been at least one hundred temples, very big temples, and you cannot find even a single inch which has not been carved, which has not been made beautiful. Naked men and women in different postures of love...

Naturally Gandhi was very much annoyed, and at first he wanted to demolish those temples. Seventy temples had already been demolished by the Mohammedans because Mohammedans have a fanatical attitude that God cannot be represented in a statue, a picture, or anything. This is perfectly okay if it is your idea, but to interfere with somebody else's idea is idiotic. Somebody wants to represent his god in a statue – who are you to interfere? But every religion thinks it is responsible for the whole of humanity and wants to impose its idea on every human being. So when the Mohammedans came they could not believe it; they destroyed seventy temples of tremendous value.

But thirty of the temples were hidden in a thick forest, so they were saved. Gandhi wanted to do the same as those Mohammedans had done. He wanted to demolish them, but for a different reason. He was afraid that the temples would show the whole world that the Indians are not very moral people, that they are not puritans.

What kind of temples are these, in which each temple has thousands of couples carved in stone? Full-sized men and women, so beautiful that once you have seen a Khajuraho temple woman, a statue, no woman will look beautiful to you. Every woman will seem just a faded memory of something real. Those stones are so real...

I used to go to Khajuraho. It was very close to my university, just a hundred miles away, so whenever I had time I would drive there. The guide, who finally became a sannyasin, was himself ashamed to show them to people, but I told him, 'You don't understand. You need not be ashamed. These pictures, these statues, these sculptures are not obscene. There is not a single hint of obscenity, even though they are absolutely naked, in loving embraces, making love. There is not a hint of obscenity, unless your mind is full of obscenity.'

A European prime minister was going to visit Khajuraho. One of my friends was the education minister of the state in which Khajuraho lies. The prime minister of India told the education minister, 'I am busy and cannot come; otherwise I would have come with the guest to show him Khajuraho. So it is your responsibility to take him there because you are the most educated minister in your state.'

My friend phoned me and said, 'I am very much ashamed of Khajuraho; it is such an embarrassing place. And when outsiders who have only seen churches in the name of religion come, they cannot believe that this is a temple, a holy place. And I myself feel guilty, so I cannot explain, and I don't know what to explain.'

I said, 'I will come.' I went there with the guest and the education minister who was shrinking inside. You cannot conceive of any possible loving posture that is not carved there, in such beauty, such tremendous beauty, that it is almost as if the stones have come alive. It seems as though the woman is going to come out of the wall on which the statue is carved. So alive...

The education minister remained outside and I took the guest in. He was amazed at the beauty, that bodies can be made so beautifully in stone, can give such life to the stone, such warmth. He had not known that such a thing exists anywhere in the world. I explained to him, 'These are on the outer side of the temple, but you should be aware that inside the temple there are no sculptures, no statues; there's just absolute silence.' He said, 'This is a revelation, this is strange. Statues should be inside the temple. Why are they outside, and inside there is nothing, just silence?'

I said to him, 'These temples were made some three thousand years ago by the greatest psychologists that have appeared on the earth.'

They were called Tantrikas; their whole approach was called Tantra. The very word *tantra* means expanding consciousness. They made these beautiful temples all around the country. Mohammedans destroyed them; it was just fortunate that these were in a thick forest, hidden. Only meditators used to go there; there is no village surrounding the temples. By a fortunate coincidence they were saved.

I told him, 'The secret is, Tantra believes that unless you have gone through all sexual experiences to the point where sex does not matter to you at all ... That is a transcendence of your energy.

At that point, you are capable of entering the inner sanctum of the temple. You are ready for the nothingness of Gautam Buddha; you are ready for pure silence.' Meditators used to meditate for months on those statues. It is a great strategy, because looking at all those statues, a moment comes when something in your unconscious disappears. Not just looking – at one time it was months, sometimes years, of training. But they were not allowed inside the temple until they became uninterested in these sexual scriptures. When their master saw that somebody had become completely uninterested – even when sitting in front of the most beautiful woman he was sitting with closed eyes – then he was allowed to enter the temple. Now, those sexual thoughts are the major thoughts in your mind.

Every three minutes the ordinary man thinks about sex at least once, and every five minutes every woman thinks at least once about sex. These are the very subtle mistakes which God made when he created the world; that's why I say there is no God, to relieve him of all this responsibility. This is a disparity which is dangerous!

When we came out, the prime minister was very much impressed. The education minister was waiting outside. Although he had not been inside, he was still feeling embarrassed. Just to hide his embarrassment, he told the guest, 'Don't take much note of it. It was a small current of thinkers who created these temples, and we are ashamed – they are so obscene.'

The guest said, 'Obscene? Then I will have to go back and take another look; I did not find anything obscene.'

Those naked statues look so innocent, so childlike; they are not there to provoke your sexuality. Obscenity is a very subtle phenomenon, it's very difficult to make the distinction whether something is obscene or not. But this should be the criterion – I think this is the only criterion: obscenity is when it provokes sexuality in you and if it does not provoke sexuality but just a sense of tremendous splendor and beauty, it is not obscene. However, it will depend on individuals. The same statue may look to someone obscene, and to someone else a beautiful piece of art.

I told the education minister, 'Your mind is full of obscenity. This guest from the outside is far clearer. He did not raise a single question about the obscenity of the temple.'

Mahatma Gandhi's mind was full of sex his whole life. When India became free, he thought that now was his chance: either dismantle the temples, destroy them, or at least do what he had been insisting on from the 1930's: if you don't want them destroyed, cover them with huge hills of mud – the temples are very high. Then they would remain there, and if, once in a while, you want to show them to some special guest from the outside, you can remove the mud, clean the place, and then put the mud back again.

It was Rabindranath Tagore who opposed Mahatma Gandhi's proposal, saying, 'It is sheer stupidity. I have seen those temples; they have inspired me to great heights. Under their inspiration I have written such beautiful poems. And they are the greatest heritage of one of the most significant schools of psychologists, who penetrated into human psychology and life energy so deeply that they found a way, a device, to transform it and make men free of sexuality.' Because Rabindranath resisted, Gandhi could not cover them with mud.

It was Rabindranath who insisted that the only definition that is exactly right is 'truth, godliness, beauty.' If something has to be dropped from the definition, you can drop truth, you can drop godliness, but you cannot drop beauty.

Beauty is the sky for the poet, for the painter, for the musician – how is it possible for the ultimate truth to be ugly? It has to be the most beautiful experience. But the definition will be applicable to only very few people. The second definition will apply to a vast majority of people.

There is one more difference that has to be remembered: the first definition is outgoing. Truth is at the center of being, then godliness surrounds it, and then there's another circle of beauty. But that beauty is not beyond the beauty of the trees and the flowers and human faces; everything that is beautiful in the world is a link to the ultimate.

Rabindranath was the first man in history who said beauty is truth. Nobody has ever said that. There have been people who said truth is beauty, but nobody who has dared to say that beauty is truth, putting beauty on the highest peak. That will be possible only for those who can feel the sensitivity of the beautiful. It is not for everyone. The second definition is not so outgoing – it does not go out at all. Truth, consciousness, bliss – all are inside you. None of these three experiences takes you out.

In psychological terminology, the first definition can be said to be of the outgoing consciousness, expanding consciousness – just as when you throw a pebble into a silent lake, and ripples start moving toward the farther shore. The first definition is expanding, outgoing. Psychologists have a special word for it – they call it *extrovert*. And certainly the poet is an extrovert because he sees the beauty of the trees and the beauty of the stars and the beauty of the birds singing. He is an extrovert. The second definition is *introvert*. It concentrates on your very being. It is enough, there is no need to go out: truth, consciousness, blissfulness.

In still other words, it can be said that the first definition is that of the bodhisattvas and the second definition is of the arhats. I have explained to you these two kinds of enlightened people. The arhats simply become pillars of silence, joy, truth, but they never share it. They never bother to initiate anyone, they never guide anyone. The bodhisattvas, the moment they have attained, start spreading like ripples all around to the farther shores of humanity. They want to reach everyone.

Your individuality already contains an inbuilt program for whether you will turn into a bodhisattva or into an arhat. Nothing can be done about it; you cannot change it, you cannot decide it. You will have to pass beyond the mind, and only then will you realize who you are: a bodhisattva or an arhat.

Sat-chit-anand is absolutely inner, introvert – your interior subjectivity. It has nothing to do with anyone else. It is another thing if somebody gets attracted to you, it is another thing if many are magnetically pulled toward you, but the arhat himself does not make a single move to transform anybody or to give him a hand to pull him out of his ditch. If somebody is interested, he can come, but the arhat does not take on the responsibility of being somebody's master. If you insist, he will say something to you, but as telegraphically as possible.

The bodhisattva functions totally differently: sharing is his joy and he wants this world to become more beautiful. He wants to contribute to the world in some way, so that when he leaves the world, he leaves it a little more beautiful than the world he had come into seventy or eighty years before. The arhat is simply not concerned with anyone. He is just a pillar of consciousness. If somebody can learn something from his lifestyle, that's another thing. He is not a master; he is only a mystic.

This second definition has to sink deep in you because, finally, most of you will find this definition. Remember this beautiful word: *sachchidanand.*

> Osho,
> Is it true that you make things happen to us according to our needs in this very moment, or does your aura cause us to choose the happenings ourselves? My mother is suffering from cancer and multiple sclerosis, and has been feeling strong healing energy in the last weeks. She thought you had been sending it. How do you manage to arrange all these learning situations and send all the necessary energy to your sannyasins all over the world?

There are a few things I would like put on record. First, I never do anything. Second, if you want, all my energies are available to you, but that is your doing. Third, it is possible if you are in deep trust and love with me to unconsciously become a transmitter to your mother of a healing energy.

But please don't make me responsible for anything. This responsibility is very dangerous – it is walking on a razor's edge. Today you find your mother is healing, and you praise me and love me and trust me. But no mother can live forever. The day she dies, your whole love, your trust in me, will simply disappear because I allowed your mother to die, because I did not give her the healing energy. That's why, from the very beginning, I want my hands to be completely clean.

I don't accept praise because I know that behind every praise there is the possibility of condemnation. All over the world I am already so condemned, at least leave a few people who don't condemn me! But you may not be aware that this is how things go wrong. People start expecting, and if by some coincidence their expectations are fulfilled, they are immensely grateful. But it is only a coincidence. If they are not fulfilled, then I am 'the god who failed.' They make me a god, only to declare later that I am the god who failed. I am simply enjoying my energy. It is overflowing and enough for anybody who wants to share it. But the whole doing is theirs.

So remember: it is *your* trust, it is *your* love, it is *your* devotion that may become a transmitting medium to your mother. Because you love me and trust me, because you love your mother and want her to be healed, it is possible for a subtle energy to reach her. But you are the doer – that is my emphasis. I am not the doer.

What you are saying is beautiful, and it will be difficult for anyone other than me to reject it. Just go to any so-called guru – India is so full of them – and if you say such a thing, he will reply, 'That's perfectly right. I am taking care of the whole world.' But as far as I am concerned, I cannot even take care of myself! I am certainly a lazy guy. I will not take such trouble to reach your mother. Otherwise it will become difficult for my sannyasins to die. And just as a symbol, I have made *samadhis* for the sannyasins who have died. So remember, I am not going to protect you.

When death comes, it is perfectly good. Let it come. I may even help death rather than you, because death will relieve you of all pain, all stupidities, all diseases and particularly the fear of death. Once you are dead, you are no longer afraid – even of death – and you will rest in your grave for eternity. So why should I prevent you? But if you go and say these things to somebody else, he will be immensely happy. These are the people who go on creating wrong concepts in people's minds.

My thing is very clear: I am available. If you trust me, you can draw as much energy as you want. If you don't trust me, you have closed the doors yourself. But it is always your doing, it is never my doing. I cannot take the credit for it; the credit goes to you. You must be in deep love with your mother and because you are in deep trust with me, you can become a medium for a healing energy to reach to your mother.

As far as I am concerned, my whole teaching is doing without doing, action in inaction. But this kind of misunderstanding happens.

Two cannibals, a father and son, are walking through the jungle checking their mantraps when they find a beautiful white girl who is in distress. The son, an impulsive boy, exclaims, 'Look, Dad! A white girl. Let us eat her right now.'

His father, who has had more experience in the world and has been to the mission school, pauses thoughtfully and says, 'No, son, let us take her home and eat your mother.'

Different people take different approaches...

When an Englishman does not get on with his wife, he goes to the pub; a Frenchman goes to his mistress, a Greek goes to sea, a German goes to war, an Australian goes to a cricket match, an Indian goes to the Himalayas, an American goes to his lawyer and a Japanese goes and commits hara-kiri.

Just different people, different understandings. But here with me ... This one is for all of you.

Rubin Moskowitz went to one of the best restaurants in New York and treated himself to a huge meal with all the trimmings, finishing up with a Havana cigar.

Finally, the waiter brought the bill on a silver tray. It came to ninety-nine dollars and ninety-nine cents, so Rubin paid with a hundred dollar bill.

About five minutes later, he called the waiter back and asked for his change. Without altering his expression, the waiter left but returned a moment later with his silver tray. On it sat a penny and a packet of condoms.

Rubin was shocked and demanded an explanation. The waiter lifted his nose in the air and said, 'Sir, it is the policy of our restaurant to encourage customers like you not to reproduce.'

2

Gratitude Is the Only Prayer

Osho,

Can one really miss you? When love and this incredible pull are there, can one really go astray?

Prem Anugraho, it seems almost impossible to miss the goal when you are just one foot away, but even then people have missed. How far away was Judas from Jesus? He was his most cultured, educated and sophisticated disciple. In fact, among all the others, he was the only one who was educated – and he was really close. But life always remains unknown; it is not something like mathematics or logic where you can come to a conclusion.

Just because he was so close, he missed. It is very illogical, but if you go deep down, you can understand the psychology of it. Because he was very close, he was hoping – perhaps unknowingly – that he would be Jesus' successor. I am not saying he was intentionally trying to be the successor. In fact, it was obvious that there was nobody else except Judas to succeed Jesus.

In every way, he was qualified; in every way, Jesus showered his love and his blessings on him, but the day Jesus said 'Nobody is going to be my successor. I have not come here to create a dynasty. My kingdom is of the other world – the Kingdom of God,' that distance of just one foot became a distance of thousands of miles. That same night, Judas betrayed Jesus. He sold him to the enemies for only thirty pieces of silver. Of course, it was done in a very emotional, hasty way – again unconsciously.

This is the trouble with man; his actions are not conscious. Hence you cannot condemn him. Like a blind man, he is groping in darkness, not knowing where he is going and why he is going. He becomes a little alert when it is too late, when he has acted. Then there is no way to undo it.

When Judas sold Jesus for thirty pieces of silver, he was not aware of what exactly he was doing and what it was going to lead to. On the day Jesus was crucified, Judas was in the crowd with tears in his eyes and he threw away those thirty pieces of silver. He didn't think that this was going to be the consequence of an act done in anger, rage, frustration – he was not thinking that it would mean crucifixion. Twenty-four hours after Jesus' crucifixion he hanged himself in a tree, committed suicide.

Christians don't talk about Judas much, but his psychology should be understood more clearly as he is not alone. It happens almost always, with every great master. Strangely enough, those who were very close have gone far away; those who were far away – had never thought, dreamed, of being very close – came close.

There is a very subtle psychological background to it. Gautam Buddha was betrayed by one of his cousin-brothers; Mahavira was betrayed by his son-in-law. In both cases the situation was the same as with Judas: because they were so close, they naturally hoped – without being conscious of it – that they were going to be successors.

Now, nobody can be a successor in enlightenment. It is not a worldly treasure, you cannot inherit it. You cannot become enlightened just because your father was enlightened. You cannot become enlightened just because you are very close to somebody who is enlightened. The distance of one foot or the distance of one mile or the distance of one light-year makes no difference – distance is distance.

I insist on this so that you will not miss. I understand your love, your gratitude, your deep commitment. You are asking, 'Can one really miss you?' It should not be so. One should not miss; there is no reason for it. But man is so unconscious that he does not function reasonably. He functions irrationally. He functions without any understanding of his own actions, intentions, hidden desires, ambitions.

You are saying, 'When love and this incredible pull are there, can one really go astray?' One should not go astray if one is conscious, but the possibility cannot be denied. You have to forgive me, the possibility cannot be denied. The closer you come to a master, the more you are lost, the more you are dissolved. In the fear of dissolution, the fear of your personality being lost, you may start backing off.

You have to understand that this fear is there. Even the moth that is magnetically attracted toward a flame does not go directly into the flame. I have been watching moths – strangely enough, they never go directly into the flame. They first go round and round, perhaps hesitating, perhaps having another thought, perhaps taking time – a little more time – before they take the jump. The jump into the flame is going to be their death on one plane, and the other plane on which they will be reborn is not yet there – it is not guaranteed.

Only your trust is the guarantee, your love is the guarantee. Other than that, you don't have any solid foundation. You are gambling by taking a jump. And the ultimate is available only to the gamblers, not to the businessmen who are continuously counting pros and cons, whether this will be profitable or this will be a loss. These people will go on counting for millions of lives. They may come across a Gautam Buddha, a Jesus or a Socrates, but seventy or eighty years are not enough for them to come to a conclusion.

Only a gambler, in a single moment, can take the jump. I hope you will be able to take the jump. Nobody can prevent you except yourself. You have asked a very significant question, a question that implies the very quantum leap of the disciple to the devotee, the quantum leap from personality to individuality, from a dewdrop to the ocean.

Have you ever seen a lotus flower with its leaves just above the water? In the night, dewdrops gather on the leaves. They look so beautiful in the early morning sun, far more beautiful than any pearls, far more alive, far more radiant. But slowly they slip from the leaves, finally dropping into the ocean. A dewdrop slipping from a lotus leaf is the situation of a disciple. So close to the ocean and yet – because of the closeness itself – a tremendous fear arises: to pull oneself back.

You are saying, 'And this incredible pull...' Just because of this incredible pull, one can start resisting, because you don't understand all the subtle workings of your mind. Nature, as it is, has to be understood if you want to transcend it.

In all the medical '-pathies' developed around the world – homeopathy or ayurveda or acupuncture – except allopathy, nobody has exactly understood the inner function of nature in man's body and mind. I say except allopathy because others may be helpful, not in a small way either – if you look at their help, it is tremendous – but they are not scientific.

In almost seventy percent of cases, ayurveda will be successful, acupuncture may be successful, homeopathy may be successful, naturopathy may be successful. But remember the seventy percent – it is no more than that because seventy percent of diseases are false. They are just in your mind, they don't really exist. That's why you don't need real medicine; any hocus-pocus will do. And seventy percent is not a small percentage so I would not like these '-pathies' to disappear from the world. I want them to be recognized, because seventy percent is big. Strangely enough, those seventy percent of the cases are the most difficult as far as allopathy is concerned.

Allopathy finds itself in difficulty: how to deal with a person who has no disease but believes he has? Allopathy has no way of helping such a person – only thirty percent remain to be helped by allopathy. It is a strange world. Thirty percent are helped by the most scientific approach and seventy percent by all kinds of hocus-pocus – superstitious approaches which really don't make any change, but they help. The most scientific approach of allopathy is based on a deep understanding of nature: the body has a resistance of its own. Because of this fact, naturopathy condemns allopathy.

Allopathy goes on injecting viruses into patients because the allopathic understanding is that the moment the body gets a virus, it immediately creates antibodies. It immediately starts fighting, it has a resistance of its own. The whole body immediately goes on red alert to destroy the disease. Naturopathy condemns it because it thinks people are being poisoned with diseases. You are supposed to take out diseases and you are, on the contrary, putting poisonous viruses into people's bodies. Naturopathy cleans people's bodies by fasting, by strange methods that you cannot believe. But they can help only those people who are not suffering from any real disease.

It is the same situation with the mind. A scientific approach to the mind will make it clear. The closer you come to the master, in deep love, in an incredible pull, your biological mind – which is thousands of years old – immediately creates an anti-pull as a protection, as a defense. You are moving toward danger: because of the danger of the death of your personality, the mind immediately pulls back.

You always keep a little distance to people you love, but you can come very close to the person you don't love because there is no fear, no question of merging or melting. You can come close to your enemy without any problem. You are not going to melt into him, so you can rub shoulders with your enemy without any fear. But with a friend, the mind always keeps a little distance. Coming too close is risky; you may not be able to come back to your old personality again – the risk is real.

You ask me, 'With this incredible pull, can one really go astray?' It's just *because* of this incredible pull that you may go astray. Just to avoid it, you may take a different route. So if you are clear about it, missing can be avoided. As far as I know, neither Jesus nor Mahavira nor Gautam Buddha ever told their disciples that it is possible to miss. They all took for granted that those who had come to them had simply come to them. But I see deeper into the nature of man, and their disciples prove what I am proposing.

Jesus never thought, even dreamed, that Judas would sell him for thirty silver pieces. He loved the man so much and Judas loved him so much – it seemed almost impossible. That's why after twenty-four hours Judas felt so repentant that the only way he saw to get out of this guilt was to commit suicide. To go on living with this guilt was more difficult than committing suicide. He also could not believe it. He loved Jesus so much. How could he have done such a thing?

The whole psychology of man has not been explored and because it has not been fully explored, there are corners – dark corners – that you go on forgetting. You simply remain attentive to the lighted spots of love and trust, but you forget completely that there are nooks and corners in your being where there is no light, no love, no trust. They are also part of you; in a strange way they are more powerful than your love and your trust.

On what grounds can I say that? I say it on a very fundamental ground – your love is spent, your trust is spent, but your dark spots are unspent. Their whole energy is gathering. They are the antibodies against your love, against your trust. They are your doubts, they are your distrust, they are your hate – and they are accumulating.

You go on sharing your love, you go on sharing your trust. What about your hate, what about your distrust, what about your doubt? These go on accumulating. Naturally, these phenomena are the phenomena of darkness. So they hide in dark corners in your being, just waiting for the chance when they can take revenge with full vengeance.

Any moment, when you start wavering a little, hesitating a little – to go one step more or wait – those forces which are repressed in you immediately take possession of you. And they are so powerful that they can pull you away from the source that was going to be a rebirth to you. They can pull you away from your love, from your trust, from your commitment. They can pull you away from the ultimate revolution that was going to happen within you.

But if you are aware, alert, watchful, not allowing any dark corners inside you, making every nook and corner of your mind full of light, then of course it is impossible to miss, impossible to go astray.

Anugraho, your very name means gratitude, and to me gratitude is the only prayer. But small words like gratitude contain so much that you should go deeper into them, so that you can become aware of the whole territory. Your gratitude should not remain a small lighted spot in your being; it should become your whole being. Only then are you absolutely safe from going astray, from missing the message, from missing the master.

Remember, I am not a missionary. I am not trying to convince you of any ideological, intellectual or philosophical theories. That is very simple. It is necessary for you to understand that not a single philosopher was betrayed by his students. I have been wondering about that: what happened? Jesus was betrayed, Mahavira was betrayed, Buddha was betrayed – what happened to the great philosophers like Aristotle, Hegel, Kant? They had thousands of students. But nobody betrayed them because they were only students, far away. They never came close because they didn't even become disciples, what to say about devotees? They never came so close, where the distance is almost negligible, nonexistential. That is the reason why they were not betrayed.

Their whole philosophical teaching was just intellectual. They were giving you arguments in support of their system of thought – and they were great intellectuals. At the most you could argue with them, but you could not win. The students who were at the side of Plato or Aristotle or Hegel or Kant were not great intellectuals. They could raise questions, they could argue a little bit, but those philosophers were tremendously logical and they had worked out their systems in such minute detail that it was impossible to win an argument with them. Every argument meant that finally the students would be even more convinced.

But it was just a communication from one head to another head. There was no question of coming close to the heart; there was no question of love or trust. I am not trying to convince you of any ideology, I am trying to impart to you a new being, a new transformation. It is more than mind can do; it is much more than words can express. It is something that goes on happening without words, without mind.

Slowly, slowly, the more you start feeling my presence, the more you become accustomed to my silences of the heart, the closer you will move. The final stop will be when you have come too close. Just for a moment you will have to think whether to go one step more or a few steps backward or move away – it is too dangerous. The moth has come very close to the flame – any closer and death is certain.

The ancient seers of the East describe the master as death: a strange definition! When I first came across it ... Death? But slowly, slowly it became clear. To me they were right, yet their definition is only half. I say, the master is death *and* resurrection. Just to stop at death is very dangerous. It will give a totally different idea to the disciple, making him even more afraid. He has to be assured of a resurrection.

That is not possible only with intellectual argumentation, but by opening your heart to the disciple, inviting him within. By and by his fear will disappear. He will start feeling a new energy arising in him, a new life and a new way of seeing things, a new approach to looking at the world. And everything becomes so psychedelically beautiful, so colorful, so blissful. Then he does not care, he knows he is on the right path.

It is not a conviction, but a realization that one is on the right path. Each moment the silence is becoming deeper, each moment the joy is becoming wider, greater. Each moment new flowers are continuously blossoming, new fragrances are surrounding you. Each moment you are coming to something tremendously valuable. But you cannot figure it out unless you have entered it.

A missionary is an ugly phenomenon. I am absolutely against anybody being a missionary. He neither knows anything, nor can he help anybody toward knowing or toward being. A master is a totally different thing. A missionary can be prepared in a school, in a college. There are colleges around the world where missionaries are prepared.

Just a few days ago I was telling you about a Catholic missionary college where a professor asked a student, 'When you have become a missionary, how are you going to deliver your sermons in the church?

'For instance,' he said, 'when you are talking about heaven, let your face show a radiance, let your eyes light up, let your whole being, your body, indicate that you are thrilled.'

The student asked, 'That's okay, but what about when we are talking about hell?'

The professor said, 'For hell, your normal face will do. You don't have to make any effort.'

A Catholic is trying to convert a Jew. He is really taking on a very difficult job. I am the only person who is deeply conversant with the Jews. Half my sannyasins are Jews. It has never happened before and it will never happen again; Jews are difficult people.

A Catholic trying to convert a Jew tells him that if he becomes a Catholic his prayers will certainly be answered, because the priest will give them to the bishop, who will give them to the cardinal, who will give them to the pope, who will shove them up into heaven through a hole in the Vatican roof – which just matches a hole in the floor of heaven – where St. Peter will take them to the Virgin Mary, who will speak on their behalf with Jesus, who will put in a good word for them with God.

The whole channel of all the right people!

The Jew repeats this whole story with an astonished air, ending with, 'You know, I guess it must be true, because I have always wondered what they do with all the shit in heaven. They must throw it down through that little hole in the Vatican roof, where the pope gives it to the cardinal, who gives it to the bishop, who gives it to the priest, who gives it to you – and now you are trying to give it to me!'

Converting anybody just with words is an absurd activity. It is not conversion, it is just salesmanship. Authentic conversion comes by experience, but experience is only possible if you allow yourself to become vulnerable, receptive, to someone who has arrived. Perhaps it was possible with Jesus, but it is not possible with the pope.

Just look at his picture! Can you think this man can radiate anything that will thrill your heart? And he is God's representative, he is the infallible representative of God. Look at his face! He is just a stupid Polack; everybody knows it. You cannot make a Polack infallible simply by choosing him as pope; that goes against all the laws of existence.

But if it happens in your life that you come close to a man who is at home, who has arrived, then don't be worried about taking any risk. Every risk is a great opportunity to have a taste of the infinite, to become one with the eternal mystery of existence. Hence I say again: there is no need to miss, but people are unconscious and go on missing. There is no need to go astray, but people are not alert, so it is very difficult to prevent them from going astray.

When somebody turns back, goes away, the master can only look on helplessly with tears in his eyes, because the master cannot interfere in your independence, in your freedom. Even if it is the freedom of going astray, the freedom of going away, he will allow it. He respects you and loves you and he cannot enforce anything on you.

Osho,
What is the difference between the master seeing the disciple and the disciple seeing the master?

The master sees you not only as you are, but also as what you can become. In your seeds, he sees the spring and the flowers. When you see the master, it will depend from what distance you are seeing. If you are just a student, you will see his beautiful words, arguments, ideology. If you are seeing him as a disciple, you will see him much more in his silences than in his words, much more in his presence than in his presentation, much more in his eyes than in the ideas and the philosophies he is talking about, much more in his gestures, in his grace. But if you are looking at him from the space of a devotee, then you will see only a mirror in which your ultimate being is reflected.

As far as you are concerned, what you see will depend on where you are, where you are standing, at what distance. As far as the master is concerned, whatever your distance, he sees only two things: what you are right now and your potential, which can explode any moment. In your bud he will see the open flower, with the fragrance released.

But there are many who are not even students, who are just spectators or curiosity-mongers – in them the master sees nothing. They are so far away in darkness that it is impossible to see who they are and what they can become. Their distance is too great and they are surrounded with such darkness. Nor will they be able to see anything in the master. Perhaps a faraway echo of his words, but nothing more.

Hymie Goldberg entered the synagogue and began to pray, 'Dear God, please let me win the lottery.'

Then he left the synagogue and went home. Nothing happened that day so he returned to the synagogue the next day.

'Please, God,' beseeched Hymie, 'please, won't you let me win the lottery?'

He went home and again there were no results, so he went back to the synagogue the following morning.

'Almighty God,' Hymie wailed, 'I beg of you, let me win the lottery!' Suddenly, he heard God's reply, 'Hymie, meet me at least halfway,'

God thundered. 'Buy a lottery ticket!'

Even without a lottery ticket he wants to win the lottery, just by asking God! Obviously, it's only to such people that God has ever spoken. They irritate him so much that he forgets that he's not supposed to speak. Now this fellow will torture him every day, and he is not even purchasing a ticket.

With the master also you have to meet him at least halfway!

Osho,

According to you, what is the most hilarious thing in the world?

According to me the most hilarious thing in the world is man. Among all the animals, trees, mountains, rivers, oceans, stars, clouds, man is the only hilarious animal.

I will give you a few examples:

Hamish MacTavish became a sergeant with a Scottish Highland regiment. One day he walked into the pharmacy and deposited an old condom on the counter. 'How much for a repair job?' he asked.

'Well,' replied the chemist, 'with washing, drying, patching, lubricating and re-rolling it comes to thirty pence.'

'My God,' said MacTavish, 'how much for a new one?'

'Fifty pence,' replied the chemist.

Tucking the condom back in his kilt, MacTavish walked out saying, 'I will talk it over with the lads at the barracks and let you know our decision tomorrow.'

One day, Paddy, who worked in the local brewery, fell into a gigantic barrel of beer and drowned. When his wife was informed of the accident she asked if she could see the scene of the tragedy.

At the brewery, the foreman explained to her, 'He was climbing this ladder when he slipped and fell into the beer and drowned.'

'How terrible!' exclaimed Maureen. 'It must have been an agonizing death.'

'I would not say exactly agonizing,' replied the foreman. 'He managed to get out twice to go to the bathroom!'

An American, an Englishman and a Frenchman are discussing a good example of savoir faire.

'Well,' said the American, 'if you came home and found your wife in bed with another man and you did not kill the son-of-a-bitch, that would be a good example of savoir faire.

'Nonsense, old chap,' says the Englishman, 'if you came home and found your wife in bed with another man and you said "Please carry on, sir," – that is savoir faire.'

'*Non, non*!' cries the Frenchman. 'If you came home and found your wife in bed with another man and you said "Please, sir, carry on," and the man was able to continue – *that* is savoir faire.'

Except man, nothing is hilarious in the world. Just look around you. There are so many examples, it is not that there are only a few. In fact every man – if he watches himself – will find himself behaving in a hilarious way in many situations. Or if you are alert enough and a witness, you will find so many people ... When there is so much hilariousness going on, you cannot believe why the world is so sad; it should be a continuous festival of laughter. That's what my concept of an authentic humanity is: it will be hilarious, enjoying every moment. It will not be serious, it will not be saintly. It will be utterly human and absolutely respectful of its humanity, its laughter, its dance, its song, everything that human beings are prone to.

Be more alert and watch and note down whenever you see something hilarious happening – and particularly in my place. Where do you think I get all these jokes? My people just go on watching each other and creating jokes and informing me. I never go out. But people are learning watchfulness, so they come across so many hilarious things in themselves and in others. They go on preparing jokes for me.

I'm never short of jokes because in my place, twenty-four hours a day, there is nothing else to do. It is a continuous carnival.

3

You Are a Pilgrim of the Unknowable

Osho,
Sitting in front of you, I feel something tremendous is happening to me which I don't understand at all. I feel so thankful, but I don't know why and for what. Tears are coming, but I cannot see any reason. I leave discourse with unsteady knees, as if I have done twenty-four hours' hard work. But what happened? Is it a matter of my undeveloped awareness that I don't grasp what is happening, or does my mind want an answer where there is no answer?

It is one of the perennial questions that you have asked. One day or another, every seeker on the path stumbles on the same question. It is the mind which wants to know everything, because the knowing mind becomes powerful through what it knows. It then becomes its own territory. But existence consists of three layers.

One is that of knowledge – that which is already known. Mind is perfectly at ease with it. The other is the territory of the unknown which, sooner or later, will become known. What is known today was unknown yesterday; what is unknown today is bound to be known tomorrow. Mind is uncomfortable with the unknown, but only a little. It knows that it is still beyond its territory, but it cannot remain beyond its territory much longer. The first territory belongs to all the religions of the world. That's why they are all past-oriented. They don't have any tomorrows, only yesterdays.

The second category belongs to the scientific world. It is perfectly at ease with the yesterdays because tomorrow is going to be based on yesterday, but its focus is on the unknown. That is the adventure of science: to go on conquering the unknown and making it known; in other words, to demystify the universe. That is the basic purpose of all scientific research. There should be no mystery in the world; everything should be known. Science is the mind's final growth, therefore it cannot go beyond mind. The very word *science* means knowledge. Hence science does not divide existence into three categories, but only into two: the known and the unknown.

Then there is a third category, which I call the unknowable. We are the pilgrims of the unknowable. To move into the unknowable feels very scary to the mind because in no way can the unknowable be made part of knowledge. It can never become the dominion and the empire of mind. It will always remain a mystery.

You can live it, but you cannot know it. You can experience it, but you cannot reduce your experience into knowledge. You can dance it, you can rejoice in it, but you cannot transform its basic quality of being mysterious into knowledgeability – knowledge is absolutely unmysterious. This is the world of the mystic. This is the world of *sat-chit-anand* – truth, consciousness, bliss.

These words are absolutely unknown to science, and these words are absolutely scary for the mind. It neither knows the truth nor does it want to know the truth; lies are so beautiful and comfortable. Truth is dangerous for the mind because the mind's whole basis is false and phony. The moment truth arrives, the mind has to leave; its time is over. The arrival of truth is instant death to the mind. Its whole empire simply disappears.

The mind is not interested in consciousness. In fact, the mind tries in every way to remain as unconscious as possible. Down the ages, every society and every culture has condemned alcohol and other intoxicating drugs, but to no effect – they have survived and they go on growing more and more influential. The reason is: mind wants to drown itself in unconsciousness, which is its only relaxation. Otherwise there is always tension because the unknowable is very close. The mind wants to forget all about the unknown, all about truth.

You will be surprised to know that science is not interested at all in discovering the truth. It is interested in discovering relative truths. Relative truths are simply relative lies. You can use those words as synonyms – just try.

If you say to someone 'I love you relatively,' what will it mean? It will simply mean that you love many more people too. Relatively, you can say 'I love you too.' You hate many people relatively; you just don't hate that person. With love, you are really saying 'I love you, relatively,' but no lover has ever made such a statement. Every lover says 'I love you totally, absolutely.'

Science is only interested in the objective world, where you can never come to the ultimate truth because from the very beginning it boycotts the subjective world. So its truth is always going to remain relative. The scientist is interested in objects but he is not interested in himself. To be interested in oneself means to be interested in truth, to be interested in consciousness, to be interested in bliss. But those are fearful, dangerous paths for the mind – any one of them. In fact, all three come together as three aspects of one experience. The moment you experience truth, you also experience a tremendous explosion of consciousness and, at the same time, an immense overflowing of bliss from your own heart.

In this flood of light, the mind finds itself even incapable of opening its eyes. It is a bird of darkness – like the owl which in the day closes its eyes and in the night its day begins. The overflowing bliss becomes almost like a flood. Bliss will take away all the dead wood that the mind has collected as knowledge; consciousness will dispel all the dark corners in which the mind is hiding – repressing desires, repressing anger, greed, lust and a thousand and one other things that have been condemned by society.

The mind's greatest fear is not death. Its greatest fear is enlightenment. Death is nothing to be worried about. It cannot take away anything from the mind, but illumination is going to destroy the mind completely.

Your question is really the mind trying to figure out what is happening to you. And what is happening to you is beyond the capacity of the mind, which is why you are afraid, shaky, worried. I will read your question: 'Sitting in front of you, I feel something tremendous is happening to me, which I don't understand at all.' Neither do I! Nor has anyone ever known what it is – no Gautam Buddha, no Jesus Christ, no Socrates. Nobody has ever known what it is, but they have all drunk of it, felt its sweetness, its fragrance, its music. Everything is so vast, so tremendous, they cannot reduce it into words so that mind can figure out what it is.

Unless something is reduced to language, the mind is incapable of understanding it. The mind is a linguist, full of words and language. That is its only treasure but if something cannot be brought into language, it remains outside the world of the mind. But the mind is only a small part of you: you are far bigger. Hence you can experience many things which the mind cannot understand.

You are saying, 'I feel so thankful...' You are experiencing the inexpressible. All that you can do is feel grateful. You cannot even say what you are grateful for because that 'what' is part of the mystery of existence. It is a good indication that what is happening to you is bringing thankfulness. And thankfulness or gratefulness is far more important than any knowledge because it transforms you; knowledge only informs you.

You can find great scholars, full of knowledge, but their lives are empty and poor. Nothing happens in their lives. Underneath the load of their knowledge, they have not lived. They are simply carrying the load because that load makes them respectable in a world of ignorant people. If those same people were surrounded by mistakes, they would be laughed at.

Mohammed used to say, 'A man of knowledgeability is just a donkey carrying holy scriptures.' He may feel very proud among other donkeys who are carrying mundane things: one carrying salt, another carrying mud, another carrying sand, another carrying wood – naturally the donkey who is carrying holy scriptures is a priest among the donkeys. He is a great scholar among the donkeys and all the donkeys are going to be respectful to him; he is no ordinary donkey.

It's the same with your scholars, great professors, great priests, great rabbis – they have wasted their lives on books. I am not against books, but you should remember that is only one dimension; it is not your whole life. If your whole life becomes full of books, you are just a bookcase, otherwise utterly empty. Books can enhance your life. If you have some life, if you have some love, you may be able to find in poetry something which even the poet may not have been aware of. If he was just a man of the mind, then what he has written is only a composition of words according to the rules of grammar and language. But a mystic can read in those words something he pours into them, something which is not there.

One of the significant qualities of the mystic is thankfulness, without even knowing for what. 'But I don't know why and for what' – that's exactly the right thing. Full of gratitude for the unknowable, full of gratitude for that which is beyond the capacity of the mind. You are touching new horizons, you are flying close to the stars. The mind cannot reach there. That's why there is thankfulness.

'Tears are coming, and I cannot see any reason.' They are not tears of rationality. In fact nobody has heard of rational tears, nobody has ever experienced that tears are flowing from his eyes because two plus two is four – my god, two plus two is four brings tears! Knowledge cannot bring tears. Tears are indicating something very deeply significant – you have touched something which can only be expressed by tears or laughter or dancing. They are all irrational; you cannot explain them rationally.

I gave Shunyo a small antique Rolex watch for Veeresh. I told her, 'Find him and give it to him.'

She came running back to me saying, 'Veeresh is really crazy. When I gave him the watch, he simply started crying and dancing. I could not believe it! He did not say anything, he is simply dancing outside!'

Because she was searching for him, she asked Anando to also look for him. After Shunyo had given the watch to Veeresh, Anando found him and she could not believe it either – 'What has happened?' Just tears and laughter together, and he was dancing, jumping. She brought him close to my room, to inform Shunyo.

Anando said, 'It is strange. What has happened to him?'

Shunyo said, 'It is nothing, just that Osho has given him a watch.'

It is irrational, but a man who knows only reason knows only a desert of a life. He does not know the roses. He does not know the beautiful sounds of the birds, which don't mean anything – they are irrational. In fact, even to call them *songs* is not quite right. The birds are just making sounds for no reason at all, just out of tremendous gratefulness to this beautiful morning, to the sun, to the trees; just for another day to breathe, to fly in the sky, to love, to sing and dance. They are making sounds because they don't know how to thank the universe in any other way.

When you also experience something of the heart, you will find a tremendous desire to cry. That crying is not out of sadness. Those tears are more valuable than any heartbeat. Those tears are still warm, those tears are still alive, and those tears are saying that you have touched something beyond words, beyond mind. They are of immense joy and gratefulness, sensitivity and helplessness – helplessness because you cannot express what you are experiencing in words. In fact, anything that is great in life has no reason.

Once Picasso was painting by the side of a rosebush and for almost an hour a man stood there, watching. Finally he could not resist the temptation and said to Picasso, 'Excuse me, sir, but I cannot see any reason in what you are painting. I have looked at it from every side but I can't figure out what it is.'

Picasso looked at him and said, 'Just look at the roses. Go to them and try to find out why *they* are there. I am harassed so much, but nobody asks the birds, nobody asks the peacock "Why this tail, with so many beautiful colors?" Nobody asks the cuckoo – whose sound is so sweet, almost incomparably sweet; nobody asks the trees "Why are you green?" But every idiot comes to me and asks, "What are you doing? What is the meaning of it?"'

'Go to God and ask him, "What is the meaning of this whole universe?" I am a small creator, he is the big creator. Just go – perhaps he knows the reason.'

But I know that if you meet God, he will not know the reason either. What reason can he supply for why he painted the peacocks feathers so beautifully? What was the reason? Why has he given a long white tail to the birds of paradise? You will find one here in my garden. It comes and goes seasonally. Just two days ago, it came again. For a few months it had disappeared. It has such a white tail, so snow-white, and the bird is very small and black. Such a small bird and carrying such a long white tail – it does not make any sense. Because of the tail, the bird can hardly fly; he simply jumps from one tree to another tree. Now what reason could there be? But he is so beautiful, just the combination of colors is so beautiful. Beauty need not be rational; neither bliss needs to be rational nor silence. Meditation is not a rational endeavor: it is basically irrational.

To be more accurate, it is supprarational: it goes beyond reason and all its concepts.

Picasso was right. He was simply saying that nobody asks God. Everybody goes to pray in the church, in the synagogue, in the temple, and nobody asks him, 'What is the purpose of it all?' The sun goes on rising every morning, creating such a beautiful sunrise over the oceans, over the mountains, creating so many beautiful colors on the horizon – for a strange reason which I don't know.

I was a student in a university which has, perhaps, the best location in the whole world – certainly in India. I have visited many universities, but the University of Sagar, a very small place, has some special quality to it – not the university, but the mountain and the lake. The university is on the mountain, a small mountain, but the lake is very vast, miles long. I have seen the horizon being painted every morning by God, every evening by God in many places around the world, but I have never seen as many psychedelic colors as those at Sagar University. I have never seen such colors as when the sun rises over the lake and when it sets over the mountains. It spreads so many colors, absolutely without reason, just out of sheer abundance!

After seeing the mornings and evenings in Sagar I have been searching for the same colors, but I have not found them anywhere. Every place seems to be poor as far as mornings and evenings are concerned. Sagar is a small place. The only remarkable thing is that it has a university in one of the most beautiful places. But why should God be so generous? There is no reason.

Even if you meet God, he cannot explain anything to you. That's why I have removed the very hypothesis of God. There is no need of God, because to accept God is to put so much burden and tension, worry and concern on the poor fellow – it is better that he is not. It is not that I'm against God; it is just out of my love and compassion. I feel he should not be. My own way of denying God is totally different from an atheist's – they are against him. I am absolutely for him, but he is not there.

Picasso was right when he became angry.

Another time it happened...

A very rich woman, super-rich, asked him to make a portrait of her. He said, 'I don't paint portraits.'

She said, 'The price is not a question at all – whatever you demand – but I want a portrait from you, just because you don't do portraits. I want something unique; nobody in the whole world except me will have a Picasso portrait. I'm ready to pay whatever price you ask, but you have to do a portrait.'

For a moment, Picasso thought to himself, 'Ask such an enormous amount that the woman will escape.' So he said, 'Five million dollars.'

The woman said, 'I will give you six. Start painting; I am already prepared.'

Now he was caught, so he had to paint the portrait. When the portrait was complete, the woman said, 'Everything is beautiful, but just tell me one thing: where is my nose? I cannot find it.'

A nose is the very center of your face. If you can find the nose, then you can figure out where the eyes are, where the mouth is, where the ears are – everything. But without finding the center...

The woman said, 'Just tell me about the nose, everything else I will figure out.'

Picasso said, 'I told you already that I don't do portraits because this kind of problem always arises later on. I don't know where your nose is. I knew when I was painting, but now all that I know ... It is a beautiful painting, so many beautiful colors – who cares about the nose? Just don't tell anybody that this is your portrait.'

Picasso, in a certain way, has come closer to mysticism than any other painter because whatever he has painted is not to be understood, only to be experienced. His colors, his combination of colors, are just unbelievable. He has defeated God many times. But don't ask the meaning, don't ask the reason, don't bring it to the mind – just enjoy!

You know it already: when you are enjoying a really good ice cream – what do you call it, tutti-frutti? – you don't ask the reason, you don't ask the meaning. And when you go to Sarjano's place for pizza, do you ask, 'What is the meaning of it?' Taste is enough. I don't even know what pizza is because I have never tasted it but I feel saliva coming into my mouth – what about you? And I can promise you I will never taste pizza because I love to keep a few things mysterious!

You are saying, 'I leave discourse with unsteady knees...' – I also leave in the same way, somehow I manage to reach my room! You are saying '...as if I had done twenty-four hours' hard work.' The reason for unsteady legs is that you are drunk with something that is not chemical drugs or alcohol, but something of consciousness, something of truth, something of bliss, which can make you as drunk, or even more drunk, as any alcoholic beverage.

And now you are asking me, 'But what happened?' Don't ask such questions. Something really happened. If you ask questions, there is a danger that it may stop happening; it is a very shy phenomenon. Allow it to happen, enjoy as much as you can, and don't be worried about unsteady knees. The more you stop asking questions, or figuring out what is happening, the less you will feel that you have worked hard for twenty-four hours. To ask about the unanswerable creates great tension. It really creates the feeling of hard work and failure because you can never succeed. Even if you work your whole life you cannot succeed.

'Is it a matter of my undeveloped awareness that I don't grasp what is happening...?' No! With developed awareness you will find your knees becoming even more unsteady. It is simply what you recognize yourself, 'Does my mind want an answer where there is no answer?'

Yes, stop doing that!

Dolores marries old Mr. Pincus because she figures she will get his money without having to put out much. On their wedding night she giggles when he takes out a condom and lays it on the night table.

'Darling,' she murmurs, 'don't you think you are being a little cautious?

After all, you are eighty-eight.'

But Mr. Pincus only sniggers and moments later takes cotton wool from the drawer and stuffs it up his nostrils. He then takes out a pair of earplugs.

'Darling,' she says, 'I understand the condom, but what are you doing now?'

'Honey,' he replies, putting in his ear plugs, 'you might as well know now that there are two things I can't stand in life. One is a woman screaming, and the other,' he says as he snaps off the light, 'is the smell of burning rubber.'

Hymie Goldberg had worked hard all his life and become very rich. But now he's on his deathbed with his wife Becky by his side, and he is dispersing his worldly possessions.

'My Cadillac,' he begins, 'with the push button motorcycle-cop detector, I leave to my son Sam.'

'Better you should leave it to Joe,' says Becky. 'He is a better driver.'

'All right,' whispers Hymie. 'My Rolls Royce I leave to my daughter Linda.'

'You had better give it to your nephew Willie,' interrupts Becky. 'He is a very careful driver.'

'All right. Give it to Willie,' continues Hymie. 'And my twelve-cylinder Jaguar, I give to my niece Sally.'

'Personally,' says Becky, 'I think Judy should get it.'

Hymie raises his head and shouts, 'Becky, please! Who is dying? You or me?'

Osho,
The deeper and deeper I go into meditation, the fatter and fatter I am getting. Am I in danger of exploding?

First a small story...

Once there was a Japanese meditator called Wu, whose master lived in a little house on the other side of the river. One morning, after a particularly 'good' meditation, Wu felt so overjoyed that he dedicated a small poem to his master.

He wrote, 'At the peak of the mountain, the sun is rising in the East. Sitting here in my lotus posture, the three worldly evils cannot affect me.'

He folded the paper and gave it to his servant to take to the master. The master looked at the paper and wrote a few words on it, telling the servant to take it back to Wu. Wu was most upset to have his poem returned, especially when he opened the paper and found three words written underneath it, 'Fat, fat, fat.'

Wu immediately ran down to the river and swam across as fast as he could to his master's house. Prostrating himself in front of the master, he said, 'Oh, master, I wrote you this poem as an expression of my love for you and look what you have done!'

'So,' said the master, 'you sit on top of the mountain and feel that the three worldly evils cannot affect you any longer, but three little words are enough to blow you right across the river.'

Don't be worried about your getting fatter.

You are saying, 'The deeper and deeper I go into meditation, the fatter and fatter I am getting. Am I in danger of exploding?' I hope so! That's the whole purpose of your being here – exploding. But becoming fat is not because of meditation. Perhaps you are meditating too much and not doing enough exercise. You will have to do one of two things. I hate exercise myself, but then you have to reduce your calories. I have to live on only six hundred calories per day. That is now. A few days ago I was living on twelve hundred calories per day.

If you don't want to exercise, then you will have to cut down on the stuff that you go on putting in your mouth. Meditators are known to become fat because they forget completely that meditation is sitting silently, doing nothing, and the fat grows ... So either start doing some exercise or cut down on your food.

Gautam Buddha had to cut out one meal completely from his disciples' diet. They could eat only once a day, not twice; and of course not five times a day with different names: breakfast, lunch, coffee break, supper, and the last – just a little bit before you go to sleep. He had to cut down from two meals, which are common in India, to one meal. That means fifty percent.

Mahavira was even more ... He was teaching longer periods of meditation than Gautam Buddha. Gautam Buddha had an alternating system: one hour meditation, one hour walking. That repeated walking one hour and meditating one hour kept the balance. And then only one meal a day. But Mahavira had no such alternating system. People were in meditation for eight hours, ten hours, twelve hours. He also insisted on one meal, but he made another condition: you had to eat it standing. Also you could not use plates; you had to use only your hands. So whatever fits into your two cupped hands – that's all. And eat it standing, because when you are sitting you are at ease, comfortable.

We make our meals as comfortable as possible: comfortable chairs, table, beautiful plates, candlelight, some fragrance, flowers, and then you go on, course after course. So if you are meditating as well, then naturally you will become fatter and fatter.

There is also a reason for this fatness other than food: a meditator slowly becomes less and less interested in sex. That has two by-products. One is: the little gymnastics that you used to do in sex are dropped and that may have been your only exercise. Secondly, the moment you drop sex, you become more interested in food. People who drop sex automatically start eating a little more.

The way life starts creates this connection. The child becomes aware of his mother's breast and the food that comes from it at the same time. Later on the breast becomes a sexual symbol, but the association with food is very deep in your unconscious. The people who drop sex – here it is otherwise; here sex drops people – start eating more to substitute because eating is connected with man's sexuality. So you have to be aware: exploding is perfectly good, but that is an exploding of consciousness, an explosion of your inner being, not an explosion of your body.

People are already afraid of coming close to me, and if you do this kind of exploding, then I am going to lose all my crazy people. So please, be kind toward yourself and be kind toward me. Cut down on your food, create an alternating system: meditation, walking, jogging, running, anything that gives your body enough exercise to absorb your food. This is tremendously significant: if you can create an alternating system your meditation will go even deeper, because when the body is tired, it quickly relaxes. When it is not tired, it does not relax quickly.

That is one of the reasons why rich people cannot sleep. Their bodies are not tired. Sleep is part of relaxation. Laborers, beggars, sleep so deeply that even emperors feel jealous. Because they are working the whole day, their bodies are so tired that it is impossible for them not to fall asleep immediately.

You will be surprised to know that there are aboriginals in India, in Burma, in Thailand, and in other Far Eastern countries, who don't dream. The reason is that their work is so hard, they are so tired, that by the time they go to sleep they fall so deeply asleep that they miss a layer of dreams. The first layer is of your waking consciousness; the second layer is of your dreaming consciousness; the third layer is of your dreamless sleep; the fourth layer is your awakening, enlightenment. Because their lives are so hard – just to have a little food, just to survive – they don't dream.

When they first came in contact with the Christian missionaries ... Christian missionaries are now being trained in psychoanalysis. Christianity is the most cunning religion in the world. Seeing that the old style of priesthood was getting out of date, they started sending their missionaries to learn psychoanalysis. They could see that in the future psychoanalysis is going to replace the priesthood. The psychoanalyst is the future priest. He is already taking the priest's place. He has become the most highly-paid professional in the world – and all he does is analyze your dreams.

So when these missionaries, trained in psychology, reached the thick forest in Burma, in Thailand, they could not believe what they found. When one of them asked the aboriginals, 'What did you dream last night?' the aboriginals looked at each other and said, 'What does he mean by "dream"?' They had never dreamed. They have not dreamed for two reasons.

One, their life is not of repression. A repressed person dreams more because the mind has to get rid of whatever is repressed in dreaming. It is a kind of catharsis – the mind unbinding itself. Secondly, it is only those who cannot go to the deeper layers of sleep who are stuck in the dreaming layer. Once in a while you slip into the deeper layer, where there is no dream. But you surface again.

Your sleep graph is not the same the whole night. Sometimes you are very superficial, sometimes you are going very deep. Sometimes you are again superficial, just on the verge of waking. Sometimes you go very deep, almost close to death. On one superficial layer is your life and on the deepest layer is your death, and just below your superficial layer is the dreaming layer. Many aboriginals completely miss dreaming.

You will be able to go deeper into your meditation, into your relaxation, because relaxation is essential for your meditation. Make it a point to jog, jump, run, and then when you feel tired, utterly tired, sit down or lie down and meditate. Then you will find that you are not getting fatter and your body is not going to explode, but your consciousness is going to explode into the tremendous phenomenon we call enlightenment.

The East has never bothered about dreams but the East has been concerned for thousands of years with consciousness. It is a strange phenomenon. The West became concerned with consciousness only one hundred years ago, and immediately it jumped on dreams. The whole psychological endeavor became dream analysis. One wonders what happened. The East has been concerned for at least ten thousand years with consciousness. Its whole genius has been focused on searching deeply into consciousness – more than has happened anywhere else. This has been the only contribution to human evolution as far as consciousness is concerned.

The East is poor. It has not developed science, it has not developed technology because it has put all its intelligence into one direction and that is consciousness. But the strange fact is: even after ten thousand years, Eastern psychology has nothing to do with psychoanalysis-type psychologies, which are concerned with dream analysis. What is the reason?

The reason is Christianity. Christianity is the most repressive religion in the world. It represses everything. And because of that repression the layer of dreams becomes thicker and thicker and thicker. Now Western psychoanalysts say that if a man sleeps eight hours per night, he dreams for six hours. For only two hours, once in a while, he goes a little deeper and does not dream. Otherwise, for six hours he is dreaming. What happened to the Eastern explorers of consciousness? They did not come to such a thick layer – six hours! And, strangely, the conclusion of Western psychology is that if you are not allowed to dream that amount of time, you will not feel refreshed in the morning.

They have done some experiments. One man is disturbed whenever he is dreaming. It is very easy to know when a person is dreaming. Whenever a person is asleep without dreams, there is no movement of the eyes under the eyelids. You can see that there is no movement. The moment he starts dreaming, he is watching a film and his eyes start moving. You can immediately check whether the person is dreaming or not – very simple.

So one person in this experiment is disturbed. Whenever he moves his eyes he is immediately woken up, then allowed to sleep again. When he goes to sleep, again he will dream. The whole night the disturbance continues. He can only sleep for those two hours when he does not dream. Another person in another room is being disturbed differently. Whenever he is not dreaming, he is disturbed, he is woken up – and then allowed to dream six hours without disturbance.

This has been repeated many times in many psychological labs around the Western world and the conclusion, the result, is very strange – nobody had ever thought such a result would come out of it, not even the psychoanalysts had thought of it. The result is that the man whose dreams are disturbed is disturbed the whole day. He feels tired, tense, sad, depressed. He feels that he has not been able to sleep, he is utterly tired and because of the continuous disturbance the whole night, he wants to sleep again. The other person, whose sleep time was disturbed but not the dream time, has no problem. He gets up rejuvenated, fresh, with no tiredness.

The conclusion is that you need dreams more than sleep. Your body, your physical well-being, depends on dreaming, not on sleep, which has been the traditional concept. Traditionally it has been understood that dreams are a kind of disturbance. Now the situation is totally different: dreams are not a disturbance, they are a tremendous help. But this is the Western mind and the experiment is confined to Western people. They should not apply their conclusion to the whole of humanity. Their conclusion belongs only to the Christians. A meditator starts dreaming less and less, and once you are at the very peak of meditation, dreams disappear.

Primitive people, aboriginals, don't dream at all. The East has not paid any attention to dreams because it would have been futile. There was not such a repressive attitude in the East before Christianity came. All the repression that you see today in India or in other Eastern countries is not part of its heritage. It has been brought by Christian missionaries. Although Hindus are not Christians, Christian ideology has penetrated every religion in the world. They may not have been able to convert everybody to Christianity, but they have fed their ideology into every mind.

Just see: Hindus were perfectly at ease with the temples of Khajuraho. They never thought that they were pornographic. And today? Even if you wear slightly fewer clothes than you do now, that's enough to disturb the Indians. It is not Indian culture; it is Indian culture polluted by Christianity. Before, Indians were never worried. All Indian gods have their wives but the Christian god has no wife.

Before Mohammedanism – which is a by-product of Judaism, just as Christianity is – India was a totally different world, absolutely unrepressed. There was no question of repression at all. With Mohammedans, repression started entering the Indian mind, and with Christianity it became absolute. The Mohammedans invaded India about thirteen centuries ago. Alexander the Great had started the influx of invaders just two hundred years after Gautam Buddha, but there were no repressive ideologies preached to people then; people were more innocent. Hence, a method like *vipassana* – which is a Buddhist method – was possible for meditation: just by watching the mind silently, meditation happens.

Meditation was not something arduous or difficult, but to the Western mind or even to the Eastern mind as it is today – absolutely overtaken by Western ideology – watching the mind is not easy. So much garbage and so much crap has been forced into the mind that you go almost crazy just watching it. It is a film which begins, but never ends. You can go on watching day in, day out, year in, year out and the mind is always ready to supply new images, new dreams.

It is because of this I had to create a few devices – Dynamic, Kundalini, and others – before you could enter a silent witnessing meditation like *vipassana*. I have made devices to help you cathart, throw out your garbage rather than waste time in watching it.

It can be thrown out by *latihan* – tremendously beautiful – but it is not a meditation; it is only a clearance. It can be done even better by Dynamic Meditation than by *latihan* – because *latihan* has some dangers which I have cut out of the meditation. Sometimes *latihan* people go mad because they cannot stop.

It is an Indonesian method which became immensely successful in the fifties in Europe and America. It never became successful in the East because in the East – particularly in Indonesia, which is a backward country – there is nothing to cathart! The man who invented Latihan was Bapak Subuh. He called his philosophy *subud.* He has taken the word *subud* from *Buddha*, which means 'the great awakening.' But *latihan* cannot bring the great awakening. It became fashionable in the West and then disappeared completely because it created many people who had to be put into mental asylums, for the simple reason that no stop is built into the process.

Once you start *latihan* you are overtaken by the process of catharsis, and it goes on and on and you don't know what to do; you are almost without control. But I have divided Dynamic Meditation into different sections. *Latihan* has to be done alone; Dynamic Meditation has to be done under instruction. Under instruction, after each ten-minute section, the process is changed. Then once you have learned it you can do it alone. So you are always in control. It never becomes so big as to take all control into its own hands. These devices are needed just to clear the rubbish that Christianity has created, and to bring you to a state of naturalness, simplicity.

From there the only way is witnessing, which Buddha called *vipassana. Vipassana* means 'looking at.' If you want to do *vipassana*, or any silent meditation, Dynamic Meditation becomes absolutely essential. Christianity has poisoned your mind, and that poison has to be thrown out. To throw it out, you have to go completely crazy; otherwise that craziness remains inside you and won't allow you to get into silent, watching, witnessing meditation.

So do some Dynamic Meditation, do some jogging, do some running, swimming and when you feel utterly tired, when you feel an intrinsic need to relax, you are free from Christianity. Then you can sit silently, then you can watch your mind – and not much is there. You have thrown out almost ninety-nine percent of it. Maybe here and there a few pieces are clinging because they are very old and have become glued to you – just watch them.

Watching is a process of ungluing those small pieces hanging here and there in the mind. Once they also disappear, you don't have a mind, you have a vast sky opening. That is the explosion, and that explosion will bring you to *sat-chit-anand*: to truth, to consciousness, to bliss.

4

Sat, Chit, Anand: Your Birthright

Osho,
When I look at my life, it is richer and more fulfilled than I could have ever expected. I am filled with gratitude through all the love, understanding and sheer joy that being with you has brought me. Why then, Osho, do I think of death so longingly?

Devageet, there are many things which have to be understood before you can see the answer to your question arising in your own consciousness. There are questions I cannot answer, but I can manage a situation around you, around your question, so that the answer arises within you. And only such answers are significant. It is a roundabout way. I could have given the answer directly, but then it wouldn't be your answer. And I want every answer to be your own.

Your question is yours: it has an individuality, a certain beauty, a certain aliveness. It comes out of your heart, just as a flower comes out of the juices of the tree. It is not something imposed from outside; it is something that grows from the very roots up to the top. Just as your question is yours, my whole effort here is that your answer should also be yours. So while I am answering you, this is the first thing to be understood: my answer is only a device to trigger your answer. I don't want my answer to become your answer; then it will be borrowed and dead.

Your question is very significant. It is not an ordinary question out of curiosity. Its significance also lies in its depth, in its existential meaningfulness. This question cannot be asked by each and everyone. Unless you have touched a certain depth within your being, only then is this question possible. Every question shows the heart of the questioner. Just by looking at your question, I can see what is happening within you. It must look very strange and absurd because you are saying, 'When I look at my life, it is richer and more fulfilled than I could have ever expected.'

This is the first thing to be remembered: whenever something beyond your expectations is fulfilled, you will always find a deep desire to die because, who knows, tomorrow may not bring the same contentment, the same joy, the same beauty, the same experience. It is better to die at this peak rather than in despair, in sadness, in misery. Why not die in a moment of celebration? Why not make death also a celebration? But that is possible only when you are at the peak of fulfillment; it is not possible when you are in the valleys and in darkness.

So whenever you feel fulfilled, contented, more contented than you ever expected, you will find arising in you a natural, very spontaneous desire: this is the right moment to die, at the highest peak of my life. What more can there be? Why go on living? It is risky to live because one can always lose this height. It is risky to live because one can become accustomed to this joy, this happiness; one may start taking it for granted. It may become just an ordinary thing. One may forget that it is extraordinary and happens only very rarely to very, very few human beings. You may not be aware of all these considerations, but these are the reasons why the desire to die at such a moment arises.

You are saying, 'I am filled with gratitude for all the love, understanding and sheer joy that being with you has brought me. Why then, Osho, do I think of death so longingly?' It is one of those contradictions of existence, those mysteries of existence. For example, the poor man is never frustrated because he has something to hope for: tomorrow may bring good news. There is a possibility that tomorrow he may not be poor. It is the rich, the super-rich man, who becomes frustrated, because tomorrow is not going to be something different or new, something more than he has already. Tomorrow has become absolutely hopeless; hence the frustration.

People in poor countries don't suffer as much as far as the mind and consciousness is concerned. As the country becomes rich, logically one would expect that the people should become happier, more contented. Now the misery has gone: there is no starvation, there is medical care. Everything is good: you cannot expect more. But suddenly there is a sadness that starts settling in the rich countries, in rich societies. The sadness comes because they start forgetting the misery of starvation and they cannot see the future bringing any new meaning, any new flowers. Everything will now be static, routine.

Hence more people commit suicide in rich countries than in poor countries. Logically it should be vice versa: in poor countries people should commit suicide, but they do not because they still have hope. Life today may not be meaningful, but who knows about tomorrow? Things change. They have seen poor people becoming rich, they have seen all kinds of changes happening. There is no need to feel hopeless because all the possibilities are open. They just have to make an effort. If they fail, it doesn't matter; they must make more effort. But the idea of suicide does not arise at all.

I have moved among the poor for decades. It is almost impossible to find a poor man asking about suicide, about meaninglessness, about frustration, about anguish, about angst. These are not their questions at all. These questions arise only at a certain stage of affluence, luxury, comfort. More people go insane in rich countries than in poor countries. The ratio is large, the difference is great.

Even if in a poor country somebody does commit suicide or go insane – which is very rare – his reasons are totally different from the reasons of a rich man. The poor man may commit suicide, but not out of frustration, not out of meaninglessness, not out of discontent. He knows nothing of contentment and he is not tired of his discontent, because there is always a possibility that discontent may become contentment, the poverty may change. The people who commit suicide in poor countries are either retarded – they cannot manage to live, their minds are not able to cope with life and its situations – or they commit suicide because they are blind, crippled, paralyzed. But these are not the reasons in a rich society.

The same is true of your spiritual life. You feel it as a question. I feel it as the sheer outcome of your joy, fulfillment, contentment. To me it is a beautiful experience, not a question, not a problem to be solved, but something to be understood. It is indicative that you are coming closer and closer to the ultimate *sat-chit-anand*, to the truth, to the explosion of consciousness, to the highest peak of bliss. Just before one is coming close to home, one starts feeling as if one has arrived. But it is only 'as if.' It is so beautiful that one cannot think things can be even better.

But I want you to still be discontented. I want you to still hope because I know there is much more that is possible for you than you can conceive. I can conceive it because I have known much more and I know that there is no limit to growth. But this point comes to every seeker and searcher at some stage. And this has to be passed, otherwise it can become a danger. It has to be transformed into an indication. It is simply an indication that you have come to the very limit of your mind.

But you are more than your mind. Beyond the mind, there are no limits at all. Then there are skies upon skies, and as you move over one peak, you have another peak immediately confronting you. This existence is inexhaustible. And when I say this, I am saying it with absolute authority, because I have passed through the moment about which you are asking. I have also felt at one time, 'What more can there be? Why go on unnecessarily breathing, why go on every day getting up, knowing perfectly well that what has to happen has happened?' Now it is sheer habit that every evening you have to go to sleep, every morning you have to get up. What is the point of it all?

But I have lived through a very strange space. I have never accepted any limit to anything. When this moment came to me, I insisted that I could not accept that this is all. Life must be much more. And what is the harm in searching? You can die tomorrow or the day after tomorrow. What is the hurry? Why today?

So the first thing is: you are free to die any time. There is no problem, but it is better to inquire more, to investigate more, to explore more. And I promise you that soon you will be surprised to find that at the moment when the desire to die was so strong, you were simply passing through the boundary line of your mind, going beyond the mind into the no-mind. In fact, once you have passed this point, you will know for the first time what real life is.

Fulfillment, contentment, feeling richer are all irrelevant. Life is much more. It cannot be confined to these small words: *gratitude, love, understanding, sheer joy*. Once you have passed through all of them, you will be surprised that there is so much to existence for which no word exists in any language, and which mind has no capacity to understand. Certainly it is not contentment – *contentment* is a very poor word. It is not just joy, it is not just love. It is so much more that I can only say that these words are like a teaspoon, and with the teaspoon you are trying to empty the ocean.

It happened...

One of the great philosophers of Greece, Plato, was a contemporary of Diogenes. They were continuously in controversy because Diogenes was a mystic and he knew things which Plato could not even dream of, although Plato was a great philosopher. In the books and the histories of philosophy, you will find Plato, but you will not find Diogenes. But the real thing was with Diogenes not with Plato, who was a great thinker, a giant intellectual. Diogenes was a simple, childlike, innocent man, but he knew something which thousands of Platos together could not know.

One day, when Plato was on a morning walk by the side of the sea, he saw a man. It was early in the morning, a little dark

– the sun had not risen yet. He could not figure out who the man was. This man was Diogenes and in a spoon he was bringing ... He would go to the ocean, take the water in the spoon – he had made a small hole in the sand – pour the water into the sand, and then go back.

Plato, standing there, saw him doing it. He looked like a madman. For a moment he thought, 'I should not interfere.' But such is the mind – it becomes curious. 'Maybe he is not mad; perhaps he is doing something meaningful and I am not aware of it. And what is wrong if I ask him?' So he said, 'Please forgive me for interrupting. I don't want to interrupt you – you may be involved in some great work – but what is going on?'

Diogenes said, 'I am trying to empty the ocean.' Plato said, 'My God, with that spoon?'

Then the sun was rising. Diogenes started laughing and said, 'Plato, are *you* doing anything else?' Then Plato recognized Diogenes. He used to live naked, but that day he was covered with a cloth, just to hide himself, so Plato did not know him at first. Otherwise he might not have interrupted.

Plato was simply stunned, he could not answer. Diogenes said, 'That's what you are trying to do. Your mind is nothing but a teaspoon and with it you are trying to exhaust the oceanic existence. What I am doing is just to remind you. I know it is not possible. You should also remember that what you are doing is impossible.'

It is fortunate to come to such a point when one feels so happy that one would like to die. But my suggestion is to wait a little, because I know something more than that. I have passed that point, and the day I passed that point, for the first time life opened all its mysteries to me. Since then, not for a single moment has the desire to die arisen in me, for the simple fact that now I know there is no death. There is more life and more life and more life – there is no end to this inexhaustible existence. Hymie and Becky are on holiday in Florida when one night a hurricane hits the coast. Becky gets extremely upset and cannot sleep a wink. Hymie, however, is sleeping soundly.

'Hymie,' cries Becky shaking him awake, 'the house is rocking as if it's going to blow away.'

'Relax,' says Hymie, 'go to sleep. We are only renting it.'

All the houses that you have rented have blown away many times. This time also you are renting a house, and it will blow away one day. But *you* are going to continue.

You are an eternal pilgrim. Your pilgrimage is not going to end anywhere.

The pilgrimage itself is the goal, there is no goal to the pilgrimage.

The elderly man goes to visit a physician for a check-up. The doctor notices that his hands are shaking like leaves in the wind. 'You must drink a lot,' says the doctor.

'No, I don't,' says the old guy, 'I spill most of it.'

Come to such a point when you start spilling most of it. Don't be contented so early. It is not even the beginning yet.

> Osho,
> Once a week I cook unfertilized fried eggs for the whole commune's breakfast in order that everybody's brain becomes sharper and more intelligent. However, after cooking one thousand fried eggs, I don't feel like eating any myself. Is it okay for me to drop improving my brain and just enjoy its lack of activity?

A writer had been out too late the night before, and in the wrong places. Nursing a magnificent hangover, he stops at a small restaurant for breakfast. 'What will you have?' asked the waiter.

'All I want is two fried eggs and some kind words,' says the bleary- eyed writer.

Presently, the waiter returns with two pale-looking fried eggs. 'Here are your eggs, sir,' he says. 'And now for the kind words: don't eat them.'

Osho,
The other morning in discourse I was overwhelmed by your clarity and your beauty and grace, and felt so grateful and vulnerable. Thank you, Osho. I also realize that I am still not seeing your total radiance and splendor. This brings sadness and frustration. Osho, is it true that without being enlightened we cannot see you as you really are – sat-chit-anand? Can we only catch a glimpse?

One has to learn a little patience. Everything that has ever happened to any human being is going to happen to you because you have all the potential. You contain all the Gautam Buddhas, all the Jesuses, all the Socrateses. You contain the whole potential of humanity within you. And if you can see in me a certain clarity, beauty, grace, and if you can feel grateful and vulnerable, then you are on the right track. That's how one starts growing slowly.

It is true when you say, 'Osho, I also realize that I am still not seeing your total radiance and splendor.' But you are fortunate even to see a glimpse; there are millions of people in the world who will not be able to see even that glimpse. On the contrary, they will only see everything evil that man has ever imagined but no glimpse of splendor, no glimpse of clarity, no glimpse of grace. They see only fear, danger – danger to their morality, danger to their religion, danger to all they think is valuable.

There are millions of people who would like to destroy me. It is really a miracle that I am still alive in spite of those millions of people whose deepest desire is expressed by the United States Attorney General. He told a press conference, 'Osho should never be seen by anyone, never be heard by anyone. In short, I want him to be completely silenced.' That's all he wants.

The way he said it was so absolutely violent that the journalist who was interviewing him asked, 'Do you want him to be murdered or assassinated?'

For a moment the Attorney General remained silent and then said, 'Not exactly. But we have more sophisticated methods to silence him.' Now he is not simply speaking his own mind. He is expressing the minds of many.

So you should be happy, not sad, that you don't belong to those millions. You should feel fortunate, not frustrated, that at least you are capable of seeing a faraway glimpse of the Himalayas. Just a little patience, a little closeness, a little more love, a little more gratitude, a little more openness, and you will start moving toward the ultimate splendor. It is not my property. It came into existence when I was no more. It is the property of existence itself.

So don't be at all sad. There are many present here who have come far closer than you, who have looked into me more deeply than you. They are not in any way more special than you. They have just been patient – years of patience, years of silence, years of meditation, but this is nothing compared to the eternity of time. One day you will find that you have come so close that you can touch the beauty, you can touch the truth, you can dance in the music of eternal consciousness. You can be showered by flowers of bliss.

Yes, *sat-chit-anand* – truth, consciousness, bliss. All are possible to you. In fact, they are your birthright. You just have to claim them; the claim needs a little patience.

There is a Sufi story...

A king was passing by a nursery that belonged to a poor gardener. He looked at the poor gardener and stopped his horse. He had stopped for a special reason. He had wanted to stop many times. He used to pass through that beautiful place where the poor gardener's nursery was because it was the most beautiful way to the palace.

Today he could not contain his curiosity. The curiosity was that the man looked so old; certainly he had passed a century. Perhaps he was one hundred and twenty or even more. He looked so old and yet he was preparing small plants and working the whole day on those plants – plants of trees which take at least one hundred years to grow to their full height.

Their life span is long; they live at least four thousand years. After one hundred years they are still children. They can count on a life span of four thousand years, but only after one hundred years do they start flowering – not before that. And after one thousand years, they start giving fruit.

The king was puzzled: this man seemed to be at least one hundred and twenty years old. 'Is he mad, or what? He cannot expect to see the flowers of those trees, to say nothing of the fruit. And he is working so hard in his old age, the whole day in the hot sun' – it was a desert land.

He stopped and went close to the old man and said, 'I watch you every day, and I see how hard you work, but a question ... Every day I go on repressing it, not wanting to interfere. But you will have to forgive me – I want to ask one thing: Do you think you will be able to see the flowers of these plants?'

The old man laughed. He said, 'No, I will not be able to see the flowers of these plants. But do you see, just behind my hut, those huge trees, thousands of years old? They are the same trees. They are giving me fruit, they are giving me flowers.'

The king said, 'I can see them, but I still don't understand. What do you mean by talking about *those* trees?'

The man said, 'If my parents or my forefathers had also thought that they would not be able to see the flowers, to say nothing about the fruit, those trees would not be there. I am not thinking about myself. I am thinking about my forefathers and about future children. I owe them something.

'If my forefathers were so patient that they could be happy that some children whom they could never know would enjoy the fruit and the flowers of those beautiful trees ... Do you think I am a worse human being than my forefathers? Can't I think also of someone, far away in the future, being thankful to me?'

The king wrote in his biography, 'The old gardener has shocked me with his patience, with his infinite love and compassion and trust.'

Somebody, someday, is bound to see the flowers, and as far as your inner growth is concerned it is not a question of somebody else seeing the flowers – *you* are going to see them. Can't you be patient – just a little patient?

Just today I received a letter from Amrito, one of my old sannyasins in Holland. He is a famous Dutch writer, with all possible qualifications, degrees, honorary degrees. He has written many books, including at least eight books on me. Today I received a letter saying he is writing another book on me and in just a few days is coming here for my blessings. The title of the book is *Ten Years of Preparation*. Ten years ago he became a sannyasin, and still he calls those ten years just a preparation.

This patience is needed. In a hurry, you can get only seasonal flowers. They come and go. The deeper your patience, the greater will be your growth, there is no need to be frustrated or to be sad. Not even a single sannyasin, if he is honest and sincere in his search, is going to fail. Success is absolutely sure and guaranteed.

But you have to remember that it is not the path of the curious, it is not the path of information gatherers. It is the path of those who are ready to go through the transformation, who are ready to drop their personalities, their defense measures, who are ready to open their hearts to receive the light that is rising on the horizon. It is simply a case of receptivity, sensitivity, sincerity, and an honest search.

Your success is sure.

Miss Bradshaw, a comely high school teacher, had saved money for several years and was finally aboard a sleek ocean liner for her long-anticipated trip to Europe.

Aboard ship she wrote: 'Dear Diary...

Monday: I felt singularly honored this evening – the captain asked me to dine at his table.

Tuesday: I spent the entire morning on the bridge with the captain.

Wednesday: the captain made proposals to me unbecoming to an officer and a gentleman.

Thursday: tonight the captain threatened to sink the ship if I do not give in to his indecent proposals.

Friday: this afternoon I saved one thousand, six hundred lives.'

Just wait. It is only a question of saving your own life, not the lives of one thousand, six hundred people. Here I am not the savior; here everybody is a savior – not of anybody else, but of himself. For the first time in the whole history of mankind we are making a new effort to give the respect, the dignity and the responsibility to every person to save himself.

For centuries this dignity was not given to human beings. Krishna was trying to save Hindus and Christ was trying to save Christians. Everybody was trying to save somebody else. And they have not been able to transform the world. Krishna failed, Buddha failed, Jesus failed, Moses failed. When I say they failed, I don't mean they failed in their own enlightenment, I mean they failed in their promises to humanity. They were absolutely successful as far as *they* were concerned.

But the moment they started telling people, 'I will save you, I am the savior, I am the prophet, I am the messenger, I am the incarnation of God,' then they misled people. People stopped seeking, searching on their own. They just hoped that if they believed in Krishna, in Buddha, in Jesus, then it would not be their responsibility to transform themselves into a new and higher state of consciousness. This has not happened. It is in this sense that I say that all the saviors of the past have failed. And I don't want to belong to the failures. I am not a savior. I have saved myself – I think that's enough. Now you save yourself.

Osho,
I have never been near so much authentic laughter as I have here in your presence. As I make myself available to the laughter happening around me, I notice myself withdraw and become serious. Inside I long to let go and to become a part of the laughter around me, but my mind and body resist.

Why do I feel incapable of authentic laughter? And, is there a way for me to regain my natural capacity to let go in a belly laugh?

Anurag Saleen, you are a victim, but you are not alone. Almost the whole of humanity is a victim: victims of pretensions, victims of having to wear masks, victims of not being natural. Being unnatural pays because society gives respect to the false; society is not respectful to the authentic and to the real. The false can be controlled, and society is deeply interested in controlling everybody. But the authentic cannot be controlled, so society is very much afraid of those people who are authentic, real, themselves, because they cannot be enforced into slavery, into obedience, into being oppressed or exploited.

The desire for reward keeps society respecting the false and because the false is respected, each small child slowly starts following the false. Parents teach this, teachers teach this: the whole effort is to mold you in a certain way that is acceptable to everybody. The end result is a phony world, where nobody is real, where smiles are false, where love is only a word.

Just today I received news from England. A survey has been made of people aged between five and twenty-five. A single question was asked, 'What two values do you think are the most significant and important in life?' And it is shocking to see the answers from the five-year-olds right up to the twenty-five-year-olds. The answers are: money and success. These two things are the most important in life: not love, not laughter, not meditation, not blissfulness, not even God – money and success.

But in a world where money and success are everything, you cannot be authentic – it is dangerous. You will have to repress your individuality and compromise at every step for success, compromise at every step for money.

I am reminded of a young man. His name was Subhash Chandra. He became a great revolutionary and I have tremendous respect for him because he was the only man in India who opposed Mahatma Gandhi. He could see that all this mahatmahood is simply politics and nothing else. Indians believe themselves to be very religious. It is just a belief – nobody is religious. Mahatma Gandhi was playing the role of a saint simply to become the leader of the majority in the country as all those who thought they were religious were bound to be in favor of Mahatma Gandhi. Just one single man, Subhash, opposed him and immediately the phoniness was apparent. What happened was this:

Mahatma Gandhi used to say, 'I am beyond love and hate. I am beyond anger, violence.' That was his whole philosophy to go beyond violence and become nonviolent, become so loving that you love even your enemy.

Subhash was well-known for not being in agreement with Mahatma Gandhi, although he was in the same party. There was only one party which was fighting for the freedom of the country, so all freedom lovers were in that party. Subhash stood as a candidate to be the president of Congress, and immediately Mahatma Gandhi's phoniness was revealed.

On the one hand he was teaching that you have to love your enemy, but on seeing that if Subhash became the president of Congress, he would be dangerous to his philosophy and to his leadership, he became a totally different kind of man. Subhash did not believe in hypocrisy, and there was a possibility of his winning. The only man who could defeat him was Mahatma Gandhi himself, but that would bring him down, right down, from his great saintliness.

So what he did was this: he supported a certain man, Doctor Pattabhi Sitaramayya, as his candidate. He thought that because he was declaring him as *his* candidate, the doctor would certainly win. Subhash was very much loved by young people, by the young blood, but this fellow, Doctor Pattabhi, was absolutely unknown. He was an obedient follower of Mahatma Gandhi, so he would serve him, but he was not known to the country.

Subhash was almost a lion. He fought and, unbelievably, he won. Gandhi forgot all his philosophy. He did not participate in the gathering where Subhash was declared president. In fact, Subhash proved to be a far greater man. Seeing that Gandhi was trying to create a split in Congress – which would be a split in the movement for the liberation of the country – he resigned from the presidency, just so that the movement would remain united. He sacrificed himself completely and not wanting to get into a fight, he moved out of the country.

He had shown this sincerity from the very beginning. He was educated in England, belonged to a very rich family of Bengal, was going to be one of the top bureaucrats. He was trained for the Indian Civil Service in Britain, as were all top bureaucrats, most of whom were English. Very rarely was an Indian chosen – not more than one percent. Otherwise, on some small excuse, Indians were rejected.

Shree Aurobindo was rejected and you will not believe on what grounds. He had come first in every subject, he was one of the geniuses of this century. Only in horse riding he could not succeed. But what has horse riding got to do with being a top officer? This was the strategy: he was a scholar and he became world famous, but he was rejected. Every method was tried to reject Indians.

But they could not manage to reject Subhash. He managed to overcome all their strategies, so very reluctantly Britain accepted Subhash for the Indian Civil Service. One thing more remained, which was a formality: every ICS officer had to appear for a personal interview before the governor- general. It was just a formality once you had passed the examination. Subhash entered the office of the governor-general.

Bengalis always carry an umbrella – no one knows why. Whether it is raining or not, whether it is hot or not, even in winter when there is no need. They may just carry it by their side, but they will carry it – an umbrella is absolutely necessary for a Bengali. If you see anybody carrying an umbrella, you understand that he is a Bengali. Now, there is no need to carry an umbrella into the office of the viceroy; at least you should leave it outside. But Bengalis will not leave their umbrellas anywhere.

Subhash kept his hat on, carried his umbrella into the office, and took a chair. The governor-general was very angry. He said, 'Young man, you don't understand manners. Who passed you in the ICS examinations?'

Subhash said, 'What manners?'

The governor-general said, 'You have not taken off your hat and you have not asked my permission to sit down.'

The governor-general was not aware what kind of man Subhash was. He immediately picked up his umbrella and hooked it round the governor- general's neck. They were alone in the office, so...

Subhash told the governor-general, 'If you want manners, then you should also learn manners. You remained sitting; you should have stood first as I was a guest. You did not remove your hat, so why should I remove mine? You did not ask my permission to go on sitting, so why should I ask your permission? Who do you think you are? At the most you can reject me for the ICS, but I will not leave it in your hands. I don't want to join the service.'

And he went out of the office, leaving the governor-general almost in shock – he had never dreamed that anybody could do such a thing.

Society is afraid of anyone who has dignity, self-respect. Society wants you to be obedient, to be servile, to be compromising, to be always ready to surrender in every situation. It does not want you to be rebellious. But individuality is intrinsically rebellious; you cannot do anything about it. The only way is to keep it under a blanket of personality, to cover it from every nook and corner, and not allow it even a window to breathe.

So everybody is suffering inside. A closed, invisible wall of personality is surrounding you that does not allow you, Anurag Saleen, to gain your naturalness, your spontaneity, to have a belly laugh, even though here nobody is preventing you. In fact, here it is impossible to go on holding yourself, controlling yourself, and not be spontaneous and relaxed. This is not your usual society. All these people are rebellious individuals. But even here, you are carrying your mind, your unconscious, your conditioning. You will have to put it aside. Others may not be able to help in your ultimate salvation, but others can help you have a belly laugh.

So whoever is sitting by the side of Anurag Saleen, please help her. Tickle her! It is just a question of breaking her barriers. So tonight, I am telling this joke for Anurag, wherever she is. If she does not want to be helped by others, she should relax and have a good laugh. Otherwise, if you see anybody who is not joining in, tickle. There may be others besides Anurag who will be helped.

Hymie Goldberg is drafted to fight in Ronald Reagan's latest war with Iran. However, he manages to convince the draft board officer that he is half blind and is sent home.

That evening, Hymie goes to the cinema and when the lights come on he notices that a member of the draft board is sitting next to him. Without a moment's hesitation Hymie taps him on the shoulder and asks, 'Excuse me, madam, is this the train for New Jersey?'

Now look for Saleen. And if you find anybody who is not laughing, tickle them. Don't be shy.

5

Instinct, Intellect, Intuition: Past, Present, and Future

Osho,
Finally I have come home to myself with a silence and serenity never known before. I feel like a flower bud ready to open, yet I do not feel in touch with the energy of love and joy that would allow this flower to bloom. It is almost as if I have not yet fully opened my heart to myself. Osho, am I missing something, or is it just a matter of time?

Flowers don't open to themselves – otherwise they could have opened in the middle of the night. They open to a rising sun in deep welcome, in gratitude and prayer. They open to the songs of the birds.

You are trying to do something utterly stupid. You are trying to open your heart to yourself. Do you understand what it means? How can you open your heart to yourself? Who are you other than your heart? If you are trying to open your heart to yourself, it will close more and more. You are the center of the heart. The petals will have to come close to you, become a bud; even the open flower will start closing.

This is something very significant to understand: you can open to existence, but not to yourself. *You* are the one who is the barrier.

But you seem to be accustomed to the old human habit of making somebody else responsible.

I will read your question: 'Finally I have come home to myself with a silence and serenity never known before.' Remember – underline the word *myself.* When one really comes home, no self is found. Gautam Buddha has to use a negative word, *anatta. Anatta* means 'no-self.' When you really come home, *you* are not to be found at all. If you are still finding yourself, you have not come home. Your absence is the home. Your ego is taking you astray, and just to prevent you from coming home it will give you the sense that you *have* come home, it will give you some false substitute of a home. But this has to be remembered as a definitive criterion: when you come home you never come to yourself. You come to the ultimate. You come to *sat-chit-anand.* You come to truth. You come to consciousness. You come to bliss.

But in the world of truth, consciousness, and bliss, where are you going to find this rat you call 'myself'? I knowingly use the word *rat* because rats have been found, scientifically, to survive under any conditions. They eat almost one-fifth of humanity's food. One-fifth – twenty percent – is a large portion, while half of humanity is starving. And rats grow fast; their birthrate is higher than India's. They don't believe in birth control at all; they are all followers of the Vatican Pope; they are all Catholics.

There has been a very revealing result of an experiment somewhere on a small island in the ocean where both America and France have been testing atomic weapons, nuclear weapons. The whole island has no population, except rats. All the trees have died. There is a tremendous amount of atomic radiation there which can kill any human being – but the rats have not died. They quickly became immune to any radiation. It was thought that in the Third World War all life would disappear. Now it is known that rats will live on, Third World War or no Third World War. All kinds of poisons have been used on rats to save crops. The rats did not die, but the people who ate those crops died.

Your ego is just like a rat. It has the immunity and the ability to adapt to any situation. You want serenity? You want silence? You want to come back home? Whatever you want, just name it and your ego will give it to you. But anything that is centered on 'myself' is going to be wrong.

Remember: no-self is your reality, your authentic reality. And how can you be silent with yourself? The self is the cause of all chaos in you, the self is the cause of all anxiety and misery in you. How can you be silent and find serenity? Your ego is deceiving you. If one has to beware of any enemy, it is the ego, it is the self. You have not come home yet.

You say, 'I feel like a flower bud ready to open, yet I do not feel in touch with the energy of love and joy that would allow this flower to bloom.' From where are you going to be in touch with the energy of love and joy? From yourself? Yourself is a false entity; it has no energy and no love. If you want energy and love for the nourishment of the bud that you feel, then you have to be open to all dimensions of existence and allow existence to reach to you: in the sunrays, in the songs of the birds – just listen to their chit-chat – to the trees, to the mountains, to the moon, to the stars, to all living beings, particularly to human beings.

You have to become a receptacle. The ego never wants to be a receptive entity – it goes against the egoistic structure, it goes against its pride. The ego can give, but it cannot take. But it has nothing to give. Unless you take from existence, you have nothing to give. Before giving you have to learn getting.

Be open to existence, to the starry night, to the day full of flowers, full of the rays of the sun, to human beings, who are all potential buddhas. Throw open all your doors and windows and the bud will start opening on its own accord. Do you think any gardener goes to a bud and tries to open it? If you try to open a bud forcibly, it will be crippled, distorted, something aborted. If you do not allow it to open on its own accord, you will destroy all possibility of having a beautiful flower. Every bud opens on its own accord. It just has to grow and be ready when the sun rises. Just wait for the sun.

Again, you are saying, 'It is almost as if I have not yet fully opened my heart to myself.' I wonder that you could not see your question and its utter stupidity. To open to yourself? That is almost like trying to fly by pulling on your shoestrings. Rather than opening the bud, you may destroy it. You will fall flat on the earth and forget all about buds and flowers.

The ways of the ego are very subtle and very clever. Then you say, 'Osho, am I missing something' – you are missing everything – 'or is it just a matter of time?' Don't throw the responsibility on time. What does poor time have to do with you? Time will not open your bud.

You need to be aware that the simple process of opening is always toward the beyond. Opening cannot be toward yourself – that's an absurdity. If you understand what I am saying, then you will be aware that you are full of words which you don't understand.

The question you have formulated has not arisen in your being. You have tried hard to make it very beautiful. You have used good words, but words are empty unless they have content. You cannot deceive me; in your question I can read your whole biography – not only the past but something of the future too. If you go on this way, you will never reach what you call your home and you will never blossom. You will never know what spring is.

You will have to change your whole approach. Right now you seem to be very knowledgeable. But knowledge is all rubbish. You don't have any experience of anything, even of the bud you are talking about. There is nothing like a bud in you. In this wrong situation which surrounds you, there cannot be. Your ego is too strong – it would crush any bud. Your ego is just like a bulldozer. Poor rosebuds cannot stand against a bulldozer. If you change from all this knowledgeability and accept your ignorance about the path, about the workings of your mind, then meditation will still be missing – and meditation needs patience.

Right now, without meditation, you are already a bud. You are already hoping to open unto yourself, which is really unique because in the whole of history, no mystic has talked about opening unto 'yourself.' Everything is possible – you just have to remove the hindrances: the greatest hindrance is the ego; the second hindrance is knowledgeability without experience; the third hindrance is imagination without seeing clearly that there is no bud yet. I can see this. I don't know where you are, who you are, but I can see through your question – the bud *cannot* be there. Your question is very revealing. You have not reached home, perhaps some caravanserai – an overnight stay – but in the morning you have to move on.

Home is when everything stops – time and mind – and nothing moves. Home is an eternal moment which begins but never ends. Home is when there is absolute nothingness: no self, no I. Only in this nothingness can buds of silence and serenity grow. And if you are open toward the universe, then it showers nourishment, and all buds start opening on their own accord.

Meditate, so that you can go beyond mind and self. Certainly meditation will take a little time because you are so full of bullshit. First you will have to clean the ground. Your misunderstanding is tremendous.

Chiang Kai-shek, the dictator of China before Mao Zedong came to power, was one of the most powerful people on the earth. When Mao removed him from power he escaped to Formosa, a private resort for the dictator.

He changed the name of Formosa to Taiwan and made it the capital of China. The whole of China was gone, but he made this small island the capital and continued to remain the dictator. There was no China in his hands, yet because of American support, Mainland China was not represented in the UN. Chiang Kai-shek's Taiwan represented China in the UN for many years – you cannot believe what kind of politicians are sitting on your chest.

This man Chiang Kai-shek when he was dethroned in utter desperation, old age, sickness – he had passed ninety – was being interviewed in Taipei by an American reporter from *Newsweek*.

'And when was the last time you had an election, General?' the reporter asked.

Chiang Kai-shek winked and said, 'Just before bleakfast.'

People's egos are such, even at the age of ninety. That idiot is saying he had an *erection* just before breakfast.

There is a loud knock on the door and the psychiatrist hurries to answer it. 'Doc,' says a frightened voice, 'I must talk to you about my brother. He breaks thermometers, drinks the mercury and throws away the glass.' 'What?' shrieks the horrified shrink. 'He throws away the glass? That's the best part!'

There are psychoanalysts who are far more insane than their patients but because they have qualifications, certificates, the ego goes on playing its games. The ego enjoys degrees – PhD's and DLitt's – very much, but psychoanalysts never look at the fact that they are either neurotic or psychotic themselves. It is a known fact that they go mad four times more often than any other profession. It is strange. These are the people who are supposed to help humanity out of all kinds of neurosis, psychosis, but they themselves go to the mental asylum four times more than any profession in the world.

And every psychiatrist – it is hilarious – once in a while goes to another psychiatrist to be psychoanalyzed. After six, eight months, they themselves need psychoanalysis. Now on what grounds can these people help those who are in real need of help? But the ego never even suspects that something may be wrong. It always pretends to be right.

The meditator is the only person in the whole world who begins his first step with a deep feeling of 'I am ignorant. I don't know anything.' With this ignorance, innocence comes side by side. With this ignorance, all the crap of your knowledge and words and imagination drops away. With this ignorance, slowly, slowly you settle into being just like a child, with a clarity, a purity, a silence, an alertness.

All that is needed is a deep recognition that you know nothing, a recognition that your ego is not you. You are simply the silence which has been taken over by the ego. You are a land conquered by an enemy and you are being identified with the enemy.

Everything is possible, but you have to begin from the right point with humbleness, with openness, with receptivity – and a silence and a patience and a trust will arise on their own accord. Yes, many, many flowers will blossom in your being too, but first you have to put things right.

Osho,

Some people do things instinctively. Is instinct the same as intuition? Or is instinct animal-like and intuition only human?

Osho, please comment on the difference, if there is a difference.

Instead of two words, you will have to understand three words, because you have a past and you have a present and you have a future. Instinct is what belongs to your animal past. It is very old, very solid. It is the inheritance of millions of years. And when I say it is animal-like, I am not condemning it. With the word *animal* the priests of all religions have associated some condemnation, but I am simply stating a fact, no condemnation at all.

Our past was an animal past. We have passed through all kinds of animals. Our evolution has been from fish to man, passing through all the species of animals. It has been a long, long journey to arrive at mankind.

Intellect is human: it is our present. That's how we function, through intellect. All our sciences, all our businesses, all our professions, whatever is going on in the world – our politics, our religion, our philosophy – are all based on intellect. Intellect is human.

Instinct is almost infallible because it is so old, so ripe, so mature. Your eyes are blinking; are you doing it? They go on doing it by themselves. Your heart is beating, your breathing is going in and out: this is instinct. It is not up to your intellect to look after all these essential things of life. They are in the hands of instinct because instinct is absolutely infallible. It never forgets to breathe, it never forgets anything.

But intellect is very fallible; it is very new, a very recent arrival. It is just groping in the dark, still trying to find out what it is, where it belongs. And because it does not have roots in experience, it substitutes experience with beliefs, philosophies, ideologies. They become the focus of intellect, but they are all fallible because they are all man-made, manufactured by some clever guy. They are not applicable in every situation. They may be right in one situation and in another situation they may not be right. But intellect is blind, it doesn't know how to deal with the new. It always brings the old answer to the new question.

Paddy and Sean are sitting opposite the local whorehouse in Dublin, discussing the virtues of the Catholic faith. Suddenly Gideon Greenberg, the local rabbi, approaches the door, looks left and right, then hurries up the stairs.

'Did you see that?' roars Paddy. 'I'm glad I am a Catholic.'

Ten minutes later, the Anglican priest approaches the door, looks around quickly, then dashes up the stairs.

'Another hypocrite,' laughs Paddy. 'Thank God I am a Catholic.'

A few minutes later Sean nudges Paddy and says, 'Hey, man, look! Father O'Murphy is coming this way.'

The two men watch in stunned silence as the Catholic priest disappears up the stairs into the whorehouse. Suddenly Paddy jumps to his feet, crosses himself and shouts at Sean, 'Where is your respect? Stand up and take off your hat. There must be a death in the house!'

Now the whole thing has changed. Intellect lives through prejudices; it is never fair. Just by its very nature it cannot be because it has no experience. Instinct is always fair and shows you exactly the natural way, the relaxed way, and the one that the universe follows. But strangely, instinct has been condemned by all religions and intellect has been praised. Of course, if everybody follows instinct, there is no need of any religion, no need of any God, no need of any priest.

Animals don't need God and they are perfectly happy. I don't see that they are missing God. Not a single animal, not a single bird, not a single tree is missing God. They are all enjoying life in its utter beauty and simplicity, with no fear of hell and no greed for heaven, no philosophical differences. There are no Catholic lions, there are no Protestant lions and no Hindu lions.

The whole of existence must be laughing at man, at what has happened to man. If birds can live without religions and churches, mosques and temples, why can't man? The birds never fight religious wars, neither do the animals nor the trees. But if you are a Mohammedan and I am a Hindu, we cannot coexist. Either you have to become converted to my religion or – be ready – I will send you to heaven immediately! The fact is, if instinct is praised, religions lose any rationality, any reason to exist. Hence they praise intellect.

And the third thing, which is your future, is intuition. These three words have to be understood.

Instinct is physical. Your past – based on the experience of millions of years, infallible – never commits any mistake and does miracles in you of which you are not even aware. How does your food become blood? How does your breathing go on functioning even when you are asleep? How does your body separate oxygen from nitrogen? How does the instinctive world of nature go on giving to every part of your body what it needs? How much oxygen is needed in your head for the mind to function? The exact amount is sent through blood running all around the body, distributing fresh oxygen, taking out the old, used, dead cells, replacing them with new ones and taking them back to places from where they can be disposed of.

Have you ever thought why you don't feel pain when you cut your nails, or why you don't feel pain when you cut your hair? They are dead cells of your body and this is the way instinct disposes of them. If they were living, then they would hurt just as if you had cut your finger. You would feel wounded and you would feel immense pain. But when you cut your hair, you don't feel anything because the hairs are already dead.

The scientists say that what instinct does for man, we are not yet capable of doing. And in a small body the instinct does so many miracles. If someday science is going to do the work of a single human body, it will need at least one square mile of factory space for a single human being and tremendous machinery. And still it will not be infallible. Machinery can break down, stop, or the electricity can go off.

But for seventy years continuously, or even one hundred years for a few people, or even one hundred and eighty years for very few people, the instinct goes on functioning perfectly well: the electricity never goes off. Not a single mistake is committed; everything goes according to plan. The plan is in every cell of your body. Scientists are trying to read it, but because it is in code language, nobody knows how to read it. They are still trying to figure it out.

The day we can read the human cells, we will be able to predict everything about a child, even before it is born, even before it is in the mother's womb. The father's sperm has a program and in that program your age, your health, what kind of diseases you will have, your genius, your intelligence, your talents, your whole destiny is contained.

On the other polarity of your being, beyond the mind – which is the world of intellect – is the world of intuition. Intuition opens its doors through meditation. Meditation is simply knocking on the doors of intuition. Intuition is complete; it does not grow. Just like instinct, you have inherited it from existence.

Intuition is your consciousness, your being; intellect is your mind; instinct is your body.

Just as instinct functions perfectly as regards the body, intuition functions perfectly as far as your consciousness is concerned. Intellect is just between these two – a passage to be passed, a bridge to be crossed. But there are many people, many millions of people, who never cross the bridge. They simply sit on the bridge thinking they have arrived home.

The home is on the further shore, beyond the bridge. The bridge joins instinct and intuition. But it all depends on you. You may start building a house on the bridge – then you have gone astray. Intellect is not going to be your home. It is a very small instrument to be used only for passing from instinct to intuition. So only the person who uses his intellect to go beyond it can be called intelligent. Intuition is existential, instinct is natural. Intellect is just groping in the dark. The faster you move beyond intellect, the better.

When Billy Graham sang 'All I want is Jesus,' five thousand people joined the Protestant church.

When Pope the Polack sang 'Ave Maria,' ten thousand people joined the Catholic church.

When Frank Sinatra sang 'There's a gold mine in the sky,' one hundred thousand Jews joined the Air Force.

Intellect functions that way. And Jews are intelligent people – if there is a gold mine in the sky, why waste time here? Immediately join the Air Force!

Intellect can be a barrier to those who think there is nothing beyond it. Intellect can be a beautiful way to those who understand that there is certainly something beyond it. Science has stopped at intellect. That's why it cannot figure out anything about consciousness.

Intellect without an awakened intuition is one of the most dangerous things in the world. And we are living under the danger of intellect because intellect has given science immense power. But the power is in the hands of children, not in the hands of wise people. Intuition makes a man wise. Call it enlightenment, call it awakening; those are simply different names for wisdom. Only in the hands of wisdom can intellect be used as a beautiful servant. And instinct and intuition function together perfectly well: one on the physical level, another on the spiritual level.

The whole problem of humanity is getting stuck in the middle, in the mind, in the intellect. Then you will have misery, you will have anxiety, you will have agony and you will have meaninglessness. You will have all kinds of tensions that seem to have no solution anywhere.

Intellect makes everything a problem and knows no solution at all. Instinct never creates any problem and does not need any solution because it simply functions naturally. Intuition is pure solution. It has no problems, whereas intellect has no solution, only problems. If you rightly see the division, it is very simple to understand: unless instinct is available, you are dead. Unless intuition is available, your life has no meaning – you just drag on. It is a kind of vegetation.

Intuition brings meaning, splendor, joy, blessings. Intuition gives you the secrets of existence, brings a tremendous silence, serenity, which cannot be disturbed and which cannot be taken away from you. And with instinct and intuition functioning together, you can also use your intellect for right purposes. Otherwise you have only means but no ends. Intellect has no idea of any ends. This has created today's situation in the world. Science goes on producing things but it does not know why. Politicians go on using those things, not knowing that they are destructive, that they are preparing for a global suicide. The world needs a tremendous rebellion that can take it beyond intellect into the silences of intuition.

The very word *intuition* has to be understood. You know the word *tuition*. Tuition comes from outside, somebody teaches you – the tutor. Intuition means something that arises within your being. It is your potential; that's why it is called intuition. Wisdom is never borrowed, and that which is borrowed is never wisdom. Unless you have your own wisdom, your own vision, your own clarity, your own eyes to see, you will not be able to understand the mystery of existence.

As far as I am concerned, I am in absolute favor of instinct. Don't disturb it. Every religion has been teaching you to disturb it. What is fasting but disturbing your instinct? Your body is hungry and asking for food, and you are starving it for spiritual reasons. A strange kind of spirituality has possessed your being. It should simply be called stupidity, not spirituality. Your instinct is asking for water, it is thirsty; your body needs it. But your religions...

Jainism does not allow anybody to even drink water in the night. Now as far as the body is concerned, it may feel thirsty, particularly in summer in a hot country like India – and Jainas exist only in India. In my childhood, I used to feel very guilty because I had to steal water in the night. I could not sleep without drinking at least once a night in hot summers. But I used to feel that I was doing something that should not be done, that I was committing a sin. Strange and stupid ideas are being forced on people.

I am in favor of the instinct and this is one of the secrets I want to reveal to you: if you are totally in favor of instinct, it will be very easy to find the way toward intuition. They are the same, just functioning on different layers: one functions on the material level, the other functions on the spiritual level.

But intellect goes on creating repressive methods for the instinct. Celibacy, for instance, creates perversions – homosexuality, sodomy – because it is not part of your instinctive program. To accept your instinctive life with absolute joy, without any guilt, will help you to open the doors of intuition. They are not different, just their planes are different. Instinct functions beautifully, silently, without any noise. So does intuition, but even more silently, far more beautifully.

Intellect is a disturbance. But it depends on us whether we make it a disturbance or use it as a stepping-stone. When you come across a stone in the street, either you can think it a hindrance or you can use it as a stepping-stone to a higher plane. Those who really understand use intellect as a stepping-stone. The masses are under the control of religions which teach them to use their intellect as a repressive force for instinct. They get involved in fighting with instinct and forget all about intuition. Their whole energy becomes involved in fighting with their own life force. And when you are continuously fighting with your instinct...

A Jaina monk is supposed to remain naked all the year round, even in the winter months, even in the cold night. He cannot use a mattress, he cannot use a blanket, he cannot use anything to cover his body, day or night. He has to fast. The longer he fasts, the greater a saint he becomes in the eyes of the same kind of conditioned people – thirty days, forty days...

Jainism is the only religion in the world which allows you to leave the body if you want to, but you cannot do it quickly by jumping into a river, or by cutting off your head, or by drinking poison. These methods are too simple. Jainism believes in austerity, arduousness. No shortcut is allowed; you have to fast to death.

If a healthy young man fasts, it takes ninety days for him to die, ninety days of utter agony. He can neither sleep nor can he be at ease for a single moment. And every day he goes on becoming thinner, every day two pounds disappear. By the time ninety days have passed, he will be just a skeleton. Only then will he die. These ninety days he suffered hell unnecessarily – but this is thought to be spiritual: this is fighting against the body; this is conquering the body and the material. This is the spirit conquering the body.

Just a few months ago a Jaina monk committed suicide like this: they call it *santhara.* I wonder why a government that is against suicide takes no notice of these people. They should be prevented. They should be put in jails with others who attempt suicide. What does it matter what means you use for suicide? Whether you die within nine minutes or ninety days does not matter. If you allow the Jaina monks, then why should you prevent others?

The prevention is also very beautiful. If someone is caught committing suicide – if he has already committed it, then nothing can be done – then he will be sent to the gallows. Strange punishment! That's what he was doing himself, so why waste unnecessary years in court cases, judges, advocates before finally sentencing him to death for trying to commit suicide? The poor fellow was doing it himself, without any expense to the country.

After that Jaina monk, one of his disciples, an old woman, started ... Because her master had gone, she did not want to live. And these people are surrounded by thousands who respect them because this is the greatest sacrifice and the greatest victory of spirituality over materialism. From all over the country, thousands of people will come to touch their feet – and all that they are doing is simply committing a crime. But they are not criminals, they are saints!

It is the same situation in all the religions, with different superstitions. They turn the energy of your intellect against your instinct and that spoils all possibilities of opening the flower of your intuition. That is the mystic rose that will lead you to the ultimate ecstasy and to immortal life. But people seem to be absolutely in the hands of the dead past. Whatever the old scriptures have told them, they go on doing it, without ever considering the whole science of man.

These three are the layers of the whole science of man. Instinct should be allowed a relaxed flow. Never, for any reason, disturb it with the intellect. Intellect should be used as an opening for intuition. It has just to give way for intuition to take over your life. Then your life is a life of immense light, of luminosity. It becomes a constant festival.

But it seems the majority of the world consists of very retarded people. They never think about their life themselves. Whatever they are told, they do. They never bother whether it comes from right sources or wrong sources. You may be born a Catholic or a Hindu or a Mohammedan, but your birth does not ensure that your religion is right; your birth and your religion have no connection. But right up till now, wherever you are born decides your religion. The child has not chosen the religion; the religion is imposed on him. And the constant repetition of all kinds of lies makes him more and more unintelligent, superstitious, retarded, idiotic.

Paddy and Sean are eating their lunch on the construction site. Suddenly Paddy says, 'Yuck! I just ate a worm with this apple.'

'Well,' says Sean, 'drink some water and wash him down.'

'To hell with him,' replies Paddy, throwing away the apple core. 'Let him walk himself.'

All over the world you are surrounded by these kinds of people. You have to stay alert and not get trapped in the same imprisonment as everybody else.

If being with me you cannot be unimprisoned, unfettered, then you will not find any other place on the earth where you can be free. To me, freedom is the most fundamental value. Only in freedom can you grow to the highest peak, can you become an Everest. Only in freedom will your intuition blossom and bring immense treasures to you.

6

In Favor of Luxury

Osho,
Sitting with you in discourse a feeling of magnificence and utter luxuriousness, which feels so different from material luxury, keeps on arising in me. Would you like to talk about the luxuriousness of being with a living master?

There are two worlds side by side: the world of matter and the world of consciousness. The world of matter is known to the mind, but the world of consciousness is only known when the mind disappears. We are all born as a mind, but existence gives us every opportunity and every challenge to go beyond it. Very few dare, but those who dare are the only people who have known life in its immense beauty, its luxury, its joy, its music, its harmony, its eternal silence and peace. Only those few people have really lived; the others are somehow just dragging themselves from the cradle to the grave.

The mind can never know what authentic luxury is. It cannot know *anything* of the real; it knows only about the unreal, about the world that is made of the same stuff as dreams are made of. The mind has its own limitations, but there is no question of condemning the mind. Your eyes can see but your eyes cannot hear; there is no reason to condemn the eyes because you cannot hear the music.

'Why can't you hear the sound of the running water? Why can't you hear the songs of the birds and the tremendous silence of the stars?' Eyes can only see, there is no question of any condemnation. Ears can only hear. It is absolutely absurd to condemn the ears because they cannot see the light of the sun and the moon, because they cannot see the rainbow and its colors, the flowers and their tremendous beauty.

All five senses have their own windows to existence, and our mind is all five senses combined. These five senses are the five doors or windows of the mind into existence. But because these five senses only go outward, you can see what is outside you but not what is inside you. You can touch what is outside you but not what is inside you.

All senses are doors opening to the outside world, but the world of consciousness is within. The mind has no way to even have a glimpse of the world that is hidden inside you. They are side by side; there is not a difference of miles or even a few steps. They meet on a boundary line, they are running parallel – and just as parallel lines never meet, they never meet. You would have to jump from one line to another line.

The mind hankers for luxury, for comfort, for joy, for love. It tries to make things that it longs for happen, but they are bound to be just outward things: a beautiful house, beautiful furniture, a beautiful garden. Everything that you can think of, the mind can manage – but only on the outside. It is only a very faraway echo of the inner beauty, of the inner luxury, of the inner richness. But the inner, which is so close, remains almost closed to millions of people. Their whole lives they are playing with toys and never come to know the real. And the real was not far away. It was just a change of gestalt.

This word *gestalt* is German. No other language has exactly the same word, hence it is used in all the languages without being translated. But it can be explained so that you can see what it indicates.

Just thirty or forty years ago a psychology came into being and became very fashionable. It was Gestalt psychology. It has faded now, but there is some significant meaning in the very word *gestalt*. The psychology may prove true or untrue – that is not my interest. My interest is in the simple word *gestalt*. That psychology has contributed a tremendously beautiful word.

In Gestalt psychology books, you will always find a picture to explain the meaning of *gestalt* and sometimes you will find that kind of picture in children's books: a line drawing of a beautiful young woman. What is expected of you is to go on staring, without blinking, at the beautiful face of the woman. And suddenly you see something has changed. Nothing *has* changed: you are the same, the book is the same, the picture is the same. But in a strange moment, in a strange way, something has transpired between your vision and the lines of the picture. Instead of a beautiful young woman, you see a very ugly old woman. You cannot believe it when it happens for the first time.

Then go on staring – it will happen again: the old woman will disappear and the young woman is there. You cannot see both together. That is a very significant point to understand. You can't see both together because they both consist of the same lines. When you start to see the beautiful woman again, the gestalt has changed; you are seeing the same lines in a different combination. But because they are the same lines, you now cannot see the old woman. When you then start seeing the old woman, once more the gestalt has changed, your vision has changed. The same lines that were making the beautiful woman, the young woman, are now constituting the old woman.

So you can see both, but only separately. Why does it happen? It's because your mind is in a constant change; it cannot remain at the same point for long. It is not accustomed to being static; it is a dynamic force. So when you are staring at the beautiful woman, the mind gets bored. It wants some change, but you don't allow any change. You go on focusing, staring, then the mind finds a way of its own. It changes the gestalt, it changes the combination of the lines until suddenly you see an old woman.

I think you will understand the meaning of gestalt: the meaning is a sudden change in your vision. That which was not in front of you, that which you were not seeing, suddenly becomes visible. And that which you were seeing suddenly disappears – and you can't see both together.

I would like you to understand something parallel, a gestalt, in the history of world philosophy. There have been philosophers like Shankara, in India, Bradley in England, Hegel in Germany, and many more all over the world. These three can be said to be the most representative of a certain gestalt. They all say that the world is illusory, it is only an appearance. It is not a reality, it is no more than a dream. The real is experienced only in your innermost being. Except for your inner being, everything that you see is just ephemeral.

In India they call it maya. The word *maya* means: as if you are seeing a magic show in which nothing is real. Or it can also mean a mirage – what happens in a desert when you are very thirsty, tired. Suddenly you see far away a beautiful small oasis, trees, a lake. You see not only the lake, you see the reflection of the trees in the lake. It is impossible to deny the reality of an oasis. But as you come close the oasis goes – simply where, you cannot say. It simply disappears. There are no trees, there is no lake and there is no reflection of the trees.

The people, the travelers, the caravans that have been passing through deserts know very well where the true oases are and where there are only ephemeral oases. But to the new traveler, it is impossible to make a distinction; they look exactly the same. The desert creates such an illusory reality, and because of your thirst you tend to believe in it. If you hadn't been thirsty, you might not have believed. You would have suspected, doubted, you would have questioned. But you were so thirsty that this was not the time to disbelieve in the oasis.

To disbelieve in the oasis is simply to accept death because of thirst. You are so thirsty you start trusting, believing in that which is just created by the rays of the sun, reflected from the sand of the desert. When the rays reflect back, they move, they shimmer

– just as water shimmers. Those shimmering rays going back to the sun create the illusion of water. In those shimmering rays a kind of mirror effect is created, and because of that mirror effect anything that is around it is reflected. This mirage is another meaning of maya. The world as seen by Shankara, by Hegel, by Bradley is rejected as only appearance, not authentically true. It is as true as a dream, but not more than that.

There is another school of philosophers. In India, the greatest of that school is Brihaspati. In Greece, the greatest of this other school is Epicurus and in Europe, Karl Marx. These three are representative of materialism. They say just the opposite. They say matter is the only reality and consciousness is illusory: what you see as objects, material – that is the only true world. Your body is true, but you are not true. Your consciousness is only an ephemeral effect, a by-product, just like the mirage in the desert.

It's strange that these two philosophies have always existed side by side. And strangely, neither a single materialist has ever crossed the line to become a spiritualist nor vice versa – they remain parallel. Not a single person has been convinced by the arguments of the other. My own standpoint is beyond both. I can see that both are too attached to one gestalt.

One is saying that the young woman is real and the old woman is just false. The other is saying the old woman is real and the young woman is just false. But as far as I am concerned, the young woman and the old woman are not separate. Either both are true or both are untrue, because they are made of the same lines. If you deny that the old woman is real, take away all the lines that make the old woman and you will find the young woman has also disappeared. Or vice versa: if you think the old woman is real, then take away the unreal young woman's lines and the old woman will disappear. They are really two ways of seeing the same reality.

To me there is no division. To me it is a question of transcending the duality of parallel lines, of not getting caught up in any gestalt, but going beyond both gestalts and seeing, as a witness, the matter and the mind – and that *you* are far away from both. Then a new world of luxury, a new world of grace, a new world of magnificence opens up.

What you are saying is immensely important. Your question is one of those few questions which everybody has to understand because everybody will have to encounter the reality implied in the question. You are saying, 'Sitting with you, a feeling of magnificence and utter luxuriousness, which feels so different from material luxury, keeps on arising in me.' Trust in it. Settle more and more deeply in it because you are on the right path. What is happening to you, sitting here with me in communion, is just your own inner world opening.

If you love me and you trust me, then there is no need to keep your heart closed. There is no need to keep your defenses up, there is no need to keep a distance, there is no need to have any fear. If love cannot destroy your fear, if trust cannot take away your security measures, then it is not worth calling it love, it is not worth calling it trust. The whole experience of being with a living master is that the disciple slowly, slowly relaxes, drops all his defenses – there is nobody who is going to hurt him – and because there is no fear, he starts coming closer.

The whole world lives in fear, in such deep fear that we have created hidden defense mechanisms. For example: in the West, people shake hands and it is thought to be a friendly gesture. It is not! It was basically out of fear that people started shaking hands with the right hand. The right hand is dangerous – you may be carrying a weapon. It is better to shake hands and be completely sure that the other is not carrying any weapon. It is a very strange world – shaking hands was a gesture of enmity not of friendship. That's why the left hand is not used in shaking hands because the right hand is your active hand. If you are carrying something dangerous, it will be in your right hand.

In the East, people were more alert and conscious because they were more cowardly than in the West. The whole philosophy of nonviolence has made them cowardly. They have found an even better way. When you shake hands you come too close. Coming too close is dangerous, as even the left hand can be used to wound you, to shoot you.

Unfortunately there are 'leftists' and their number is not small – ten percent of the whole population. Most of them have been forced to use their right hands. That's why you don't see so many left-handed people because in school the teachers force them saying, 'Write with your right hand; the right hand is right and the left hand is wrong.' And they become a laughingstock. So the children start using their right hand, although it is difficult for them because they were born 'leftist.' But slowly, slowly, if you try, the right hand starts working. It will never be as good as that of the born 'rightists.' It will always remain secondary. But in a right-handed world, what can you do?

Ninety percent of people are right-handed. Only ten percent of people are left-handed. They are such a small minority that most of them disappear into the right-handed crowd. Very few remain left-handed their whole life. It needs a little individuality, it needs a little courage to declare, 'If my left hand is active, I am not going to unnecessarily force the right hand on my nature.' But there are very few people who will take that stand against the whole of society.

Coming too close is dangerous, but still the left hand is left out. It can carry a small knife and that may be enough to kill you. The East has found a better way. Rather than shaking hands, it puts both hands together, to show you that *both* hands are empty, and there is no need to come very close. You are there, I am here, you are showing that both your hands are empty, I am showing that both my hands are empty.

Slowly, slowly in the East it took on not only a meaning of friendliness, but even a meaning of spirituality, 'We are bowing down with folded hands to the godliness within you.' But the reality was just the opposite. It was a defense measure to make you aware, 'I am not your enemy, I also want assurance that you are not my enemy.' But you still keep your distance. Who knows? The person may be hiding a knife in his clothes, he may not show it in his hands. And it has happened; it is not that it is only a fear.

Even great kings, hugging another king – as if in deep friendship and love – have killed. When they were hugging, they were also carrying a knife, a small knife in their hands. And it was enough – if you wound the person in the right place, you can kill him even with a small knife. There are many cases on record. So-called great emperors and kings have behaved in such an ugly way, inviting another king as a friend and then killing him. If emperors can do that, what about ordinary people?

I am just telling you one example – there are of course many more – of a defense that you use without knowing it, which has just been handed down by the older generation.

My grandfather used to have a dog and he never went anywhere without the dog. Even if he was going to a marriage ceremony, to a party, he went with his dog. His dog would be sitting by his side. I would be sitting by his other side.

I said, 'This looks very bad: I am reduced to the category of your dog! When you want me to come with you, at least you can leave your dog at home.'

He said, 'You are too young to understand.'

I said, 'When will I be old enough so that I can understand? Just tell me. I have been listening to everyone: "You are too young." Always too young. When will I be able to understand?'

He said, 'That's a good point. In fact, we use this strategy just to avoid unnecessary inquiries.'

So I said, 'Just tell me today. I'm old enough to understand.'

He said, 'The reality is I always take my dog with me if I am invited to eat food anywhere. First I give it to the dog. Unless I'm sure that there is no poison...'

I said, 'You are taking it too seriously. Who is going to poison you?'

He said, 'You don't know. I have seen people poisoned.'

I now realize that he was right. After I was poisoned myself, I remembered the old man – he was right. If I had had a dog with me ... But I am not allowed to have a dog. That is the difficulty, my doctors don't allow it. They say I am allergic. No defense at all!

And then when I read that Gautam Buddha was poisoned, and it was food poisoning ... My grandfather was dead, but I thought if he had been alive, I would have gone to him and asked his forgiveness for laughing at him. If Gautam Buddha had had his dog with him...

You are living in a very murderous society, where every kind of crime is happening. Naturally man has learned to close himself from every side, out of sheer defense. But when you come to a master, there is no need to have any defense. And slowly, slowly, as you become more and more in tune with the master, your defenses drop – windows open, fresh breezes and fresh sunrays enter.

The master is not a master if he is not a fresh breeze. A master is not a master if he is not a sunrise to your being. A master is not a master if he does not come into your heart as a song, as a dance, as a celebration – there cannot be anything more luxurious, more graceful, more delicious.

Slowly, slowly you start learning a new lesson. It is not only to the master that you have to be open, you have to be open to the trees too; they are not going to harm you. You have to be open to the stars too; they are not going to harm you. This vast universe is here. You have just to be open to this whole universe and suddenly all the stars descend and come close to you, dancing within your heart. The trees start having a certain communication with you – and the flowers smile.

There are strange stories – I used to think they were only stories, but slowly, slowly my own experience told me that they were not stories.

About Mohammed the story is: when he was in the desert of Saudi Arabia, wherever he went a cloud always moved over his head. It seems to be very unlikely that clouds would be so sensitive. But every contemporary source ... Mohammed is not very ancient, only fourteen hundred years have passed, not long. All contemporary sources of Mohammed describe this fact. Even people who were opposing him have described the miracle: 'We may be in disagreement with his philosophy and religion but we cannot deny the fact; we have seen it with our own eyes. Wherever he goes in the desert, a cloud is always moving with him, giving him shade, always keeping him in the cool shade.'

About Gautam Buddha there are stories. Perhaps they are historical facts. Perhaps one day – sooner than you think – science is going to authenticate these stories, which up to now have been thought to be only mythological. It is said that when Gautam Buddha sat under a tree – just to rest – even if it was not the season, flowers would immediately blossom, and many flowers would shower on Gautam Buddha.

As scientists understand more and more about the sensitivity of trees, it seems possible that the openness of Gautam Buddha may have had a deep effect on the very heart of the tree. Even the poor tree could not resist the temptation to welcome Gautam Buddha with a few flowers, although it was not the season.

This whole existence can become a luxury. You just have to learn the art of being open.

In the university where I was teaching for almost nine years, there was a long row of trees between two university buildings: one for the arts faculty, the other for the science faculty. Between these two buildings there was this row of very beautiful trees. They gave deep shade, and in the summer they had so many flowers – red flowers – that the trees seemed to be on fire. When there are hundreds of these trees, it looks as if the whole forest is on fire. So many flowers come to them simultaneously that you cannot see the leaves anymore, just flowers, such beautiful flowers.

There were at least two dozen trees between the two buildings and just a small road joining them. The idea must have been to cover that small road with these lush, green, beautiful trees – cover the whole road between the two buildings – so that there would be shade, even in the hottest summer.

No one knows what happened. When I joined the university all the trees were alive. I had chosen the most beautiful tree to park my car under. Nobody was parking their car there because a parking lot was available on the other side of the building. I was even told that this was not the place to park.

I said, 'Unless you show me any ordinance from the university that I cannot park my car under this tree, I am going to park my car there. Even if I have to leave the university, I will leave, but I'm going to park here as long as I am part of the university.'

The vice-chancellor understood, 'It is unnecessary to quarrel with this man. He may resign just for this reason, and there is no harm. Let him park there.'

It was just outside his office – he could see me and my car from his window. My idea to park the car there had a reason. Because I was mostly out of town without leave, I told my chauffeur, 'Every day at eleven thirty, before the vice-chancellor comes to the university at around twelve, park my car under the tree. That will keep him thinking that I am in the university. And just after he leaves you can drive the car back home.'

It was because of his window that I had chosen that tree. He was not aware of the fact that it was really the window not the tree. I kept insisting, 'I love this tree and I will keep my car under this tree as long as I am in this university.' And he used to look out of his window and remained happy, thinking that I was in the university.

Slowly, slowly some kind of disease happened to those trees. All the trees died, except the tree I was parking my car under. All the other trees died completely: they were without leaves, barren, and new leaves never came. The vice-chancellor was very much surprised.

One day, when I was parking the car, he came to the window and called me, waved to me and said, 'It is very strange. I am sorry I was preventing you from parking your car. Not only me, but many people feel that it is just because of you and your car that this tree has remained alive. All the other trees have died, not a single exception, just *your* tree.'

It had become known as my tree. Nobody else dared to park his car there; everybody knew that it was my tree. And the vice-chancellor himself said, 'I am sorry that I was preventing you. If you had listened to me, this tree also would have died. And it is the only tree I can see from my window.' I myself did not think that it had anything to do with me. Then I left the university. After two years I went back again, just to meet the vice-chancellor, my friends and colleagues. I was passing through the city and I thought...

When I went there, I saw that my tree had also died. I also became a little suspicious – perhaps the vice-chancellor and those other people were right. When I reached his office he reminded me. He said, 'I knew it would happen. The day you resigned I looked at the tree and I felt that it was going to happen. And within three months – just three months – the tree died.'

I had left the tree absolutely young, a luscious green, full of flowers. Perhaps there was something happening in the being of the tree: some love, some trust, some opening, some friendliness.

Modern researchers say that trees are more sensitive than human beings. They go through the whole range of emotions: fear, love, anger, compassion. They go through all these emotions far more deeply than human beings.

So it is not only a question of being open to a master. It is really a question of being open. The master is only an excuse. Use the master as an excuse, so that you can learn the language of trust, the language of openness, the language of communion with existence. Then you will find that your life will become inwardly rich – every day more and more. And you will find a grace in your being that you were never aware was possible.

I am in favor of this luxury, this richness. People have always misunderstood me – perhaps that is my destiny. I have been condemned all around the world as the guru of the rich. If understood in my sense, I am certainly the master of the richest, the most sensitive, the most loving, the most luxurious people in the world. But those who have been condemning me, they are condemning not in my sense. They cannot even understand that *inner* luxury is possible. To them luxury means outside things; richness means money. But to my people it has to mean the inner, always the inner. Whatever I am saying is for the inner, not for the outer.

On the outside, there is nothing of much value, just the mundane world, with all kinds of greed, struggle, competitiveness, violence. The outside is ugly. I would like the outside also to be beautiful and rich and luxurious, but it can happen only when the inside has changed. The first and the foremost change has to be inner. The outer will follow.

A shipwrecked sailor, who has been living alone on an island for five years, wakes up one morning to see a ship anchored close by and a small boat coming toward the shore.

He races to the beach and is greeted by an officer who steps out of the boat and hands him a packet of newspapers.

'What are these for?' he asks, amazed.

'With the captain's compliments, sir,' replies the officer. 'He suggests that you read what the newspapers say about the world first and then tell us if you still want to be rescued.'

What do you think: did the man decide to be rescued or not? I have been thinking about him, but I cannot imagine that he decided to be rescued. If you read five years of newspapers, the only conclusion will be to get rid of this world. It is not worth living. It is not worth being with these people. As far as I am concerned I have forgotten the world of the newspapers completely. I have found my people. I have found my world.

I have found a small planet of my own, where love is the only law, where laughter is prayer, where dancing is divine, where every moment is sacred, and where to be natural is the only spirituality. Because I could manage to find my people, I am alive. Otherwise, I would have managed long ago to be crucified by all kinds of idiots, who are always willing ... They would have been very happy and I would have been very happy because it does not seem to be worth living in this world. And what I have done is very difficult, is almost unprecedented: finding my own kind of people who can understand me, who can have a rapport with my innermost being. Otherwise there is nothing but misunderstanding in the world.

A very proper Englishman goes into a bar one night, sits down, but does not order a drink. The bartender, an unusually friendly guy, asks him if he would like a drink on the house.

The Englishman shakes his head.

'I tried liquor once,' he said. 'Did not like it.'

Still trying to be friendly, the bartender asks him if he would like to join a couple of the boys for a few hands of poker.

The Englishman shakes his head. 'Tried gambling once,' he says, 'didn't like it. In fact, I would not be sitting in this place at all, but I promised my son I would meet him here.'

'I see,' says the bartender. 'Your only child, I assume.'

Because he tries everything only once and then – finished!

Osho,

Watching your people arrive in larger numbers every day makes me feel so humble, and full of joyful tears, knowing that we all have this one thing in common: our love for you.

It is such a gift to be just one of all these loving smiles who sit at your feet each day in Chuang Tzu.

Osho, again and again, thank you for being here.

Jivan Mary, I am reminded...

Mulla Nasruddin was coming home. The sun had set. There was still some light, but it was getting darker every moment. He was passing by the side of the graveyard when he saw, far away, a few people coming on horses. He could make out that they had swords. He immediately concluded that there was danger: 'It seems my last moment has come.'

So he jumped over the wall of the graveyard and there was a freshly- dug grave. To avoid the dangers that were coming, he lay down in the grave, closed his eyes and stopped breathing.

But those people had already seen this fellow, and they also saw him jump over the wall. They thought, 'He seems to be a thief or something.'

It was a marriage party, and in many places in the East – particularly Mohammedan countries – when people go to a marriage party, they go on their horses and carry their swords.

This again reminds me of shaking hands. In the beginning, the marriage party was really a party of enemies who were going to force some family at the point of a sword to give their daughter to their son. It was not a friendly affair. In the beginning, marriage was an invention, a question of conquering, forcing a certain family, whether they were willing or not; it was a power struggle. This must have happened thousands of years ago, but even now the marriage party still carries swords.

In India, being a very nonviolent country, the whole marriage party does not carry swords. The man who is going to be married doesn't carry a sword, but a small knife – just symbolic.

I have asked many of my friends when they were getting married, 'Why do you go on carrying that small knife? I don't see any point in it.'

They said, 'Neither do we see any point in it, but traditionally...'

I said, 'At least you should have inquired. There must have been some reason, some time back.'

Then I told them, 'This is just the last remnant of a historical fact. Thousands of years ago, women were thought to be commodities and they had to be conquered. There was no other way except force. It is ugly to carry these knives because they are symbolic of that old, primitive, barbaric stage.'

They said, 'But our parents, family, everybody will be very annoyed and even the other party will not like it. They have also forgotten that this is a symbol of antagonism, not a symbol of any friendship or love.'

It was a marriage party, but Mulla thought, 'So many swords, there is danger.'

And those people thought, 'This man seems to be a thief or something. Suddenly, when he saw us, he jumped over the wall.'

So they all came nearer, jumped over the wall and looked all around – 'Where has that man disappeared to?'

Mulla was looking at them silently. Because one cannot continue to stop one's breathing, once in a while he was breathing and then watching to see what would finally happen.

Finally they walked all around the grave and they saw that this was not the way a man had to be buried. He was uncovered, fully dressed, had his shoes on, even his umbrella with him. They had never seen a dead body carrying an umbrella, wearing shoes, and then lying like this. The cold night was coming ... Who were the people who had left the body uncovered?

Mohammedans don't make graves like Christians, their graves are just pure mud. They just pour the mud on top of it, that's enough. They are poor people. They cannot manage to have marble – at the most a small stone on which they put the name of the person, that's all.

But what kind of thing was this? When they looked closely, they saw that once in a while the body was breathing. When they were all surrounding him silently, Mulla opened one eye. They could not believe what kind of fellow he was, and they were very angry.

They asked him, 'Why are you here?'

Mulla said, 'I can ask you the same question. Why are *you* here? Perhaps you don't know the answer, so I will answer from both sides. I am here because of you! You are here because of me!'

Jivan Mary, I am here because of you. You are here because of me. It is absolutely irrational, but truth is truth!

You have not asked any question, so I decided that, since for many days I have not given you any sutras to meditate on, I should use this great opportunity that Jivan Mary has given me.

A few sutras for her, for all of you, to meditate on...

A woman who looks like a dream usually gives a man insomnia.

Some people sleep with one eye open; others wake with both eyes shut.

If at first you don't succeed, try someone else.

Two is company, three is the result.

The best way to make your dreams come true is to wake up.

Sometimes the best way to liven up the party is to leave.

It is better to be in the missionary position than never to have any religion at all.

The only time most people look like their passport photographs is during a hijack.

In these days of jet travel, the only journeys that take a long time are the ones from your house to the airport.

A husband who gets his breakfast in bed is in hospital.

Married life is like sitting in a bathtub – after a while, it is not so hot.

Marriage is like a violin. After the beautiful music is over, the strings are still attached.

Nobody is ever satisfied. Poor men wish they were rich, rich men wish they were handsome, bachelors wish they were married, and married men wish they were dead.

The fastest way to discover your bad habits is to move in with your lover.

God gave black men rhythm because he made such a mess of their hair.

And the last:

Sex is the most fun you can have without laughing.

7

The Five Sacred Mantras

Osho,
Sat-chit-anand … Meaning or no meaning, just the sound of it touches my heart deeply.

Sat-chit-anand is one of those few expressions in all languages of the world which have descended from the highest peak of consciousness. They are pure music, they are absolute poetry; they are no ordinary words. If they touch your heart without even knowing the exact meaning, the reason is that they are re-echoing the soundless sound of those who have entered that space. Sanskrit can be proud that it has never been a living language used in the marketplace.

Sanskrit lovers try to prove just the contrary. They try to prove that once it was a living language which people spoke, just like any other ordinary dialect. But I insist on my difference. I want to know why they insist on Sanskrit being a living language used by ordinary people. They think if a language is not used by ordinary people, then it loses something of importance, it is a dead language. Certainly it has never been used by the people, but it is not a dead language. It is the language of the mystics. It is the language of those who know.

It is not worldly, that's true. It is something otherworldly – and this is not a criticism. In fact, the extraordinariness of the language is that it was only used by very few people of tremendous understanding. Their every word has immense significance because it is coming out of a deep experience of the reality of their own being. The so-called living languages are mundane. They are for the marketplace, for day-to-day use: naturally, they cannot contain something of the beyond. Perhaps Sanskrit is the only language ... It is also the mother language of all the civilized languages of the world.

Sanskrit is rare in the sense that the people who formulated it were not thinking of the material side of existence, but were more concerned that the words used would reflect something of consciousness, heights of consciousness, of love, of compassion, of ecstasy. Their words are mantras, sacred, they are coming from the very source of our life. This is possible.

You say, '*Sat-chit-anand* ... Meaning or no meaning, just the sound of it touches my heart deeply.' It is a soundless sound; or, in other words, the sound of silence, the sound of the ultimate experience, the sound when *you* are no more – only the universe remains.

Certainly you can avoid meaning. You can say 'meaning or no meaning' because meaning is of the mind. But *sat-chit-anand* has a significance which goes far higher than meaning. It is just a fragrance which has left the flower. The flower is visible – part of this world, part of matter – but you cannot catch hold of the fragrance. You can feel it, it can touch you deeply, it can reach your innermost core – but still you cannot figure out the meaning of it. You cannot figure out what it is in reality.

The meaning is irrelevant here; significance becomes the relevance. Not that it has *no* meaning, but basically it has only significance. And the significance is that the very sound, *sat-chit-anand*, penetrates the heart, breaking down all the barriers, all the bars and all the defense mechanisms. It resounds within your being, creating a subtle harmony, a deep peace, a strange feeling of fulfillment, of being at ease with the world, with the universe, with existence itself – at ease not only with existence, but with yourself too.

It is a pure silence, as if water can be condensed to ice, and the ice can be again melted into water. That is the reality of such beautiful sounds. They can be condensed to meaning, but their basic reality is to melt within you and to reach each fiber of your being, to each cell, to give it a dance.

These are the mystic sounds. They are very few. I have talked to you about *satyam-shivam-sundaram*, *sat-chit-anand*, *hari-om-tat-sat*, *om-mani-padme-hum*, *om-shantih-shantih-shantih*. These five I have chosen as the most significant, as the most deep-going. I will try to give you the meaning also, because that meaning will help the significance to become deeper. That meaning will not only touch your heart, it will also touch your intelligence – and you have to be touched in your totality to be transformed.

I will begin with the last one. That is the sound every Eastern scripture ends with: *om-shantih-shantih-shantih*. It means 'The soundless sound, or the sound of silence, peace, peace, peace' – just giving you the sense of the whole scripture in these few telegraphic words. Every scripture in the East ends the same. It may be Hindu, it may be Buddhist, it may be Jaina – it doesn't matter. They are all different in their philosophies. They are all different in their theologies. They are different religions, continuously in controversy for at least ten thousand years. But strangely, they all end their scriptures with 'the sound of silence: peace, peace, peace.' It seems they are all different roots of this experience.

They may differ about their roots, about the description of their roots. They may quarrel, they may contradict each other, but as far as the end is concerned, when they reach the highest peak of consciousness, all that is found is the sound of silence and utter peace, so deep that they have to repeat it three times: peace, peace, peace.

The fourth is used by the Tibetans, although it takes almost all the words from Sanskrit: *om-mani-padme-hum*. It is a very mystic statement. It says: 'The sound of silence, the diamond in the lotus.' You cannot conceive a more beautiful thing than a beautiful diamond in the most beautiful flower on the earth, the lotus. They are trying to convey to you the beyond in some way comprehensible to the mind: the sound of silence – om – the diamond in the lotus. I have loved it from my very childhood. Just the words 'the diamond in the lotus' have managed to express the beyond in the most beautiful way.

The third is *hari-om-tat-sat* – 'the sound of silence, this is the only truth.'

The second is *sat-chit-anand* – 'truth, consciousness, bliss.'

And the first is *satyam shivam sundaram* – 'truth, godliness, beauty.'

These five, I can say to you, belong to the universal religious consciousness, not to any organized religion because they have come from individual mystics. They have poured their heart, they have poured their enlightenment, they have poured their awakening into these five mantras.

There is no word in English to translate *mantra*. It means a sacred word, not of any use in the day-to-day life experience, but only significant when you go beyond this visible world and enter the invisible consciousness. A mantra is a secret key. It opens the door to the ultimate.

But the meaning is also significant because you are in the mind. The sound may have gone deep into your heart, thrilled you, but still it is good not to leave the mind completely out of your experience because it can become a disturbance; it can become very vengeful.

Don't antagonize your mind. It can disturb everything. Have you watched how it disturbs your body? When you are in anger, your whole body is disturbed: your stomach is disturbed, your blood pressure goes up, suddenly you start perspiring – even in an air-conditioned place. There have been many cases of heart attacks in intense anger. The heart suddenly stops. The mind can disturb the body on the one hand, on the other hand it can disturb the heart. Very few people know its disturbances in the heart because it is not a common experience.

But if you don't know the meaning, if the mind is not satisfied, soon it will start creating suspicion, doubt, skepticism. Soon it will start saying to you that you are being irrational – and you will be affected. If the mind is not in cooperation, the impact of *sat-chit-anand* on your heart will start disappearing. My whole effort is to transform your total being, not leaving anything outside because nature does not intend it so. When the mind can be persuaded to go along with you, there is no need to create an opposition. I am against any kind of unnecessary conflict and split in your being. It is better to create a bridge between mind, body and being.

And the meaning is also tremendously beautiful. *Sat* means truth. Man's longest search has been for that, because without knowing the truth, we know nothing. Truth is the very meaning of our existence. Without knowing truth we are just accidental, we don't have any meaning.

Perhaps something has gone wrong in nature and we are the product of it – freaks. Unless you know the meaning of yourself you cannot have a deep relationship with the cosmos. The meaning is going to become a bridge with the cosmos. Unless you feel some meaning, some truth in your being, you are not yet aware of a deep communion with the whole.

Truth is the experience of being in deep communion with the eternity of existence, with the wholeness and the perfection and the grandeur and the magnificence of that which is. Truth simply means that which is. It is pure isness – and the revelation of this truth to you is only possible if your *chit*, your consciousness, rises to its ultimate flowering.

It is consciousness that is going to discover the truth. Hence, meditation is emphasized. Meditation will not give you the truth, but it will give you more and more consciousness, and, finally, consciousness gives you two things: on one hand, truth, and on the other hand, a tremendous bliss. You become almost like a bird with two wings. Truth is your one wing, bliss is your other wing – and you are pure consciousness.

In this experience you can fly like an eagle across the sun into the unknown. Then this whole universe belongs to you; then wherever you are, you are at home; then whatever you are, you are in utter peace – whatever happens is beautiful and brings tremendous gratitude to you. Prayer becomes your very heartbeat. You don't pray in synagogues,

in churches, in temples or in mosques. Those are for the irreligious; those are for the hypocrites; those are for the pretenders. The authentic religious man has prayer in his heartbeats. He is continuously feeling a tremendous gratitude to all that existence has made available to us – life, love, laughter.

Osho,
Is man really the most hilarious animal? Would you give us a few more examples?

Devageet, this is more like you. The other day you were asking about death. That is not at all a reflection of your individuality. You are a man who can understand laughter as one of the most religious qualities. It has never been accepted by any religion as a religious quality. But I am never in agreement with any superstition, however old and ancient it may be. And I don't care at all what others have believed, lived. I trust my own experience more than any holy scripture, more than any great saint or sage.

My experience about laughter is that it is the most purifying, the most healthy, the most rejuvenating, the most refreshing, and the most total experience. It can be your first experience of totality. You can laugh totally. And there is another beautiful thing about it: it is not only of the mind. The mind may trigger it, but soon it spreads all over you. It is overwhelming. There are beauties upon beauties as far as laughter is concerned. When you are laughing, one of the greatest things is that the mind cannot think. If you are alert, you can experience a space of no- thought, which is the experience of meditation.

Laughter gives you a childlike innocence. It helps to unburden you of unnecessary seriousness which all the religions have been burdening you with. They have even taken away the smiles from your lips – what to say about laughter? They have been preaching seriousness. They are afraid, as if God will feel offended if you laugh. And I cannot conceive of God in any other position, in any other posture, than laughing. If he exists at all, he must be laughing twenty-four hours a day at the hilariousness of humanity. We don't know the whole of humanity, we know only a few people here and there. God must be watching all over humanity, and so many circuses going on.

Friedrich Nietzsche said, 'God is dead.' But the question is, 'Who killed him? Or, if he died naturally, what was the disease?' Sometimes I have this idea: perhaps, laughing since eternity, he just popped off as there is a limit to everything. You must all feel compassionate toward poor God. But in another way, he enjoyed more than anybody else.

He may have been disturbed once in a while – 'What kind of man have I created?' It is a well-established fact that after man he stopped creating. Seeing man, he must have become aware – 'I have committed a mistake. Now it is time to stop creation.' He did not stop at horses, he did not stop at buffaloes, he did not stop at millions of species of birds and insects and animals and trees. But suddenly, since the day he created man, nothing has been heard of him. He became so worried about what he had done, he either died from too much laughter, or, seeing what these creatures he has created in his own image were doing, he committed suicide.

A beautiful young woman is strolling through the zoo, and finally stops in front of the monkey cage. Seeing no monkeys around, she asks the keeper, 'Where are all the monkeys today?'

'They are inside their house, miss,' he replies. 'It is the mating season.'

'Will they come out if I throw them some peanuts?' she asks.

The keeper scratches his head and says, 'I don't know, miss. Would you?'

The great novelist has been locked away in a mental asylum for years. But at last there seems to be some hope of recovery. For three months he sits at his typewriter in his room, writing a new novel. Finally he announces that it is complete and brings it to the top shrink who grabs it eagerly and starts to read, 'General Jones leaped on his faithful horse and yelled, "Giddyap up! Giddyap! Giddyap!"'

Then the shrink thumbs through the rest of the book. 'Why, there is nothing here but five hundred pages of *git ups*!' he says.

'I know,' says the writer. 'Stubborn horse.'

Lord Dottingham returns home from fox hunting a little earlier than usual and finds Lady Dottingham in bed with his best friend, Sir Arthur Carpley. His lordship stands stiffly in the bedroom doorway and loudly berates his wife for her unfaithfulness.

With thunder in his voice he reminds her that he had taken her from a miserable existence in the London slums, given her a fine home with servants, expensive clothes and jewels.

As Lady Dottingham is by this time crying loudly, his lordship turns his wrath on his supposed friend. 'And as for you, Carpley,' he shouts, 'you might at least stop while I am talking!'

Osho,

The other day I fell in love with Milarepa. It was so beautiful, but after ten minutes it was gone.

Osho, is this the way things really go?

Lolita, I wonder that the love affair continued for as long as ten minutes. With Milarepa, things are more speedy. Of course, this is the way things really go. But with Milarepa they go with express speed. His love affairs are just hit and run.

He is really a great guy – my musician. Only music seems to be his really permanent love affair. Everything else is just in the margin; ten minutes are more than enough. And he never repeats any mistakes; he commits mistakes every day, but always new ones.

I have sometimes thought about the word *mistake*. Who made that word? That's what he goes on doing. Take this Miss, take that Miss. He understands exactly the meaning of the word *miss-takes*.

For you I feel really sad, but there is no problem. Here almost all are Milarepas. My people are the misfits of the world; this is a gathering of the misfits. But they fit with each other perfectly well, so don't be worried: fall in love again. Remember the American motto: 'Try it again, and again, and again.'

I don't know if it is ever going to happen, but the trying is beautiful in itself. Hoping that it is going to happen keeps you alive, keeps you young. The day a woman thinks it is not going to happen, she becomes old – and no woman wants to become old.

I have heard...

A politician was asking a friend at a meeting of women, 'How do I keep them quiet just for five minutes? Because I feel so embarrassed – I am delivering my election campaign speech and they are all talking. Nobody is listening. But they are voters so I have to talk to them, but how to keep them quiet?'

The friend said, 'It is not difficult. The first thing is: you should shout loudly "Who is the oldest of you all?" Then there will be utter silence, and in that silence deliver your speech.'

They say that a woman takes at least six years passing from thirty-five to thirty-six. So don't be worried. You are young and you have the tremendously beautiful name of Lolita, a romantic name. I think some other Milarepa is going to meet you after this meeting. Many Milarepas may already be thinking, 'Who is this Lolita?' Even Milarepa himself may be thinking, 'Have I committed a mistake?' But this is the way things happen.

During the geography class, the teacher looks at little Ernie and says, 'What is the matter, Ernest? Why are you looking so unhappy?'

'I didn't get no breakfast,' Ernie replies.

'You poor dear, but to get on with our geography lesson' says the teacher pointing to the map, 'where is the Mexican border?'

'In bed with Mama,' says Ernie. 'That's why I didn't get no breakfast.'

Mrs. Applebottom becomes angry with the French maid, and after a series of stinging remarks about her abilities she dismisses her. But the French girl will not allow such abuse to go unanswered.

'Your husband,' she cries, 'considers me a better cook and housekeeper than you, madam! He told me so himself.'

Mrs. Applebottom looks at the girl scornfully and makes no comment. 'Also,' says the angry girl, 'I am better than you in bed!'

'And I suppose,' snaps Mrs. Applebottom, 'my husband told you that too!'

'No, madam,' says the maid, 'the chauffeur did.'

But in a way, Lolita, you are fortunate that you got rid of Milarepa in just ten minutes. I know a few other great lovers who got into trouble with Milarepa and for years they went dragging on. And Milarepa is not one to look back.

A man pinned under his wrecked car is being questioned by a policeman.

'Are you married?' asks the cop.

'No,' replies the man, 'this is the worst fix I have ever been in.'

You are out of the worst fix. Rejoice. But never stop falling in love, because unless you fall in love, how are you going to rise again? Falling is a strategy of rising again and again. Finally, when you are risen the way Jesus Christ has risen, there will be no need to fall again with any Milarepa. Love is good, love is nice – even for ten minutes. Don't count the minutes. A single minute of love is equal to eternity; ten minutes is equal to ten eternities.

Try my other Milarepas, Lolita. It is a little difficult because other Lolitas have already made them so fed up that the moment they see anybody coming closer to them to fall in love, they escape. Any excuse and they fly away.

I receive letters every day from my sannyasins asking, 'What has happened to your male sannyasins? In the whole world it is the man who hangs around a woman, chases her. In your commune it is just the opposite. It is the woman who has to chase the man and the man seems to be utterly enlightened.'

But the men are enlightened because of you all – poor sannyasins have never been chased by so many women. So rather than getting into another hell of an affair, they simply close their eyes.

Even a man like Devageet is thinking of dying. I did not tell you the real reason that day, but I cannot keep secrets!

8

You Cannot Avoid Misunderstanding

Osho,
What is misunderstanding?

Misunderstanding is obviously the mother superior of mistakes. Man lives almost half awake, half asleep. Hence whatever he understands is only half. With each of his understandings there is a shadow, a deep unconsciousness which continues to misinterpret, to distort, to confuse whatever small light, whatever small consciousness he has got.

His consciousness is certainly very small – just a thin layer, not more than skin-deep, but his unconsciousness is thick, deep, nine times larger than his consciousness. That dark night is within you; it has never seen the light of the day. So whatever your consciousness tries to see, to hear, your unconsciousness, which is nine times larger – its weight, its pressure is tremendous – distorts it.

You think you have understood something, but finally it is always a misunderstanding. The misunderstanding is not coming from outside, neither is it coming from your conscious mind. It is coming from your darkness within. Unless that darkness disappears, there is no way to get rid of misunderstandings. Understanding is almost equal to wisdom, almost synonymous with awakening. It is a transformation of your whole unconsciousness into consciousness, as if suddenly the sun has risen and the whole night with all its darkness has disappeared.

Ordinarily we think that we sometimes misunderstand, but that most of the time we understand. I want to emphasize: *all* the time you misunderstand. It is not your fault, it is just the very situation. Because you are only a very thin consciousness with such a thick layer of darkness, you cannot do anything else than perhaps sometimes understand something.

Almost all the time, everything is distorted, but not distorting it is not under your control. What *is* under your control is to start getting deeper into your being, bringing more awareness to the dark parts of your being. Awareness is just like light. As the light goes deeper into you, the darkness, the unconsciousness, will disappear. The moment you are fully conscious, no misunderstanding will be possible.

People who are awakened have been asked again and again, 'Can the awakened one misunderstand?' And the answer has always been 'No.' It is impossible for the awakened one to misunderstand. It is just not possible. Just as the man with eyes goes through the door, not through the wall, a man of fully enlightened being naturally understands everything as it is, its true nature. In other words, the moment you are your true self you will be able to understand everything in its true authenticity. Before that, you cannot avoid misunderstanding.

It is good to understand that you cannot avoid misunderstanding. That will help you in many ways: it will make you humble; it will take away your arrogance; it will take away your so-called knowledgeability; it will put aside your ego, which depends on all kinds of misconceptions. It will bring more innocence to you – and in innocence, meditation becomes easier.

When the ego is not there a great barrier is removed. When you are humble you can see that by the very nature of your being – as you are now – in ten situations, nine times there is misunderstanding.

Perhaps one time there may be understanding. But you cannot figure out when it is understanding and when it is misunderstanding. Your light is so dim; everything is vague. One moment, just like a flash of lightning, you see something, but the next moment all is darkness.

What you have seen seems to be just like a dream. Perhaps it is right, perhaps it is not. In fact, if you are alert enough, you will start using the word *perhaps* more. If you are asked about anything, you will not be so deterministic, you will not be so definitive, you will not be so arrogantly certain. You will not talk in terms of absolutes, you will become more relative, you will say *perhaps*. 'Perhaps it is so. It is very difficult...'

For example, you feel you are in love with someone. It is very difficult to say 'Perhaps I love you.' But it is true. In the state man is in, more than that is not possible. Your love is only a perhaps, because what is love today can turn into hate tomorrow. Or maybe tomorrow is too far away. What is love this moment may disappear the next moment. Just a moment before you were so absolutely certain, but a moment afterward you yourself cannot believe what has happened to you. Have you gone mad? What made you so certain?

You trusted too much in the one-tenth part of your mind. You completely forgot about the unconscious mind, which is so vast, so dark, that you don't know what is going on there, what is cooking there. Just on the surface you are thinking of love and deep down there is hate, anger, jealousy, and all kinds of wild sentiments, emotions, prejudices. And you are sitting on the volcano. If you are alert...

One great enlightened man, Mahavira, even after his enlightenment – when he could be absolute in his statements without any conditions – continued to use the word *perhaps* about every question that he answered. He was the first man in the whole history of mankind to bring in the concept of relativity. All that we can say is only relatively true – perhaps for the moment, but we cannot say it's forever. We cannot make any unconditional statements.

His *perhaps* is one of the reasons why he could not gather a very big gathering of disciples – one of the greatest enlightened persons. But people want certainty; they are living in uncertain lives. People want beliefs; they are drowning.

Their situation is like that of the old Jew who had fallen on the street with sunstroke and was almost dying. A Christian priest saw the crowd. He entered the crowd and he said, 'The old man needs me. Just let me come through. He is dying!'

He went by the side of the Jew, not knowing that he was a Jew, and whispered in his ear, 'This is the moment! Remember God, God the Father, the Holy Ghost, Jesus Christ the Son, the only begotten Son of God. Remember.'

The old Jew opened his eyes and he looked at the crowd and said, 'Who is this crazy man? I am dying and he is talking in puzzles. What God? What Holy Ghost? Who is the only begotten son? I am dying here and this idiot...'

People do not want puzzles. People want clear-cut belief systems. But Mahavira never gave a single belief system to anyone. If you ask him if God is, he will say 'Perhaps.' But a God who is a perhaps is not much of a God. You cannot worship a God who is a perhaps. Then your prayer will be perhaps. You cannot create a religion out of the idea of relativity. Ifs and buts are prohibited from religious systems. People don't want anything that will create more confusion in their minds, however great the source from which it may be coming. They are searching for some small belief that can give them a kind of security, safety, a God who will be their protector, to whom they can pray in difficult times – and almost all the time is a difficult time!

If you don't even have a God to pray to, you are left in deep aloneness. And a man like Mahavira, rather than giving you some comfort, some consolation, tells you *perhaps* about everything. No consolation. But he has a great insight about you. He knows even if you believe in God, your belief is only an *if*. It cannot be more than that, because your unconscious knows nothing about God. Have you ever dreamed about God?

I have asked many, many people, 'Have you ever dreamed about God?' They say 'No.' The unconscious has not even heard the word *God.* Nobody has repressed God so deeply in himself that he becomes part of the unconscious and uncoils in his dream, like a genie coming out of a bottle. And you will meet neither Jesus Christ nor Buddha there. It is very strange.

Your unconscious is your greater reality, and Mahavira is correct when he says *perhaps* about everything. He is making you aware that in your situation nothing can be more certain than that. Change the situation, make your whole being full of light. It does not mean that you will become absolutely certain. It simply means all questions will disappear; there will be no answer. In authentic totality of consciousness, there is no question. You don't ask about God or hell or heaven. You simply don't ask about anything. You are so silent. Out of your silence, questions cannot come. Questions grow in the mind, and you are so far away and beyond the mind – in your innermost center – where there is no question and there is no answer. You are tremendously fulfilled, contented, at ease: with existence, with yourself, with everything.

Questions mean that you have some kind of tension, some kind of not-at-easeness; some trouble is there that brings the question. Something is haunting you and you are incapable of figuring it out. But when your whole being is full of light, when all darkness has disappeared, you are so in tune with existence that even to say you are in tune with existence is not right. It will be right to say that you are one with existence. Or it will be even better to say: you *are* existence. All separation has disappeared.

There is no questioner. There is no quest. You have arrived home. In that state there is understanding but there is nothing to understand.

This is the strange situation of man. When he wants to understand, he cannot. When he is capable of understanding, there is nothing to understand.

The newlyweds walk up to the hotel desk and ask for a suite.

'Bridal?' asks the clerk, noticing the 'Just Married' signs on their luggage.

The young bride blushes and says, 'No thanks. I will hold his shoulders until I get used to it.'

This is misunderstanding.

Old man Finkelstein was brought to court on charges of sexually molesting a teenage girl.

The judge dismissed the case because the evidence would not stand up in court.

Mendel Kravitz returns home one day to find a stranger on top of his naked wife, his head resting between her ample breasts.

'Hey!' yells Mendel. 'Just what are you doing?'

'Why, er, I'm listening to music,' replies the stranger.

Mendel puts his head beside the stranger's head and declares, 'I don't hear any music.'

'Of course you don't,' replies the stranger. 'You're not plugged in!'

Osho,
Finally it has hit me too!

Sex and relationship have dropped me. Just when I felt that I was in the juiciest relationship, enjoying sex like never before, suddenly I couldn't stand it anymore. All the longing for the other, for sex and intimacy, has gone. I am feeling so good and relaxed by myself, with a lot of love in my heart, but without any direction.

Osho, can you explain what is happening? How come it is hitting so many of us all at once? Is it contagious? Has it to do with the star constellation? Or are you cooking something?

Nandan, you are here not as a separate ego, but as part of one phenomenon. So when anything starts happening, it is bound to happen to many others simultaneously. It will have a chain effect.

It does not happen in the world because people are not in any way deeply connected with each other. There is no communion. There are communities, but there is no communion. This is a commune. The whole purpose of your being here is to melt and merge with all who are present here. There is no friend, no enemy. All are in love with me. Their sole purpose is exactly what somebody said the other day, 'Our whole purpose here is one, we all love you.'

It is a loving commune where you are all equal, where you are no longer competitive, where there is no struggle of any kind going on, just a tremendous music and a silence drowning you all into oneness, without your even knowing it. You are slipping deeper into a whole.

This wholeness brings a new health and a new joy and a new kind of love. Sex is a very primitive thing. It is an animal heritage. Nothing is wrong in it, it is just very old. As you grow more and more mature, you start searching for something new and greater, something better and higher, something superior. Sex seems to be something below you – a little childish, a little immature.

It is good. There is a time when you can fool around. While you are meditating, your maturity comes sooner, your centering comes sooner, your awareness about things becomes clearer every day. Sex is going to be the first victim of your awareness – other things will follow – because sex is the very root of your animality.

Once sex drops, it's as if a tree has lost its roots. Then the branches cannot remain green any longer; the flowers cannot remain alive any longer. In fact, the tree has died with the roots. For a few days, perhaps, it may manage to remain standing; for a few days the leaves will remain green, and perhaps for a few days the flowers will remain apparently alive. But basically the tree is dead the moment the roots are cut.

Your anger, your jealousy, your violence, your inferiority complex, your superiority complex – all kinds of neuroses, psychoses – are just branches. They will start dying by themselves. Once you have gone beyond sex without fighting with it...

That's my basic difference to all religions. They have been trying to drop sex. I am not telling you to drop it. I am telling you to be more mature, to be more meditative. While you are not mature, sex is perfectly right. Nothing is wrong in it, there is no condemnation. Be playful and rejoice in it. Here, for the first time, a totally original experiment is going on: sex is accepted with deep respect. It is our heritage; we are born out of it. It is in our every fiber and every cell. To condemn it is to condemn oneself.

Trying to drop it means only repressing it into the unconscious. Then things become more and more complex and perverted. Once you start repressing sex into your unconscious ... There is no other place in you – whatever you repress goes into the unconscious. The unconscious is your basement where you go on throwing all that you don't want, that you don't want to show to the world. But whatever you throw into the unconscious creates a very strange problem: you start becoming afraid of your own unconscious. You cannot go there, even with a lamp in your hand, because you know what you are going to encounter.

I was staying in a friend's home. They were a little old-fashioned, so their bathroom and their toilets were not attached to the house but at a little distance behind the house. There was a small lawn, and beyond the lawn were their toilets and bathroom.

They had one small boy, just one child. His mother said to me, 'While you are here, somehow help us to teach this boy that there is nothing to fear. Each time he has to go to the bathroom or to the toilet, somebody has to follow him. While he is inside, the doors have to be kept open and the person has to stand there – if it is night, with a lamp. And the doors have to be kept open so that the person who is standing outside does not disappear.'

I talked to the boy. I asked, 'What is the problem?'

He said, 'I am very much afraid of ghosts.'

I said, 'How did you become afraid of ghosts?'

It was the parents themselves who had made him afraid of ghosts.

He said, 'When I don't want to go to sleep, they force me to go to sleep. When I don't want to get up early in the morning, they force me to get up early. And to make this happen, they frighten me with ghosts saying, "If you don't go to bed early, ghosts may trouble you in the night. And if you don't get up early in the morning ... Remember – we are warning you – there are ghosts all around sitting in the trees, invisible people."'

'They have convinced me, so I am afraid of going to the bathroom or the toilet, particularly in the night. Now they want me to go alone, and nobody is interested in standing outside while I am inside. Because of this I have to keep the doors open.'

I said, 'Why don't you do one thing: take the lamp yourself. And when there is light, you can see if a ghost is anywhere.'

He said, 'Please don't tell me such a thing. I can go in darkness but I can never go with a lamp.'

I asked, 'What is the reason?'

He said, 'The reason is clear. In darkness somehow I can dodge the ghosts. But when I carry a lamp, they all see me. Don't suggest that idea. If I have to go, I will go in darkness. At least then they can't see me. And if I feel that something is there, I can run, I can dodge, I can shout, I can do something. But with a lamp, all the ghosts in all the trees will see me and say "He is going now. This is a good time."'

I said, 'This is right. Your logic is perfect.'

I have always remembered this whenever I have talked about your unconscious and your repressions. If you repress all that you have been told is ugly, then there is no possibility of your ever becoming a meditator, no possibility of your ever becoming enlightened. That is the reason why in the West enlightenment has not happened. Half the world has remained absolutely unaware of the greatest experience in life, for the simple reason that Christianity is the most repressive religion in the world. It goes on forcing ... And other religions are not much different, just a little more lenient.

It is not surprising that all the psychologists, psychoanalysts, psychiatrists are born in the West, not in the East. It was a necessity in the West. Christianity has created the necessity because it has created the disease. It has created the repressive mind. It was absolutely necessary for Sigmund Freud, Carl Gustav Jung and Alfred Adler to somehow help the Western part of humanity become acquainted with the unconscious. Christianity has completely cut off humanity from the unconscious. Unless the unconscious becomes part of the conscious, becomes conscious itself, there is no way of your ever being beyond the animal you are repressing within yourself.

Sex should never be repressed. Sex should be lived in its totality, with joy, without any guilt. Then what you are saying – and what so many sannyasins have been feeling – comes one day. You were rejoicing in it so much, and suddenly it drops away.

Now all the religions have been against me, are still against me, and they will remain against me for at least five centuries. Such is the stupidity of humanity. They cannot see that this simple experiment is so successful. Nandan, who is saying that she is having the juiciest affair of her life, enjoying sex like never before, is not aware that this is how sex drops.

I don't tell you the real secrets because then you may become afraid and you may not enjoy. You will remain a little less juicy, just to prolong the journey a little longer. But when you are enjoying sex at the highest peak, that's when it suddenly slips out of your hands. It is a beautiful experience, one of the most beautiful experiences: the moment sex drops on its own accord.

It happens only to those few people who have lived with intensity, have loved with intensity, have not felt guilty at all, have not listened to any religion or any tradition or any past, who have lived almost like Adam and Eve – as if they are the first people on the earth and they don't know anything of repression. No priest has been able to pollute them; no religions have poisoned their minds. If you can be ... And that's my whole effort here: to make you into

Adam and Eve, as if you are the first people on the earth, fresh, just driven out of the Garden of Eden.

What Nandan is saying is tremendously important. I will read it to you. 'Just when I felt that I was in the juiciest relationship, enjoying sex like never before, suddenly I could not stand it anymore.' One can get free from sex only when one has seen the whole scene in its totality and there is nothing more to be discovered, when one has inquired, lived all the possibilities of sexual relationships. Then what can you do except let it go? You are finished with it. You have come to the end of the book.

You are saying, 'Suddenly, I could not stand it anymore. All the longing for the other, for sex and intimacy, has gone. I am feeling so good and relaxed by myself, with a lot of love in my heart, but without any direction.' The disappearance of sex does not mean disappearance of love. It really means *appearance* of love. Sex was a very primitive phenomenon. There was not much love in it, only biological infatuation. If you have observed animals making love, you may have noticed one thing: they don't look happy. They look almost as if they are in torture. In fact, that is the reality: it is a biological slavery, just a biological, hormonal, chemical slavery. It hurts those who have a little more consciousness.

As your meditation grows, you will see more and more that it is not a sin; it is simply stupidity. There is no need to be forgiven for it because it is not a crime and there is nobody to forgive you. And you have not committed anything for which you should feel guilty and ashamed.

But the moment you are free of it, suddenly you will feel a tremendous relaxation, because sex is a tension. You may not have felt it before. It was constantly there, so one becomes accustomed and immune to it. The moment it disappears, suddenly a great relaxation. Sex is the need of the other. In the very need of the other, there is dependence.

That's why no wife can really respect the husband nor can the husband respect the wife. They hate each other. Psychologists are perfectly right when they say that husbands and wives are intimate enemies. And the reason? The reason is: you cannot love someone on whom you have to depend. The man has to depend on the wife; he has a sexual need and the wife takes every opportunity to torture him. That is her only opportunity to torture him. The man tortures her in many other ways. She is dependent financially. She doesn't have the freedom to move in society; she doesn't have the freedom to feel independent, liberated. Even the women who think they are liberated are not liberated. They are only reacting. They are still in the same old grip, only they have gone to the other extreme.

The moment you feel you are no longer dependent on anyone, a deep coolness and a deep silence settles inside, a relaxed let-go. It does not mean you stop loving. On the contrary, for the first time you know a new quality, a new dimension of love: a love which is no longer biological, a love which is closer to friendliness than any relationship. That's why I am not even using the word *friendship*, because that ship has drowned so many people.

Your love becomes more like an aura around you which can be shared with anyone, even with a stranger. In fact, it is not a question of doing anything when you are sharing; it simply becomes your nature. You are just loving. In the past you used to fall in love with some individual. Now you don't fall *in* love with anyone – you *are* love. Wherever you are, you carry your fragrance. Wherever you are, you carry your fresh breeze, your relaxed coolness. You will feel tremendous freedom.

This is true liberation of women, of men, because both are slaves of each other. The women's liberation movement does not take account of the fact that she is not alone in bondage. Man is also in bondage because both are dependent on each other. After the whole day at work, the man comes home, and the woman immediately lies down and has a headache. The whole day there was no head, no headache, nothing. The moment she hears her husband's car driving into the car porch, immediately, strangely, the headache comes with the husband; they both come simultaneously.

Just a few days ago I was telling you...

One day Hymie Goldberg came home and just shook his wife awake and gave her two aspirins.

She said, 'What for?'

He said, 'Take them!'

She said, 'But I don't have a headache!'

He said, 'That's great. So let's go!'

Now he has tricked the woman. Now she cannot say she has a headache. She has refused the aspirin, not knowing Hymie Goldberg's subtle logical strategy.

Once this longing for the other – the dependence on the other – disappears, your life takes off onto a new plane of existence. It is beautiful when you are in a commune like this, where life is accepted in its totality without any condemnation, where there is no god except life. Naturally this experience will go on spreading because you are so close to each other. Not that somebody is your husband, somebody is your son, somebody is your mother and somebody is your father – no, but for the simple reason that in the center you have someone who disappeared a long time ago.

But your love is still directed toward that same entity which has become only a presence, is no longer a person. The closer you come to me, the closer you will be coming to each other, but it will not create any relationship. It will be simply freedom: freedom to love, freedom to be friendly, freedom to rejoice in each other's happiness, freedom to dance, not even knowing with whom you are dancing. There is no need. It is perfectly beautiful to dance with a stranger.

Here, nobody knows from what country you come, nobody knows with what religion you have been conditioned, nobody knows to what caste you belong. Nobody bothers about all these stupidities humanity has been burdened with for centuries. Suddenly just a pure humanness, a pure consciousness, a song that goes from heart to heart, a rhythm that spreads like ripples in a lake. So if something happens to one of you, it is going to happen to many.

Certainly I have been cooking it for many years. I am waiting for that day when you are free of all kinds of slaveries – and sex is the greatest slavery. Your greatest anxiety, your greatest jealousy, your greatest violence – all are rooted in sex. But still I want you to live it, not repress it. One day it will disappear.

It is joyful, Nandan, that you have not become afraid or worried, because people who are coming from the West are in a difficulty. They have become accustomed to think of life and sex as synonymous. They are not. Life is vast; sex is a small thing. In the West when sex drops, the person may think of committing suicide. Now, what is the point anymore?

Just the other day I heard you all had an evening with my therapist, Veeresh. Neelam may have suggested to him ... Being my secretary, it was her duty to suggest that Veeresh not talk about sex and drugs. Veeresh said, 'My god, then what is there to talk about? These are the only two things, that's all, the whole of life!'

In the West, the idea has become very settled – in a subtle way, deep down in every being – that the moment your sex is gone ... Now, what are you doing? Just take your gun and shoot yourself. I have heard a statement: 'You know you are getting old when you have been with a boy all night and all that comes is the morning.' It seems to be almost a tragedy in the West. In fact, there should be rejoicing that all that comes is the morning. Now Nandan, all that will come will be the morning! Start enjoying the morning.

A tremendous harm has been done to humanity by the people – whether in the West or in the East – who have been against life, against sex, because they are the ones who keep people filled with sexuality for their whole lives. They are the ones who are responsible for so much sexuality, so much pornography, so much obscenity in the whole world. But nobody blames them, nobody even thinks there is a relation, or thinks about who has made humanity so stupid that even an eighty-year-old man thinks only of sex. A tremendous misunderstanding...

Sex certainly has to disappear, not by force but by a deep understanding that only comes through experience. Then a celibacy which has a beauty of its own arises. The Hindu celibate monks, the Jaina celibate monks, the Catholic celibate monks cannot understand the beauty of the celibacy that will happen to my sannyasins. Just the word will be the same, but the levels will be so far away from each other. The celibacy of a Catholic monk is nothing but perverted sex. It will create all kinds of complexities in his being.

The celibacy that is happening to you and to all my people is a freedom, freedom from all complexities. It is a growth beyond biology. Because the enlightened people and the sages of the past went beyond sex, the ordinary man misunderstood the whole thing. He thought perhaps they have attained that great wisdom because they have left sex behind, so if we leave sex, we will also attain wisdom. It looks logical, but it is fallacious.

People like Gautam Buddha have not repressed sex. They have lived it in its totality. I don't think anybody in the whole world has lived a life of sex so totally, so intensely, as Gautam Buddha. By his twenty-ninth year he had come to the situation you are in: sex simply became meaningless, just an old game. How long can you go on playing it? And it's not a very clean game either.

The misunderstanding has continued for twenty-five centuries in the East, even with his own monks. They thought that because he had left sex ... They could not see the difference between leaving sex and sex leaving you – from the outside it appears the same. One thing was certain: sex was no longer part of his interest, his longings, his desires, but sex was not repressed by him.

But those who were seeing from the outside the great wisdom that arose, the great radiance, the great beauty, the explosion of *sat-chit-anand*, their simplistic logic was, 'This man has left sex. That's why he has attained truth, consciousness, bliss. So if we also leave sex, we too will attain the same state of being.' For twenty-five centuries the monks have been doing that, but not a single Gautam Buddha has been produced.

I have been condemned my whole life, so much so that I have started enjoying it. When for a few days nobody condemns me for something, I start thinking 'What has happened to the world?' And the condemnation has been basically on a single point. I was telling people, 'Live sex joyously and it will leave you one day, so silently that you will not even hear the footsteps when it is going away. You will suddenly see yourself on a totally different plane of existence.' But that old fallacy persists; not only persists, all the vested interests of all the religions of the world want it to continue.

A big, tall Cherokee Indian named Brown Bear comes into the bar with a six-shooter tucked in his belt. He is a giant of a man, so no one asks him why he is carrying a bucket full of horse manure in one hand and a black cat in the other. He puts down the bucket.

'I will have a whiskey!' he roars at the bartender.

After drinking it, in one gulp, he orders another and then another.

All of a sudden, Brown Bear pulls out his gun and starts shooting the bucket, drops the cat and chases it around the bar on his hands and knees. When Brown Bear finally catches it, the trembling bartender raises his head above the bar and asks, 'What the hell was that all about?'

Brown Bear replies, 'My father told me to be more like a white man, so I came here to have a few drinks, shoot the shit and chase a little pussy.'

A little French boy comes to England in order to learn English. As his plane leaves Paris he learns the word *take-off*. During the flight he is looking through a magazine about Africa and learns the word *zebra*. When he arrives in England, the family he is staying with have a new baby and he learns the word *baby*.

The next day he comes to the school and the pretty young teacher asks him if he has learnt any English words yet, and the little boy replies, 'Take-off ze bra, baby.'

Little Ernie took his paper up to the teacher for marking and as she bent over the desk, he looked down the front of her blouse and said, 'Teacher, I see something.'

The teacher was extremely embarrassed and said, 'Ernie, that is very rude. Tomorrow, don't come to school.'

The next week Ernie was sitting in the front row when the teacher was writing on the blackboard. She dropped her chalk and, with her back to Ernie, bent down to pick it up.

Ernie got up and without a word headed for the door.

'Where are you going?' asked the teacher sternly.

'Teacher,' said Ernie, 'my schooldays are over.'

9

An Infinite Universe Is Within You

Osho,
The beautiful statement sat-chit-anand has truth first, consciousness second and bliss third. Is there some inevitable sequence among them?

There is no sequence among truth, consciousness, and bliss. They are not steps of a hierarchy, but they come one after another. Neither of them is higher than the other two, so – in the way we understand it – there is no sequence. The actual experience of *sat-chit-anand* happens simultaneously. In fact, these three words, *sat-chit-anand* – truth, consciousness, bliss – do not indicate three experiences. It is just the poverty of language that we cannot contain the whole experience in one word. Our words are so poor. The experience is absolutely an organic whole: whatever happens, happens simultaneously.

But perhaps as far as the human mind is concerned, a very different kind of sequence may be needed to comprehend what happens. In the statement *sat-chit-anand*, truth comes first. The natural tendency of the logical, rational mind is that truth must come first in experience and then consciousness and then bliss. In actual experience you start with meditation, which brings you wider and wider consciousness. At the ultimate peak, when the explosion happens, suddenly you find yourself fully conscious. Then on the one hand you find truth and on the other hand you find bliss. This all happens in a split second. Perhaps it is better to say it happens in no time. Even a split second takes some time. It happens in timelessness.

But for the mind's understanding – which is not the ultimate understanding but only a relative understanding – you can say the enlightened person experiences consciousness. As the consciousness comes into existence, suddenly he becomes aware of the truth that was hidden in the unconscious – because now there is no unconscious – and the bliss that was also hidden in the unconscious. I have told you it is almost like a bird, a single unity. The bird has two wings: truth, bliss, and the bird's own body can be called consciousness. But you cannot divide them: you cannot say what comes first and what comes second; the whole bird comes. Without the wings, the bird cannot come and without the bird, the wings cannot come.

Or take another example: you suddenly switch on the light in a dark room. Do you think that first you see the table, then you see the chairs, then you see the wall and then you see this and that? – so many things are in the room. But when the light comes on, they all suddenly become clear to you without any sequence – nothing is first, nothing is second. They were all hidden in darkness. Once light is there, darkness is no more. You immediately become aware of the existence of everything that is there.

Your being is certainly a bird. The ancient seers have called it 'the golden bird' – consciousness as the body, truth and bliss as the wings, and the whole sky full of stars is yours. Not only this sky; the mystics have been aware of skies beyond skies. Now even the scientist agrees that this sky cannot be the only sky.

The expansion of scientific consciousness has also brought a vast universe. There was a time in the Middle Ages when it was thought the earth is the center and the sun and all the stars are moving around it. It was a very small, cozy world, and nobody bothered about what was beyond it. As scientific exploration goes deeper and deeper, they become more and more mystical in their statements. Now they know existence has no limits.

And what we think of as stars are not stars. Each star is a bigger sun than our sun. Our sun is a very mediocre sun, although it is very big in comparison to the earth. It is over one hundred times bigger than the earth. It looks vast next to the earth, but only in comparison to the faraway stars, which look so small that we call them 'twinkle twinkle little stars.' They are not 'twinkle twinkle *little* stars'; they are far greater suns than our sun.

Our sun has its own solar system, made up of Earth, the moon and all the other planets. Each sun has its own solar system, and up to now they have counted at least three million suns. Among these millions of stars, the most mystical experience that has been encountered by the scientists is that they all are moving away from the center – as far as possible, at tremendous speed. It means the sky is available for them, they can go on ... They have been going on for billions of years and their speed is the same as the speed of light.

The speed of light is the ultimate speed, physicists have concluded. There is no higher speed according to them. It is tremendous. You will have to work it out. In one second, light travels 186,000 miles. You have to multiply it by 60 – that will be the distance light travels in one minute. Then you have to multiply it by 60 again – so you will have one hour of the light's travel. Then 24 – that is one day's travel of light. Then 365 – that is one light year. And that is the lowest unit of measurement as far as light and its speed is concerned.

One light year is just like one meter, one yard, one foot. There are stars thousands of light years away. The nearest star is four light years away. Even to reach this star seems to be impossible. Four light years – we don't have any vehicle, any rocket, that can go at the speed of light. And the trouble is intrinsic. The trouble is that at the speed of light, everything melts. Because it is so fast and the friction is so great, everything burns out and melts into light. We don't have any metal, artificial or natural, that can remain intact at the speed of light. And without the speed of light, there is no possibility of reaching to those stars which are millions of light years away.

Scientists say that this earth was separated from the sun about four million years ago. There are stars which will never know that this earth ever existed because the day this earth was born, their light started coming toward it, but has not yet arrived – even at that tremendous speed – and scientists reckon the earth may go out of existence before those light rays reach here. Just in-between two light rays the whole of the earth's life begins, comes to a peak and ends. Those stars have infinite space available – that is the sky. And now it is absolutely certain that there is no limit. Those stars can go on forever, as far as they want. We are citizens of an unlimited universe.

Existence is always in balance. Just as there is this vastness outside, the same tremendous expanse is within you. The within will be exactly as vast – as infinite – as the without, because the within and without should be in balance.

Physicists are the mystics of matter and the mystics are the physicists of consciousness. In this small statement of *sat-chit-anand*, the mystics are saying that a whole infinite universe within you becomes available simultaneously in an explosion of consciousness. The explosion of consciousness only brings light. Everything is there already – has been there forever – waiting for you to be awake.

There is no sequence the way we understand sequence, but there is a certain secret to be understood: without consciousness coming to its peak, you will not become aware of either truth or bliss. But once you have become aware, you know they are all one. This is a far more meaningful, significant, trinity than the Christian one. Their trinity seems to be fictitious: God, the Son, the Holy Ghost – it is good for children's books because they cannot understand *sat-chit-anand*. They say they can understand the Holy Ghost, they can understand the father, they can understand the son. But that is a very stupid fiction. With no rationale, with no evidence, Christianity goes on claiming it. Its whole structure depends on it.

The mystics' trinity seems to be based far more on experience, on truth. It is not a fiction – and it is available to you without any prayer, without any holy scripture. Just *you* are enough because you contain that infinity. All that is needed is to look inward. Allow your consciousness to grow so that it fills you with light and dispels all darkness, and you will find the most precious treasure within yourself. In that experience, there will not be any division between truth, consciousness, and bliss. It will come all at once, showering on you.

But the moment you bring that experience into language, you have to make one into three – so as not to be unfair to the tremendous experience that has happened. No single word can say anything about it. It will be a very partial statement, and any partial truth is more dangerous than a lie. At least the lie can be detected. The partial truth is very dangerous because it may not be detected; it gives you the feeling that it is true.

These three words contain almost three universes. Each is a sky unto itself. There is no limit to your consciousness. You can go in the inner world just as far away as stars are going in the outer world. Neither does bliss have any limits, nor does truth have any limits – and when three things don't have any limits, they cannot be three. Three unlimited things are bound to become one. So the experience is of one organic whole, not in sequence. But in language the difficulty is that we have to write words in sequence.

Languages like Chinese, Japanese, Korean – Far Eastern languages – are far better than alphabetical languages because alphabetical languages have to put everything in a sequence, in a sentence. One thing will be followed by another and then by another, one word by another word, one line by another line, one paragraph by another paragraph, everything in sequence. The nonalphabetical languages have disappeared from the world, except in the Far East.

In the beginning, all languages in the world were nonalphabetical, they were pictorial. For example, if you see an elephant, you see the whole elephant as one unity. But if you have to describe the elephant, you cannot describe it as one unit. You will have to tell about its legs like pillars, you will have to tell about its ears like big fans and so on and so forth. It is a big animal. And in reading your sentence about the elephant, one who has never seen an elephant is bound to think that there is a sequence. In Chinese, the situation is different. The elephant is not described the way we write about it. There is only a symbol of the elephant.

I remember one symbol I cannot forget: a symbol of a roof of a house, just a plain roof – anybody can understand the roof – and two women sitting under the roof. One of my friends was learning Chinese. I asked him, 'What is it?' He said, 'This symbol means *fight, war*.' Two women under one roof? There is going to be a Third World War without any doubt. Whoever made the symbol must have been a great psychologist. Knowingly or unknowingly, he has expressed so much in such a small symbol. If you have to write about it in an alphabetical language, you will have to use a few sentences to say the whole thing.

The mystic has always been in tremendous difficulty: how to say the unsayable? But he has tried, and he has tried his best in the East, because the East has known the mystic for almost ten thousand years. Ten thousand years is the minimum time that I am talking about.

The whole genius of the East has been concentrated on only one point: the discovery of oneself. That discovery – whether the mystic was in China, or in India, or in Arabia, or in Japan, makes no difference – the mystery has brought them to the same point, has always culminated in *sat-chit-anand*. They have all found tremendous bliss. Their lives have become absolutely authentic and truthful, and their beings have become absolutely conscious. There are no longer any unconscious parts lingering in them.

This can be seen by people who have receptivity, sensitivity and intelligence – who have eyes to see it, who are not standing with closed eyes saying 'There is no light.' You will have to open your eyes. Any mystic belonging to any age, to any country, to any part of the globe, reveals the same truth because truth is the unchanging, unmovable center of the whole of existence.

If you can find yourself in company with a mystic, and you can be unafraid, and open your heart so that he can pour his experience into you, he can only give to you. You need not be worried. He is not going to take anything from you. You don't have anything in the first place – and what you have, you are unaware of. The mystic can pour his light into you and can make you aware of all that is hidden in you – your hidden splendor. This is the authentic relationship between the master and the disciple. The master does not teach anything. He simply pours his light into the heart of the disciple. There is no philosophy to be taught, there is no teaching that the student has to be converted to – there is only an experience that has to be transferred.

For centuries it has been known as the transmission of the lamp. It is a beautiful expression: *transmission of the lamp*. The master simply allows you to have his fire, to make your dark house also light. He loses nothing, but you gain tremendously. Hence the great gratitude that has been felt by the disciples for the master, because you cannot repay him – there is no way. What he has given to you is invaluable. All that you can do is feel a heartfelt gratitude. This gratitude is the only authentic connection between the disciple and the master. And as the disciple also becomes aware, he rises to the same status as the master.

A beautiful story...

When the master of a great seeker, Rinzai, saw that the moment had come when Rinzai was going to be of the same status as the master himself, he called Rinzai and slapped him hard. Rinzai said, 'But I have not done anything, I have not even said anything. You have been beating me for years.'

It is a very loving gesture, this beating. Only Zen has come to understand that it is out of sheer love that the master slaps the disciple.

The master said to Rinzai, 'This is my last slap to you. I could not resist the temptation of enjoying it once more, because from tomorrow you will be a master yourself.'

So playful. Both laughed, both enjoyed it. Rinzai remembered it his whole life. He became a much better-known master than his own master, but he never forgot the last slap that the master had given him. He continuously remembered, 'My master loved me so much that there was not a single day that he would not beat me – on any excuse.'

It looks very strange to the logical mind, but logic has nothing to do with the inner world. Rinzai said, 'Now I understand how much effort that old man was making in slapping me. In fact, his hands were hurting more than I was hurting because I was young, healthy. He was very old, but he did not miss. As I was reaching close to my enlightenment, he knew it before I knew it.'

Naturally, the master knows before the disciple that you are just on the brink. And that slap was not just a slap. To the outsiders it was a slap, but to both the master and the disciple that slap was a push beyond the boundary that was making him still think of himself as a disciple. With the last slap, he was recognized as a master, not with certificates – they are so inhuman, so dead – but with a living contact.

Then both the men, the old man and the young, laughed late into the night, and the whole monastery thought, 'What is happening?' People were looking from every window and door – 'What is happening?' And both were laughing tears of joy.

The next day, the master did not appear for his morning sermon. He sent word to Rinzai, 'Now you can go. Now, you can do what I have done to you. You can transmit the lamp to others. I am too old – just take the whole responsibility of the monastery.'

Rinzai said, 'When you said you were hitting me for the last time, I immediately understood that now I have to be responsible for this whole monastery. With your last slap, you have retired. That's why I was crying, because you are retiring. Without you, I do not want to be enlightened. Let me remain a disciple. Don't retire. But you have done it already. I was perfectly happy and I was not thinking that it was going to happen so soon.'

What had he experienced, when the master slapped him the last time? Just a sudden explosion: *sat-chit-anand.*

There is no sequence. It is all simultaneous. It is all together. It is one without any order.

> Osho,
> Last night, I noticed your beard. It is really a magnificent thing; it reminds me of a lion's mane. Does a beard like yours come with enlightenment? Or do you have to be born with it?

Such a beard comes with your birth. Enlightenment cannot give you such a beard – don't be fooled!

You can see it: Gautam Buddha has no beard, not only no beard, no mustache either. Great masters of the Jainas, called *tirthankaras*, are without any beard, without any mustache. In fact, both traditions – the Jaina and the Buddha tradition – have a strange idea which their scholars have not been able to explain, which has been questioned for twenty-five centuries at least. But I don't belong to any tradition. That's why I have a certain objective insight into things. I can give the reason.

It was not that they were shaving themselves twice a day – just that they had no beards and no mustaches from their very birth. They never grew them. In fact, in Jainism, it has become a part of the definition: unless a master is without a mustache and beard, he is not a master, because their twenty-four great masters are all without beards, without mustaches. I cannot believe that all these people were missing some hormones which create the beard, which create the mustache in man and not in women. Once in a while some women may have – particularly in old age – a little mustache, a little beard. Sometimes it happens in young age also.

I knew a very beautiful young girl. She was the daughter of the principal of one of the Leonard Theosophical Colleges of the Christians. The principal was very much interested in me – that's how I came to know the girl. She was very intelligent, very beautiful. She got married in America, got a DLitt from America and now teaches in America – but all her beauty was in trouble because of a beard. She had to shave it twice a day, but still there was a black spot. If you came close to her, and she was so beautiful ... That black spot was making her feel very inferior.

When I saw her last with her husband, they had both come for six months to teach in the Leonard Theosophical College in Jabalpur, and then six months in some other theosophical college in America. The last time I saw them must have been thirty years ago.

I told her, 'You will suffer unnecessarily your whole life from inferiority because of this beard. The more you shave it, the bigger it becomes and you are in America. It is a simple thing – just a little change in your hormones and it will disappear. You need some more female hormones. You have too many male hormones. The balance is not right.'

She said, 'I never thought about it and nobody ever told me.'

Then I received her letter a few months after she had gone to America saying, 'I am very grateful that my beard has disappeared.'

It is a question of hormones. In old age, women start growing beards because their female hormones are finished, but their male hormones are still there, active. They have lived the life of a woman, but they have not used their male part, so the balance has changed. In old age, many women start growing a beard. But in old age, nobody takes much notice. I cannot believe that all these twenty-four *tirthankaras*, spread over five thousand years, all had unbalanced hormones. What could be the reason? And the same was the question about Buddha. I don't believe that they did not have mustaches or beards. My own understanding is that it is only a symbolic expression, that as you become more and more aware, you become more and more delicate – as graceful as a woman. Instead of having male qualities, which are the qualities of a warrior or a soldier, you start having the qualities of compassion and love and grace and beauty of a woman.

Those statues, the twenty-four *tirthankaras* of the Jainas, don't represent the people exactly; they represent only a metaphor. They are not photographs. They are very objective pieces of art. You can go into any Jaina temple. If it is big enough, it will have twenty-four *tirthankaras*. If it is not big enough, then they place three statues and mirrors on both the sides and small windows for you to look through.

When you look into those mirrors, they go on reflecting each other. So instead of three, you see a line of hundreds, as far as you can see. The first mirror reflects the second mirror, then that mirror reflects the other mirror, and this goes on and on. So as far as you can see and strangely, you can see exactly twenty-four *tirthankaras* – a great artistic device. But if the temple is very poor, then you will find only one statue of Mahavira.

But one thing is – it is striking that Jainas have also not been able to explain this – all the statues look similar, exactly similar. The only difference is a small symbol underneath their legs – a line represents Mahavira. Even the priest cannot say which is Mahavira. First he has to look. You may not understand how he manages to tell that this is Mahavira, this is Abhinava and this is Meminaka. There are different symbols for each master, but their statues are exactly the same.

That too is impossible. Twenty-four people exactly the same? The same height, the same nose, the same eyes, the same face, the same body – it is not possible. For centuries they have been at a loss to answer because they have been looking at those statues as factual. I look at those statues as symbols. Those statues say nothing about the bodies of those twenty- four masters. They say something about their having exactly the same experience. Their same faces, their same eyes, their same heights indicate only one thing: what has happened within them is the same.

Now, how to say it in a sculpture? The great artist must have found a tremendously beautiful way to say through their statues, 'We are not making their portraits; we are not photographers. Through the statue we are trying to represent their inner experience.' And because the inner experience was the same – *sat-chit-anand* – there was no need to make any differences in the bodies.

You are a little bit crazy, but not more than me. I insist: if you want this kind of beard, you will have to be born with it. It does not come with enlightenment. Enlightenment has no concern with your beard. Even a woman can become enlightened but that does not mean she will have a beard. This kind of beautiful beard comes only with your birth.

I was very reluctant to listen to my parents. They were all insisting that this does not look right, 'You should cut off your beard.'

I said, 'I want to keep the original hairs just as existence has given them to me. I am going to return them to existence in exactly the same way. I am not going into this stupid business of shaving every day. Moreover, I am so lazy – someday I may shave off half, and the other half...'

The priest had been invited to preach at a mental hospital. During the sermon he noticed that one of the patients was paying very close attention, his eyes fixed on the priest's face, his body bent eagerly forward. Such interest was most flattering. After the service the priest noticed that the man was speaking to one of the attendants. So, as soon as possible, the priest asked him, 'Did that man speak to you about my sermon?'

'Yes,' said the attendant.

'Would you mind telling me what he said?' asked the priest.

'Well,' said the man reluctantly, 'what the man said was, "Just think, he is out, and I am in."'

We are all in. There is no out. We have dropped out. You are my people – insiders.

Osho,
Standing in the queue for breakfast this morning I overheard two German girls talking, 'Who the hell is this guy Milarepa anyway? Osho gives him so much juice!' The other replied, 'Oh, he's no one really! Don't you know? Osho just invented him as a joke!'

Just then, Lolita walked up, put her arms around me, looked deep into my eyes and said in a sexy voice, 'Hi, schnooksy, did you hear the discourse this morning?' One look in her eyes and I knew I was in trouble again. I forgot all about my breakfast, excused myself, and ran back to my room. I closed my eyes and began repeating, 'Vimal, Vimal, Vimal.'

Osho, am I having what psychologists call an 'identity crisis?' I am also wondering, who the hell is this guy Milarepa?

Milarepa, you have created more trouble than you are aware of, because Jivan Mary committed a mistake in typing the name of Lokita. She typed the name *Lolita*. And then such a chaos began; the boyfriend of Lolita was immensely freaked out. He suspected that this Lolita was having a love affair with Milarepa. And Lolita was crying and weeping and trying to convince him.

Hearing about Lolita's beauty, many new lovers started knocking on her door, saying 'Don't be worried. If Milarepa has left you after ten minutes, we are here. For what are we here?' And the boyfriend freaked out even more. Lokita was enjoying immensely. She changed her name to Lolita. She dropped her own name, Lokita. So many were following her.

Milarepa, the girl who hugged you was not Lolita; it was Lokita who has changed herself into Lolita. But you are such a fool that you have forgotten completely who this woman is. And naturally, just a ten-minute love affair – who remembers the name or the face?

I have heard about a man who married ten times. And when he married the tenth time, after three months he discovered that he had married this woman once before. When you marry ten times, memory has its limitations. You are not a computer.

Milarepa changes girlfriends ten times every day. So naturally, when Lokita hugged him again, telling him that she was Lolita, he thought, 'My God. I am again in trouble.' You will remain in trouble always, Milarepa.

Now these two girls were asking 'Who the hell is this guy Milarepa anyway?' and 'Osho gives him so much juice.' I have to give it to him because the poor fellow has to distribute his juice all around. If I don't give him juice, you will find him lying flat on the bed, finished. I have to keep him alive. Do you have any objections?

It is too much that the other replied, 'Oh, he's no one really.' He is one of my craziest disciples and I will not tolerate such insulting remarks. And she said, 'Don't you know? Osho just invented him as a joke.' He is not a joke, although his whole life is full of jokes. But he is a real person, just sitting here, keeping his head down, avoiding the girls.

He is becoming a little old – I may take him out of the circus. But I never take anybody out of the circus unless he requests it, and Milarepa has not requested it yet. So I feel he needs a little more experience, a little more anxiety, a little more tension, a little more trouble. Let him have it to his heart's content.

The old bull's active days are over – soon Milarepa's days will also be over – but the farmer permits him to stay in the pasture with the cows. Of course, the farmer lets a young bull loose in the field as well, and he goes to work immediately.

Watching this, the old bull starts snorting and pawing the ground with his hooves. 'You are wasting your time,' says the farmer. 'You are too old for that sort of thing now.'

'I know,' says the old bull, 'but I can show him I am not a cow, can't I?'

Poor Milarepa is not a joke, just an old bull that I am keeping in the pasture with the cows. Not to be caught, he finishes his love affairs quickly – ten minutes. That must be the minimum time in the whole world. A love affair finished in ten minutes! Perhaps three minutes honeymoon, two minutes married life, five minutes trouble, and it is finished. The fact is: now he is getting old. Everybody is getting old. But he has to go on proving that at least everybody should know he is not a cow.

And as for you, Milarepa – you need not be afraid of the cows. You need not go to your room and lock it and feel that again another crisis has arisen and start repeating 'Vimal, Vimal, Vimal.' *Vimal* is not a transcendental meditation; it is not going to help. And don't be so afraid of women – just a little longer.

I came across a statement just the other day: 'There is nothing in the world better than the love of a good woman unless, of course, it is the love of a bad woman.' Here you will find the greatest women in the world – fed up with the world. They have come here to meditate. But a woman is fundamentally love. Her meditation cannot be without love. A woman is not much interested in sex. She is much more interested in warmth, in cuddling, in friendliness, in love. Man is much more interested in sex. These are the fallacies which show that God never created the world, because nothing fits together. He does not seem to understand that man and woman have to live together. They should be made in such a way that they fit with each other, but they are absolutely misfitting. Man's sexuality is genital and local. It's like local anesthesia.

When my personal physician took my blood, in the beginning he used to tell me, 'Now, the prick.' Finally he understood that what he is doing is nonsense. It is not the prick. Now he does not say that. I have been watching while he changed his idea. Now he does it silently without saying anything.

But man is nothing but the prick. Women have a totally different kind of being. Her whole body needs love. It is not sexuality. Her whole body is orgasmic. That's why there is tremendous trouble. Man comes to orgasm quickly – within two minutes – and the woman has not even started. The woman takes a little time. Her whole body has to become ready, ecstatic. Her whole body has to join the dance. Only then can she feel orgasmic joy. So she is not actually interested in the prick. She is more interested in hugging, in being close to you, in the warmth of your body. She wants to be surrounded by your love, she wants to surround you with her love.

More and more people will be feeling that sex is dropping away, but that does not mean that you have to escape when you see a woman approaching you, shut yourself in your room and repeat the transcendental mantra: *Vimal, Vimal, Vimal.* You have to change your old idea of love. It was not love, it was pure sex. When sex drops, you can meet the woman on a higher level for which she has always been longing and suffering.

For millions of years women have suffered because man has not been able to give them what they need. Man has simply used them for his sexuality. They feel almost like a commodity to be used, and then the man turns over and goes to sleep and starts snoring. This is so ugly and the woman has tears in her eyes, is crying. After each lovemaking the woman cries because she has not got anything. Her standard of love is higher than the standard of man.

As more and more sannyasins will be dropping out of sex, they should start learning the language of love, of warmth, of friendliness. No woman is going to feel offended that you have dropped sex. In fact, she is going to be immensely happy that now love can move to a higher level, which was always her deepest longing.

This difference between women's and men's orgasmic capacities has been one of the causes of the greatest misery of humanity, and nobody has ever tried to bridge it. Either the woman has to be brought lower – which is impossible, because her whole body is orgasmic; she cannot become locally orgasmic. Or – the only way possible – the man learns the language of love and becomes the same as the woman, his whole body needing a shower of love. That will take almost ninety percent of the misery from the world.

But it can happen only if the man comes to a point where sex drops by itself, because this is the deepest reason for man's and woman's conflict. But they are not aware of it, so they fight on any other excuse – continuously misunderstanding. Man says something, the woman understands something else. The woman says something, the man understands something else. It is almost impossible to have an intelligent conversation between two lovers. I have never heard of anything like that. You can have an intelligent conversation with somebody else's woman, but not with your own woman. With your own woman you can only fight – or you can read your newspaper.

Two Italians meet each other in the pizzeria.
'Are you going to Goa?' asks the first.
'No, I'm-a going to stay-a,' replies the friend.

The pope was giving another of his speeches to a lively crowd of Italian youngsters. He was trying hard to make his point. 'You must not use-a the pill!'

A young, pretty signorina stepped forward and said, 'Look, Polack! You no play-a da game, you no make-a da rules.'

This goes on, this misunderstanding. But with my people I hope to create a very deep understanding of all that is hidden in the darkness inside. I am trying to bring it out in every possible way, so that you can become aware of your whole being and what the real authentic cause of your misery is. And if you are thinking of some false causes for your misery, you are not going to get out of misery.

Nancy Reagan comes back from her medical examination with a smile on her face.

'Why the grin?' asks Ronald Reagan with a sour face.

'Because,' she boasts, 'Dr. White told me I have the figure of a woman half my age.'

'Oh, yeah? And what about your seventy-year-old ass?'

'Come to think of it,' replies Nancy, 'he didn't say a thing about you.'

10

Each Moment Is the Goal

Osho,
Is not the inquiry into sat-chit-anand the same as Badarayana's 'Athato brahman jigyasa'?

Badarayana's statement, '*Athato brahman jigyasa*' is one of the most potential statements ever made. It means, 'Now begins the inquiry into the ultimate.' It is the first statement in his *Brahma Sutra* – *Maxims about the Ultimate* – one of the greatest mystic books in the world. This is the first sentence of that strange book, but one of the most significant books that has ever been written.

I call it strange because Badarayana is not well-known around the world, although in India he is the only mystic on whose maxims thousands of commentaries have been written. Each of his statements is so pregnant with meaning that you can go on commenting on it in a thousand-and-one ways. Still it seems something inexhaustible has remained. This is the only book which has commentaries, then commentaries on commentaries, then again commentaries on those commentaries.

For almost two thousand years, all the great geniuses of this great country have been in some way or other connected with Badarayana. And still his name is not known in the world. Perhaps the reason is that nothing is known about him except the book. About his personal life absolutely nothing is known. Whether he was a historical person or not is very difficult to say. But one thing is certain: whoever wrote the book – whatever his name was – was certainly one of the greatest mystics of the world. So what is the problem in calling him Badarayana?

Whoever wrote the book, one more thing is certain: the book is historical. It has existed for two thousand years and is one of the books – the only one – which has spread due to so many commentaries. It has so many complexities that almost every philosopher in India became involved in some way or other. There is no other book in the world which has been commented upon so much. It can mean only one thing: his statements are almost mines of meaning. You can go on digging and you will go on finding more and more – fresher sources of water, fresher sources of meaning and significance.

Sat-chit-anand is not equivalent to *athato brahma jigyasa. Athato brahma jigyasa* – now begins the inquiry into the ultimate – is the first step and *sat-chit- anand* is the last step. What begins as an inquiry ... *Sat-chit-anand* is not an inquiry, it is the ultimate result of the inquiry: you have come to the conclusion. The statement of Badarayana is the beginning and *sat-chit-anand* is the end. They are not synonymous, although they are deeply connected with each other. Without the inquiry, there is no possibility of realizing the conclusion. Hence Badarayana comes first. This small statement has to be understood because it is for every beginner.

As far as the ultimate is concerned, one is always a beginner. One is always coming close to it, closer and closer and closer, but something always remains inviting you, calling you forth, challenging you, a higher peak. You were thinking you have arrived but still there is something left. And this pilgrimage continues. I have started saying that there is no goal, only the pilgrimage. In other words, the pilgrimage in itself is so divine, so holy, that to be bothered and to be anxious about the end of it can only mean one thing: you are not interested in the journey, you are interested in the end of the journey. You are not enjoying each moment of your pilgrimage. You are looking forward, ahead, for the time when you will have reached and then you will celebrate – and that is a wrong approach from the very beginning.

Each moment is the journey and each moment is the goal. You have to live as if you have already arrived, although there will never be a moment when you can say 'I have arrived.' You can only say 'I am coming home. I can see the home coming closer and closer.' But it is good that you never come. Once you have come, you come to a full stop, and life knows no full stops. Yes, colons, semicolons, commas, everything is allowed – but a full stop? – absolutely no, a hundred times no, because a full stop will mean that life has come to an end, life has come to the grave. Life never comes to an end. It never terminates in death. It is an ongoing process.

Hence, Badarayana's statement has to be understood very lovingly and very deeply. Each word of it is pure gold.

First, it has been commented on by different commentators, giving different colors to it. You are not accustomed to this because in the West the very phenomenon of commentaries has not happened. Nobody comments on Kant, nobody comments on Hegel, even on Socrates nobody comments, nobody comments on the Bible. The very phenomenon of commentaries is absolutely Eastern. The reason is that the great philosophers of the West came into existence after writing had arrived, when it was no longer a question of memorizing – you could write a treatise.

When philosophers like Kant or Hegel or Feuerbach write, they write with all the possible implications, complexities, meanings. They keep in mind what the points are if somebody is going to contradict them. They also keep in mind what the arguments of the opposite philosophy can be, and they are already replying to them – although nobody has opposed them, nobody has even understood what they are writing about. So their writings are very complete in a way, full and entire. They have not left anything for anybody else to add.

In the East, commentaries started for a certain historical reason. It is at least ten thousand years old – that is the very orthodox view about the history of philosophical development in the East. There are people who think it is far more ancient than ten thousand years. Because there was no writing – writing had not yet been invented – every master had to speak in small maxims, not elaborate treatises but in small sutras. The word *sutra* means *the thread*.

They are giving you the very minimum to remember, because to remember a vast amount of a great philosophical treatise will not be possible. And there is a danger of forgetting something, there is a danger of adding something of your own. So the way of the sutras was the only possibility – to write in such a condensed way that every disciple of any master can remember the small, seed-like maxims.

But they are only seeds. They indicate the way, they indicate a certain direction. Unless your heart becomes a soil for those seeds, they will not sprout into leaves, into branches, into flowers, into fruit. Those seeds contain everything that is going to happen, they have the whole inbuilt program. If you allow that seed to enter your being, as it sinks deeper and deeper, you will realize all that is contained in it. It will become a reality in you. But because individuals are different, because individuals are unique, each individual heart is not the same soil, not the same territory, not the same land. The seed will have to grow according to the soil.

Somebody's heart may be very fertile, creative. The tree may become very huge, the foliage may be very green, and when the spring comes there will be thousands of flowers and fruit. But somebody else's heart may be very hard. The seed is the same, but the soil is not going to help the seed much. The seed has to grow against all odds, against all hindrances. The heart is not going to help, on the contrary it will hinder. It is just a seed which has fallen onto ground full of stones. It may grow, but it won't be the same as in a fertile creative heart. It may not attain the same height; it may even be a bit crippled; it may not have much foliage; only a few flowers may come. But the uniquenesses are such...

Somebody is a poet and the seed may become poetry, somebody is a musician and the seed may become music, and somebody is a sculptor and the seed may become a beauty in stone. It will all depend in which kind of heart the seed falls. There are many more implications.

It is possible that one heart may be very fertile and it may bring forth thousands of flowers and one heart may not be so fertile and it may not bring forth thousands of flowers but just one flower – very huge, very big. Those thousand flowers will not be in any way competitive to this one flower. In number they may be many, but the beauty of this one flower has almost accumulated the whole beauty of thousands of flowers.

For many years, while I was teaching in the university, I had one gardener. I had a beautiful garden. And this old man I had chosen for a certain reason – he was somebody else's gardener, some army officer's gardener. Every year, he had won the competition for growing the biggest roses. I used to go to see it because the whole city was involved in the competition. All the rich people – officers, bureaucrats, professors, doctors, those who could afford a garden – were participants.

But I was not interested in the people who were participating. I was interested in finding out who the gardener was. The poor gardener was not even mentioned when the trophy was given to the winner; it was given to the owner of the garden. I was looking out for the gardener – this army officer could not be a gardener himself – but the poor gardener was not even there.

I followed the army officer's car. I looked around his house, I watched, and I found the gardener working. When the officer went in, he did not even tell the gardener, 'I have won the trophy because of you. In fact, it belongs to you.' He simply went into his garage and then into his house.

I went into his garden. The old man, a poor man, was working. I asked him, 'Have you heard that your roses have been chosen as the best for this year?'

He said, 'Nobody has told me yet.'

I asked, 'How much is this army officer giving you as salary?'

He said, 'Not very much.'

I said, 'Whatever he is giving, I will give you double. You can tell me later how much he is giving you. Just bring whatever you have into my car and come with me.'

He said, 'But he is a dangerous man. He will search for me with his gun.'

I said, 'Don't be worried, I am no less dangerous. Don't you worry.'

So I brought him into my own house and I told him, 'You start working, and every year I will not be going to the competition, you will be going. And all the trophies that you win will be in the house that I have given to you.'

He could not believe it. He asked, 'But what about the army officer?'

I said, 'I will take care of him. You need not be worried about it.'

Then I saw how he was winning. His whole art was never to allow any rosebush more than one flower. He would cut off all the buds and leave only the biggest bud.

I asked him, 'What is the secret of it?'

He said, 'The secret is simple. The rosebush has a certain amount of juice. It can be distributed to one hundred flowers, but if you don't allow it to be distributed, it is bound to assert itself into one flower.'

I remained nine years in that university. For nine years continuously he was the winner. And his secret was just to allow one flower to grow.

So it is possible. These are the uniquenesses I am talking about – that the same seeds in different hearts will bring different manifestations.

That is how commentaries begin. The master dies. He had thousands of disciples who have listened to him. Now they start thinking – what is the significance of a certain statement or of a certain word?

In the East, it has been a very delicate affair – not brutal logic, but a very subtle, very feminine art.

The word *athato* can mean *now*, it can mean *here now*, it can mean *from now*, it can mean *from this point onward*. Because of these different meanings growing in different hearts, the whole meaning of the sentence will change. Just the first word will change the whole meaning. For example, to a man or a woman whose heart is the heart of a devotee, the heart of a lover, *athato* will mean 'Enough of love; now begins the inquiry into the ultimate. Enough of this world and its pleasures, now begins the inquiry into the ultimate.'

To the logician, the same word will mean 'Enough of logic, enough of rationality, enough of philosophy; now begins the real inquiry into the existential' – not into words, not into philosophical investigations, but into an existential experience. To a poet it may mean 'Enough of poetry, enough of all that life I have lived up to now; the time has come to enter the path in search of light, in search of the truth. I have sung songs of joy, I have sung songs of beauty.'

But a time comes when you are tired even of your own creativity. How long...? Just as you become tired of the woman you loved so much, of the man you loved so much, you become tired of your creative dimension for which you would have sacrificed your life. A moment comes when it seems that you have been playing like a child, collecting seashells on the sea beach, or making castles of sand. Beautiful utopias – but it is enough.

You have not gained anything of the eternal, of the timeless, of the immortal. How long are you going to wait? Now is the moment to change the direction of all your genius and intelligence. Then *athato* will mean something different, different from what it can mean to a businessman, to what it can mean to a king. He has been on a power trip, he has conquered as much as he wanted, he is tired.

I am reminded of one of the greatest emperors, perhaps in the whole of world history.

His name was Ashoka. He could have become a world conqueror far more easily than Alexander the Great. He had far bigger armies, far more developed technology, far more riches. He was on the way to becoming a world conqueror, but the first victory was enough. He conquered what is now the state of Orissa. In his days it was called the land of Kalinga. He conquered the country of Kalinga.

Millions of people had to be killed, massacred, because the people of that place were ready to die but not to be conquered. The situation was such that the fight would have continued until not a single man remained and Ashoka would have been victorious only over millions of corpses. Halfway, Ashoka trembled, seeing millions of people massacred, and seeing the point that these were not the people who were going to give way. Either life in freedom or death – there was no other alternative for them. They would not accept any kind of slavery.

When he became absolutely certain of it, he thought for a moment – just in the middle of millions of corpses – 'Is it worthwhile? What is the point? Killing these brave people and just becoming victorious over a country of the dead. You will feel repentant your whole life because you have destroyed so much life. And not the life of ordinary people, but people of tremendous courage, who have given you absolute alternatives: "Either we will live in freedom or we will die in freedom. Slavery is not acceptable. You may be a great king, you may have great power, but at least we have the power to die – you cannot take it away from us."'

The country was poor. It was not in any way comparable to the vast empire of Ashoka. Ashoka's empire was the biggest India has ever seen – from Afghanistan, which is now a separate country, Pakistan, which is now a separate country, Sri Lanka, which is now a separate country, Burma, which is now a separate country, to Nepal, Bhutan, Sikkim, Ladakh ... India has never had so large a map as it had at the time of Ashoka.

Just this small country of Kalinga was independent, and they were poor. They did not have an army or the technology, just courage – such a courage that they had only two simple alternatives: 'We will live in freedom or we will die in freedom; we don't know any other alternative.' In fact, Ashoka had become challenged in a way – he had to see how, for centuries, these people had been free without an army, with just human courage and dignity and pride. It was a great challenge to the great emperor, who could have crushed them without any effort. He had already killed half of the country.

But then suddenly a turn came to his consciousness, and he saw that this was simply being stupid, 'You are destroying a beautiful, proud people and you are able to destroy them because you have bigger armies, you have more weapons, better weapons, you have better horses, but you don't have better human beings than those you are destroying. Your people are simply servants who are fighting because they are being paid. These people are fighting without arms, without horses, just because they love freedom. It is ugly to destroy these people – this will be destroying a beautiful variety.'

He returned home. His generals asked, 'What is the matter? We are winning.'

Ashoka said, 'This is not victory, this is simply murder. And I am not a murderer. If I cannot conquer them alive, I don't want to conquer them. I don't want to be called in history a conqueror of corpses. Forget about it.'

The whole thing became such a nightmare in Ashoka's mind that the moment he reached his palace he came to a transformation point: he renounced the empire. He said, 'Of what use is this whole empire? Enough of it! I don't want any conquering or anybody to conquer, anybody to invade, and I don't want any empire.'

Ashoka became a disciple of Gautam Buddha. Gautam Buddha had died two hundred years earlier, but his disciples were alive, his enlightened disciples were still there. It may have been the third or fourth generation, but there were people who had the same flavor and the same charisma, the same magic.

Ashoka became a disciple, renounced the world, started living like a beggar in his own capital, begging for his food every day in his own capital. And because he became a sannyasin, this word *athato* would bring to his mind a totally different meaning than it could bring to the mind of a poet, or to the mind of a creative artist, or to a painter.

And the meaning of *brahma jigyasa* will be like the meaning of *athato*. To the theist, *brahma* will mean *God*; to the atheist, *brahma* will mean *the ultimate reality* – not a personal God, but an impersonal reality. *Jigyasa*, inquiry, will also take different forms. To somebody it may become meditation, to somebody else it may become yoga, to somebody else it may become prayer. It will depend on your potentiality – and according to your potential the seed will take form.

This simple sentence has been commented upon by almost one thousand commentators. I have gone through so many commentaries and it has been such a joy to see the same small sentence – just three words – take such different meanings. And the whole commentary on all other sutras, all other maxims, will depend on the different meanings of this first sentence.

It is not equivalent to *sat-chit-anand*, but it is the beginning. And *sat- chit-anand* – truth, consciousness, bliss – is the ultimate realization of this small beginning that becomes deeper and deeper and bigger and bigger, and sooner or later becomes your whole life. Badarayana's sutra is only a hint that it is time to change. It is time to become a seeker; it is time to behave like a mature person; it is time not to waste your life anymore on mundane activities. It is time for the pilgrimage. Your boat has arrived. It is time to go into the unexplored seas, to the untraveled path; to be alone and to go within; to be alone and to be absolutely free and independent; to find your roots in existence.

The day you start finding your roots in existence will be the moment when you have touched the edge of your very life spring. That will be the time of a certain conclusion. Your life is no longer a question, but becomes an answer. And that answer is *sat-chit-anand.* Those three words are irrefutable.

God can be argued against. In fact, half of the world is now communist and does not believe in God. Buddhism, which is the third-greatest religion after Christianity and Mohammedanism, doesn't believe in God; Jainism, which is a minority religion, doesn't believe in God either. In fact, if you accumulate all the numbers, there are more atheists in the world than theists. It has never been so before. The world was always a theist majority and an atheist minority. The balance has reversed. Today there are more atheists in the world than theists.

And the theist is not much of a theist either. He is theist just by name; scratch his skin a little and you will find a doubt inside. He believes in God, he goes to church, he goes to the temple, but his is not a faith which has no doubt within it. It is a faith which has been sitting on repressed doubt. It is a belief – just underneath is doubt. I have never come across a single theist who *really* believes. He may say 'I really believe,' but the more he says 'I really believe,' the more he exposes himself. When you say to someone 'I really love you,' what do you mean? Is not love enough? This emphasis of 'really' makes the whole thing bogus. It is like in a movie – it is not true, it is a Hollywood love affair.

Truth cannot be denied either by theists or by atheists or by agnostics. These are the only three possibilities, the only three alternatives. The agnostic is the most intelligent of all three. The agnostic says, 'I don't know, I am still trying to know. I am on the path, but I have not come to any conclusion yet.' He is the most honest of the three – not really getting into either belief or unbelief. Keeping himself neutral so that he is not prejudiced, so that he is not carrying a certain opinion already. Just keeping himself without any prejudice, without any opinion, so that when he comes across the truth, he can realize it as it is, not as he wants it to be. An opinion will give color, distortion; an opinion will create its own illusions, hallucinations.

The agnostic is the most significant seeker of truth. But there are very few agnostics in the world. Perhaps most of them are here, going onto the path with open eyes and with a clean heart, ready to accept truth as it is, with no desire to project anything onto the truth. The agnostic cannot deny the beauty of *sat-chit-anand*. He can say 'I am searching,' but he cannot say anything against it.

Neither can the theist deny it. He may say 'This is what I mean by God: my God is truth, my God is consciousness, my God is bliss.' There is no problem – it is just a question of words that only idiots fight about. If this is what you mean by God, then it is perfectly okay. But then don't pray, because there is no person who is going to listen and say hello to you.

Sat-chit-anand is just an experience. If you want it to be synonymous with your idea of God, there is no harm, but remember, there is no need to create temples and mosques and synagogues and churches for it. It is an experience that is going to happen within you, not without.

Nor can the atheist deny it. He can deny God as a creator. He can laugh at the very idea of a personal God because there is no evidence and no proof for it. It is simply pure fiction invented by cunning priests for the gullible, for those who are still childish and have some father fixation – they need somebody to protect them, a great father.

Not even the atheist can deny the reality of truth, nor can he deny the reality of consciousness because he is already a little bit conscious. If this much consciousness is possible, what is the problem? Why can't more grow? This small consciousness that we have is enough proof that there is a possibility of growth, of expansion.

We may not know bliss, but we have known moments of peace, we have known moments of silence, we have known moments of joy. Bliss is altogether something tremendously vast. But if you have seen a dewdrop, you have seen all the oceans: a small dewdrop is enough proof that water exists. And if there is a dewdrop, what is the problem? There may be oceans. The formula that makes the dewdrop, H2O, makes all the oceans. It is the same formula, the same foundation.

These are the three kinds of people in the world. None of them can deny *sat-chit-anand*. That's the beauty of mystical experiences. Theological belief systems don't have this greatness. They can be denied, refuted, laughed at. There is no way to defend them. There is no way to prove them. But the mystical experiences belong to a totally different category.

It is something that would be absolutely inhuman for anybody to question, because to question it is to question the very meaning of life. To question it is to question your very existence, your very consciousness, your very experience of pleasure, peace, silence, joy. It is not possible.

Just a few days ago the records of the Nobel Prize committee were made available; the public is allowed to see them every fifty years. Fifty years of records: how many people were considered for the Nobel Prize; why certain people were rejected for the Nobel Prize; why it was given to certain people. All those records were opened just a few days ago. And I came across the strangest thing. I could not believe that they could have done such an ugly and nasty thing: Leo Tolstoy was denied the Nobel Prize on the grounds that he was a kind of mystic.

I have never thought that it can be a crime that one of the greatest creative artists ... His novels are incomparable – perhaps no one will ever be able to write such a great novel as *War and Peace*. The man was not only a novelist, but a man who lived whatever he was preaching. His preaching may be under dispute, you may not agree with him – that's another thing. I myself don't agree with him because he was preaching poverty.

He was a very rich man, he was a faraway cousin of the Czar. He belonged to the royal family of Russia and he had immense land, thousands of slaves. Everything that was possible in those days was available to him, but he did not use anything, he lived like a poor man. His whole family lived like a royal family, but he used to live in the servants' quarters, not in the palace. At least he was a sincere man: whatever he thought was right, he did.

The Nobel Prize committee mentions it – he was a Christian. He has written the most beautiful books on Christianity. I don't think there has ever been any theologian who has written so beautifully about Christianity. But the Nobel Prize committee declared that the Nobel Prize was not to be given to him because his ideas about Christianity were not orthodox, they were very much his own.

Tolstoy believed in a mystical Christianity. He did not believe in the orthodox, traditional Christianity. He had his own ideas about Christianity – as if to have one's own ideas about religion is a crime. He was not accepted because his Christianity was a kind of mystic Christianity. This mysticism became the barrier. His name was proposed and rejected. There have been many other names which have been rejected on strange grounds – and even politicians have been given the Nobel Prize.

It is very strange. Leo Tolstoy is as important a person as Jesus Christ himself, but I think Jesus Christ would also have been denied the Nobel Prize because he was not an orthodox Jew. He was proposing his own ideas about religion – mystical Judaism. Naturally, you cannot give a Nobel Prize to a man who was finally crucified. He cannot be accepted as a respectable, prestigious person. He was hanged on the cross just like any other criminal. On each side of him there was a criminal. He was treated exactly like any other criminal, or even worse. No other criminal was forced to carry his own cross.

It was certainly difficult. I know this from my own experience. When I was in America, against their own constitution and all their own laws, they handcuffed me, they chained my legs. Not only that – they were not satisfied – they put another chain around my waist. Even that was not enough: they put both my hands in handcuffs and chained them to the chain on my waist so I could not even move my hands. I could not wave to the crowds who were greeting me. That was their strategy – that I could not even wave my hands to the crowds who had come to greet me. And they chained my feet so close together that walking was impossible.

So I know how difficult it must have been for Jesus to carry a cross in such a situation, a heavy cross. Perhaps because he was only thirty- three, young, healthy, and a son of a carpenter, accustomed to carrying big logs from the forest to his father's workshop, continuously working with wood, he was able to somehow carry the cross. But three times on the way, he fell, and whenever he fell with the cross, they hit him hard with their sticks, lashed him, and forced him to get up and take the cross on his back. Certainly a Nobel Prize cannot be given to such a man! It will be very insulting to the Nobel Prize committee.

We are living in an insane asylum. Mysticism is the highest flowering of human consciousness. To deny Leo Tolstoy the Nobel Prize on the grounds that he is a mystical person is so absurd but so indicative of the insanity of humanity and of the people who are powerful because they are members of the Nobel Prize committee. The King of Sweden is the chairman and all the others are highly respectable, prestigious people. I don't think any one of them is even worth the dust under the feet of Leo Tolstoy. But they are denying that man who has created novels which are sheer poetry. The beauty of his novels is so alive that if you want to choose just ten great novels of all the languages of the world, you will have to include at least two novels by Leo Tolstoy in those ten.

It is a strange phenomenon that Leo Tolstoy, Anton Chekhov, Fyodor Dostoevsky, Maxim Gorky, Turgenev – five great novelists – were contemporaries. If you are going to choose ten novels, five will be from these five people. Perhaps all ten will be from these five people, because they have all written such great novels: *The Mother* by Maxim Gorky has no comparison in the whole world; or *Fathers and Sons* by Turgenev; or *The Brothers Karamazov* by Dostoevsky; or *Anna Karenina* by Leo Tolstoy. Perhaps these five people will cover almost all ten places – they will not leave room for anybody else. But none of them received the Nobel Prize – not only

Leo Tolstoy, none of them, and each was better than the winner. It is very difficult out of these five to vote who is the best.

They were all friends. They lived in the same city – Moscow. It was a strange combination, it had never happened before: five such unique geniuses in the same city, creating novels such that you cannot choose which is better. And defeating the whole world – past, present, and perhaps future – because there seems to be no possibility to improve on *The Brothers Karamazov* or Maxim Gorky's *The Mother*. But none of them got the Nobel Prize.

I have come to know only about Leo Tolstoy. I don't know why the others were refused. Perhaps Maxim Gorky was refused because he was pro-Communist; Turgenev may have been refused because he was an atheist. These are just my assumptions. I don't know their records. But these names must have come before the committee. It is impossible that they were not proposed and rejected.

But the same grounds will do for all. They were all mystics in their own ways. They were all seekers of the ultimate in different directions, but they were all moving toward *sat-chit-anand*. They had all come to the point of *athato brahma jigyasa* – now is the time to begin the inquiry. And their novels reflect their inquiry.

They are not ordinary novels, the way that novels are written today. Today novels are written to be read just once and thrown away. You cannot read a modern novel twice unless you are utterly stupid. I have not come across a single modern novel that can be read twice by any intelligent man. But these five people – their novels you will have to read many times to grasp the meaning. The first time you will be simply acquainted with the superficial story, but you will become aware that there is much more that you are missing. You will have to read them twice, and suddenly you will become aware how much you had missed the first time. Perhaps the third time you may be able to touch their depth.

It is a constant joy, once in a while – after two, three, four years – to read them again. In these three or four years your consciousness has developed, your experience has developed. You are no longer the same. The novel is the same, but you are no longer the same. Now you can see better, now you can understand more, now you can dig deeper. These are novels which have to be read all your life, again and again. Every time you will find something new that you had missed, something great – and you will be shocked that you missed it.

That is the beauty of all the ancient sutras. They are so condensed in meaning that you can go on reading again and again and you will find new meanings. And as your consciousness grows, those meanings will become deeper and deeper. As your experience on the path becomes richer, those sutras will have a new music, a new dance for you.

I have been thinking of speaking on Badarayana's *Brahma Sutras*, but I am keeping that for the last. Once I speak on Badarayana's *Brahma Sutras*, then I will not speak again because there is nothing that can be better than Badarayana's *Brahma Sutras* – that is the end. So I am keeping it aside. If you want me to continue to speak, don't let me speak on Badarayana! If you allow me to speak on Badarayana, then remember ... Just once in a while, here and there, you can ask questions, but the whole sutras I have kept for my last communion with you, my last transmission of the lamp.

> Osho,
> The musicians are playing. We are waiting for you to be with us. There is a moment when the auditorium is filled with silence. Then you come. Osho, what is this magic of waiting?

There is certainly a deep magic – almost a miracle – when you are in silence, in trust, in love, just waiting. The moments of waiting are moments of meditation. Because you are waiting, expectant, your mind stops functioning. You are so concentrated in your waiting that there is no energy left for the mind – that is the secret, the magic.

Waiting for me is just a taste of the ultimate waiting for truth. If just waiting for me you feel so much that it is inexpressible, so much that you can only call it magic, learn something from it. The same waiting is needed for the ultimate to happen to you. It also comes like a guest.

People have a wrong idea, and the wrong idea is created by people just like me, without any intention of creating it. In fact, nobody wants to create it, but somehow language interferes, distorts, and creates something which was never intended. The difficulty is: How to say the right thing? Language seems to be perfectly good for saying the wrong thing. The moment you start saying the right thing, it doesn't fit with language, with grammar, with...

For example, everybody thinks he is going in search of truth. The reality is that you are not going anywhere, you are just going to remain here-and-now. Truth and consciousness and bliss are going to come to you. They are going to be your guests. You are the host. All that you need is an open door, waiting, just like one waits for one's friend, or for one's beloved, looking far away, as far as the eyes can see, looking toward the faraway horizon, waiting.

I am reminded of a Sufi story. It is not just a story, it is a historical fact.

Another great emperor of India was Akbar. Mohammedans pray five times a day and Akbar was very particular. One day he had gone hunting in the forest with all his friends, and they all got lost.

Evening was descending, the sun was setting, and it was time to pray. So Akbar stopped under a huge tree, tied his horse to the tree, and sat on the ground to do his last prayer of the day. As he was praying, a woman, a young woman, ran just by his side, giving him such a shock – it seemed as if she was mad or blind – that Akbar fell down. Still, she did not look back.

Naturally Akbar was very angry. Mohammedans in prayer are very particular; nobody should disturb them. It can become a very dangerous thing and for the emperor ... An ordinary village girl, not caring at all, was running like mad and hitting the emperor. The emperor fell down. Mohammedans pray sitting on their knees, so it is very easy just to push them a little and they will fall down.

It is very difficult to push a Buddhist or a Hindu when he is praying because he is sitting in a lotus posture. It is a very locked posture – you cannot just push him. He is very strong in his posture. But to push the Mohammedan is very easy, however strong he may be – his posture is such, sitting on his knees.

Akbar finished his prayer quickly because he wanted to catch hold of the girl. She could not be allowed to do such things. If she could behave with the emperor in such a way, what to say about other people? But it was getting dark, so he could not figure out where she had gone. He waited, thinking she had to come back to the village. He was just outside the village. Finally she came.

Akbar stopped her and said, 'Do you remember what you have done?'

She said, 'I don't remember anything. Do you?'

Akbar said, 'You seem to be very strange. You don't understand. You are talking with the emperor of the country.'

She said, 'I understand, but I don't remember anything of what you are talking about.'

He said, 'What I am talking about? I was praying here and you ran in such a way that you pushed me, and I fell down. You disturbed my prayer.'

She said, 'Perhaps if you say so, it must have been so, but you have to forgive me. I was going to wait for my lover just on the road which runs through the forest. I wanted to greet him – he is coming after many years – just outside the village. I could not remain sitting in the house and waiting. It is just one mile distant, but he will be waiting, thinking that I must be standing just by the side of a tree where we used to meet when we were young. That's why I was concentrating so much that I did not know I had committed any mistake. Please forgive me, it must have been committed without my knowing at all.'

She was so innocent and tears came to her eyes because she had hurt her own emperor. 'You can give me any punishment, otherwise it will remain heavy on my heart. But just one question before you punish me: you were in prayer – still you were not so much in concentration as I was, because I don't remember it at all. It cannot be that I hit you; it cannot be one-sided. Your body must also have touched my body, but I don't remember having seen anybody on the way – praying or falling or anything. I don't remember that anybody touched my body. So I am puzzled, and I would like to be clear about it. Is your prayer not as strong as my love?'

Akbar remembers it in his autobiography, *Akbarnama*. He says, 'I had to ask forgiveness from that village girl. I have never forgotten her face, and I have never forgotten that my prayer is just formal. If I am lost in my prayer and my love, in my gratitude toward the ultimate, how can I be aware that somebody has touched me, pushed me, or that my body has fallen? I would not have been aware of anything. But I *was* aware and that makes it certain that my prayer is just superficial.

'That girl's love was far deeper. She was closer to the ultimate than I was, although she was not concerned with the ultimate at all.' A tremendous statement of understanding...

You are saying, 'The musicians are playing. We are waiting for you to be with us. There is a moment when the auditorium is filled with silence. Then you come ... Osho, what is the magic of waiting?' It is prayer. It is love. It is trust. It is gratitude: it is the whole of religion.

If you can learn waiting, and if waiting can become your moment- to-moment experience, whenever you are not involved in ordinary things, and you can find time ... Anytime, day or night, just in your bed, sit silently and wait. Wait for the guest. And I promise you: the guest has always come. The waiting has never failed. It has always been an absolute success, but not the success of your ego – it is the success of your humbleness.

It is the victory of your being, not the victory of your mind. It is the victory of your silence, of your love. Learn waiting and you have learned all about meditation.

11

Communication Happens Beyond the Mind

Osho,
Why is communication so difficult, particularly between lovers?

Communication as such is difficult. Of course it is more difficult between lovers. But first you have to understand the general difficulty of communication.

Each mind has been conditioned by different parents, different teachers, different priests, different politicians. It is a different world in itself. When two minds try to communicate as far as the ordinary mundane things are concerned, there is no difficulty. But the moment they start moving beyond things into the world of concepts, communication starts becoming more and more difficult.

For example, Gautam the Buddha does not have any God in his philosophy. He is far freer of God than even Frederick Nietzsche. Frederick Nietzsche states that God is dead. The implication is clear: God used to be alive, now he is dead. Gautam Buddha does not talk about God at all. It is so irrelevant that he does not pay any attention to the subject.

Now, to a Christian, or to a Hindu, or to a Mohammedan, it is impossible to conceive of a religion without God. God is the center of most of the religions. Only three religions are free of God; one is Gautam Buddha's, another is Mahavira's, and the third is Lao Tzu's.

When Christian missionaries came into contact with Buddhist scriptures for the first time, they could not even conceive of the idea that a religion could be without God. What kind of religion will there be if there is no God? To whom are you going to pray? Who is going to send his prophets and his only begotten Son? Who is going to send saviors for you? Who is going to judge whether you are to be sent to hell or heaven? God removed, hell and heaven are also removed. God removed, punishment and reward are also removed. God removed, the very idea of judgment is removed. Then there is no sin and no virtue. Who will decide it?

They were even more surprised that Gautam Buddha was known by his disciples – and now even by those who are not disciples – as Bhagwan Gautam Buddha. Now *Bhagwan* means God. This was very puzzling. Gautam Buddha did not believe in any God. Why did he allow his disciples to address him as Bhagwan?

The same is the situation with Jainism. They are even more strict about the absence of God. Buddha simply ignored the whole subject. It was not worth any consideration. Jainism did not leave it because once Mahavira was gone there was a danger of the whole thing cropping up again. He wanted it to be clearly stated that there is no God, there never has been any God and there is no creation because there is no creator. It is an evolving world.

What Charles Darwin found two thousand years later was known to Mahavira. It is not a creation, it is an evolving world – it has been here forever and will be here forever. The whole concept of creation and a creator is just idiotic. Mahavira was very strict; he did not want God to pop up in some disguise when he was gone just because people have a certain unconscious hankering for it. It gives a certain false consolation to people. If you really want to be consoled, it is absolutely necessary to avoid the false consolation. If you authentically want to be at peace with existence, then all that is false and based only on belief has to be discarded.

But again the problem – the followers of Mahavira addressed him as Bhagwan. Now communication becomes difficult because Bhagwan means a totally different thing to the Buddhists and the Jainas than it does to the Hindus, Mohammedans, Christians, Jews. Their whole concept developed in a totally different way.

For the religions which are God-centered, God comes in the beginning, before everything. He creates the world and nobody bothers from where he comes. If there was no world at all, how did he manage to exist and where? There must have been a small island, or some cloud – something. God cannot exist in nothingness, and if God can exist in nothingness, then what is the problem? Why bring him in unnecessarily? Existence is perfectly good, autonomous, not dependent on a despot you call God.

According to those who do not believe, he is whimsical because for eternity he just remained silent. What was he doing? Smoking? Taking drugs? Or just dreaming? Sleeping? In a coma? What is the situation? – because according to Christians he created the world only six thousand years ago. And six thousand years is such a stupid idea because India has scriptures which are far more ancient than the Christian God.

The Rig Veda according to the Hindu scholars – and I support them on that point ... I don't think the Rig Veda is something great, perhaps two percent of it has something beautiful and spiritual, ninety-eight percent is simply crap. So I don't agree with their idea that the Rig Veda is written by God, but I certainly agree with their concept that the Rig Veda is ninety thousand years old because the proof and evidence are intrinsic. Ninety thousand years ago, there occurred a certain constellation of stars which has not happened again since then. That constellation of stars is described in the Rig Veda in absolute and perfect detail. Now, there is an astronomical argument which is irrefutable; you cannot do anything. The whole of astronomy supports it – this kind of constellation happened.

According to their measurements it happened ninety thousand years ago, and also according to the Hindu scholars it happened ninety thousand years ago. Because it is described in such detail it cannot be said that the Rig Veda was written just three thousand or at the most five thousand years ago, as Christians think. People who were writing the Rig Veda five thousand years ago cannot in any way describe something which happened eighty-five thousand years earlier. There was no astronomical technology in their hands, and anyway somebody would be needed to remember it. Who is going to remember what happened eighty-five thousand years ago? Just think how long you can remember back: your father, your grandfather, perhaps your great-grandfather ... Beyond that it is vague. It is not that the world began with your great-grandfather just because you cannot remember further back.

These religions – Hinduism, Judaism, Mohammedanism, Christianity – are all God-oriented. They believe God created the world. In fact they are believers in the concept of creation. And, naturally, creation needs a creator. But the whole scientific approach proves just the opposite. It is not a creation. Creation means complete. That's what the Bible says: in six days God created the world in its perfection, and then on the seventh day he rested, and nobody knows what happened to him. Where did he go? Because the world was perfect, there was no need for him.

Evolution means the world is never perfect: it is trying to be perfect. It is evolving. Creation is something dead: everything has come to a full stop. That is a very dead idea about existence. Existence is a constant flow toward higher beings, higher consciousnesses. Certainly God did not create Gautam Buddha, and you cannot say that Adam and Eve had the same consciousness and the same *sat-chit-anand* as Gautam Buddha. Gautam Buddha was a very evolved being and the evolution was going on without God managing it. Existence is accepted by Buddhism, Jainism, and Taoism as autonomous and eternal. That looks meaningful. But God is removed completely.

The Christians who were translating Buddhist scriptures were worried why Buddha did not prevent his disciples from calling him

Bhagwan. They could not understand that in Buddhism, *Bhagwan* takes on a totally different meaning. It means 'the blessed one.' The same is true about Jainism. God-oriented religions have their God in the beginning and then not even a trace is found of that God. Atheists have been challenging him, but he seems to be either deaf or perhaps Nietzsche is right, he is dead. Or perhaps Gautam Buddha is right that he never existed. Who can give the proof?

One great English atheist, Edmund Burke, asked a very simple thing. Addressing a big meeting of an atheist association, he said, 'If God exists, I will wait for five minutes' – looking at his watch – 'and I don't want him to do something as great as he did for Moses.'

God had separated the ocean into two parts and made a path for Moses and his followers to pass through the ocean surging on both sides. No walls, just water. A valley miles deep and on both sides water standing on its own.

Burke said, 'I don't want to give him that much trouble. All I want is for him to stop my watch within five minutes, then I will believe.' And God could not even do that.

Atheists have been continuously challenging God, but no answer. In fact he has not left his address with us. Even if you want to write a letter you cannot. Those who think the whole hypothesis of God is nonsense find your prayers very childish. Whom are you addressing? Where is he? You have not seen him. You know nobody who has seen him.

In Jainism and Buddhism, God comes at the end of evolution, and that is a more significant meaning. Then there is not a single God. It is also significant to remember that a single God is bound to become a dictator. And the world cannot be really free under a dictator – a Joseph Stalin, Adolf Hitler, Ronald Reagan. God is not elected by you. You are just puppets in his hands. As he created you out of mud, any day he can bulldoze you back into mud. There is no higher court of appeal. The whole idea of creation is whimsical. Buddhism says every living being is on the way to becoming a god. God is the ultimate evolution of consciousness.

That's why Buddha did not prevent his disciples from addressing him as Bhagwan. Nor did Mahavira. They are Bhagwan, but their meaning is totally different. They are not creators of the world; they don't claim any stupid, ridiculous idea. They are very straightforward. They are simply saying that consciousness evolves from animal to man, from man to God. So every living being one day is going to become God. The whole world will be full of Gods. And this seems to be more scientific – just one solitary God, and existence looks so poor. And that solitary God, what will he do? Marijuana? Hashish? Or play cards with the Holy Ghost? What is he going to do from eternity to eternity?

But that's how communication becomes difficult. The Hindu papers in India never write my name as Bhagwan. That is a taboo because Bhagwan means one who created the world. I certainly am not so mad as to create this world.

Christians will be worried...

When I was in my first jail in America, I was sharing the cell with a criminal who had been there for many years. I was puzzled; I was first lying and resting – what else to do? But that man would get up – he had his Bible – and he would put the Bible on the bed, sit on the floor, put his head on the Bible and pray to God. His name was Bobby.

So one day I shook him and I said, 'Bobby, what are you doing? If you were such a great Christian, you would not be in jail. You have murdered and you never thought about God, and about the Bible and everything. God cannot help because for four years you have been praying – and have you ever looked inside this Bible? Just putting your head on the Bible is not going to move the Bible into your head. It is not a creeping thing, it is just dead words.'

He was very much shocked. And he said, 'I also wanted to ask you. When I heard that you are called Bhagwan, I was very surprised. Certainly you have not created the world.'

I said, 'If I had created the world, you would not have been in it. You are enough proof I have not created this world.'

He was very shocked. He said, 'You seem to be a very strange person.'

I said, 'God has to be a strange person. And you are stupid, Bobby. I am sitting here and you are putting your head on a dead book. Turn toward me.'

He said, 'But you are not a Christian.'

I said, 'I am a god. Are you interested in God, or in a Christian God?'

He said, 'You are raising problems that I have never thought about. Yes, it is true, I am interested in God, but if you are a god, then why are you in jail?'

I said, 'This is nothing, Bobby. Who was Jesus Christ?'

He said, 'He was God – God's only begotten Son.'

And I said, 'If he can be crucified, what is the problem of my being in jail? Your Christian God would also have been in jail, but because he has not been found yet, he is out of jail.'

He said, 'That seems to be logical because Jesus Christ was crucified.'

He became friendly, very friendly. Just three or four days ago I received a letter from another jail. Bobby had been moved. He told his new cell- mate about me, and told him, 'Write a letter to Bhagwan to tell him that poor Bobby remembers him.' He also said, 'Bhagwan will have forgotten my name, but he shattered all my beliefs. Just being five days with him was enough.'

God created the world in six days. Bobby was finished in five days because I explained to him a simple fact, 'God is the final evolution. Bobby, one day you are going to be a god. But it is not going to happen by prayer.'

The religions that believe in God are bound to believe in prayer. That's why in the West, meditation has never developed. Only religions that don't believe in God have developed meditation. Because

God is out there somewhere, you have to pray, you have to depend on him. If he listens – good; if he does not listen – what can you do?

Meditation is developed by those whose god is inside. That's where I find people like Jesus Christ contradictory. On the one hand he says 'The Kingdom of God is within,' and then every day he prays to a God somewhere above in the skies. This is a simple contradiction which cannot be explained in any way. If God is within, then meditation is the way, not prayer. Prayer to whom? To yourself. That is the only way of getting deeper into your consciousness and finding the godliness which I call *sat-chit-anand*.

So when a Buddhist or a Jaina is talking to a Hindu or a Christian, if they mention the word God, there will be no communication at all. The Christian will hear one thing: he will hear about the God who created the world six thousand and four years ago, on the first of January of course, a Monday – because he cannot create in the middle of the calendar. There was no calendar before he created the world. The calendar starts with the world. You can't have a calendar when there is no universe. Where will you hang it? Simple problems! Where will you print it? So Christians don't say January the first, Monday. *I* am saying it. But if he ever created the world, at the same time he must have created the calendar.

The moment the Christian thinks of God, he immediately thinks of this whole thing that is lined up in his mind. When a Buddhist says 'Bhagwan,' there is no question of creation. He is not looking backward, he is not looking into the past, he is looking forward. He is looking forward to everybody's evolution, into the ultimate flowering of consciousness, truth and bliss. Each living being, sooner or later, is going to become a god. One day the whole of existence will be full of gods. And that will be its ultimate evolution.

How to communicate? On each single word you have different opinions, prejudices, conditions. The words are the same, but the moment you say them and the other hears them, he is not hearing the same meaning, he is hearing a different meaning. Of course the word is the same, but the word triggers a totally different meaning.

So if your communication is about higher things, it is more difficult, almost impossible.

As far as lovers are concerned, they have still more difficulty in communicating because the feminine mind functions differently, and the masculine mind functions differently. The man has been conditioned by the society in a different way to how the woman has been conditioned. And they have to live together, twenty-four hours a day; it becomes heavy. It becomes heavy because whatever the man says, the woman hears something else. The woman is not much in the head, she is much more in the heart: the man is much more in the head. That creates a great disparity. The man is perfectly good in arguments.

A man and wife were fighting and the man said, 'Sit down, be calm and quiet and let us reason it out.'

The wife said, 'Never, because whenever we reason anything out, you are victorious. No reasoning! I am going to break things like furniture, burn clothes, if you are not going to agree with me.'

And the man said, 'Wait. You are right. It is not a question of reasoning because each time I say "Calm down, sit quietly and let us argue it out," you are the winner.'

The woman has her own arguments: breaking plates. Of course those plates are ones which need to be broken. She never breaks the really beautiful ones. She hits the man with the pillow, but hitting somebody with a pillow is not violent. It is a very nonviolent fight, a soft pillow. She throws things at the man, but never aims at him. She aims here and there. But that is enough to create havoc in the neighborhood. That's what she wants: the whole neighborhood should know what is happening. That humbles the husband. He starts crawling and saying, 'Forgive me. I was wrong from the very beginning. I knew it.'

As couples settle, the husband forgets all about arguing. When he enters the house, he takes a deep breath, and prepares himself for any irrational thing that is going to happen.

A man saw written on a board in front of a restaurant, 'Here you will feel at home.' Reading it, he entered.

The waitress came and asked, 'What can I do for you?'

He said, 'First, bring me chapatis, but all burned.'

The waitress could not understand.

'Vegetables, without any salt. Milk which has gone sour.' The woman thought this man seems to be mad. 'And then come here and sit beside me and nag.'

The waitress thought, 'A strange customer, but let us try.' What can be done?

She brought burned chapatis, rotten vegetables without any salt, milk which was no longer milk, it was almost curd. And then the man said, 'Sit beside me and start nagging.'

The woman said, 'What kind of person are you?'

He said, 'What kind of person? Go out and look at the board you have put in front of the restaurant, "Here you will feel at home." This is how I can feel at home, otherwise not. This is what my wife has been doing to me for years. Now I have become accustomed to it. If you don't nag me, I cannot eat, I have no appetite at all. Once you start nagging, I immediately start feeling hungry.'

It is conditioning. With lovers it becomes difficult, more difficult than for ordinary people because the ways a woman comes to conclusions are not logical, they are hunches. But they are mostly right. Logic may fail, but her hunches don't fail. She has an intuitive approach – man has only an intellectual approach – and certainly the intuitive approach has a back door to know reality. Intellect simply goes knocking on the front door and nobody opens it. The back door is always open.

It is just after midnight and there is a knock on the doctor's door. Dragging himself out of bed, and poking his head out of the window, he peers down at the figure on the doorstep. 'Well?' he asks.

The woman looks up and says, 'No, sick.'

Even in small words like *well*, the woman functions differently. Once that is understood then some kind of communication is possible.

A man goes into the pharmacy and says to the aging female assistant, 'I'd like ten condoms please, miss.'

'Don't you "miss" me!' snaps the assistant. 'Okay,' he replies. 'Then give me eleven.'

'No! No! A hundred times no!' cried the centipede to his wife, crossing his legs.

It is not only in the human world; even among the animals you will find the same conflict going on all over the world.

Old man Finkelstein is desperate to get married, but so far he has not met with any success.

Finally he advertises for a wife in the local newspaper. He gets almost two hundred replies, most of them from men, who write: 'You can have mine.'

The pompous judge glares over the courtroom at the woman tramp who has been dragged into court on a charge of vagrancy.

'Have you ever earned an honest dollar in your life, you good- for-nothing?'

'Yes, your honor,' replies the woman. 'I voted for you in the last election.'

Unless lovers come to a state of meditative consciousness, they will not be able to communicate. Their communication will always be a conflict; it will never be a communion. The only possibility is: if both evolve their consciousness to a point where it goes beyond the mind, then all conditionings are left behind. Even the biological differences are left behind. The consciousness that goes beyond the mind is no longer male, no longer female. Now there is a possibility to have not only conversation but some communion. A deep understanding is possible. But without meditation no such possibility exists.

For thousands of years, man has lived in this situation of no communication and he has become accustomed to it: man has become accustomed, the woman has become accustomed – and they think nothing can be done about it. In fact, I am the first man who is saying something *can* be done about it. Neither Gautam Buddha, nor Jesus, nor Moses, nor Lao Tzu – none of them even thought about it. Yet it is one of the greatest problems.

Every house is full of this conflict. Children grow up in the atmosphere of this noncommunication, then naturally they start learning the same strategies as their parents. It is almost as if every husband has forced the woman into slavery, and every woman has taken revenge. It is natural. She has reduced every husband to a hen-pecked husband.

It is a very vicious circle. Man has taken away the freedom of woman, has taken away her education, has taken away her culture, has taken away her freedom of movement in society, has taken away her financial independence. Naturally she is burning with anger, and has been for centuries. Whatever she could do as a personal reaction to this was to torture the husband in a thousand-and-one ways. She has invented her own ways. If she is unhappy, the husband is going to get cold tea, may have to miss his lunch, or when he opens his lunchbox tiffin in the office, he may find that there is nothing in it.

It is said...

Akbar once asked his courtiers, 'Do you think in the capital there are a few strong men who are not hen-pecked?'

All the courtiers said, 'We think this is a vast capital. There may be at least a few people.'

But Birbal, the most intelligent man of this court, said, 'My Lord, I think there is not a single man on the whole earth who is not hen-pecked. *Husband* means hen-pecked.'

The emperor was a little angry. He said, 'What do you mean?'

Birbal said, 'I mean exactly what I have said. These courtiers, these great warriors, your generals, they are saying there may be some people in the capital. None of them has raised his hand claiming he is not a hen-pecked husband. You yourself are asking the question, but can you raise your hand and say that you are not hen-pecked? And remember Allah: don't lie.'

The emperor was completely stunned and he said, 'I cannot lie, that's true. About me, it is true. My wife tortures me. That is the only place where I am no longer emperor. But these people are saying "a few people".'

Birbal said, 'I am ready to investigate the whole capital. Give me your two beautiful Arabian horses. You have one white, one black. I will take those two horses and go for an investigation.'

He went to many people, strong people, wrestlers, professional fighters, warriors, but they all said...

He told them, 'If you can say that you are not hen-pecked, you will have to come to the court and declare it. Then you can choose one of the horses. These are the greatest horses in the world. This is the very best breed which you will never manage to find, you could never afford. They have been brought from Arabia only for the emperor. One horse is yours; you can choose.'

But they said, 'We love the horses. They look great, but we are sorry we cannot say anything. If our wives come to know that we have declared we are not hen-pecked, there will be great difficulty – much more difficulty than any horse is worth.'

Finally he came to a gardener's hut, where a poor, but very strong, man – seven feet tall – was digging a hole. Birbal asked, 'Are you hen-pecked?' He did not answer, but showed his muscles which were almost like steel.

He said, 'Put your hand in my hand.'

Birbal himself was a warrior, a fighter. He gave his hand, but the gardener's hand was almost like steel. As he pressed Birbal's hand, Birbal hit the roof. He said, 'Let go. You will kill me.' Certainly it seemed so, because he had not even answered about being hen-pecked or anything. He was simply saying, 'Don't dare to ask such a question of me!'

Birbal said, 'Then you can choose one horse, whichever you like. Certainly you are not hen-pecked.' And the gardener called inside for his wife to come out.

She was a small woman, very thin. He asked her, 'Which horse should I choose? – because I don't want any quarrel later on. You tell me the color.'

Birbal said, 'Stop! Now you don't choose any. It is finished. You are a hen-pecked husband.' Even Birbal wondered how this small woman was harassing this giant of a man.

He came back to the court with two horses and told the emperor, 'There is not a single person.'

It has deep roots in the psychology of man. Because man has misbehaved for centuries with women, women have found their own small strategies. They cannot revolt because they are so dependent. They have been crippled, they cannot become a class separate from man like the proletariat and the bourgeoisie – the poor and the rich – who can fight and have a great revolution like the Communist revolution in Russia. That is not possible. Because each woman is attached to a single man, women can't function as a class, so they cannot go against man as a class. But each single woman finds her own strategy for torture.

It is very easy for her to torture. The fundamentals of the strategy are: first she makes the man completely dependent on her for his food, for his clothes, for his bed, for everything. This is absolutely unconscious. When the man becomes completely dependent on the woman, if there is any conflict, he does not get any food – and he cannot cook. He will not get fresh clothes because he cannot wash them himself because he knows nothing about it. He will not get a bed prepared for him because he has never prepared it. He does not know what to do. In the house the woman rules so totally that at any moment she can withdraw. That's enough; she doesn't have to do anything active and violent, she can simply withdraw. Then the man becomes almost a helpless child.

Communication is only possible between equals, and communication is only possible beyond the mind. Here, with my people, you will find, slowly, slowly, a communication is developing. As their consciousness goes higher, they will start understanding many things which they were not able to understand before. They will not only understand their own unconscious, they will also understand the woman's unconscious. They will not only understand their own minds, they will also understand the feminine mind – and vice versa. And because they are both beyond, there is a possibility of tremendous understanding.

The world will be at peace only when man and woman have come to a deep understanding. And with that deep understanding there will be great love, great compassion, great friendliness. It is an absolute to be achieved. Without it man can never become civilized.

Osho,
My spelling error, 'Lolita' for 'Lokita,' has created havoc around here! Lovers of Lolita are tearing around calling, 'Where is my Lolita?' and Lokita is dying to be called Lolita, and Milarepa doesn't know which is Lolita and which is Lokita! This would have to be a 'once' mistake!

Jivan Mary, they say history repeats itself, and history repeats itself because man is unconscious. So he goes on committing the same mistakes again and again. Although he decides every time that he is not going to commit the same mistake, the decision remains hanging in the conscious; it never reaches the unconscious from where all actions arise. And there is no communication between the conscious and the unconscious. There is no bridge; they don't know each other. Nobody has ever introduced them to each other. And you will find this everywhere.

A smoker decides: 'This is my last cigarette. Enough is enough. I am not going to smoke again.' And within two or three hours he feels so uneasy, so uncomfortable, so tense and under stress, he forgets all about the decision. He thinks, 'Just one more cigarette is not going to kill me.' This has been going on for years. He decides, and even while he is deciding he knows this is not going to happen – 'Let me try one more time, perhaps...' The problem is that the mistakes are unconscious. Unless your consciousness becomes deep enough so that it reaches the very bottom of your unconscious, you will have to repeat mistakes.

I was once an editor of a daily newspaper. In this small life I have done so many things. There I became aware of what they call 'proofreader's blindness.' I have seen it myself that the proofreader goes on making the same mistake again and again. It seems to be strange that he goes on missing the same word. There seems to be some unconscious reason behind it that pulls him back, or makes him blind, and he passes the word without exactly reading it, or passes it quickly. And once he has committed that mistake he can read the whole passage with the wrong word many times; he will simply be unaware of it.

There may be some deep wound inside. For example, a man who has failed utterly in love, for whom love has left only a wound in his being, he will quickly pass the word *love* without realizing it. He will see that it is written perfectly correctly with the right spelling, but he is not looking at it. He does not want to look at it because it opens his wound. The same is the situation of the typist. It is not a different thing. One can commit the same mistake again and again because man is not conscious, his whole life is a repetition.

Just the other day I was telling you about a man who married ten women. He left them fast – three months, four months, was more than he could live with one woman. But finally he not only found that the tenth woman was a woman he had married once before, he also found that he always ended up with the same kind of woman. After three or four months he becomes fed up and divorces her, but when he falls in love again within two or three days he finds, 'My God! Although she is a different woman, she has the same character.' He does not know that his choice is coming from the unconscious, and his decision is coming from the conscious. They are two separate parts of his being.

He loves a certain kind of woman – a certain hairstyle, a certain kind of eyes – a certain color – a certain face, a certain nose, a certain curvature of the body. He is not aware of why he falls in love with a certain woman, but it is always going to be the same woman in a different dress, with a different name. It is his choice because he is the chooser, but he again finds the same kind of woman, and the same kind of woman will show the same kind of character sooner or later.

The man was puzzled as to what was happening, but he was not aware it was happening because of his unconscious. This is our whole life story. We go on making the same mistake. We are bound to do it because we have not done anything to change the very structure of our consciousness. Jivan Mary, it is possible not to commit the same mistake again. But you will need to be not only more alert in typing, you will have to be more conscious in your whole life – each moment. You will have to be more meditative. Then even to commit a mistake once becomes difficult – you can commit once, that is allowed; twice you cannot. Your whole being knows there is no division, your house is not divided; your house is one, you are one, you are not split.

But what do we go on doing? With one hand we make something, and with the other hand we destroy it. And we are not aware that both are *our* hands. It needs a tremendous revolution in your consciousness.

Hymie Goldberg gets a phone call from his lawyer. 'What do you want to hear first, the bad news or the terrible news?' the lawyer asks.

'Hell!' says Hymie. 'Give me the bad news first.'

'Okay,' replies the lawyer. 'The bad news is that your wife has found a picture worth a hundred thousand dollars.'

'That is bad news?' cries Hymie. 'In that case, I can't wait to hear the terrible news.'

'The terrible news,' replies the lawyer, 'is that the picture is of you and your secretary on Miami Beach!'

An old chicken farmer is very proud of his brood, so when two smartly- dressed city gentlemen ask to look at them, he quickly obliges.

'A very fine bunch of chickens,' says one of the men.

'Thank you, sir,' replies the farmer.

'And what do you feed them on?' asks the second man.

'Special chicken fertilizer, imported from China,' says the old man, proudly.

'A-ha!' cries the first man. 'Just as we suspected, that is illegal. You will be fined two thousand dollars.'

A month later, two more well-dressed men show up and ask the farmer what he feeds to his magnificent chickens. The old man, wiser than the first time, says, 'I just feed them on shit.'

'A-ha!' say the men. 'We are from the Health and Hygiene Department, and what you are doing is illegal. You will be fined two thousand dollars.'

A few weeks later, another city gentleman arrives and asks the same question. This time the farmer shrugs and says, 'Listen, mister, I just give them fifty cents each and tell them to go to the market and buy what the hell they want!'

12

I Am the Ultimate

Osho,
The most fundamental Upanishadic statement is 'Aham brahmasmi'.
Is it connected in any way to sat-chit-anand?

The statement in the Upanishads, '*Aham brahmasmi*,' is perhaps the most fundamental and the most essential experience of all the mystics of the world. The Upanishads are the only books which are considered not to belong to any religion, yet they are the very essence of religiousness.

This statement, '*Aham brahmasmi*,' is a declaration of enlightenment – literally it means, 'I am the divine, I am the ultimate, I am the absolute.' It is a declaration: 'There is no other God than my own inner being.' This does not mean that it is a declaration of a single individual about himself. It is a declaration, of course, by one individual, but it declares the potential of every individual.

It denies God as a separate entity. It denies God as a creator. It denies God as a ruler. It simply denies the existence of God, other than in our own existence. It is the whole search of the Eastern genius. In thousands of years they have discovered only one thing: don't look for God outside your own being. If you can find him, you can find him only in one place and that is in you – other than *you* all the temples and all the mosques and all the synagogues and all the churches are inventions of the priests to exploit you. They are not in the service of God; on the contrary, they are exploiting all the potential gods.

Aham brahmasmi is perhaps the boldest statement ever made by any human being in any age in any part of the world, and I don't think it can be improved upon in the future – ever. Its courage is so absolute and perfect that you cannot refine it, you cannot polish it. It is so fundamental that you cannot go deeper than this, neither can you go higher than this.

In Sanskrit, this simple statement *aham brahmasmi* is only two words. In English, it can be translated with these few words: *I am the ultimate*. Beyond me there is nothing; there is no height that is not within me and there is no depth which is not within me. If I can explore myself, I have explored the whole mystery of existence.

But, unfortunately, even the people of this country – where this statement was made some five thousand years ago – have forgotten all about the dignity of human beings. This statement is nothing but the ultimate manifesto of man and his dignity. Even in this country, where such individuals existed who reached the ultimate awakening and illumination, there are people who are worshipping stones. There are people who are enslaved by ignorant priests. There are people who are living in the bondage of a certain religion, creed or cult. They have forgotten the golden age of the Upanishads.

Perhaps that was the most innocent time in the history of man. At that time the West was almost barbarous, and that barbarousness has somehow remained as an undercurrent in the Western consciousness. Otherwise, it cannot be just coincidental that the two great world wars have happened in the West. And preparation for the third is also happening in the West – just within a small span of half a century.

The days of the Upanishads in this land were the most glorious. The only search, the only seeking, the only longing, was to know oneself – no other ambition ruled mankind. Riches, success, power, everything was absolutely mundane. Those who were ambitious, those who were running after riches, those who wanted to be powerful, were considered to be psychologically sick. And the only search of those who were really healthy psychologically, spiritually healthy, was to know themselves and to be themselves and to declare the innermost secret to the whole universe. That secret is contained in this statement, *aham brahmasmi.* In a way, the people who followed the days of the Upanishads have fallen into a dark age.

You will be surprised to know that the idea of *in*volution has not appeared in the Western mind at all, only the idea of *e*volution, only the idea of progress. But the mystics of the Upanishads have a more perfect and more comprehensive approach. Nothing can go on evolving forever. Evolution has been conceived by the Upanishads as a circle. In fact, in existence everything moves in a circle: stars move in circles, the sun moves in a circle, the earth moves in a circle, the moon moves in a circle, climates move in a circle, life moves in a circle.

The whole of existence knows only one way of movement, and that is circular. That which seems to be going up one day will soon be going down. Again it will come up – it is just like a wheel and the spokes of the wheel. The same spoke will come up, will go down, will come up, will go down.

Evolution is incomplete if there is not any complementary idea of involution. Materially man has evolved. Certainly there were no railway trains and there were no atomic weapons and there was no nuclear war material, there was no electricity, there was nothing of the technology that we have become accustomed to living with. Materially, man has certainly evolved, but spiritually, the situation is totally different. Spiritually, man has not evolved.

According to the Upanishads, man has gone deeper into darkness. He has lost his innocence and he has lost his blissfulness and he has lost the simple experience of 'I am the mysterious, I am the miraculous; I am the whole cosmos in a miniature form, just as a dewdrop is the whole ocean in a miniature form.' The dewdrop can declare 'I am the ocean,' and there will not be anything wrong in it. Certainly a particular individual is only a dewdrop, but he can declare '*Aham brahmasmi*,' and there is nothing wrong in it. He is simply saying the truth.

The Upanishads talk about four stages of man's fall, not of evolution. The first stage, when the Upanishads came into being, is called the 'Age of Truth.' People were simply truthful, just as small children are simply truthful. To lie, one needs some experience. Lying is a complicated phenomenon, truth is not. To lie you need a developed memory, you have to remember what kind of thing you have said to one person and what kind of thing you have said to another person. A lying person needs a good memory. A man of truth needs no memory because he is simply saying that which is the case.

The child has no experience other than the truth, other than what he experiences. He cannot lie. The days of the Upanishads are the days of man's childhood, of purity and innocence, of deep love and trust. The first age the Upanishads call Satyuga, the Age of Truth. Truth was not a long journey. You hadn't to go anywhere to find it. You were living in it.

The situation was exactly expressed by Kabir in a symbolic parable: A fish in the ocean, who must have had a philosophic bent, started inquiring of other fish, 'I have heard so much about the ocean, I want to know where it is.'

The poor fish that she asked had also heard about the ocean but they were not so curious, so they never bothered about where it was. They said, 'We have also heard about the ocean, but where it is we have never bothered to ask, and we don't know the answer.'

The young philosopher fish went on asking everybody, 'Where is the ocean?' And they were all stunned. They had heard about it from their forefathers – it had always been known – but as far as an exact description or experience was concerned, nobody was able to explain it to the young fish.

Finally, when nobody could give her an answer, the young fish declared, 'You are all stupid. There is no ocean at all.'

Kabir says the same is the situation of man. Man goes on asking, 'Have you seen God? Have you seen the mysterious, the miraculous?' – and all he hears is: 'We have *heard* about it, we have *read* about it...' But there was a day when people were so innocent, childlike, that they *knew* that they are surrounded by the ocean, that the ocean is not to be searched for, it is within and without. They are part of it, they are born in it, they live in it, they breathe in it, and they will one day disappear into it. They are part and parcel of the ocean.

But every child has to grow. And just as every child has to grow, Satyuga, the Age of Truth, could not remain forever. It produced the great scriptures called the Upanishads – the word is so beautiful: it simply means 'sitting by the side of the master' – recordings from the notes of disciples who were sitting in silence by the side of the master. Once in a while, out of his meditation, he would say something; out of his heart something would be transferred to the disciple, and the disciple would take a note. Those notes are the Upanishads.

Satyuga disappeared – the child grew. The second stage is called Treta – it is compared to a table. The first, Satyuga, was almost like a table with four legs, absolutely balanced. *Treta* means three. One leg of the table has disappeared. Now it is no longer a table with four legs, with that certainty, with that trust, with that grounding, with that centering, with that great balance. Now it is only a tripod, three legs.

Certainly something is missing. It is not so certain. Some doubt has arisen, trust is no longer complete and perfect, love is no more unpolluted. The disciple's question is not coming from his whole being, but out of his head. But still, much was yet to happen. The child went on growing. As far as age is concerned, it seems a growth, but as far as innocence is concerned it is an involution. Both are moving side by side: evolution as far as age and body are concerned, and involution as far as innocence, trust and love are concerned.

After Treta, humanity fell still more. The stage after Treta is called Dwapar. One leg is lost again – now everything is unbalanced. Standing on two legs, how can a table have trust, certainty, security, safety, balance? Fear became the predominant quality rather than love, rather than trust. Insecurity became more prominent than a tremendous feeling of being at home. But things went on growing in one direction: as far as material growth is concerned, there was evolution; in another direction as far as consciousness is concerned, there was a continuous fall.

After Dwapar, the age of two legs, is the age we are living in. It is called Kaliyuga, the 'Age of Darkness.' Even the last leg has disappeared. Man is almost in a state of insanity. Instead of innocence, insanity has become our normal state. In some way or other everybody is psychologically sick.

I am talking about these four ages for a particular reason, because the statement that was made in innocence in the days of the Upanishads has become absolutely incomprehensible to our people, to our contemporaries. Even the people who are the inheritors of the Upanishads are afraid to declare 'I am God, I am the absolute' – what to say about others? Others have their own prejudices.

For example, when Christians started translating the Upanishads they were shocked. They could not believe that such tremendously poetic, beautiful scriptures are in existence. But what they are saying goes against Christianity, against Judaism, against Mohammedanism, even against today's Hinduism. Even the Hindu is not capable today of declaring 'I am God.' He has also become impressed and influenced by Christianity to such an extent.

Christian missionaries started condemning the Upanishads because if the Upanishads are right, then what to do with the Bible? The Bible absolutely declares – just as the Koran declares – that there is only one God. If the Upanishads are right then there are as many gods as there are living beings. Some may have come to manifestation, some may be on the way, some may not have started the journey yet, but will start finally.

How long can you delay? You can miss one train, you can miss another train, but every moment the train is coming. How long can you go on sitting in the waiting room? And people go on becoming buddhas, and people go on becoming seers and sages, and you are still waiting in the waiting room with your suitcases. How long can you do that? – there is a limit. When you see that so many people have left already – the whole platform is empty – you will take courage, perhaps it is time to move.

For Christianity the problem was that everybody cannot be God. They cannot even accept everybody as the *son* of God, what to say about God? Only Jesus is the son of God.

You are only puppets made of earth. God made man with mud and breathed life into it. It is just a manufactured thing, and if a puppet starts declaring '*Aham brahmasmi*' – 'I am God' – the puppeteer will laugh. 'Idiots! You are just puppets and your strings are in my hands. When I want you to dance, you dance; when I want you to lie down, you lie down; when I want you to breathe, you breathe; when I want you not to breathe, you can't do anything.'

For Christianity it was a tremendous challenge, and they started finding arguments against it. The Christian missionaries started saying ... Their first argument was: the person, the seer, the sage – whoever he may be, the name is not mentioned in the Upanishads – who declared for the first time '*Aham brahmasmi*,' was a megalomaniac, that he was suffering from a big ego. They were full of prejudice. They could not see the simple fact that it was not the ego that was declaring – because the Upanishads say it clearly: unless your ego disappears, you cannot even understand the meaning of 'I am the ultimate.'

It is not the declaration of ego. This declaration is possible only on the death of ego. That is a clear-cut statement in the Upanishads. But Christian missionaries went on misinterpreting the Upanishads to the West, distorting and commenting that these people were almost mad. Obviously, to a Mohammedan or to a Christian, the idea that somebody says 'I am God,' is very shocking.

I have told you the story...

It happened in Baghdad in the days of Khalif Omar. He is the most famous Khalif of the Mohammedans, and he is thought to be a very understanding and very moderate, liberal man. But you will see his 'liberality' in the story.

A man was brought to him who had been declaring in the marketplace, 'God has sent me as his prophet, just as he sent Hazrat Mohammed as his prophet a thousand years ago. But now things have changed, questions have changed, new answers are needed. Now I bring the latest dissemination, the latest edition of God's message to the world. I accept Mohammed was a prophet, I accept that Jesus was a prophet.'

Mohammedans don't accept Jesus as a son of God. They accept Jesus as a prophet of God, because to accept Jesus as a son of God would mean that their prophet, Hazrat Mohammed, becomes secondary. He is just a prophet, not a son, not even a son-in-law. Religions are continually interpreting each other with their prejudices. This has been a contention between Mohammedans and Christians: Mohammedans are willing to accept that he was a prophet, a great prophet – there is no doubt about it – but don't say that he was the son of God!

This man in Baghdad declared, 'I have come with the latest message,' but Mohammedans have closed the door with Hazrat Mohammed, as Jainas have closed the door with Mahavira, as Buddhists have closed the door with Buddha. Every religion is a closed religion. It does not allow anybody else to improve upon it. The fear is that somebody, someday, will declare, 'I am bringing the latest message.' Then even the holy Koran will become just like yesterday's newspaper. What can you do with it?

To avoid this humiliation Mohammed declared, 'This is the last message given by God to the world; now there will be no more prophets. Before me there have been prophets, but now they are all out of date. I bring the last message.'

Jainas are not ready to accept another after Mahavira – the twenty- fourth *tirthankara*, the twenty-fourth prophet of the Jainas.

They don't accept a twenty-fifth because a twenty-fifth may turn things upside down. But after twenty-five centuries, things have to be turned upside down, because everything has changed. It is sheer stupidity to go on following someone who had answered questions that were relevant twenty-five centuries ago. Now those questions are not relevant. New questions have arisen, new doubts have arisen, they have to be satisfied and you cannot satisfy them with the old.

That's why every new generation finds itself slipping out of the hands of the older generation; the new generation can see the irrelevance. Their questions are different and you are answering something which they have not asked in the first place. But every religion has been the same in the sense that they all close the doors – no more improvement.

That man was immediately caught and brought to the court of Omar. This is the most heinous crime in a Mohammedan country because Mohammed has said, 'There is only one God – the God that I preach – and there is only one holy book – the book that I preach – and there is only one prophet who is the final statement, and I am that. After me everything will remain the same, no changes will be acceptable.'

When the man was brought to Omar's court, Omar told him, 'Take back your statement that you are a prophet.'

That man laughed. He said, 'It is not in my hands. I have been chosen by God to be the prophet. Only he can take it back.'

Mohammed's follower and representative, his pope – that's what Omar was – said, 'Remember you are playing with fire. There is no other punishment except death. I give you seven days to consider.'

And he told his soldiers, 'Take this man to the jail, strip him naked, bind him to a pillar and beat him continuously for seven days – no food, no water, no sleep. After the seventh day I will come to the jail to inquire whether he has changed his mind or not.'

And this is a liberal, moderate, considerate, very understanding Mohammedan! What to say about the fanatic? Just don't talk about the fanatic.

The soldiers did as they were told. After seven days Omar arrived. The man was just wounds and more wounds – blood and nothing else. He was almost dying and Omar asked him, 'Have you changed your mind or not?'

The man said, 'When I was coming from heaven, God told me, "Remember: to be a prophet is not an easy profession. You will be stoned, you will be condemned, you will be punished, you may be put into jail, you may even be sentenced to death. Be prepared. To be a prophet of God is a very dangerous thing." You have proved that God was right – I am his prophet.'

Even Omar was stunned: this man seems to be utterly mad. And just then he heard, from another pillar, another naked man who had been caught one month before because he was declaring, 'I myself am God.'

Now Mohammedans cannot tolerate that at all. A 'prophet' perhaps, that too only if a Mohammedan is very literate, very cultured, non-fanatic. Then he may say 'perhaps.' If Mohammed can be a prophet, if Jesus can be a prophet, if Buddha can be a prophet, if Moses can be a prophet ... All these, Buddha included, have been accepted by Hazrat Mohammed, then what is the problem? Why cannot this poor fellow be a prophet? First listen to him – what message has he brought? Nobody is listening to his message, and people are trying to kill him even before he has delivered his message. Maybe there is something in his message. If there is nothing in his message, there is no harm. Let him think himself a prophet. But if he has some essential message, then it will be very wrong on our part.

But if somebody says 'I am God,' the way the Upanishads are saying it, this is simply, absolutely unacceptable. And that man had been caught one month before and Omar had completely forgotten that he had been put into jail to consider.

The man shouted, 'Omar, remember, this man is lying because I never sent him as my prophet. After Mohammed I have never sent anybody as my prophet. I am God, Mohammed is the prophet, and the holy Koran is the message. This man is absolutely mad.' This is a historical fact. Omar could not believe it. What to do now?

When Christians – particularly the learned, scholarly missionaries – started translating the Upanishads, they distorted it in every way and they made comments like 'This is a statement of somebody who is utterly insane, whose ego is too big. And he is not religious at all, because a religious man should be humble. How can a religious man declare "I am God"?'

This is very strange about religions. They can see the faults of each other but they cannot see their own faults. When Jesus declares 'I am the only begotten Son of God,' they don't see any ego – it is humbleness. The Upanishads are not egoistic. They are not saying that the one sage who declares 'I am God,' is saying something only about himself. He is saying that you are also God – just as I am God, you are God. We are all part of a godliness. We are all part of the same ocean. This fish and that fish are not different; they are all born out of the same ocean and they will all disappear into the same ocean.

The Upanishads' statement is not egoistic at all, but religions which are God-centered cannot accept it easily. Even Hindus, whose forefathers made this statement, have become so cowardly that now they do not dare to make such a statement. They themselves think that it seems to be egoistic. Christianity and Mohammedanism have even impressed so much on the Hindu mind that it is no longer pure Hindu. You will be surprised to know that three times in his life even the greatest Hindu of this century, Mahatma Gandhi, was almost on the verge of becoming a Christian – he was ready to be converted into a Christian.

I have tried to figure out Mahatma Gandhi. He is ninety percent Christian, nine percent Jaina and one percent Hindu. He was born in Gujarat, which is still the area most significantly under the impression of Jainism. So from his very childhood, although he was born a Hindu, Jainism was impressed on him. All his nonviolence is not a Hindu idea; it is a Jaina idea. All his five great principles that were to be followed by his ashramites are the five great principles of the Jainas – nothing of the Hindus, although he used to read the Bhagavadgita every morning, every evening in front of his twenty, twenty-five disciples.

His ashram was not like this place. It looked just like any slum, where twenty percent lived without even mosquito nets. Instead of mosquito nets, kerosene oil was delivered to them. For what? To put on their faces, on their hands. Any exposed part of the body was rubbed with the kerosene oil. Even mosquitoes don't come close to you. How can you sleep? The smell is such a stink – even mosquitoes stay away and you have to sleep.

I remained only for one day, and when I heard that this was going to happen, I said, 'I am going. This is not the place for me.' From where did he learn this kind of stupidity? Not from the Bhagavadgita, although to convince the Hindus that he is the Mahatma of the Hindus he read the Bhagavadgita every morning, every evening.

The Bhagavadgita is one of the most significant philosophies of violence, not of nonviolence. It was perfectly in tune with Adolf Hitler, with Benito Mussolini, with Joseph Stalin, with Mao Zedong, but not with any religious person. And it is such a strange thing that during his long life not a single man ever asked Mahatma Gandhi, 'Why do you go on calling that Bhagavadgita "my mother"?' It was just a political stunt so the Hindus would remain behind him.

But the whole philosophy of the Bhagavadgita is of violence. Krishna is teaching war. Through the whole Bhagavadgita – from the first sentence to the last – he is convincing somebody of only one single thing: war. He is speaking to Arjuna, his disciple, who wants to escape from war. In fact, Arjuna seems to be more of a Jaina than Krishna, because while Krishna goes on trying to convince him, Arjuna goes on arguing against war, against violence.

Finally he says, 'I don't see the point. Millions of people will be killed, just for my ambition to sit on the golden throne. I don't think that I will feel happy when I see millions of corpses around me, including my brothers, my relatives, my friends, my colleagues, my elders, my teachers. I don't see the point in killing all these people just to become a king.'

He said, 'I will feel so embarrassed, so repentant, that I may commit suicide. I should move to the Himalayas, that would be better. I am finished with the world if this is the way the world has to run. I am no longer part of it. I want to become a sannyasin.'

But Krishna prevented him, prevented him in a very cunning way. He said to him, 'It is God's intention that you should fight; going away from the war is denying God's intention.' Because Arjuna believed that Krishna was a prophet of God, he had to submit – unwillingly, reluctantly.

This was the book Gandhi was reading day and night. He even made a commentary on it, and naturally he was in a difficulty – how to make any sense of nonviolence in a book which is completely based on violence? So he says it is only a metaphor; the war never happened. That is the strategy that he takes in his commentary on Bhagavadgita: the war never happened.

This is the first time in five thousand years that anybody has said that this war never happened. It denies five thousand years of conviction that the war happened. The war not only happened, it destroyed the whole of India – its spine was broken. The war was so great and the impact of it was so big that it made the whole of India cowardly. Because of this war that Krishna preached, India became a slave country for two thousand years. It lost its nerve, it lost its dignity, it became so nervous about war because it saw what had happened in this war – almost half the country was killed. Every family was in mourning. From every family somebody was massacred; not a single family remained out of the war.

That war's nightmare has followed India for five thousand years. It has created such a fear. It is almost like the people who have seen Hiroshima and Nagasaki. If you talk about war with them, what do you think their reaction, their response, will be? Certainly they don't want any more wars – they have seen the worst.

But Mahatma Gandhi, in a very cunning and political way, at the very beginning said that this whole episode of war was just a metaphor: it was a war between the good and the bad, it was a war between the right and the wrong, it was a war between the light and the darkness. It was not a historical thing, hence there was no question of violence. A war between light and darkness is certainly not going to be a bloodshed – neither light nor darkness has any blood.

This man, Mahatma Gandhi, admitted that three times he was on the verge of becoming a Christian. Only the politics of India prevented him, because if he was going to become a Christian, then he would not be the leader of the Hindus. He would be hated by the Hindus, and they were the majority in the country. It was just politics that prevented him from becoming a Christian. He himself would not have accepted this Upanishadic saying; he never talked about the Upanishads. He must have been afraid to talk about the Upanishads because what will he make of the statement *aham brahmasmi*? It cannot be said that it is a metaphor. It is an actual, realized fact.

You are asking what the connection is between this great statement – it is actually called *mahavakya*, 'the great statement' – with another statement of the same significance, *sat-chit-anand. Sat-chit-anand* consists of three words, as I have told you: *sat* – truth, *chit* – consciousness, *anand* – bliss. These three experiences make one capable of asserting the great statement, *aham brahmasmi*. They are deeply connected. In fact, if *sat-chit-anand* is the flower, then *aham brahmasmi* is the fragrance, so deep is the connection between the two.

Certainly 'I am the ultimate' is the very conclusion of the whole search of the East – of all the buddhas, of all the mystics. A single sentence can be called the conclusion of the whole of India. But God-centered religions will not be ready to accept it. That simply shows that their understanding is not of truth, not of consciousness, not of bliss.

Their understanding is of a very low order: it is not an experience, but only a belief. One is a Christian only by belief; a Jew only by belief; a Mohammedan only by belief. What the Upanishads are saying is not a belief – it is direct, immediate experience. And they are so poetic, so mystic, that there is no comparison in the whole world's literature.

But this final flowering and fragrance is possible only if you start with meditation and not with prayer. These two ways will take you to different conclusions: prayer will take you more and more into fiction and meditation will take you more and more into truth. Meditation is to go withinward, and prayer is to look upward, into the empty sky, with all your desires and greed and demands, with all your fears and insecurities. God is to you – if you are on the path of prayer – a consolation and nothing more. But if you are on the path of meditation, one day God will become your very own self, your very own existence.

One day a meek little man is kneeling in church praying. 'Please, God,' he mumbles, 'please make my boss give me a raise so that I can keep up the payments on my house, and so that my children don't go hungry.'

Just then the church door bursts open and a big black guy in sunglasses strolls in whistling a tune. He goes up to the altar, raises his hands and says, 'Hey, man. You up there, God! I really dig you, man. Give me a beautiful new woman, a big new car, and a huge new mansion to live in. And I want it fast.'

He then turns around and walks out. The little man is shocked and continues to pray.

Next week the little man is back, still praying for the same things, when he is startled by a screech of brakes outside the church. In walks the big black guy with a gorgeous woman by his side. He strides up to the altar and says, 'Hey, God! Thanks, man, for the car and the girl. And hey, man, the house is superb!'

After the black guy has gone, the little man goes up to the altar and says, 'Dear God, you answered his prayers. Why don't you answer mine?'

A voice booms out from behind the altar, 'Sorry, man, I just don't dig you!'

If you want fictions, prayer is the path. All the religions that are based on prayer are not authentic religions. Meditation is a totally different route. It takes you inward; it takes you away from the world toward your own being. It is not a demand, it is not a desire, it is not greed, it is not asking or requesting anything. It is simply being silent, utterly silent, moving deeper and deeper into silence. A moment of sublime silence comes, and then a sudden explosion of light and you will feel yourself saying '*Aham brahmasmi*.' Not outward because you are not saying it to anybody in particular. It will be just a feeling in the deepest core of your being. No language is needed, just an experience of 'I am the whole, I am the all. And just as I am the whole, everybody else is.' There is no question of any ego or megalomania.

The Christian missionaries who interpreted the Upanishads were absolutely prejudiced and had no understanding about meditation and no understanding about the higher qualities of a true religion. They knew only an organized church. In comparison to the Upanishads, every religion of the world looks so pygmy-like, so childish. Those organized religions don't give you freedom. On the contrary, they give you deeper and deeper bondage and slavery. In the name of God, you have to surrender; in the name of God, you have to become a sheep and allow a Jesus or a Mohammed to be a shepherd. It is so disgusting, the very idea is so self-disrespectful that I cannot call it even pseudo-religious. It is simply irreligious.

The Upanishads are the highest flights of consciousness. They don't belong to any religion. The people who made these great statements have not even mentioned their names. They don't belong to any nation, they don't belong to any religion, they don't belong to those who are in search of some mundane thing. They belong to the authentic seekers of truth. They belong to you. They belong to my people.

13

Belief Is Based on Ignorance

Osho,

Again and again, everything I want to say seems unsayable. Question after question burns fiercely and vanishes as quickly. And yet, there's an uncontrollable longing for you to point me in the right direction. Otherwise, how can I know that I'm not already astray?

Anand Savita, you may have been astray, but certainly now you are not astray. If questions arise and disappear it is a great symbolic indication. If you want to ask something and you find it unsayable, it means something from beyond the mind is longing to be expressed; words fail, the mind cannot manage to bring it down to the world of language.

And this is something to be remembered by you all: if you are getting more silent, more peaceful, more calm and cool, it is an intrinsic indication that you are in the right direction. If things are otherwise – you are becoming more disturbed, more anxiety-ridden, feeling more anguish, feeling as if you are falling apart – it is a sure indication that you have gone astray.

I want you to remember the criterion yourself, because the criterion is intrinsic. It is not imposed from outside, it is not arbitrary. You can see it very clearly – according to the symptoms. If silence, blissfulness, a kind of peace that passes understanding are there, then you need not worry at all, as these things can happen only on the right path. They never happen if you go astray. If you are miserable, feeling meaningless, feeling no significance in life, if your life has no music, no poetry, but is just a stale, dead dragging, you have clear-cut symptoms in your hands that you are no longer on the right path.

The right path is just as if you are coming closer to a beautiful garden. You may not see it, it may not yet be visible, but far away you can start smelling the fragrance, you can start feeling the cool breeze, you can start hearing the birds singing in the trees. You start seeing that things are becoming greener, livelier; you are approaching closer to the garden. But if things are becoming dry, losing all juice, the trees are becoming bare, without foliage, without flowers, and the path is becoming sandier and sandier and all coolness is disappearing – instead you are feeling hot and perspiring – you know you are moving toward the desert.

This is exactly what happens in your inner world. There is a desert called the mind and there is a garden called the heart. If you are moving toward the heart, everything is right, because the heart is the bridge to your being. The heart is not the goal, but it is a sure indication that you have left the mind behind, that the desert has been left behind.

The heart joins the mind and being just like a bridge. As you start moving on the path of the heart, things start becoming more beautiful, more loving. You are surrounded by a new energy, a new life, as if you are being rejuvenated every moment. And the day you reach your center, there you will experience *sat-chit-anand*. But before that experience of truth, consciousness, bliss, these small indications will help you on the path. They are the milestones.

As far as I can see, you are going perfectly right because you are feeling things which cannot be said – they must be coming from the heart. Only the heart is without language. It is silent, it speaks in silence. You can say that silence is its language. And you find it difficult to say them because saying is the function of the mind. The feeling is in the heart and the mechanism of expression is in the mind. So if something is arising in the heart, the mind feels absolutely impotent. This is good news.

And your questions, you say, 'appear one after another, burn fiercely and vanish as quickly.' That's how it happens to every meditator. You don't have to ask them! Even before you can ask them they are no longer there. It means you are coming closer to the answer within yourself. It may not be very clear to you what the answer is, but the question disappears without torturing you, without becoming a nightmare, without being stubborn, persistent, harassing you to ask it: that would show you are enclosed in the mind. Mind knows only questions; the heart knows only answers – and the being is beyond both. It knows neither questions nor answers. It is simply beyond all kinds of duality.

I have told you many times, but I love the incident so much, because in the contemporary world, and particularly in the West, nothing like it has ever happened. In the East it has been happening to the Sufis, to the Zen monks, to the masters of meditation, but in the West this small incident stands unique – just like a burning torch in a dark night.

Gertrude Stein, a great poetess, was dying, she was breathing her last breath. She was loved by many people, she had many friends. She was a woman of tremendous creative qualities. Her poetry comes closest to the haikus of the Zen masters or to the poetry of Kabir, Nanak, Farid. Her poetry has something essentially of the East; she had some glimpses of the mystic experience.

At the last moment – it was evening and the sun had set and darkness was settling – she opened her eyes and asked, 'What is the answer?'

And those who had gathered to say good-bye to her were puzzled. 'Has she gone senile, insane? Perhaps death has shocked her and she has lost her rationality.'

Certainly no man with a reasonable mind will ask 'What is the answer?' because unless you have asked a question, asking 'What is the answer?' is very irrational.

There was silence for a moment. Then one very close friend asked, 'But you have not asked the question. How can we answer?'

And Gertrude Stein had a faint smile and said, 'Okay, so tell me, what is the question?'

And then she died, so they had no time left to say, 'This question is as absurd as your first. First you asked for the answer without asking the question; now you are also asking us for the question! There are thousands and millions of questions. Who knows what question you want to be answered?'

In fact, Gertrude Stein was passing beyond the mind when she asked, 'What is the answer?' She was passing beyond the heart when she asked – reluctantly, smilingly – 'Okay, what is the question?' And then she passed beyond.

It was one of the most beautiful deaths in the West. In the East we have known many beautiful deaths. It is very difficult for people to make a beautiful life.

But there have been people who have lived beautifully and died even more beautifully. Because to them death comes as a culmination, as a climax of life, as if the whole life becomes a flame of fire – in a single moment, in total intensity – before disappearing into the universal. She was not losing her mind in the sense that it is usually understood, but she was certainly going beyond the mind and she was also going beyond the heart.

Beyond these two diametrically opposite centers in you is a being which is utterly innocent of any questions or of any answers. It is so fulfilled in itself, so completely contented that there is nothing left to ask and there is nothing left to answer.

My own understanding is that Gertrude Stein died enlightened. The West has no understanding of enlightenment. They simply thought she was going crazy. But it was not craziness, it was a moment of great celebration. What she could not attain in her life, she attained in her death. And she gave the sure indications: no question, no answer and you have arrived home.

Savita, you are perfectly good. I have been watching you, looking into your eyes, into your face – it has changed so much. I remember when you came the first time to me, years ago. I remember it exactly – how hard your face was, how intellectual your questions were. You have a beautiful face and a beautiful being, but you could not manage to hide the hardness. It was beyond you, you were in your head. Then the face loses all grace.

It is still beautiful as far as the shape is concerned, but it loses something essential to beauty: the grace. Now I see that your heart must have taken over your head. Your face shows a grace, your eyes show a silence, you show a certain grounding, a certain centering – small things.

When you first came to me I could see how fidgety you were. Even for a few minutes you could not sit in the same position. It is not only a question of the body. It is the mind that is continuously moving, that is continuously changing – that affects the body. Now I see you sitting almost like a marble statue: no movement, and your face is so radiant with love. You are surrounded with a new experience. You are perfectly on the right path. And the day will not be far away when your face will start radiating the light of illumination. Meanwhile, rejoice as much as you can and be grateful to existence with your total being.

Just one thing I would like to add: you have become very silent. So silent that perhaps you find laughter a little disturbing. I would like you to remember always that silence is not disturbed by laughter, it is deepened. Laughter to me is an essential quality of religious experience. It involves you totally.

But it happens when people are on the path, growing, there comes a moment when their silence becomes a little serious. It is natural. They have never known silence. It becomes a little shadowed with seriousness. And hiding behind seriousness there is a little sadness. Both can be destroyed if you learn a little laughing, a little singing, a little dancing.

I want you to reach the ultimate as a child, giggling with joy – that's the only way to greet existence when you meet the ultimate. You should enter with laughter, dancing, singing, because only your laughter and your singing and your dancing can show your gratitude. No other words are possible.

Just for you, Savita...

Yossel Moskowitz has four daughters and insists on meeting each of their boyfriends before he allows them to be taken out. The first boy arrives and says, 'My name is Jim and I have come to take Kim for a swim. Is she in?'

He seems nice enough, so Yossel lets them go. The second lad arrives and says, 'My name is Joe, and I have come to take Flo to the show. Can we go?' He, too, is given permission.

Soon there is a third boy at the door who says, 'My name is Lance and I have come to take Nance to the dance. Any chance?' So off they go.

Half an hour later a drunk staggers to the door and says, 'Hi! My name is Buck...'

But Yossel shouts, 'She is not in!'

The circus audience holds its breath as the crocodile trainer cracks his whip. The crocodile opens its huge mouth and the trainer puts his arm inside it. He cracks the whip again and the crocodile shuts its mouth with terrific force, but stops an inch from the trainer's arm. The audience gasps and then goes wild with applause.

Next, the trainer takes out his prick, cracks his whip and the crocodile opens its mouth. Then he puts his prick inside the crocodile's mouth and cracks the whip again. The crocodile shuts its mouth with tremendous force, but again stops an inch away.

The crowd gasps as the trainer takes a huge wooden mallet and hits the crocodile over the head as hard as he can. But still the animal won't bite. He then cracks his whip, removes his unscratched prick and the crowd goes wild.

Then the trainer asks the audience if anyone else would like to try this trick. A little old lady rushes into the ring and says, 'Yes, yes, let me try! But please don't hit me so hard with the hammer!'

> Osho,
> I am deeply grateful to existence that I can be here beside you and that you are available to me.
>
> I believe you are my only authentic mirror. All the other mirrors around me seem to reflect my masks and the roles I'm playing. How can I become more sensitive toward myself?
>
> How can I say yes to what I am, and no to what I am not?

It is one of the great problems for the seeker – to be caught in duality; and the duality comes in such a way that you may not recognize it at all. It seems so right, it seems that it is going to help you in your growth, but no duality can help you grow. All duality has to be left behind: neither yes nor no, neither you nor me, neither your false self nor your idea of your authentic self. Both have to be left behind.

In essence, the moment you are not divided in any kind of duality you suddenly fall into tune with existence. Existence knows no *yes*, no *no*. It knows no duality. It is absolutely simple. There is no complexity in it.

Now, what you are asking is a complex question. You are asking, 'How can I say yes to what I am, and no to what I am not?' You don't have to – you simply stop saying anything! You go into a non-saying silence within yourself. Otherwise you will get into such complexities that they will hold you back from going in.

These are all mind questions. In fact, every question is a mind question. Sometimes they are so beautiful that you may think they are coming from beyond the mind. But no question ever comes from beyond the mind; this is unquestioningly in tune with existence.

I will read your question. You say, 'I am deeply grateful to existence that I can be here beside you and that you are available to me.' Do you see the duality? It is very subtle. First, you are making a distinction between yourself and existence by being grateful to existence, as if you are apart. Do you think my hand can be grateful to me? Do you think my eyes can be grateful to me? Do you think I have to be grateful to my heart? I am one whole. In fact, to feel one with existence is the only gratitude, but that will not be expressed in words. It will overwhelm you. You may dance with joy that you have arrived, but you will not say anything.

You are saying, 'I am deeply grateful to existence...' That is where you are making your first duality. If you are really grateful to existence you will disappear. There will not be anyone to say 'Thank you' to existence – and that is true thankfulness. Secondly you say, '...that I can be here beside you and that you are available to me.' Another duality! Again your mind is making a distinction between yourself and me. Is there any need to make the distinction? Can't you come close, so close that you cannot see the other? To see the other as the other, you need a distance.

Then you say, 'I believe you are my only authentic mirror.' You are too much in the mind. I am insisting every moment, each day when I am with you: religion is not a question of belief. I want you to be free from all beliefs, but the mind is very much attached to beliefs. That's its way, its strategy, to prevent you from reaching the truth. Truth is an experience, not a belief.

The moment you say 'I believe,' without your knowing, you are declaring your ignorance. Belief is based on ignorance. A man says 'I believe in God.' He knows nothing about God, whether he exists or not. It is his belief, he is projecting his belief. When somebody says 'I believe I am in love with you,' what do you think of him? He *believes* that he is in love with you. He does not know exactly, he has not felt it throughout his being. His heart has not danced with the feeling of love. It is still a belief in the head.

You say, 'I believe...' and that shows nothing but an imprisonment in the mind. *Belief* is a word belonging to the mind. Beyond the mind there is no question of belief. Either you know or you don't. And then, '...that you are my only authentic mirror.' How can you come to this conclusion with a belief? Have you seen all the mirrors in the world? How can you decide I am your only authentic mirror? And that too based on a belief? Just look how your mind is playing tricks on you! What is the reason that mind is giving you to make you believe I am your only authentic mirror?

I have heard about a woman who was ugly, really ugly, repulsively ugly. She was very much against mirrors. Her idea was that all those mirrors were making her ugly, because whenever she was *not* looking in the mirror she was not ugly. She was so against mirrors that in her own house there were no mirrors, and she used to immediately break other people's mirrors, hit them hard. She used to carry a staff with her; if somebody, somewhere, had a mirror, she never bothered that it was not her possession. She would immediately hit the mirror, breaking it into pieces.

The whole village where the woman lived was in utter despair. They said, 'In the first place, this woman is so repulsive. Secondly, she goes on destroying our mirrors. We are poor people, but her argument is: "These mirrors are making me ugly! It is a conspiracy of the mirror manufacturers. Because when there is no mirror, I am perfectly okay."'

Finally one clever guy in the village went to the city, to the factory where mirrors were produced, and he asked them to produce a mirror in which an ugly woman starts looking beautiful.

Mirrors can be made in many ways. If you have seen ... There are many places in big cities where you can go into a mirror house where there are different kinds of mirrors: a few make you thin and tall; a few make you very fat and very short; a few make your nose so long that not even a Jew could have it; a few make your nose almost disappear – flat, no nose; a few make one of your eyes small and the other big ... There are thousands of kinds of mirrors.

In Indore, one of the big cities of India, there is a mirror house. One of the richest men of India – he is dead now – was Sir Seth Hukum Chand. He was given as many titles by the British government as you can conceive. It needed at least half a page to write all his titles. He was Sir Seth – Seth is Hindi, it comes from the Sanskrit root *shreshth*. It means 'the best.' And the British government was giving titles to only a few people. I think he was the only Sir Seth in the whole of India: best amongst the best!

He was not a king, but he was given the title of Raja – the king. He owned almost three-quarters of the buildings in the whole city. Even the Maharaja – Indore was a state, a beautiful state – had to borrow money from Sir Seth Hukum Chand. He had a huge amount of money and he made Indore as beautiful as possible – he was not a miserly man.

He had a beautiful collection of horses, such as I have never seen. I have seen many horses in many places, but the horses that he had were absolutely unique and rare: such proud horses, so strong. He had made a big palace for the horses, a marble palace. He was the only person in the whole world who had a Rolls Royce made completely of twenty-four carat gold – even the engine! Nothing was to be used except gold. And he had made a beautiful temple, completely of glass.

He had also made a mirror house. In his mirror house there must have been at least a thousand or more mirrors. It took hours to move from one room to another room, from one mirror to another mirror. You could not believe that mirrors could be of so many curves, so many different types – they can change you so much.

So the factory produced a mirror which would make the woman look beautiful. The man brought the mirror to the woman and said, 'Before you break it, just have a look in it. This is a very authentic mirror!'

The woman looked into it and she was so beautiful, she hugged the mirror, she kissed the mirror. She said, 'I was absolutely right in destroying all the false mirrors. This is the only real mirror.'

Now, this was the false mirror. How do you decide that I am your only authentic mirror? Perhaps close to me you feel beautiful, close to me you feel silent, close to me you feel meditative, close to me you feel joyous. Your mind is supplying the reason, 'The mirrors around me seem to reflect my masks and the roles I am playing.'

How do you know which is the mask and which is the original face? Are you certain? How can you be certain – because a belief can never be certain – that what you feel near me is your original face? Perhaps my presence and my people's presence and the silence that surrounds this strange temple – godless, but so full of godliness; prayerless, but so full of prayerfulness ... You start feeling these things, they infiltrate into your being and you feel happy, thinking 'Perhaps this is my reality, this is my original face. Everybody else reflects only my mask.'

But if you are really experiencing it, why do you go on keeping your masks? Throw them away! Then no mirror will be able to reflect that which is not. If you see that this is a mask, immediately destroy it. Not the mirror, mind you – destroy the mask!

I have heard...

A man was reading the newspaper and his wife was standing behind him, looking at what he was reading – wives are very suspicious. The wife read that a famous doctor had declared how many diseases happen because of alcohol. And she immediately jumped.

Every wife seems to be appointed by God himself to cure her husband. I don't see that there is any other purpose for a wife. Her whole life she devotes to curing the husband of all kinds of wrong habits: cigarettes, alcohol, other women. And all that they succeed in doing is to create a hypocrite!

She immediately told the husband, 'Why are you reading all this nonsense? Read this – what the famous doctor is saying: "Alcohol can cause all these diseases; it will take ten years off your life." Stop drinking alcohol!'

The man said, 'Okay, from tomorrow.'

The woman could not believe it. She had been torturing him since they had married. It must have been twenty years, and he had never agreed to drop it – and so suddenly. He said, 'Okay, from tomorrow.'

Tomorrow morning came, but the newspaper did not come. The wife asked, 'What happened to the newspaper?'

He said, 'I have told you, I will stop from tomorrow, not the alcohol but such stupid newspapers!'

Don't destroy any mirrors, because the mirror is innocent. If it shows you your mask, drop the mask! Then every mirror will reflect your authentic face. And when every mirror starts reflecting your authentic face – the mirror of your servant, the mirror of your wife, the mirrors of your children, the mirrors of your parents, the mirrors of your friends, even the mirrors of your enemies – when they all reflect the same face, only then can you be certain that you have come to the original. Otherwise, you go on changing masks.

The same man: with his wife, he has a mask made in England – long face, so serious, grumpy, utterly fed up with the world, everything is wrong. And then you see him with somebody else's wife and he is smiling so much. He has dropped the English face completely; he has become an Italian. You just watch how *you* change your mask. In front of your servant you have one mask – you are the boss. But in front of your master, your own boss, you have a different mask.

Even animals learn tricks with human beings. Otherwise, they are simple people. Have you seen dogs? If they know that somebody is welcome in the house, they will also welcome him with their tails wagging. If they know that somebody is not welcome in the house, they will not wag their tails. They will bark and keep the stranger away. But sometimes poor dogs, not being capable of much discrimination, find themselves in a fix. Somebody comes and they don't know exactly whether he has to be welcomed or chased away. So they do both things: on the one hand they go on barking, on the other they go on wagging their tail – diplomatic! They are waiting for the response of their boss. When their master comes out, if he shakes hands with the person, the barking stops, the wagging of the tail continues. But if the master is angry and says 'Why have you entered the garden? Get out!' the dog's tail stops completely and he rushes to chase the man out of the garden, barking as loudly as he can.

Diplomacy is a contagious disease. In front of your boss...

You may not have a tail, though Darwin says that once you had one. He even found the joint in your backbone where the tail was joined, where it was plugged in. That is certain proof that you once had a tail because otherwise why should you have this place where a tail can be plugged in? This was his basic argument to prove that man has come from apes. The only thing missing is the tail. He studied skeletons and found that there had been a tail – the part where it used to be attached is still in your body.

It is fortunate that you have lost the tail. Otherwise, when you see your boss or your wife, you will immediately start wagging it. And it will look very odd to have buttons on both sides of your pants, as you will have to keep your tail hidden. It would not be for everybody, only for special people, VIPs. For ordinary people, there will be no need to bring your tail out.

But your face shows the same expression. The boss may be shouting at you – you go on smiling, your lips are spread ear to ear. Deep down you want to kill that man immediately, to shoot that man. Deep down you are calling him 'bastard.' But on your face, that ear-to-ear smile, although he is harassing you, calling you all kinds of names, saying that you are lazy, that you are always a latecomer and it cannot be tolerated anymore, that you have to mend your ways, otherwise you will be fired.

If you watch ... With a friend, you have a different mask, with the enemy, you have a different mask, with a stranger you have a different mask. The authentic original face is only possible when you remove all masks, when you start behaving humanly and equally to all. He may be a servant or he may be a master: both are human beings and both need their dignity and respect. Whether it is your friend or your enemy, it doesn't matter: both are human beings and both need their dignity and respect.

You will find your original face only when you have destroyed all your masks – not in a mirror. My effort is not to give you a mirror which gives you a good feeling that you have a beautiful face, that this is your original face. I want you to find your original face, and the only way is that when every mirror you come across...

Every human being is a mirror. Have you ever watched a beggar? He will not ask you for anything if you are alone on the street because he knows that alone you are not going to give him anything except the advice, 'You are strong enough, you don't have to be a beggar. Don't be a parasite, just go and find some work. You are the people who have destroyed this country.'

The beggar will follow you, and when there are people around, *then* he will ask, *then* he will hold your legs, your feet, saying, 'Give me something. I am dying. For three days I have not eaten anything!' And you will give.

Deep down you hate him, deep down you want to hit that beggar. But you will give him something because you want to keep your prestige, your mask, in front of those people, so they will think 'He is a very generous man, a great man, very religious. He knows what charity is.' But they don't know what is going on inside you.

You know that fellow. Every day he has been saying the same thing to you – 'For three days I have not eaten anything.' And still he gets away with it in a crowd. So you will find beggars in places where there is a crowd: in the marketplace, near the movie hall, near your customers if you are a shopkeeper, in front of your friends or anybody to whom you have been bragging about your kindness and your compassion and your greatness.

Beggars know perfectly well – it is not one-sided – that not only are you saying something else inside while giving him some money, the beggar is also saying something else inside; he also has masks. He knows that he has got the idiot in the right place. He knows that now you cannot escape. He is thinking he is making a fool of you, but on the surface he is telling you, 'Great will be your reward in paradise. God will give you a thousand times more.'

I was in Allahabad, speaking at the Allahabad University, and as I was entering the university a beggar caught hold of me. Allahabad is one of the most prominent Hindu religious cities, because it is where three holy rivers meet. Hindus think that where three rivers meet – they call it *sangam*, the meeting – that place becomes holy. And in a holy place you will find more beggars than anywhere else because naturally everybody who comes there pretends to be holy, and to prove it he has to give to the beggars. The more he gives, the holier he is.

The beggar caught hold of me, thinking I was just like anybody else. The professors who were waiting to receive me were there, so he must have thought, 'This is the right time.'

He said, 'If you give me just one rupee, God will give you a million times more.'

I said, 'If you have such an intimate relationship with God, ask directly! Why put me in between unnecessarily. I don't have any contact with God and I don't want a million rupees – what will I do with them?'

The beggar said, 'My God! I have never seen such a man! You don't need one million?'

I said, 'I don't need even one rupee, and I don't have one!' He looked at me, surprised.

I said, 'You have to believe me; you can check. I don't even have pockets. Where to keep one rupee?'

He looked at my robe. There were no pockets. He said, 'You are the worst fellow I have come across. And it seems you don't believe in God.'

I said, 'You are right. I neither believe in money nor in God. You have to find somebody else who believes in money and who believes in God and who believes in respectability.'

I don't believe in anything. All these professors ... I didn't care. Because I don't brag, I said to the beggar, 'If this is the way a transaction is made, you give *me* one rupee and get one million rupees from God.'

He looked at me and he said, 'This is too much! Not a single man in my whole life has asked me for one rupee. There have been people who have not given, but asking...!'

I said, 'According to your ideology, I am just giving you a chance of getting one million rupees in paradise. Don't miss the opportunity! You have given the opportunity to many people in your life. I am giving *you* the opportunity, I am the only man who is missing out on one million rupees for just one rupee. Do it. It is a bargain!'

He simply turned his face from me and ran away. I said, 'Where are you going? I will be coming wherever you go unless you give me one rupee. And I am going to stay in this city for ten days!'

The professors said, 'You have done a miracle. We have been trying to get rid of this beggar. He stands just in front of the door. It looks so ugly, and he harasses everybody, and everybody has to give something. But you have done something great. He has run away! We have been trying, but he is a strong fellow. And every professor was afraid that he may be vengeful, thinking: "When I go out of the university, he may give me a good lesson, so it is better not to bother him." He is almost a wrestler, but he has run away!'

For ten days he didn't appear at the university gate. When I left the university I told the professor in charge, who had arranged my lectures at the university, 'Please send me a card if he returns.'

He said, 'What do you mean? Are you coming back?'

I said, 'No, I just want to know whether he comes back or not.'

And after three or four days I received the news that after exactly ten days – on the eleventh – he was present, 'He is again torturing us.'

You have to find the original face that you brought with you when you were born, when you were without the crippling by society, without the impositions of masks by your parents, without the diplomacy learned in life. You can find it, but you will have to find it in all the people you meet. And whenever you see any mask, drop it.

Those masks are not going to help you. Those masks are the barriers between you and the ultimate. Once those masks are dropped, suddenly you find there was no other barrier, you are one with the universal energy, you are one with the cosmos.

Little Ernie has been driving his mother crazy, so she starts visiting a psychiatrist. On her second visit the shrink asks her, 'Have the tranquilizers calmed you down?'

'Yes,' replies Ernie's mother.

'And how is your little Ernie?' he asks.

She looks up and says, 'Who cares?'

So be silent, calm and quiet – meditation is a nonmedicinal tranquilizer – and then you will not care whether you are facing your servant or your boss, friend or enemy. Who cares? They are all human beings, equally respectable, equally beautiful. There is no need to make any judgment.

And finally you are asking, 'How can I become more sensitive toward myself?' First start becoming sensitive toward trees, rivers, mountains, oceans, because they will not in any way be attacking you. So you need not have defense measures. Your insensitivity is nothing but your defense. People become hard just to protect themselves. So first start with the beautiful existence around you. Trees won't attack you; be a little more sensitive. Stars won't attack you; be a little more available. There is no need to be afraid. Mountains, clouds, the sun and the moon – just become open to them.

I'm giving you the first step in becoming sensitive – *why* are you insensitive? That has to be looked into. You are insensitive because it is a very tough society with tough competition. For the whole of life everybody is at everybody else's throat; cut as many throats as possible and you will be a great man.

Just the other day I was looking at data: Genghis Khan alone killed forty million people; Nadir Shah alone killed thirty million people; Tamerlane also killed seventeen million people, and statistics are not available for Alexander the Great or Napoleon Bonaparte. But the data is available for Joseph Stalin: he killed thirty million Russians after the revolution. Adolf Hitler killed six million Jews in Germany, and in total – because of him – fifty million people were killed in the Second World War. It is a very insane society. One has to protect oneself, otherwise you will be killed for small things.

My eye specialist is here. He has brought me a beautiful pair of glasses and he told me a story about those beautiful glasses. They have become so precious and so valuable – their design is unique – that just in New York six people were killed because they had those sunglasses. It is very difficult to get them. The price is very high and the waiting list is long – six months, eight months. Who is going to wait for eight months? Not in New York! Things have to be done quickly, people want everything to be done with speed. Instant coffee – that is the motto. Six people were killed, just for a pair of glasses. It is unbelievable.

But this is how things are going on. You may not be clearly aware of it, for your unconscious goes on protecting you. That's what makes you insensitive.

I used to live with a friend. He was a very rich man. I watched his strange behavior: when he came into the house, he would walk very fast and he would not look here or there. The servants were working in the garden, the gardeners were working, his children were playing, and whenever he came all his children would become serious. He would keep that same hardness even with his wife.

After watching for two or three days, I had to tell him, 'It is strange behavior.'

He said, 'You don't know ... If I just relax a little bit my wife says: "We need a new car. This car is one year old. New models have come out." I have to keep a hard, stony face. That keeps her afraid to mention the new car. If I relax a little bit every child starts asking for money. Servants, if I even just stand a little bit...'

He never looked at his own garden, he never looked at the beautiful flowers.

I said, 'What is the purpose of this garden? You never go in the garden, you never look at the roses, you never sit on the lawn. And you have the most beautiful lawn.'

He said, 'It is dangerous; once I go into the garden the *mali* comes, asks for a raise in his monthly salary. If I say anything about the roses like, "You have grown beautiful roses," that's enough! I don't want to raise the salaries, so I have to avoid my own garden!'

He was a totally different person outside his house than he was inside his house. I knew him only outside his house. That's why I accepted his invitation when he said, 'I have a big bungalow – half is empty. Why don't you come? And you love a garden. I have a beautiful garden and you can have half the bungalow.'

I said, 'What will I do with half the bungalow? Just one room is enough for me.'

He said, 'But you can have it for guests or others.'

So I moved into his house. Then I came to see a totally different man. I told him, 'This is an ugly attitude. You have enough money to purchase a new car, you have enough money to raise those poor servants' salaries a little bit, you have enough money to give some to your own children for toys or for sweets or something. It is not going to make you bankrupt.'

I gave him an absolute ultimatum. 'If you don't change, I cannot live in your house. Only if you change will I live in your house. I cannot see this ugly behavior with your own children. They are so happy, running, enjoying. The moment you come they all become serious, they all start reading their books, doing their homework.

'I see your wife is so relaxed when you are not here. She brings things for me – tea or coffee – or if she prepares some sweets she brings some for me. She is such a lovely lady, but the moment you enter the house, she becomes just a mirror image of you.

'This I cannot tolerate. I give you three days. Either you change or I will change houses. I was perfectly happy in my own house. You dragged me here unnecessarily and not only will I leave the house, you will lose a friend, too.'

He said, 'But three days is too short a time to change such a long habit.'

I said, 'How many days do you want?'

He said, 'It is difficult to say. I will try my best, but don't make a deadline. I am unkind to these people, I accept; don't you be unkind to me.'

I said, 'That's okay, I will remain here. I will not make a deadline, but it is better that you be quick. Otherwise I will not inform you – any night I can disappear.'

It took him almost six months to relax in his own house although he was perfectly relaxed outside it.

Your sensitivity first has to learn to be sensitive with the universe, which is not attacking you. You need not be afraid. Then be sensitive with human beings. That will be a little difficult. You may find yourself in the same position as my friend. But it is worth it. And only when you are sensitive to the universe, to human beings, to the animals, can you at last be sensitive to yourself. That is going to be the final step.

You have been condemned from the very beginning – you have been taught, 'You are worthless, you don't even deserve to exist, you have to earn respectability, prestige...' You have become very hard upon yourself. This is called discipline; this is used to create men with steel spines. Every society is trying, every parent is trying, so that his children will become *stalins* – that is the Russian word for a man of steel – because they are preparing you for a world where you will find only struggle, cunningness, cheating, hypocrites, all kinds of conmen. So you have become very hard inside.

Relax from the outer circumference of your being and then go on moving inward. Finally you will be able to relax in your deepest core and that is the meeting with existence.

Finally you ask, 'How can I say yes to what I am, and no to what I am not?' There is no need. When you know what you are, it is enough. That which you are not will disappear. It is you who are clinging to it. It is not your false personality that is clinging to you. To know the real is to be free from the unreal. There is no question of choice. It is not that you have to choose that this is the real, and that is the unreal, how to say yes to the real, how to say no to the unreal.

In the very understanding that something is unreal, you have said no to it. In the very understanding that something is authentic and real, you have already said yes to it, without saying a single word. Just knowing the difference between the false and the authentic, between the mask and the original face, is enough.

Meditate deeply and all that I have said to you will become absolutely clear. Don't start thinking about it, otherwise you will get more into puzzles, more into complexities.

Just sit silently and meditate on whatever I have said to you. A great clarity is bound to come; it always comes. It has come to many of my people. There is no reason why it will not come to you.

14

Freedom from Chains; Freedom for Creativity

Osho,
Often these days I feel as if I am pregnant. It is not a down-pulling burden. It rather feels like a weightless, but expansive something in my belly and my chest. It is a very strange sensation for a man. I am not showing any signs of pregnancy yet – my belly is still flat as usual but now I have exposed myself, and there is no Holy Ghost to blame and I am certainly not the Virgin Mary. Osho, what is it that I am pregnant with? Is it you?

I hope it is me. In fact, every disciple has to come to this stage where he feels almost pregnant with the divine. It is a spiritual pregnancy. But because we are so identified with the body, it may even seem that the body is also pregnant.

But something *is* growing within you. It is not part of the body, you need not be a Virgin Mary. And, of course, holy ghosts are not available anymore, only unholy ghosts – there are a few. One lives with Anando, another has been found in a godown, but they are all unholy ghosts – they don't do holy things, so you need not be worried about them. Moreover, even the Holy Ghost has not been able up to now to do a miracle – to make a man pregnant. It would have been more in tune with the Christian ideology if Joseph, rather than Mary, had become pregnant. That would have been a great miracle. The Virgin Mary, a poor girl, becoming pregnant is not a great miracle; anybody can do it.

The disciple certainly passes through a stage of immense value and beauty. Something transcendental – something more than you have ever thought about yourself, something beyond the grasp of your mind – is growing within you. This is the lotus I have been talking to you about. This is the flowering that brings a man or a woman to the ultimate opening toward the unknown, unknowable, inexpressible.

In a way, through this pregnancy you are born again. You give birth to your own authentic self, which up to now has been only a seed. But the seed longs to become a flower. On the way, you will feel something very similar to pregnancy. You will feel light – you will not be feeling heavy like a pregnant woman – because it is not something material that is growing in you. It is something spiritual, nonmaterial, that is opening within you. It will bring you more and more light, make you more and more unfettered, more and more free.

Meditators for centuries have felt that when deep in meditation, they suddenly find as if they have lost all weight, as if gravitation no more functions on them. In a certain way, it is right. It no longer functions on their spiritual being. The spiritual being is not matter, hence gravitation cannot have any pull on it. And the weight arises because of the gravitation and its pull.

You don't have weight, not even your body has weight. *Weight* is the normal name for a scientific fact and that scientific fact is the gravitation force on the earth. You are pulled by that force. It is good for you – otherwise you would become like balloons, moving upward, and you would not be able to find how to come back down to the earth.

It happens to astronauts when they move beyond the gravitational field. The gravitational field of the earth is two hundred miles around the earth. The moment the rocket passes two hundred miles, the strangest experience happens to the astronauts. They suddenly lose all weight. If they are not sitting with their belts on, they start floating inside the rocket, just like birds. Even birds feel the gravitation, that's why they become tired. They can fly only for a certain time. Then they have to rest. But the astronaut in the rocket has no gravitational pull.

When the astronauts landed on the moon, they had another very strange experience: as the moon has only one fourth of the gravitation of the earth – it is four times smaller than the earth, hence its forces of pulling are also four times less – the astronauts felt very light, not as light as they were feeling on the way to the moon, but still four times less.

If you are eighty kilos, you feel only twenty kilos. Because the astronaut feels four times less weight, he can jump four times further. He can simply jump over your house, just from this street to another street. He can jump to your terrace with no difficulty. There is no problem, because it is only the pull of the earth that is preventing him.

They had to walk very carefully on the moon. They were afraid because they were feeling so light. If the same thing happened as was happening on the way – in the rocket – then they would be finished. On the way, between the moon and the earth, they were able to come out of the rocket, they could float outside the rocket. Tremendous experiences, but still they are physical.

But as your spiritual being starts growing within you or starts coming into your vision – just a faraway vision of a mountain peak, covered with eternal snow – suddenly you can start feeling, even from far away, a certain coolness, a certain ancientness and a certain eternity. As you become more aware of your inner being, it will appear – as now – as if you are pregnant. You will see that you are not pregnant with anybody else, but that your own potential, your own ultimate possibility, is trying to unfold its petals.

You must have seen Gautam Buddha's statues. He's always sitting on a lotus flower. In the East, the lotus has always been the symbol of ultimate flowering because there is no other flower so big and so beautiful and so symbolically significant. The lotus grows in mud, dirty mud. That is one of the similarities: your body is nothing but dirty mud, and the lotus grows in the dirty mud. The lotus emerges from the water and its petals are so silky that the water cannot touch them. They remain always untouched by water, even from the dewdrops that settle on them in the night – particularly in winter. In the morning you can see the dewdrop sitting on the petals of the lotus, but the lotus is not wet. The dewdrop and the lotus are still separate. And soon a little breeze ... The dewdrop will start falling off the lotus leaves or the lotus petals.

That is the second symbol for a spiritual man who lives in the world: just like a lotus flower he is untouched by the world, as the lotus flower is not touched by the water in which it grows, in which it lives, in which it dies – it remains untouched by it.

These two things – growing in the dirty mud, growing beyond the dirty mud and the water, and still never being touched – are the essential qualities of a sannyasin. Being in the world, but not of the world; being in the world, but not allowing the world even to touch you. The authentic sannyasin does not escape from the world. He is not a coward. But in the past, unfortunately the cowards became sannyasins and they gave a bad name to the whole spiritual regeneration of man.

Cowards found it very rational that they were leaving the world because the world corrupts. But the world corrupts you only if you are corruptible, the world corrupts you because you are ready to be corrupted; in fact, you are hankering to be corrupted. If you are not ready to be corrupted, nothing can corrupt you.

These cowards created a strange situation for future humanity – for you, for everybody. They created a kind of rift between the ordinary world and themselves. They were spiritual beings because they left the ordinary mundane marketplace and moved to the Himalayas or to the forests or to some desert. But they were really moving away from a situation of which they were afraid. They knew that if they remained in the world they were going to be corrupted. They were fully aware of their tendencies: their desires, their lust, their greed, their anger, their violence. They were fully aware of the whole range of things that corrupt your spirituality, that bring you down, deep into the mud.

But just escaping from reality does not transform you. You may live for thirty years in the Himalayas, but if you come back to the world, you will find yourself the same man, with the same greed, with the same ambition, with the same anger, with the same lust. Perhaps in those thirty years you will have gathered much of everything that made you afraid. You are more cerebrally sexual than you were before, because thirty years of repression is going to collect the sexual energy and the sexual dreams and the sexual mind. It will become such a great force that it will be beyond you. It is going to drive you insane. And the same is true about all that is ugly – the greed, the desire for power, domination, anger, violence.

Remember one thing always: whatever any man has ever done, you are also capable of it. If somebody has murdered, never think that you are not capable of doing it. If somebody has committed suicide, never think for a single moment that you are incapable of doing it. If somebody has gone mad, don't feel good that you have not gone mad – you are also carrying the same possibility.

But as we all have the possibilities for evil, so we have the possibilities of becoming a Gautam Buddha. If one man was capable of becoming a buddha, an awakened one, every man from that very moment should remember he is capable of the same. But unfortunately, in the past, being a sannyasin became almost synonymous with renouncing the world. It was a very ugly and unfortunate association.

My whole effort is for you to remember that you have to become a lotus flower, not a coward. You have to live in the world, yet live in such a way that you remain untouched. If everybody starts renouncing the world, where will you go? If everybody goes to the Himalayas, then buses will be reaching there – tea shops, restaurants will be needed. The whole marketplace will be there. And for all these people you will need a movie house too, and television sets and transistors. Every sannyasin having his own transistor in his ear, deep in the Himalayas. It will be simply stupid. The whole idea is wrong. Where can you escape to if everybody goes there?

You can see it happening in the West. On every weekend, on every beach, there is not a single inch of space. All kinds of ugly bodies filling the whole beautiful beach and they are doing the same things they were doing at home: they are lying down and reading the same newspaper, looking at the same *Playboy*, listening to the same radio. And they have been driving for eight hours, bumper to bumper – tortured, irritated, annoyed.

It is very difficult for a driver not to be angry. If you can drive without any anger – particularly in America – you are a saint. Just a few days ago, I heard that people have started carrying guns in their cars because there is too much traffic and horns don't help. Just a few weeks ago, six people were shot dead just because there is a limit to patience. You go on honking the horn and the person ahead does not listen, but he is not responsible because there is somebody ahead of him who is not listening. Thousands of cars, and the speed has gone back to the primitive age. Now a bullock cart in India goes faster than the best car does in America. You can walk, and you will reach your destination earlier than if you were driving.

People became so angry that six people were shot with no enmity – they were strangers. And there is a fear that this will spread. Last week, the news came to me that just in the last three weeks, millions of people have purchased guns. It has been the all-time biggest sale of guns. The government has relaxed the rules, has become very lenient. At first it was taking care to whom it gave a license. Now it is not much of a problem at all; anybody can get a gun if he has the money. And millions of people have purchased guns. They are carrying their guns perfectly visible to the other drivers – listen to the honk, otherwise...

Great traffic, and where are you going? To the sea beach – for what? To be alone? For once at least, to be alone, at the weekend to lie down on the sea beach and to rest and relax – with the gun. Eight or twelve hours' driving and then one hour's rest in that ugly crowd – then back home, twelve hours' driving.

In the whole world more accidents happen on weekends than on any working day. More people are murdered on weekends than on any other day. More people commit suicide on weekends than any other day. Working days are more peaceful. But what is the problem: is everybody renouncing the world and going to the beach...?

It is good that people have not become renouncers. They have listened to all kinds of teaching. A few crazy people went to the monasteries, a few crazy people went to the Himalayas, but only a very small minority. Most of the people simply felt a little guilty, and to cover that guilt they worship those people who have renounced the world.

But I don't teach you renouncing the world. I teach you rejoicing in the world. This is an absolutely new method, a new definition of sannyas: not renunciation, but rejoicing, and still remaining beyond everything that surrounds you. This is your true spiritual birth.

You are pregnant with your own potential. You are pregnant with your own new life, new birth. This is going to happen to everybody. It is something to feel blessed about. It is something to sing and dance about, and celebrate.

> Osho,
> Being your sannyasin has given me the sense of freedom of not belonging to any particular place, country or even nationality. It's really great. I've felt able to move about without much fear and to be committed without feeling imprisoned. Why then, after nine years, do I feel a bitter sadness mixed with this sense of freedom?

Freedom has two sides and if you have only one side of it, a single side, you will feel freedom mixed with sadness. So you have to understand the whole psychology of freedom.

The first side is freedom *from*: from nationality, from a certain church, from a certain race, from a certain political ideology. This is the first part of freedom, the foundation of freedom. It is always from something. Once you have attained this freedom, you will feel very light and very good and very happy. For the first time you will start rejoicing in your own individuality, because your individuality was covered with all those things that you have become free of.

But this is only one half and then sadness will come because the other half is missing. Freedom *from* is fulfilled, but freedom *for* what? Freedom in itself has no meaning unless it is freedom for something, something creative – freedom to sculpt, freedom to dance, freedom to create music, poetry, painting. Unless your freedom turns into a creative realization, you will feel sad. You will see that you are free: your chains are broken, you no longer have any handcuffs, you no longer have any chains, you don't have any prison, you are standing under the starry night, completely free – but where to go? Then comes a sudden sadness. What path to choose?

Up to now there was no question of going anywhere – you were imprisoned. Your whole consciousness was concentrated on how to get free, your only anxiety was how to get free. Now that you are free, a new kind of problem has to be encountered. What to do now that you are free? Just freedom in itself does not mean anything, unless you choose a creative path. Either you go deeper into meditation for self-realization – that's what I was talking about: unless you become pregnant – or if you have a certain kind of talent that has not been allowed to develop because of your fetters ... You could not compose music because your hands were in chains, you could not dance because your feet were in chains. If you have a talent to be a dancer, then be a dancer. Then your freedom is complete, then the circle is complete.

Freedom *from* and freedom *for* – this is not something new that you are facing. It is being faced by every person who struggles first for freedom and then suddenly finds, 'Now that I am free, what am I going to do?' Up to now, he was so occupied, so engaged, so very busy. Even in his dreams he was thinking only of freedom. He never thought about what he was going to do when he achieved freedom.

What has happened is beautiful, but something more is needed. You have to become a creator. You have to find some creativity that fulfills your freedom, otherwise the freedom is empty. You need either to create something or to discover something. Either bring your potential to actuality or go inward to find yourself – but *do* something with your freedom.

Freedom is only an opportunity. It is not in itself the goal. It simply gives you the whole opportunity to do whatever you want to do. Now you are free and you are feeling sad because you have not used this opportunity yet. Meditation will do, music will do, sculpture will do, dancing will do, love will do. But do something with your freedom. Just don't sit with your freedom, otherwise you will become sad.

Freedom has to be a creative force in your life, not just a negative kind of freedom. The first part is negative: it is simply getting rid of the prison, it is getting rid of the chains. That you have done: now you are standing underneath the sky, completely lost.

Perhaps you have never realized that the imprisoned person has a certain reason for remaining imprisoned. That's why millions of people in the world remain prisoners of religion, of caste, creed, nation, color. They go on tolerating all kinds of prisons – not without reason. Their reason is that when they are imprisoned they don't have any responsibility, they don't have to be creators, they don't have to find some positivity in their freedom. It is enough for them to remain imprisoned because then others will go on taking care.

Why are people Hindus? Why are people Mohammedans? Why are people Christians? – because Jesus will take care. You need not be worried. All that you have to be is just a slave of the Christian church and then the Christian church will take care of all your sins, of all that is needed. One feels absolutely unburdened with responsibility – no responsibility.

But remember one thing fundamental to the whole question of freedom: responsibility and freedom are together. If you don't want to have responsibility, you can't have freedom either. They both come together or they both go together. If you leave responsibility, you have to accept slavery in some way or other.

Now, you had dreamed about freedom without ever thinking of the great responsibility that will follow. Freedom you have, but you have not fulfilled the responsibility; hence, a sadness lingers around you. You are absolutely capable of destroying this sadness. If you were capable of destroying your slavery, your chains, you are certainly capable of being creative. If you were able to destroy prisons, you can certainly make, create, something beautiful.

My own experience is: unless you become a creator in some way, your life will remain empty and sad. The only blissful people are the creators. It may be simply the creation of more consciousness, more experience of *sat-chit-anand*, more truth, more consciousness, more bliss. It may be simply an inner world of creativity or it may be something outer. But freedom has to become responsible, positive.

Your freedom is still negative. It is good that you are out of the prison, but it is not enough. Now you have to earn your bread. Up to now, *they* were supplying the bread. With the chains, they were supplying you a shelter, they were giving you clothes.

In American jails I asked many prisoners who were with me, 'How long have you been here?' One young man was with me in the first prison. I asked him how long he had been in, because he was not more than twenty-five. He said, 'I was twelve when I was first brought to prison for selling drugs.

But in prison, I found that I am free of all responsibility. Everything is supplied, medical care is available. No problem, no worries about tomorrow – from where the bread will be coming tomorrow. There is no worry. So since then, I have been coming again and again back to the prison. When they release me, I commit some small crime and I am back. And I love the place and I love the people. The first time I was afraid, but soon I found this is a better home.' This is how people become jailbirds. He was absolutely happy.

Everybody knew him – the doctor, the nurses, the jailer – and he was a nice person. He was very interested in health. I watched him because there was nothing else except him to watch. As many times as he would find time from television ... Otherwise, he was sitting in front of the television, and even while watching the television he started doing pushups.

He was known as 'the prince' by the other prisoners because he was a nice person – no bad habits, nothing. He just found that the jail seems to be the most simple way of living. And I asked the nurses, 'Why do you call him "the prince"?'

They said, 'He wants the best clothes, and he fights for them and he gets them – because he is known to everybody. He wants the best food. He wants everything that is available for the prisoners. He does not allow anybody else to be his partner in the cell, because he has so many of his own things. One bed is for sleeping in and on the other bed he has all kinds of things.

'He leaves those things with the nurses when he has to go out of the jail. He says, "I will be coming back, within a week at the most, so keep my things as I will be coming." And within a week he is back, and the magistrates know and everybody knows that he will be coming back – there is no point to it.'

Even the doctor told me, 'There is no point in sending him out because he comes back hungry, with dirty clothes. Nobody gives him a job, nobody gives him any employment. Again he becomes a street person. Here, he is the healthiest prisoner because he does so much exercise the whole day.' Even while looking at the television, he was also doing exercises.

And he slept without any anxiety for tomorrow, as everything would be available the next morning.

So many people inside the churches, inside synagogues, inside temples, attending mass ... Almost everybody is a member of a religion, a member of a nation, a member of a family, a member of an association, a political party, Rotary Club, Lions Club. People go on finding more and more chains. It seems to be very cozy. You have so much protection and no responsibility.

Freedom means you will have to be responsible for every act, for every breath; whatever you do or don't do, you will be responsible.

People are really in deep fear of freedom, although they talk about freedom. But my own experience is that very few people really want freedom because they are subconsciously aware that freedom will bring many problems that they are not ready to encounter. It is better to remain in a cozy imprisonment. It is warmer, and what will you do with freedom? Unless you are ready to be a seeker, a searcher, a creator ... Very few people want to go on a pilgrimage or to go into deeper silences of the heart, or to take the responsibility of love. The implications are great.

You will have to dispel that darkness, otherwise sooner or later you will enter some prison. You cannot go on burdening yourself with sadness. Before the burden becomes too much and forces you back into some slavery, into some imprisonment, change the whole situation by being a creative person. Just find out what is your joy in life, what you would like to create, what you would like to be, what you want to be your definition.

Freedom is simply an opportunity to find a definition for yourself, a true, authentic individuality, and a joy in making the world around you a little better, a little more beautiful – a few more roses, a little more greenery, a few more oases.

I am reminded of Madame Blavatsky, the founder of the Theosophical Society. She used to carry two bags in her hands, always. Either going for a morning walk or traveling in a train – those two bags were always in her hands. And she was throwing something out of those bags – from the window while sitting in the train – onto the footpath outside, by the side of the train. People used to ask, 'Why do you go on doing this?'

She laughed and said, 'This has been my whole life's habit. These are seasonal flower seeds. I may not come back on this route again' – she was a world traveler – 'but that does not matter. When the season comes and the flowers blossom, thousands of people who pass every day in this line of railway trains will see those flowers, those colors. They will not know me. That does not matter.

'One thing is certain: I am making a few people happy somewhere. That much I know. It does not matter whether they know it or not. What matters is that I have been doing something which will make somebody happy. Some children may come and pluck a few flowers and go home. Some lovers may come and make garlands for each other. And without their knowing, I will be part of their love. And I will be part of the joy of the children. And I will be part of those who will be simply passing by the path, seeing the beautiful flowers.'

A man who understands that freedom is nothing but an opportunity to make the world a little more beautiful, and to make himself a little more conscious, will not find himself sad.

It is good that you asked because if you had not asked, you might have carried this sadness which would slowly have poisoned your very freedom. A negative freedom is not very substantial, it can disappear. A freedom has to become positive.

Osho,
Is it true that women really think differently from men? Or is it just superstition?

It is not just superstition. And it is beautiful that it is not a superstition. The world needs the variety. Just think – a world where only men exist or a world where only women exist will be a poor world, very poor. Man and woman are polarities. It is between them that the world becomes colorful, beautiful.

Yes, there are problems too. Flowers don't come alone, they come with their thorns also. Days don't come alone, they bring their nights with them. Existence believes in polarities. It functions by what Karl Marx has called 'the dialectic.' The very process of evolution is dialectical. It is between the polarities that the whole of existence develops.

The woman is more intuitive, more instinctive. If she is not a meditator, she will be only instinctive. She thinks with her body. She is more rooted in the body than man, she is more aware of her body than man; and the body is our whole experience of the past evolution of millions of years. Man is more in the mind, more intellectual. But intellect is a very late development. While instinct is very ancient and very deep, intellect is very superficial and very new, very childish.

If man becomes meditative, he will find it more difficult to get rid of the intellect, because his whole education and upbringing is based in the mind, in the intellect – and to be a meditator, he has to drop all that he knows. The woman can become more easily a meditator because the jump from instinct to intuition is very simple. The jump from intellect to intuition is very difficult. But unfortunately, through the centuries the woman has not been allowed to participate in the world of meditation. She has, in fact, been rejected by almost all religions. The reason is clear: all religions were against the body, and the woman is body-oriented. Rejecting the woman, they were really rejecting the body orientation. They were all against the body. All their religious ideologies were intellectual.

And certainly the woman cannot participate easily in intellectual activities. She feels bored, she thinks, 'What nonsense does man go on talking about when there are so many juicy things happening?'

Man thinks the woman is good for just being used for her sexual body. But she is not good for any intellectual conversation, or any philosophical conversation. Men and women both know that the other is a little off the wall; they both agree on that point.

I have heard it said that man was made before woman to give him time to think of an answer to her first question.

Mendel Kravitz is stark naked in front of the open window doing his morning exercises. His wife enters the room and calls out, 'Mendel, you idiot! Draw those curtains. I don't want the neighbors to think that I married you for your money.'

Absolutely a different logic – that man may not have thought about it.

The priest with a reputation for his sermons on hellfire was leaving the neighborhood.

One old lady comes up to him and says, 'I am sorry you are leaving, Father. We never knew what sin was until you came.'

A handsome tomcat had just moved into the neighborhood, and all the other cats were very interested. One of them has the first date. 'Well,' they all cry the next morning, 'how did you get on?'

'A completely wasted evening,' replies the pretty cat. 'All he could talk about was his operation.'

There is certainly a great difference between man's and woman's ways of thinking, looking at things. But it makes life juicier, spicier. The world needs all kinds of musical instruments to create an orchestra. Just one kind of musical instrument will be really boring. The woman has not been respected in the past. That has kept the world in many ways poor, because the woman has not been allowed to express her way of looking at things.

She has been forced to think like man, to behave like man, to be just a shadow of man, but not to be herself. This was something absolutely ugly and to be condemned. I condemn it unconditionally. The woman should be allowed her way. She has not to be a carbon copy of man, she has not to think like the man. She has to think like herself, she has to be herself, and this will give the world a greater polarity.

And the further apart the individualities of man and woman are, the deeper will be the attraction between them. They should be strangers to each other – only then can they fall in love with each other. They should remain forever mysteries to each other. Only then can their love be a joy, a continuous discovery.

But the woman has been crushed. Her mysteries have been crushed. She has been used only as a production factory – not given the human rights which are basic. And that has made the world boring, ugly. Man has dominated to such an extent that the whole history is filled only with wars. If the woman had been allowed as much equality of opportunity for growth, the world would not have seen so many wars. In every war it is man who is killed, but it is woman who suffers.

It is easy to be killed, it is far more difficult to suffer. The mother suffers for her sons who are killed. The wife suffers when her loved ones are killed. The sister suffers when her brothers are killed. And their agony is going to last for their whole life. For those who are killed, it is a very small thing. It happens within seconds – and you are gone. But for centuries the woman has been just suffering.

No woman wants war because she is the ultimate victim, not man. It is man who creates war, it is man who fights war, but it is the woman who suffers. The woman is half of the world. If this half of the world had also been allowed to have its say, history would have been different. It would have been more peaceful, more loving, more sensitive, more aesthetic. There is still time to allow woman to be purely herself, unpolluted, unimpressed by man. And we will have a better world and a better humanity.

It is not unfortunate that they think differently. It is immensely significant and something to be deeply rejoiced in. But the woman needs her whole freedom. The world has lived under man's domination too long. It is time that woman had her share in participating in everything that is happening in the world. She has to contribute her part, which is going to be different from man's part.

And it will create a more harmonious whole than we have been able to create up to now. It has been a half circle. It has to be made a full circle. Life has to become total – man and woman together, contributing to the world all that they are born with: their different potentials, their different languages, their different ways of thinking, seeing, being.

15

The New Generation Is the Future

Osho,

What is the generation gap?

The generation gap is a very new thing in the world. Just half a century ago, nobody had even heard the term *generation gap*. Man has been here for thousands of years, but no society, no culture, no civilization was bothered about the generation gap. So, a few things have to be understood: how it came into existence, what it is, and what its final implications are.

In the past, by the age of six or seven at the most, children used to follow their fathers' professions, whatever it was, and howsoever little they could help ... If the father was a carpenter, the boy would try to bring wood, to help him in his own little way. And this was the only way that was available for the child to learn.

Always the older generation was the wiser generation. Just being old was enough to be wise, because knowing came only through one door – and that was experience. But experience needs time. Obviously the children were so new they did not have enough time to compete with the older generation. The older generation knew much more about everything – it had lived longer. That was the only measurement.

Those who had lived a long time became more and more respected because they were more experienced. They knew more things than others. This created the phenomenon of respect for the old. So whatever the older people were saying was bound to be right. There was no hesitation, there was no question, there was no doubt in the minds of the younger people. They believed in the older generation's religion, they believed in the older generation's superstitions, they believed in everything that the older generation was handing over to them.

The generation gap was not there, the generations overlapped. Before retiring, the older generation prepared the newer generation to take over the work. So there was an overlapping time of twenty years, thirty years, in which the younger generation was working under the older. And the older generation had all the power, all the prestige, and it molded the new generation according to its own ideals, morality, manners, etiquette.

There was no opportunity for the youth to declare their individuality. They were part and parcel of the older generation. They had come out of the womb of the mother, but they never came out of the womb of the older generation. By the time the older generation was retiring, becoming very old or dying, they became individuals. But by that time they themselves were old and they had to take care of the new generation that had come into being. So it was a very deeply connected world.

How did the generation gap come into being? It is dependent on many factors. Scientific progress has given people time for their children to be educated in the schools, colleges, universities. Now a new door has opened for learning. In the whole past there was only one possibility to learn and that was from the older generation. Now a new door has opened for learning, fast learning.

Experience moves at a very slow pace, but education depends on your intelligence. You don't have to depend on the pace at which education is moving. And during these twenty-five years of education, you are no longer under the control of your parents, of your society, of your priests.

In these twenty-five years you have no responsibility, you are not married. In the past, marriage used to happen too early – seven years, eight years, ten years, was old enough to get married. A ten-year-old boy gets married to a seven-year-old girl, and with the phenomenon of marriage comes a tremendous responsibility – they have almost become adults.

In other words, what I want to say is that in the past there has never been anything like youth. From children, people became adults. Youth was missing. Youth is a new phenomenon, the younger generation is a new phenomenon. It is a by-product of scientific progress. Scientific progress has given us so much technology and children are allowed to have many years in the universities to learn.

Secondly, when there was no science – and it was not long ago, just three hundred years – nothing was changing. Everything was as it had always been. The bullock cart had been there for centuries. It was still the only vehicle. So the older generation knew everything because everything was old.

With scientific progress the world of great books has completely disappeared. And progress is going faster and faster, so fast that scientists no longer write big books out of fear that if you write a big book, by the time it is completed it will be out of date; scientists are simply writing papers in the periodicals.

It was perfectly good for Charles Darwin to take thirty years to write a single book. Now it would simply be stupidity. By the time you are finished, all that you have written is wrong. Science has gone further, and the speed of science is so great that you cannot write with the same speed.

And science has developed into such a huge tree, with so many branches, that now to call anyone just a scientist is not right. It does not give you the right definition. He may be a physicist, he may be a chemist, he may be a mathematician. And the branches go on dividing into new branches. Now there is a new chemistry which has its own independent world – biochemistry.

Mathematics is no longer just one science. The old mathematics which is used in the ordinary world is no longer relevant for nuclear physics. It needs a new mathematics. So there are new mathematicians. The theorems of Euclidean geometry are no longer relevant. Now there is a totally new science opposing them, non-Euclidean geometry, which does not believe in any definitions of Euclid. For two thousand years Euclid was valid.

For two thousand years Aristotle's logic was the only logic. It is no longer the case. There is non-Aristotelian logic, there is non-Euclidean geometry, and every day sciences go on growing into different dimensions. And each dimension is so vast that the man who knows nuclear physics may not be aware at all of what chemistry is doing, or what is happening in the world of biology, or what is happening in the world of medical science. The scientist is no longer a man working alone, but only a specialist. Because of this specialization, things are moving very fast. Everybody has taken a small part and is developing it to its ultimate end.

When the student comes back home after five years at the university, he knows more than the older generation. That is the problem, that is what is creating the generation gap. To him, even his own parents look foolish, out of date, knowing nothing. This has taken away the respect that was taken for granted in the past. You cannot respect someone who looks to you completely out of date, out of tune, who does not know what has happened in the last twenty-five years.

The growth and the pace of growth is such that what before did not happen in twenty-five centuries now happens in twenty-five years. Naturally, a tremendous gap between the older and the newer generation is bound to happen. It is inevitable. The newer generation knows more, for the first time in the history of man, than the older generation.

If a student is intelligent enough, he can know more than the professors. He just has to spend more time in the library and be acquainted with the latest developments. The professor is already twenty years behind. All the professors, all the teachers, all the parents, all together are complaining of one thing: the newer generation is not respectful toward them. But they can't see one simple thing: the whole reason for respect has disappeared. You have to accept it, there is no other way. The person who knows more cannot respect the people who don't know that much.

And this gap is widening. It has stopped the communication between the older generation and the newer generation because conversation is so difficult. The parents have their own egos. They are not going to sit at the feet of their own children and learn from them. The children have *their* own egos, they know more: why should they sit at the feet of their parents and learn from them things which have proved to be completely wrong? They almost speak different languages. The influence of the older generation on the newer generation has completely gone. The relationship has become more and more formal. It is just a remnant of the past, but its substance, its soul, is dead. And this is going to happen more and more because every day science is developing with greater speed in all dimensions.

Specialization is a new thing in the world. In the past, you used to have a family doctor. Now you cannot have one because there are all kinds of specialists. The family doctor used to treat you as a whole organism, but now you have been divided into parts because each part is so detailed that a person goes on researching it his whole life, and yet he does not come to the end. So there are specialists who will be only taking care of your eyes. To you, eyes look small, but once you enter the world of specialization, the eyes have their own whole world. It is not a small thing, it is a very complicated phenomenon. There is a specialist who understands the brain. There is the specialist who takes care of your skin. Dermatology in itself is such a big science that there is no time for the person to think of other things. Somebody takes care of your ears, somebody takes care of your tuberculosis, somebody takes care of your cancer.

You can't have a single person taking care of you anymore, because there is no such thing as a physician, just purely a physician. In fact, there are only consultants who direct you ... Their whole work is to direct you to the specialist you should see, because specialization has gone to such minute detail that you need a consultant to decide to which specialist you should go. Your body is no longer taken as a whole organism, it has been dissected.

Science dissects everything into segments because each segment is so big that the whole body cannot be understood by one man alone. So when a student specializing in eyes comes home, he is not going to listen to his father's or mother's old recipes for cures for the eyes. He knows so much more that they seem simply ignorant and their recipes simply foolish, superstitious.

The older generation will have to learn one thing: to no longer expect respect. On the contrary, if you want to be still respected, give respect to your own children. This advice is meaningful only because of this generation gap. In the past it would have been meaningless. The older generation used to give love and the younger generation used to give respect. That was a settled thing for thousands of years. Now everything is unsettled; it is a chaos. And because the older generation is not getting the respect, they are withdrawing their love. The whole communication, the old relationship, is on the rocks. The new generation is still expected to respect, to listen, to follow – which is impossible.

In fact, the older generation will have to listen now and will have to give respect to the new people. And only if the older generation is humble enough to give respect to their own children, will the children perhaps be able to give respect. There is no other possibility. All communication lines are broken because they speak different languages. And it is not their fault, it is simply the situation.

'I never slept with a man before I slept with your father,' declares the stern mother to her wild daughter. 'Will you be able to say the same thing to your daughter?'

'Yes,' replies the girl, 'but not with such a straight face!'

'Just look at me!' declares old man Rubenstein. 'I don't smoke, drink or chase women, and tomorrow I will celebrate my eightieth birthday.'

'You will?' asked his son curiously. 'How? You neither smoke, nor drink, nor chase women. How are you going to celebrate?'

All lines of communication are completely blocked, but what old people are doing – condemning the new generation – is wrong. I can see the reason why things have changed. The new generation is not responsible. It is not their crime. It is simply a totally different set of circumstances. The older generation should show a little more understanding, a little more clarity, a little more readiness to listen to the new generation because they are the future. In the past, the past used to rule the future. Now things are otherwise; the future is going to rule over everything.

I have been a teacher and I have attended conferences of professors of the universities. The whole problem to them was how to create discipline, how to create respect. The students were getting out of hand, no discipline, no respect. I was the only exception. Because I said to them 'The whole responsibility is yours' they finally started dropping me from their conferences.

In the past, there were children who were married before they were ten. Sometimes children were even married when they were still in their mother's womb. Just two friends would decide: 'As our wives are pregnant, if one gives birth to a boy and the other gives birth to a girl, then the marriage is settled, promised.' The question of asking the boy and the girl did not arise at all. They were not even born yet. And for the parents there was no certainty: both might be girls, both might be boys. But if one was a boy and another was a girl, the marriage was settled. And people kept their word, their promises.

My own mother was married when she was seven years old. Her parents had to tie her to a pillar inside the house when the marriage party was coming and there were fireworks. At the reception there was music and dance, and everybody was out of the house.

My mother still reminds me, 'I could not understand why only I was left inside the house and tied! They wouldn't let me go out.' She had no understanding what marriage was. Like any child, she wanted to see all the beautiful things happening outside – the whole village had gathered, and she was crying.

My father was not more than ten years old, and he had no understanding of what was happening. I used to ask him, 'What was the most significant thing that you enjoyed at your wedding?'

He said, 'Riding on the horse.'

Naturally, for the first time he was dressed like a king, with a knife hanging by his side, and he was sitting on the horse, and everybody was walking around him. He enjoyed it tremendously. That was the most important thing that he enjoyed at his wedding.

A honeymoon was out of the question. Where will you send a ten- year-old boy and a seven-year-old girl for a honeymoon? So in India the honeymoon never used to exist and, in the past, nowhere else in the world either.

When my father was ten years old and my mother was seven years old, my father's mother died. After the marriage, perhaps one or two years afterward, the whole responsibility fell on my mother, who was only nine years old. My father's mother had left two small daughters and two small boys. So four children – and the responsibility on a nine-year-old girl and a twelve-year-old son. My grandfather never liked to live in the city where he had his shop. He loved the countryside. He had his own beautiful horse. When his wife died he was absolutely free.

You will not believe it, but in his time – and it is not long ago – the government used to give land to people for free because there was a lot of land but not so many people to cultivate it. So my grandfather got fifty acres of land free from the government. He loved living sixteen miles away from the city where he had left the whole shop in the hands of his children – my father and mother

– who were only twelve and nine years old. He enjoyed creating a garden, creating a farm, and he loved to live there in the open air. He hated the city.

Now, how can you think that there could be a generation gap? My father never had any experience of the freedom of young people of today. He was never young in that way. Before he could be young, he was already old, taking care of his younger brothers and sisters and the shop. And by the time he was twenty he had to arrange marriages for his sisters, marriages and education for his brothers.

I have never called my mother *mother* because before I was born she was taking care of four children who used to call her *bhabhi*. *Bhabhi* means 'brother's wife.' Because four children were already calling my mother *bhabhi*, I also started calling her *bhabhi*. Even today I call her *bhabhi*, but she is my mother, not my brother's wife. They have tried hard to make me change, but it comes so natural to me to call her *bhabhi*. All my brothers and sisters call her mother. Only I am crazy enough to call her *bhabhi*. But I learned it from the very beginning, when four other children...

And then I had a rapport with my uncles and with my father's sisters, a friendliness. They were a little older than me, but there was not much distance. I never thought of respect; they never thought of receiving respect. They loved me, I loved them.

It was a totally different world just seventy years ago. Generations were overlapping, and there used to be no youth. Now youth has come into existence and it will be growing bigger because as machines are going to take more and more jobs in the factories, in the offices, what are you going to do with people? They cannot be left doing nothing, otherwise they will do something absurd, something irrational, something insane. They will go mad. So you have to extend the period of their education. From twenty-five, soon it will be thirty-five. Then you will have to give them only a very small period of employment.

My own understanding is that there is going to be a second layer of university. After ten years of work, not more than that, you will be retired. By the time you are forty-five, you are retired. The best way will be to have another university that begins at the age of forty-five. It will be good, beneficial to the world, because knowledge will expand with such tremendous speed. But it will be very difficult as far as human relationships are concerned. They change with small things. You may not even think...

For example, in the past when there were no cars, it was impossible to fall in love with a girl who did not live in your own neighborhood. And then too it was very difficult because all the neighbors knew you, all the neighbors knew the girl, all the neighbors knew your parents, the girl's parents. Immediately you would be reported. You could not go far away. The moment the car came into existence and was put into the hands of the young people, love became a tremendous phenomenon.

Now taking your girl to any faraway place where nobody knows you, nobody knows the girl, nobody is going to complain to your parents, has become very easy. It has also become very easy to take out a different girl every day because the first girl will never know where you have gone. The car has managed a totally new world of love affairs. The inventors of the car never thought that it would change the whole structure of society.

In America, the average person lives in one city for not more than three years, remains in one job for not more than three years, remains in one marriage for not more than three years. Strange, but things are changing so fast. When you change your job, it is not only the job that changes. You have to change the city, the place you live in, the house. You become acquainted with new secretaries, new typists. You were getting fed up with the old ones, but the new ones bring new life to you.

One of my attorneys was going to come this week but then he informed me, 'I am sorry, I will not be able to come because my wife is divorcing me, so I am going through the process of divorce. And I will end up almost a pauper because she is a powerful woman. Everything is in her name – the house, the car – so once we are divorced, I am on the streets. She is going to take everything. And living with her has become so difficult that I would prefer to be on the streets than continue living with her. The person who is going to marry her I think of as my best friend, because he is taking on the whole responsibility, not realizing what is going to happen to him soon.'

In the past people lived in one village their whole lives. Perhaps they went once in a while to the nearby town or city. But even today in India there are millions of people who have not seen a railway train because they have never gone that far from their small village. They are perfectly satisfied in their village. They are poor, but they don't have the longing to go anywhere. They have a small piece of land and they are too attached to it – they cannot leave it.

America is continuously on the move. It is the car that keeps people moving. When I was in America I wanted to see trains, but I could not see any. Five years I was there. I inquired, 'I don't see any railway trains. I never come across railway crossings.' I was informed that most of the people fly. The remaining ones who enjoy traveling use their cars. Trains are almost old-fashioned. It takes seven days for a train to cross America. Who is going to waste seven days in a train? The distance can be covered by plane within two hours. You can have your supper in London, your lunch in Mumbai, your coffee break in Tokyo, your supper in New York.

With this speed, there are bound to be many implications; old ties cannot remain. So people have their girlfriends all around the world. It was not possible in the past to have a girlfriend if you were married. Even if you were not married, then too it was not possible to have a girlfriend. It was against the older generation's morality. They never gave you the chance. Before you could even think of any girl, you were married. Marriage came almost naturally. Just as you got your sister, your brother, you got your wife. Before you became aware what was happening, you were already caught. There was no question of choice.

There is a certain human psychology. If you are living, for example, with your sisters, with your brothers, you simply love them. Not that they are very beautiful or something unique. They are just your sisters, they are your brothers, and you have lived so long together that a liking naturally arises. In the past, love had no existence, it was only liking. You lived together with your wife for years before you could make love to her, and a certain liking ... There was no alternative, so you were almost in chains.

You could not have any friendship with any woman. That was prohibited. Your only possible relationship was with your own wife, and that, too, deep in the darkness of the night when everybody was asleep. You could not even whisper. Somebody might wake up because families were extended families with fifty people, forty people living under one roof.

It was good in a way because you never saw the woman, her whole topography. You never saw the man. Everything was happening in the dark. You never got fed up. Now everything is happening under electric light and there are idiots who even have cameras fixed in their bedroom to take pictures of what kind of stupidity they are doing, so later on they can enjoy them in their photo album.

Small things make such long-lasting and deep changes in life that one is not aware that this is going to happen. The new generation is going to have a greater future and, for the first time, the older generation has to learn to be humble, loving. Perhaps if they are humble and loving they may still be respected for their love and for their humbleness, and there may continue a certain communication. But they have to understand clearly that they represent the past and the new generation represents the future – and the gap is large.

If they go on sticking to their ideologies and to their churches and to their superstitions, the gap will become bigger. It looks strange to learn from your own children, but I don't think it is strange – just the situation has changed. For thousands of years, children have learned from you. Now it is time to have a change. Start learning from your children. Start looking at the world through the eyes of your children, and the gap will disappear. But the gap will disappear only if the older generation changes its attitudes. It is not going to disappear the way they are behaving all over the world.

They are trying to force the new generation to go according to them, as they have always been going. But they don't see that the whole world has changed. Nothing is anymore the same. New things have brought new possibilities. The inventors had no idea what their inventions would do, but small things can have a tremendous effect. The world cannot be the old way again. People cannot leave all the facilities, comforts and luxuries that technology and science have given to them.

So the gap is going to become bigger and bigger, unless the older generation proves more prudent. Now is the time to prove that you are really wise. Up to now, it was just taken for granted. This is the challenge to the older generation to behave wisely and intelligently. Then the gap can be bridged. But it will be bridged from the side of the older generation, not the younger generation.

Osho,
When I see you, sometimes I see a twinkle of childlike innocence, a warmth that I call love. And sometimes I see a vast emptiness, as cool and crystal clear and impersonal as the night sky. Are both these qualities in you? Are both these qualities in me? It seems impossible but true.

You have stumbled on a very significant truth. The childlike innocence and the warmth of love that you see are not contradictory to '...a vast emptiness as cool and crystal clear and impersonal as the night sky.' In fact, they are both sides of the same coin. If you become childlike, innocent, there will be a warmth and love in you. But on the other side of the coin, you will be just like the cool, impersonal nothingness, just like a starry night.

Both these things happen together. The first happens – the coolness, the nothingness – and then the innocence of the child brings the warmth. But it is always difficult for the intellect to figure it out when it sees something which appears to be the opposite.

For example, if you dig up the roots of a rosebush, you cannot conceive that these roots are connected with the roseflowers. The roots are ugly. There seems to be no likeness in any way possible between the roseflowers and the roots. But the roots are giving all the juice and life to the roseflower. It is the roots which are giving the color, the liveliness, the warmth, the beauty to the roseflower. Life is full of such apparent opposites. This is your inner opposite: if inside you, you become as cool as the starry night – nothingness, impersonal – this will be your root; then your childlike innocence, warmth, love will be your expression as a flower. They cannot exist separately.

This is in me and these qualities are in you too. Once you have become aware of the phenomenon, it won't take long for you to realize the same roots and the roses within you. Only when you experience it within you, will you be able to understand – not just intellectually, but existentially. But you have certainly stumbled on a tremendously great truth.

You are saying, 'It seems impossible but true.' Truth *is* impossible, but anyway it happens. It only appears impossible, but it is our very potential. Existence is so full of mysteries: never think in terms of impossibilities. Everything is possible. The impossible is only an idea of the mind.

Can you understand how these green trees are growing upward, against gravitation? It is impossible. But they are managing perfectly well – all the trees of the world – and they have never thought about gravitation, they don't care about it. Scientists have been very troubled that trees grow one hundred and fifty feet high. And not only the trees, but the juice, the water, has to go upward without any pumping system in the tree. How is it managing? You cannot take water one hundred and fifty feet high without an electric pump.

But these trees have their own mystery, and it is so subtle that when scientists became aware of it they could not believe it: for millions of years these trees – ignorant, uneducated, not knowing anything of science – have been doing a miracle. The miracle is that on the top where every tree is searching for the sun ... That is the trick: every tree is searching for the sun. So whenever the trees grow thick, the trees will also go higher. It is a competition. Whoever goes higher will survive longer.

They are seeking the sun so the sun can evaporate water from their tops. And it is a connecting link; they function like blotting paper. When on the top the sun takes the water as vapor, the top becomes dry, the blotting paper becomes dry. It goes on taking the water from underneath and the second layer of blotting paper becomes dry. And because the second layer has become dry, it takes water from a lower one. In this way, for one hundred and fifty feet the tree goes on carrying its water without any pumping system. But it needs the sun, otherwise it will die.

It is the sun against gravitation. The tree is managing a conspiracy against gravitation in combination with the sun. With the help of the sun it is going higher, taking juices from the roots. It has been found that roots have a certain sensitivity which even we don't have. A few people have it. You must have heard of a few people who can just walk around and tell you where you will find water. But these people also take help from the trees, which you may not have noticed. They always carry a branch, a fresh branch cut from the tree, in their hands. The whole trick is that they carry the branch in their hands. Their hands are very sensitive. They don't know anything about water, but the tree branch knows. So wherever the tree branch gives them a jerk – just so slight that you cannot see it, but they can feel the jerk – the tree branch is interested, there is water.

They are deceiving people, they are trying to show that they are working a great miracle. It is not a miracle; it is a simple method the trees have been using. Wherever the water is, the branch is bound to move. And they have only to be sensitive to the branch, where it moves, which side, where it points. They will go round and round, again and again, at the same point, to make completely sure where the point is, where you will find water.

It has been found that the roots of trees move hundreds of feet away just to find water. But how do they manage to know that a hundred feet south or north there is water and, strangely enough, even water in a water pipe, a hundred feet away? The tree roots are so sensitive toward water that although the water may be going through a pipe, they become aware of it. And it has been found that they break the pipe. They enter the pipe and they start drinking *your* water for their own purposes, sending it one hundred and fifty feet high. It is stealing, and they don't pay any taxes! They don't care about your water corporation. But they manage.

In the commune in America we were living in a desert. Only one type of tree grows in that desert. That tree has learned ways to exist in the desert, it has adapted itself to desert life. As the camel is adapted to the desert, those trees are also adapted.

Their whole strategy is – because they don't have any water as far as their roots are concerned – to gather moisture from the air, particularly in the night when the desert becomes cool and there is moisture, humidity. From each leaf, from every branch, they suck in the moisture, and that is their only way of existence. They don't use their roots because as far as the roots are concerned, it is pure desert; there is no water at all. But they learned a new method – just the opposite – of absorbing moisture through the leaves.

Ordinary trees everywhere evaporate water from the leaves and suck water from the roots. But desert trees function in a totally opposite way. They don't use their roots. They use their roots only to keep them standing, just as a support for them to stand – that's all. It is sheer intelligence: in the night they will suck in all the moisture from the air –and they live perfectly well.

It is a wrong idea that existence is unintelligent. It is more intelligent than you can think. Its whole functioning is full of intelligence and nothing is impossible. You just have to find the right way and then impossibles become possibles. Your mind is a little cowardly. Your mind wants things according to it, it wants everything in accordance with its own conditioning. That makes many things impossible. You have to learn not to force existence to be in accordance with you. That is the irreligious way, and you are not going to win.

The religious way is to be humble and function according to existence. Be natural and let nature decide the course of your being. And nature is tremendously intelligent. It gives you birth, it gives you life, it gives you your intelligence. Unless it is an ocean of intelligence, from where can you get your intelligence? – which is small, certainly, in comparison to the universal intelligence.

It is my experience that both these things come together. A silent nothingness, impersonal coolness ... But remember not to hear me saying 'coldness'; I am simply calling it 'coolness.' Coldness is a totally different thing: coldness is a closedness. Coolness is not a closed experience. It is very lively, very open, a fresh breeze passing through you continuously. You are being renewed every moment – that's why you are cool.

And because you are impersonal, you are innocent. Otherwise you cannot be innocent. And because you are innocent and alive and fresh every moment, there comes a certain loving warmth in you which is unaddressed to anybody – just like a fragrance. Anybody can rejoice in it who is capable of being receptive.

I want my people to make this impossible possible. When this impossible becomes possible, you will have the total existential understanding of *sat-chit-anand*, of truth, of consciousness, of bliss.

16

God Is Your Concentrated Fear

Osho,
When I was coming for discourse, my heart was trembling with fear; I felt as if I was going to die. Death seemed to be very close.

Later in the discourse, I felt an infinite joy from some unknown source. Are these just two colors of love for you, or is it something else? Will you please comment?

Death is always close by. It is almost like your shadow. You may be aware, you may not be aware, but it follows you from the first moment of your life to the very last moment. Death is a process just as life is a process, and they are almost together, like two wheels of a bullock cart. Life cannot exist without death; nor can death exist without life. Our minds have an insane desire: we want only life and not death.

We don't look at the existential truth, we always cling to our own insane desire. Any desire that goes against nature is insane. And this desire is in almost every living creature, not only human beings. Even the trees are afraid of death, but trees can be forgiven. They are not conscious beings, they are only unconscious – fast asleep.

But you are a little bit awake: you can sense the presence of death. Hence the possibility opens for a deeper understanding: life and death are both together, two extremes of one energy. Life is the active force and death is the inactive force. Life is the positive electricity and death is the negative electricity, but they cannot be separated.

You are saying, 'When I was coming for discourse, my heart was trembling with fear; I felt as if I was going to die.' Those who are aware, are aware that death is possible at any moment – the very next moment and you may be gone. This awareness is going to help you to live this moment as deeply as possible, because death can cut your roots without informing you, without any previous intimation of 'I am coming.' It simply comes. You know only when it has happened. But it is not the greatest misery. The greatest misery is when there was the chance and the opportunity, you did not live – you went on postponing.

Life is an opportunity. Death is the end of the rope. If you understand death, your life will become intense and total. But instead of understanding death, you become overwhelmed by it. Hence the heart starts trembling with fear. Fear is not going to help at all, fear is going to cloud your mind even more. There has never been any understanding out of fear.

So whenever you feel fear, it is a tremendous opportunity to understand that life is momentary, it is ephemeral, it is made of the same stuff as dreams are made of. How real the dream looks when you are asleep – in fact, more real than your experiences when you are awake. You may have never thought about it, but while you are awake you can doubt: 'Perhaps what I am seeing may be just a dream.' I may be a dream, you may be a dream, this whole communion may be happening just as a dream. Soon you will be awake and you will find, 'My God! It was just a dream.'

There is a possibility when you are awake to suspect, to doubt the reality that surrounds you. But when you are asleep, you cannot even doubt the existence of the dream. It is so real, it is more real than reality. Have you ever doubted any dream, thinking that perhaps what you are seeing is a dream? The moment you doubt, you are awake, and the dream is immediately finished. The dream can remain there only if you are totally asleep, so deep that no doubt, no suspicion, can arise in you.

But to those who have understood both life and death as nothing but two aspects of one reality, the dream and the so-called reality of your waking consciousness are not basically different. Just as in the morning you wake up and the dream life is finished, one day in death you wake up into another reality and all that was real up to then – for seventy years – becomes just a dream. Not even a trace of it is left anywhere in your consciousness.

Death is a constant reminder – 'I can come any moment. Be prepared.' And what is the preparation? The preparation is: live life so totally, so intensely, be so aflame with it that when death comes there is no complaint, there is no grudge. You are absolutely ready because you have lived life so totally, you have known all its mysteries – there is no point in living anymore. Death has come exactly at the right time, when you may have thought to die yourself. I call that death perfect which comes at the moment when you yourself may have thought, 'It is enough.'

Death comes, and you understand that life has been lived totally, so now there is no point to go on breathing and go on waking and sleeping unnecessarily – because nothing new is going to happen. Now everything is past and there is no future. In such a moment, death is a welcome guest. And unless you are ready to welcome death, know well that you have missed life. Those who feel sadness and fear about death are the people who have missed the train. But in our unconsciousness, we are all continuously missing the train. The train is moving every moment, just in front of you, but somehow you go on missing.

I have told you about those three professors, all belonging to the Department of Philosophy...

They were talking, standing on the platform. They had come to send off one of them on a long journey. But they got so involved in their talking and discussions that the train left. It was only when the last compartment was moving just in front of them that all three became aware of it. They all ran. Two jumped into the compartment, one could not.

An old man, a porter on the railway station, was watching the whole scene. And this man standing there was looking so sad that the old man said, 'I can understand that you missed the train, but don't be worried, because within two hours another train will be coming.'

He said, 'I am not worried about myself. I am worried about those two fellows who have entered the compartment. They had come to send *me* off...'

But such was the rush – and everything had to be done so quickly.

This is our state. It can happen to anybody, just because our actions arise out of our unconsciousness. Your heart trembling with fear is nothing but your misunderstanding. As far as death is concerned, what you experienced is true for everybody, every moment, until you die. It is not true only for those who are already dead. In one thing they are better off than you: they cannot die anymore – no fear, no trembling of the heart. They just lie down and rest in their graves. Nothing is going to happen to them anymore.

But as long as you are alive, the possibility of death is absolutely certain. Only the timing is not certain. But the happening is absolutely certain. What does it matter whether you die after seven days or seven years or seventy years? One thing is certain: you are going to die. Life is not something that you can go on missing. Otherwise at the moment of death you will feel the greatest misery and pain, the deepest agony, from missing the whole opportunity that was given to you.

Existence gives so abundantly, it is not miserly. You are just not alert enough to use the opportunity to transform yourself into something immortal, eternal, into some experience which will make you beyond the reach of death. Just fearing death is not of any help. If you see that death is following you, it is time to start searching deeper into yourself for that point which is beyond death. We have been calling that point *sat-chit-anand*: the truth of your being, the ultimate consciousness of your life, and the tremendous blessing of your coming to flower.

You are also saying that as you sat in the discourse you felt '...an infinite joy from some unknown source.' There is nothing mysterious about it. You came to the discourse trembling, overwhelmed by the fear of death, and here you saw laughter and music and you became one with the commune. You forgot your tiny ego and its fear of dying. You fell into deep harmony with all who are present here. This harmony is the source of your joy, not any unknown source. This harmony is the source of your infinite joy, and this harmony is also the source of your deep feeling of love for me.

It is not something unknown, it is something very clear, you just have to be a little more conscious. Then this clarity will give you all the clues to things that go on happening in your being, but you won't know from where they come, where they are going. Everything seems to be a misunderstanding. But out of harmony, out of love, out of joy, arises understanding.

One day a psychiatrist was invited by the local women's club to give a talk about sex. He accepts the invitation, but because his wife is a bit of a prude, he tells her he is going to talk about fishing. The next day the psychiatrist's wife happens to meet the sponsor of the talk in the local supermarket.

'Your husband,' gushes the woman, 'gave a splendid speech last night.'

'I am surprised to hear that,' replies the wife. 'After all, he has no experience in that area.'

'Come on, now,' says the other woman blushing, 'he seemed to know a great deal about the subject.'

'Maybe,' replies the wife, 'but he only tried it twice. The first time he threw up after eating what he caught and the second time he lost his rod!'

But that kind of misunderstanding goes on. You have to be a little more clear.

> Osho,
> Again I feel this fear inside me: the fear of connecting with you really deeply; the fear of falling apart, and then not being able to function anymore in this world; the fear of being helpless and absolutely vulnerable.
> What to do? My mind is already set that enlightenment is not going to happen to me before the death of my body. Is this okay?

Fear arises in many situations. Deep down it is always there, but not active. It is inactive, so that you don't become aware of it. But fear is the very foundation of unconscious life. All your actions arise out of it. You want money, you want power, you want prestige. What are all your ambitions except to cover up your deep hidden fear? Perhaps money may be a security, perhaps power may make you more protected, secure, safe. Perhaps respectability, society, your religion, God ... All these are by-products of fear.

Why do you believe in God? You have not seen him, you don't have any evidence that any such thing exists anywhere. But you know that without God you will not be able to repress your fear. Your fear needs God. It is a fear-oriented hypothesis. Your fear needs a father figure to protect you in dangerous situations, to help you when you need the help, to become a light in your darkness, to support you when you feel you are falling into an abysmal abyss. God is your concentrated fear.

And there are lesser gods. Money is a lesser god – more visible, hence more people cling to money. But they don't want to take any chances, so they also go on donating to the church, just to keep a bank balance in God's bank. And here they go on clinging to the money because in life it seems money gives a certain security. At least tomorrow is certain. You will have food, you will have the house, you will have your wife, you will have your husband, you will have your children.

Our whole life seems to be circling around the center of fear. It is present twenty-four hours a day, but we become aware of it only in certain situations. You start feeling the presence of death. Perhaps you have seen somebody dying, perhaps you have seen somebody very old on the road and it has reminded you about the next step. That fellow is going to step into a grave soon. You are also in the same queue, but how far are you? Maybe a little longer distance, but sooner or later – and the queue is becoming shorter every moment. You are coming to the window.

Anything may trigger the idea of death in you – just a dry leaf falling from the tree is enough to remind you of death. Just a few days ago it was so green and so young, so beautiful. It used to dance in the morning sun. What has happened? A dying leaf falling from the tree was the cause of Lao Tzu's enlightenment. Seeing the dry leaf falling, he accepted his death so totally that there was no question of any fear. If this is how life functions, then there is no question of fear.

Have you ever thought that death is the only certainty in life? Everything else may fail. Love may fail, money ... Nothing is certain. You know what is happening in America. Just a few days ago the dollar was on top, the biggest and the strongest currency in the world. It will never be again. It has gone down the drain. There is no possibility for it to rise again. It will have to go even lower. And how proud the dollar was! And now its place has been taken by the German mark or by the Japanese yen. The Japanese yen is now the topmost, but it cannot remain at the top.

Nobody can remain at the top forever. Once you have reached the top, the next thing is to fall. How long can you balance? It is almost like in a circus when somebody is balancing on the rope. How long? Just for a few seconds it is possible to manage it, and that too needs tremendous exercise and rehearsals. And still the fear is there. Underneath there is a net, because even after so many rehearsals, so much practice, nobody knows – anything is possible. The rope may break, the rope has not been trained not to break. Just any small thing: the woman who is walking on the rope may sneeze just in the middle. You cannot know – anything is possible. You cannot prevent a sneeze.

Money is more visible. People believe in money more than in God. They may pretend that they believe in God more, but their actual life shows something else. But the reason is the same. Whether it is money or power or prestige or God or religion, the reason is the same. You are living in fear and you are trying to protect yourself somehow.

But death is only one of the reasons you are aware of fear. Love can also make you aware of fear, because love is also a kind of death. Your ego has to die, only then is love possible. It is a very partial death, but still something close to death. Hence people talk about love, but are very afraid of love. They talk about love because they feel very lonely. That loneliness creates fear.

Man is really in great trouble. The old proverb is right which says 'Life is not a bed of roses.' It is not. Such great dilemmas! Loneliness creates fear. Out of that fear you want to be in love, to be intimate with someone so that your loneliness disappears. But as you come closer to somebody, again another fear – you may be lost.

You have to be humble enough to reach somebody's heart, otherwise there is no way. The ego will be a barrier, it will keep a distance. And love is possible only when there is no distance at all – the ego has to give way. That ego giving way appears to be almost a death because you have been so identified with the ego.

So man is split. Half of him wants to love, half of him pulls back – don't go any further, you are too close, there is danger. Your fear is that if you come in deeper communion with me, you will fall apart. Naturally, nobody wants to fall apart. And a great fear arises. But there is a strong magnetic pull also. Deep down you know that whatever can fall apart is not you. And whatever can fall apart is going to fall apart sooner or later. How long can you hold it? It is not your authentic reality. It is just all false personality which needs continuous holding. Not even for a moment can you leave it alone, otherwise it will fall apart.

I know a few people who are even afraid to sleep.

When I came to know the first person who was afraid to sleep, I could not think what the problem might be. I went because his son had come to me – he was my student. He said, 'My father is in tremendous misery. Apart from that, he is a successful man. He is rich enough, there is no need to worry.'

Then I asked, 'What is the problem?'

He said, 'The problem is, he is afraid of sleep. He says, "What is the guarantee that I will wake up?"'

Now, how to give this man a guarantee? And naturally the fear seems to be logical. There is no guarantee. You may not wake up. Many people have not woken up. Once they have gone to sleep, they have gone. But if you become afraid of such things, life becomes absolutely impossible. So he keeps himself awake and he keeps his whole family awake. He is driving everybody mad.

His son said to me, 'Do something, because to keep himself awake, everybody else has to be awake. He will not let anybody sleep. He knocks on everybody's doors asking "Are you awake?" Just a few minutes of sleep and his knock comes. If everybody sleeps in the house, it will be very difficult for him to remain awake. All the lights have to be on. And he goes on making everybody stay awake because there is danger.'

Now this man looks insane, but if you try to understand, you will see that this is your fear also. You are saying you are afraid that you will fall apart. And I guarantee: you *will* fall apart! So what is the fear? Do it once – once and for all! Then there will be no fear. Fall apart and let us see what falls apart. Not your legs, not your hands, nor your eyes ... Nothing that is really yours is going to fall apart, only your false notions about yourself: your personality, your ego, your knowledgeability, these are the things which are going to fall apart. But they are not worth holding on to.

Once they are gone you will have a far more beautiful space available to you. Don't cling to things which don't have any authentic reality. And the authentic reality need not be supported by you. It is there, it is not going to fall apart. Only the false can disappear, only your shadow – not you. But why should you be afraid if your shadow disappears? Your shadow is not you. Your shadow has nothing to do with you. It has no reality, it has no existence, it has no meaning in your life. But you have become too identified with your shadows.

I have read *Aesop's Fables* more deeply than the greatest holy scriptures of the world because *Aesop's Fables* have more significance and more meaning, and tremendous psychological truths which are completely missing in your holy scriptures.

One of the parables of Aesop is...

A fox gets up early in the morning as the sun is rising. She comes out of the cave looking for some breakfast. But then, just as she comes out, she sees her shadow. In the early morning sun the shadow is very long. She says, 'My God! I am this big! Even a camel will not be enough for breakfast.' She starts searching for a camel – it will be even better if she can get an elephant.

But time passes and she does not come across any elephant, any camel, and it is getting hot, and in fact the time for breakfast has passed. It is time for lunch and she is feeling really hungry. The sun has come just above her head. She looks another time at her shadow. It has shrunken completely, it is just under her.

She says, 'My God, I never thought that hunger can do that much. I have shrunken. I used to be so long – just in the morning – so huge and just missing one breakfast ... Now even if I can only get a rat that will do for lunch.'

Just a small parable written for children, but if even an old man can understand it ... It has a tremendous psychological truth. We are all living identified with our shadows and the fear that the shadow may disappear. It is better not to come too close to someone who can make your shadow disappear, who can make you aware of what is false in you and what is not false, because the moment you become aware about the false, it falls apart. But my suggestion to you is: rather than trembling your whole life about the false, being afraid about its death, it is better once and for all to get it finished.

And you are saying, '...and then not being able to function any more in this world.' Strange fears! I have been functioning perfectly well in this world. My family was also worried, my neighbors were also worried, my friends were worried, my professors, my teachers, 'How are you going to manage?' Everybody was worried, except me.

I used to tell them, 'Trees can manage, animals can manage. I don't think there is much of a problem. The whole of existence is managing. I will also find some way.'

But my father was very much concerned. Almost in tears he would say to me, 'I am worried. I have loved you so much, although you have given me more trouble than any of my children. But perhaps because of that I have loved you more than any of my children.' And he had enough children – eleven children. Whenever he would find me alone he would say, 'I continuously think of your future because you are going to be good for nothing.'

I said, 'You are right. I am going to be good for nothing. But you need not be worried, because I don't see any problem in being good for nothing. Existence will take care.'

And he proved right. I turned out to be good for nothing. I have never done anything – neither good nor bad – but I have lived perfectly, totally, intensely. The way I wanted to live, I have lived that way, without caring even if the whole world was against me. I have not cared. I have lived my own way, my style, because I don't think that I have to listen to anyone. I have my life and I am responsible only to myself, to nobody else.

Why are you so afraid that you cannot function anymore in the world if you come closer to me? All these people are closer to me and they are all functioning perfectly well, better than anybody else. And then you ask me, 'What to do?' First thing, just fall apart. Come closer, become good for nothing, and just see how existence takes care of you. A little trust.

And then, fear upon fear, 'My mind is already set that enlightenment is not going to happen to me before the death of my body.' Here there are so many enlightened people. They don't tell it because if they tell it, people will laugh about it. So they keep it secret, but they know perfectly well that they are enlightened. They are all alive, more alive than you will find people anywhere else. And their enlightenment has not disturbed anything.

My enlightenment is not a small thing that can be disturbed because you smoke cigarettes. You can smoke, just smoke in an enlightened way! My enlightenment does not prevent you from anything – just change the quality. It does not teach you to escape from the world. I am absolutely in favor of the world.

I call those people cowards whom you have worshipped as saints. I call them people who have betrayed the beautiful earth. And I want my people not to betray the earth. You can reduce my whole vision of life to a single sentence: not to betray the earth. Trust it, it is your mother, it is your very source of life.

And why should you be so certain that you will not become enlightened before the death of your body? If so many people can become enlightened ... Just remember one thing: become enlightened and don't tell it to anybody; telling creates trouble. Then people start asking questions: 'You are enlightened, so why are you doing this? And why are you doing that? And why are you going to the Blue Diamond Restaurant?' Once you say you are enlightened, you are in trouble.

Once it happened...

I was going from one meeting to another meeting in Mumbai, and one of my very close friends was driving me and we came to a bistro, a beautiful place. He just jokingly asked me, 'Should we go in?'

I said, 'That's a great idea.'

He still thought that I was not going to go in, but he wanted to see how far the thing would go. So he stopped his car. I got out of the car. He started feeling a little nervous.

I said, 'Come on!'

He said, 'But if somebody knows you and knows me there will be trouble.'

I said, 'Don't be worried. You just come behind me.'

He had to come because I entered. There was a striptease going on; a woman was dancing nude. I pulled up a chair just in front of her. The manager had heard me speak somewhere. He came running to touch my feet and my friend was perspiring ... It was air-conditioned.

I said, 'You are not enlightened. I am enlightened. Why are you perspiring? And he is touching my feet, not yours.' Even the naked woman came to touch my feet. When the manager came, naturally...

My friend was almost having a nervous breakdown.

You will not believe it – I had to drive because he was not in a position to drive. He was lying back, just resting, getting better before we reached the next place.

He said, 'This is the last time. I will never drive you anywhere. You have almost killed me!' Because not only the manager came, the woman came and all the customers, and there were about three hundred people in the bistro. 'And there were many who recognized you, who recognized me.'

There was great silence, all the music stopped, everything went topsy-turvy.

The manager asked me, 'What can I do?'

I said, 'Just bring good ice cream.'

So I ate the ice cream. He hadn't even the courage to ask for payment and we went out. You don't ask payment from an enlightened man!

But since that time my friend has stopped driving me. Before that he used to drive me in Mumbai from one place to another place. Since that day he lost his nerve.

What is the problem? Just become enlightened but don't tell anybody! And then you are free to do anything you want. Inside you are enlightened. Outside you are free to act. I am not taking you away from the world. I am teaching you the art of how to be in the world and yet not be part of it.

You are hoping to get enlightened when your body dies so that you don't commit any mistake. But if you are committing so many mistakes, you can commit them even when you are dead. Committing mistakes is something which becomes habitual. If you have been committing mistakes all your life, do you think just by death you will stop committing mistakes? You will commit them somewhere else, but you will continue. Don't wait – death will come. But you don't have to postpone enlightenment until after death.

The reason is clear: you are worried that enlightenment means that, just like me, you will have to remain in one room. This is *my* way. It is not necessary for you to be in your room. You can be in anybody's room. Here it is happening every day. People see somebody suddenly coming out from somebody else's room. They cannot believe what is happening. In fact, it seems no room belongs to anybody. People are simply changing every night. And all are enlightened people. I don't take enlightenment seriously. It is the most hilarious thing in the world.

Paddy decides to go rabbit shooting, but when he gets to his favorite field he sees the village priest is already there. Paddy watches with fascination as the priest holds his finger over a rabbit hole and immediately a rabbit pops out. The priest grabs it and puts it into a sack. He repeats this unusual but very successful technique until his sack is full of rabbits. Paddy stops the priest and asks him how he does it.

'Easy,' says the priest. 'Put your finger on your wife's pussy and then hold it over a rabbit hole. They can't resist the smell, so when they come out, grab them!'

As this sounds much easier than shooting, Paddy rushes home to find Maureen bent over scrubbing the floor. He lifts up her skirt and applies his finger as instructed.

Without looking up, Maureen giggles, 'Holy Moses, Father! Rabbit hunting again?'

17

Politicians Are Great Criminals

Osho,

Is there any difference between the criminals and the politicians?

The criminal is poor; he is uneducated, unsophisticated and simple-hearted. The politician is a hypocrite – cunning, diplomatic, sophisticated. But their essential reality is the same. In other words, the criminal is a politician who could not succeed, and the politician is a criminal who has succeeded in attaining power. But their psychologies are not different. They both want power and domination; they both want to do things without any concern for the consequences; they are both end-oriented, they don't bother about the means.

Their basic philosophy is the same: the ends justify the means. If you succeed, then how you have succeeded – using right means or wrong means – does not matter. Success proves that your means were right. It is the end that proves your means were right. They are both violent. But if you have to choose between the two, the criminal is certainly the better. He does harm, but his harm is very limited – maybe he kills someone. Genghis Khan alone killed forty million people; Tamerlane killed seventeen million people; Nadir Shah killed thirty million people. The exact numbers Alexander the Great, Napoleon Bonaparte and Ivan the Terrible killed are not available. But they must have succeeded in killing far more than Tamerlane, Genghis Khan, Nadir Shah. But numbers for Joseph Stalin and Adolf Hitler are available. Joseph Stalin killed thirty million people after the revolution in Russia. Adolf Hitler killed six million Jews inside Germany, and in the whole Second World War he killed about fifty million people. Criminals have a very limited score.

Politicians are great criminals, so great that you accept them as your heroes, so great that they create history. I have known politicians in the highest posts and I have seen criminals. And I was amazed by the fact that criminals have done whatever wrong they have done out of innocence; they were not aware of the law. They were temperamental – in a certain moment of rage and anger they became mad and they did something. But their act was not premeditated. That makes a tremendous difference. The politicians I have known have done far greater harm to humanity.

And they go on doing harm, because they have the power of all the armies, of the bureaucracy. They do not do it out of innocence. Their actions, howsoever ugly, are preconsidered, well planned. But they belong to the same category; politicians are bigger criminals, that is the only difference – the difference of quantity. The criminals are simple human beings. Their only fault is their unconsciousness. They don't take note of what the outcome of their action will be. They don't plan it well.

One of my teachers, an old Mohammedan, always used to be in charge of the examinations. He was a very beautiful man. He never married. I asked him once, 'Why have you never married? You are such a beautiful man. You could have got a very beautiful woman.'

He said, 'It is difficult. I can afford only one thing. It is difficult to maintain both a wife...' He loved clothes so much that he had three hundred and sixty-five robes – every day a different robe.

He said, 'I am a poor teacher. In one year's time, the turn of a robe will come, and by that time people will have forgotten about it.' So he was always looking at new robes – very costly. His whole salary was going into clothes. But he lived in a beautiful small house, very well-decorated with a beautiful garden.

He was very much respected and because of that respect he was always chosen to be in charge of the examinations. Before the examinations he would tell the students, 'Remember one thing: to do wrong is not wrong, but to be caught doing it is wrong. You are free to do whatever you want to do – copying, cheating. You may be carrying books inside your clothes, notes ... Everything is allowed, just don't get caught red-handed. I am going to do my work. I will make every effort to catch you. So I warn you; don't blame me later on.

'If you are courageous enough and you are certain that you are cunning enough to get away with whatever you are doing, it is perfectly okay. But if you are caught, you are finished – your year is lost. So I will give you two minutes to think. Either you bring all your notes, all your books, that you are hiding in your clothes – anything that you are doing which is not allowed in the examination ... Just bring it here. I will keep my eyes closed so you don't feel embarrassed, because I don't want anybody to feel embarrassed. After two minutes it is your responsibility.'

And he would sit with closed eyes, a very sincere man. He simply did not want to embarrass anybody. And students would come with books and notes. Some would even come with notes written inside their shirts and they would have to sit the whole time without shirts. But they knew the man was very clever, you could not deceive him.

When people started going to him, others would lose their nerve and they would also go. Within two minutes his table was full of notes, clothes, handkerchiefs ... People had to run out to wash their hands, because they had written notes on their hands.

After two minutes everything was clean, and he would ask, 'Can I open my eyes or are you still doing it?'

He was saying something immensely important: the politician is the criminal who has not been caught, and the criminal is the politician who is not clever enough, who has been caught. And the criminal was doing a very small thing, on a small scale. But basically they are not different. The politicians are ugly creatures in the sense that they go on interfering in other people's lives.

One night Hymie Goldberg is coming home. It is a dark night and he is late. And a man comes close to him and says to him, 'I have been robbed. The robbers have taken away everything. All that I have is this gun.' He puts the gun on Hymie Goldberg's chest and says, 'Now, you have two alternatives: either you give me money or I give you death.'

There was a long silence. Even the murderer started feeling a little nervous because Goldberg was just standing there.

He asked, 'Have you heard me or not?'

Hymie said, 'I have heard, but let me think.'

But it is very rare to find such people who decide between money or death. Probably most people would give you the money because if you are dead, anyway the money will be gone. What is there to think about? But Goldberg has a thousand years of heritage. He is a perfect Jew.

The ordinary criminal uses direct means. That's why he is caught. The politician uses very indirect means. It is very difficult to catch hold of him. Indira Gandhi told me once, 'I never write anything, I simply phone, because writing can be used as a proof against me any day.' This is great planning. She would call the governor of a state and say 'Do it.' But she would never write anything. Now, there is no record of a verbal communication. She also said, 'There are stupid politicians who go on writing things when they are in power.' And she showed me a whole file. That was her whole power.

The file had come as an inheritance from her father, who was the first prime minister of India. He was collecting material against all the politicians – although they were men of his own party – proof that could be exposed any moment if the man tried anything against the party or against the party leader. If anyone wanted to leave the party he could not leave because Nehru knew ... The file became such a terror that even the great leaders of this country were afraid of it. Nobody knew exactly what was collected in the file, because everybody was doing all kinds of wrong things. Just a few days ago...

There was one president, Sardar Zail Singh, and he had ample proof against the prime minister, Rajiv Gandhi, that he was not listening to him, he was not even asking him for necessary signatures. Without those signatures, nothing can be done. The president is only a nominal head in India, but his power is the signature. And things were happening without Singh's signature.

But he could not do anything because when he was chief minister of Punjab, he had been caught red-handed taking a big bribe. The investigation was started, completed, and it was proved that he was a criminal, but Rajiv never passed on that file to Singh. He never said a single word about it to the newspapers or to the country. This was a key thing.

So, when Zail Singh wanted to say some things to the country which were going to be against the prime minister, he was told, 'It is perfectly okay, you can speak but your file is in my hands: all will be exposed. You will be immediately arrested.'

He could not ask for an extension to be the president again. And even though he is no longer a president, he cannot say anything against the government – though he knows everything – for the simple reason that his own crime will be immediately exposed. When he was president he was immune, he could not be arrested. But now he is an ordinary citizen. He will be arrested, harassed; harm can be done to him.

Politicians work in criminal ways. Ronald Reagan was saying to the senate that he would not sell armaments to Iran because, of course, Iran is anti- American. 'How can I sell armaments to Iran which can be used one day against America?' He was saying this to the senate and underneath, in the darkness, armaments were being sold to Iran. Nobody would have known it. Because all those armaments were being sold without his own senate and the country knowing about it, all the money must have been going into his own pocket. He has been caught red-handed: when Iran and America had a conflict a few months ago, Iran used American armaments against America. It was a puzzle: how did they get American armaments?

And it was clear to the senate that Ronald Reagan had done another tremendously criminal thing: he has put billions, trillions of dollars into very sophisticated armaments that he does not have people trained to operate, and he has been selling the old armaments which his whole army is trained to use. Now this is creating the situation where, if America gets into a war with a country like Russia, there is no chance for America to win. It will have all the sophisticated arms, but no experts to operate them because it has sold all the old armaments for which the whole army is trained.

Even a small country like Iran managed to fight with America, for the simple reason that it knows perfectly well that what Ronald Reagan is doing is against America, against his own country – just for his own interest, because he cannot run again for president. He has been president twice already, so this is the last chance to gather as much money as he can manage, by any means.

Now this is the ugliest thing that one can do to one's own country. Do you understand the facts? People are not trained and you have wasted trillions of dollars on arms which scientists have recently invented, for which years of training will be needed, and you have taken away and sold all the old armaments for which people are trained. You have sold them because you think that you have got better armaments, so there is no need for the old armaments. But just having the better armaments is not enough – you need people to operate them.

In just a small conflict with Iran, it became clear. America had the best missiles, but they all missed, because the people who were using them had no idea what to do with them, how to use them. The more sophisticated the armament, the more training and expertise is needed. Reagan has put the whole country into the most dangerous situation.

Just the other day I received a letter from a very well-known fighter for human rights. He has exposed what Ronald Reagan and his company are doing: they are trying to distort the whole constitution. In America, religion and state should remain separate – that is the constitution of a secular state. And every religion should have the same opportunity; no single religion should be the dominant religion. It is not a religious state.

But Ronald Reagan is a fundamentalist Christian. That is the most fanatical group of Christians. And he has conspired with all the Christian bishops, Christian divine healers, and now he has in his hands the majority of the people. The country is Christian and he is trying in every way to impose Christianity on American citizens. He has been trying for a long time, as he was when I was there. And the Supreme Court refused. He was trying to make the Christian prayer – approved by the church – compulsory in every school, in every college, in every university: every educational institution should start the workday only after they have said the Christian prayer.

But he failed, because the Supreme Court decided that this is against the constitution. He went roundabout: he said, 'It is against the constitution if the government enforces it. Right. But if the parents enforce it, the constitution has no power over it.' So, he argued, in non- governmental institutions which get governmental support – they are semi-governmental, not under the government's direct control – like colleges, even universities, schools in the thousands, the parents can decide because they are the trustees of those institutions. They can decide, 'In our institution, the Christian prayer will be the beginning point.' This was going in a roundabout way.

Now a few judges have become very old, so he has changed them. There are nine judges: all that he needs is five judges in his favor. Four judges have become old and have retired. The American constitution allows the president to appoint the Supreme Court judges. The people who made the constitution could never have conceived a situation where suddenly four judges would retire. If one judge retires, it does not make any difference. The president can place his own man, but the eight remaining judges will be there to oppose him – he will not have the majority. It is the first time in the whole history of America that four judges have been appointed by the president. One judge who is very sick, very old, insists on remaining because he says he is the only defense of constitutional rights. If he retires, then the fifth judge will also be Ronald Reagan's. Then five judges are enough, and whatever he wants, he can do. He can overrule the constitution, he can even change the constitution.

That old man is being harassed from every side to retire. He is sick, in a hospital, but he is reluctant to retire. 'Because,' he says, 'once I retire, America loses all its constitutional rights. It becomes a Christian country. No other religions will have the independence to exist. They will be dominated by the Christians.' But how long can that man last?

Because Ronald Reagan's term is coming to an end soon, that man can be killed, that man can be poisoned, that man can be declared naturally dead – he is old and in hospital. And I have every suspicion that before Ronald Reagan retires that man is going to die. Either he will retire or he will die. And they will find ways, which are very easy, to kill that man, just to get Reagan's man appointed.

The chance may never come again for a president to appoint five judges. He can change the whole constitution, he can change everything that is beautiful in the American constitution. One religion can become dominant over the whole country – one single cult, one single creed.

Politicians are criminals with very clever, cunning, planning minds. Criminals are poor people, small politicians, not knowing how to do things. They go on doing things and getting caught.

Ronald Reagan and his entourage are flying to Japan when the plane is forced to land in the Pacific Ocean. Escaping from the plane they are washed up on a desert island and find themselves without food or water.

The next morning they notice the wreckage of the plane only two hundred yards from the shore, but they also see sharks.

'I'll swim out and get some food,' volunteers one man. 'I used to be a lifeguard.' He dives into the water but the sharks soon find him and he is forced to return.

Another man steps forward. 'I am the President's bodyguard and those sharks had better watch out!' He gets twenty yards into the surf before racing back to the beach with sharks snapping at his heels.

Suddenly Reagan jumps up. 'I am the President and I can manage it. I will bring back some food,' he declares. No one takes much notice, but when he strides down to the beach everyone becomes alarmed.

He enters the water and immediately eight sharks form a two-lane escort and help him to the plane and back again.

'It is a miracle!' cries Nancy.

'Nonsense!' snaps Reagan. 'It is just professional courtesy.'

Just the same category of people. What those sharks are doing on a small scale, the great president is doing on a greater scale. Naturally the poor sharks show professional courtesy. A great hero – they escort him like bodyguards, take him to the plane and back. There is not much difference in their approach, in their attitude.

The world will be a far better place if politicians and criminals – who belong to the same category – disappear from the world. And it will be easy to make criminals disappear because their demands are not high. Perhaps their situation is forcing them to be criminals. Somebody cannot manage to buy medicines for his dying wife so he steals. You cannot call him a criminal. In fact, the society is criminal which does not make arrangements for a dying wife. That man is simply breaking the rule of a criminal society. But he will be called a criminal because the society owns the courts, the judges, the law, the constitution, everything.

Most of the criminals are created by situations. Most of the politicians are created by their own ambition. Hence they are the most dangerous people in the world. If the world wants to be at peace, politicians should disappear entirely from this planet. And once they disappear, criminals will disappear without much effort. They are simply shadows of the politicians. The politicians have created a society which is basically criminal.

I have told you a story about Lao Tzu. He was made Chief Justice by a Chinese emperor who thought that he was the wisest and the most respected human being in the whole empire. He could not find a better chief justice.

Lao Tzu told him, 'It won't last long. If you say so, I will accept the post. But you don't know me, you have just heard about me.'

But the emperor was stubborn as emperors are supposed to be. He said, 'No. You have to accept this post.'

The first case that came before Lao Tzu was about a great thief who had stolen a lot of money and armaments from the richest man of the empire. The man was so rich that he was lending money to the emperor; he was far richer than the emperor himself. Naturally, he never expected what happened.

The man – the thief – was caught red-handed. So there was no question that he should not be punished. Lao Tzu heard the whole thing, both sides, and gave the judgment: 'Both the thief and the rich man should be sent to jail for six months.'

The rich man could not believe his ears. He said, 'What is going on, what kind of justice is this? I have been robbed and you are sending me to jail?'

Lao Tzu said, 'According to me, you are the real criminal. He is just your shadow. You have accumulated the whole wealth of the country, you have left everybody poor, beggars. You have exploited so much that now it is a natural consequence: people will steal from you. I cannot send your shadow to jail without sending you also. The shadow alone cannot go to jail. It will go only with you.'

The rich man said, 'Then I want to have an audience with the emperor before you implement your judgment.' He told the emperor what kind of madman he had chosen.

'Just try to understand. If today he is sending me to jail, tomorrow you will be my companion in jail, because we belong to the same profession. I exploit people, you exploit people. Our whole profession is to be parasites. And you have put that crazy guy who ... Never in history has such a judgment happened.'

The emperor also was alerted and thought, 'This is dangerous. Perhaps that man was right when he said "You don't understand me, and you don't understand my way of thinking. You are taking an unnecessary risk by appointing me your chief justice."'

Lao Tzu was immediately relieved of the post.

Osho,
Why do you always laugh at the pope? Are you against him for any personal reasons?

I have no antagonism against anybody in the world for personal reasons.

I laugh at the pope for absolutely impersonal reasons.

First, he pretends to be the only infallible man in the whole world, which is absolutely absurd because the whole history of popes shows that is not right. One pope burned Joan of Arc because she had become so powerful, so respected by people, that the pope started feeling jealous. She had freed France from slavery. And certainly a young girl with such courage had never been seen in the whole of history. It was obvious that she would have tremendous love and respect from the people. She had brought freedom to them as a gift.

The pope was very jealous. In fact, he felt that people had been paying more attention to her than to him. He declared her a witch and once the pope declared any woman a witch, the only punishment was to be burned alive. And Joan of Arc was burned alive. It was very shocking to the whole of Europe.

And slowly, slowly the sympathy toward her became so strong that after three hundred years, another pope came along who saw that it was impossible to remain as the highest and the most important person unless something was done about Joan of Arc – her glory had become far greater than it was before she was burned.

The pope decided that it was a mistake to think of her as a witch. 'She is a saint,' he declared. 'From now onward, she will be known as Saint Joan of Arc.' And her grave was opened – just burned bones were there. Those bones were taken out after nearly five hundred years, worshipped, taken to the special graveyard where only saints have their graves, and the pope himself came for this great moment to confer sainthood on those dead bones. The woman had been burned nearly five hundred years ago. On what grounds can the pope say that he is infallible?

There are many such cases. If one pope decides she is a witch and another pope decides she is a saint, both cannot be right. Both can be wrong, but both cannot be right. If one is right, then the other is wrong. The idea of infallibility is laughable. It is sheer arrogance. And the pope declares that he is the direct representative of Jesus. The truth is that the tradition of popes started three hundred years after Jesus' crucifixion. There is a gap between the beginning of the tradition of the popes and Jesus. The gap is of three hundred years. How could Jesus have appointed them to be his representatives? But nobody asks them because they are surrounded with Christians who simply believe whatever they say.

The pope before this pope was a homosexual. It was known to everybody because before becoming a pope, he was a cardinal in Milan, where he was continuously moving with his homosexual boyfriend. And the whole of Milan knew it. It was the talk of the town. It was so ugly.

Then he was chosen to be the pope. And immediately, the first thing he did was to appoint his boyfriend as a secretary. Secretaries seem to be strange people, but to have a woman as a secretary is understandable. And that boyfriend was hanging around him – no secretarial job or anything. That was just a facade to keep him in the

Vatican. And these people go on talking about infallibility; they go on talking about their direct connection with God.

I don't have any personal antagonism and particularly toward this pope, although he is the worst that has ever happened in the long line of popes.

When Nathan Nussbaum returns to America from Europe, his partner in the men's clothing store wants to hear everything about the trip.

'And I even went in a group to see the Vatican,' says Nathan, 'where we were blessed by the pope.'

'The pope?' exclaims the partner. 'What does he look like?'
'Nothing special,' answers Nathan. 'I would figure a size forty-four, short.'

A tailor has his own understanding about things. I also have my understanding and I am not a tailor...

I can see the whole stupidity of all the popes that have been in power.

One pope forced Galileo to change in his book his lifelong research proving that the earth moves around the sun. 'Change it, otherwise you will be punished by being burned alive. Because the Bible says – and the Bible can never be wrong, because it is the written word of God himself ... You have to change it and write that the sun goes around the earth.'

Galileo was very old and sick. He said, 'There is no problem. I will change it. Just one thing you have to remember: my changing it does not make any difference. The earth will still go around the sun. Neither the earth reads my books, nor the sun reads my books. If you say ... I am not a stubborn person and I don't care which one moves. This is my research. Even if I change it, tomorrow somebody is going to discover it again because this is the fact.'

For the pope the question was totally different. If one thing is found wrong in the Bible, then the whole Bible comes under suspicion. Who knows? If one thing is wrong, other things may also be wrong. And if God can write wrong things – is fallible – where does the pope stand? And particularly this pope, who is a Polack...

I am worried, immensely worried, about what they are going to find after this pope dies, although he will live longer than they think. Popes in the past have not lived more than one year, or two years, because they became pope at the very end of their life. It is a long hierarchy. They start as the lowest of priests, they become bishops, they become cardinals, and then finally, two hundred cardinals choose the pope. It is very rare and only very old people are chosen, for the simple reason that they will be dying within a year or two, when another cardinal can be chosen.

This is a simple strategy in politics. But they forgot ... This Polack has completely forgotten to die. He was chosen with the hope that he would follow the tradition because he was old. But he is so enjoying being the pope that he has been becoming younger, not older. And now all the cardinals are in a fix – what to do? And where are they going to find somebody after the Polack dies? You will have to find someone more stupid, more idiotic, and I don't think there are people outside Poland who can manage to be more stupid than this man.

Two Polacks are leaving school to go out into the world. One of them asks the other, 'And what are you going to do with your life?'

'Well,' replies the other, 'I have decided to be a chicken farmer.'

Five years later they meet on the street and the first Polack asks, 'How is the chicken farm going?'

'My God,' replies the other, 'it was a complete disaster. All my chickens died.'

'Why,' asks his friend, 'what happened?'

'I am not sure,' the other Polack replies. 'I either planted them too deep or too close together!'

Polacks have a specialty – his was the farming of chickens. I am not against the pope, I am against the whole ideology that the pope represents. I am against the idea of God, I am against the idea of the son of God. I am against the idea of any human being pretending to have a direct phone connection to God. The whole Christian theology is so poor that if you understand religion a little bit as an experience, you will be surprised that Christianity is counted as a religion at all. There is nothing religious in it. No meditation – not a single pope has been enlightened. Even the man who created the whole of Christianity was not enlightened.

Christianity was not created by Jesus. He remained a Jew his whole life. He was born a Jew, lived a Jew, died a Jew. He never knew that he was a Christian. He was not trying to create a new religion at all. There is not a single statement by him to that effect. He was continuously trying to prove himself a Jewish prophet for whom the Jews had been waiting for thousands of years, the awaited great prophet after Moses – and the Jews were angry because of this.

If he had created a new religion, there would have been no problem. If he had wanted to create a new religion, the Jews might have laughed at the whole thing, that a son of a carpenter whose birth is suspicious ... Holy ghosts don't exist, at least in Judaism. Some hooligan may have done the trick. They would have laughed, but because he was continuously harassing them to accept him as their prophet ... That was impossible.

Sometimes it is good to understand things from their background psychology. Why was it so difficult for the Jews to accept Jesus as their last prophet? Obviously he was not educated, he was not even a rabbi, he had no learning about the Jews' scriptures. At the most, he was suffering from megalomania. But these were superficial reasons to reject him.

The deeper reason is: the last prophet was their hope. And the hope was that the last prophet would redeem them from their misery, from their suffering. Jews have suffered more than any race in the world. And they were living with the hope that the last prophet would come one day and the coming of the last prophet would be the end of the dark night.

They believed – because of Moses – that they were the chosen people of God. And the chosen people of God having a carpenter's son as their last prophet, of whom it is well known that he is not the son of his own father ... He was born after the marriage, but before nine months, so certainly he was not the son of Joseph!

Mohammedans never refer to Jesus as the son of Joseph. They also don't believe in the Holy Ghost. The Holy Ghost has been invented by Christianity just to cover up an old slander. Mohammedans call Jesus, *ibn Mariam*: Jesus, the son of Mary. This seems to be more sincere. They don't bring anything else into it, they simply drop Joseph out. One thing is certain – he is the son of Mary. The Arabic for Mary is Mariam. And in Arabic, everybody has to write his name and his father's name. Because the father is uncertain they write Jesus' mother's name: Jesus ibn Mariam – the son of Mariam.

The Jews were hoping for a prophet, a great prophet who was going to deliver them from all their suffering. And Jesus was not doing anything to redeem them from all of their suffering. They could not accept him, because to accept him would have destroyed their hope. And that hope was the only thing they were living for. It is a very strange phenomenon.

Hymie Goldberg was on a ship – his first journey – and was suffering from seasickness. The captain came to him and told him, 'Don't be worried, because never in the whole history of shipping has anybody died of seasickness.'

Goldberg said, 'Please don't say such a thing. Death is the only hope that I am living for, hoping that I will die. This sickness – and you are telling me ... You think you are consoling me, but you are taking away my only hope.'

Nobody wants their hopes destroyed. Because life is so empty, we are filling it with hopes. The poor man is thinking he will become rich. The uneducated person is thinking if he cannot become educated, at least his children will become educated. But everybody is living through hope because the present is absolutely empty. They can only imagine a fulfilled future.

Jesus did not give that fulfillment. That was given by the hope that one day the prophet will come. Of course, they will never accept anyone, because no man is capable of redeeming you from suffering; it is not only Jesus. Nobody else after him has tried because seeing the result ... Otherwise, the Jews will crucify the other fellow also because you cannot redeem anybody from his suffering.

It is a simple thing: everybody creates his own suffering and only he is capable of redeeming himself. You cannot throw the responsibility on some prophet who will come and redeem you from all misery, all anguish. The Jews are utterly tired, but hope is the only light in their dark night – and Jesus wanted to take away that hope also. This was the underlying psychology. They cannot accept Jesus.

It is a strange thing that the founder of Christianity was a Jew who never knew anything about Christianity. He never founded it. It was founded by a man who was against Jesus. His name was, in the beginning, Saul. He was so much against Jesus that he was traveling toward Jerusalem to convert people who had become Christians back to Judaism. Jesus was gone, he was dead. This man Saul was moving ... He was a fanatic Jew, and he wanted to reconvert those Jews who had been converted into Christians. But something happened on the way.

My own understanding is that it was sunstroke. He was a very violent and angry man, very hot. And the sun was also very hot. He was passing through the desert, day and night moving toward Jerusalem. One day, just in the middle of the day, when the sun was at its hottest and he was burning with a deep desire to convert back all the Christians, he got a double sunstroke. He fell into a coma.

And in his coma, he saw Jesus Christ. The reason is very simple: if you are so much against Jesus Christ you will continuously be thinking only of Jesus Christ. In that coma he saw Jesus Christ coming in all his glory. It was just a dream, but it transformed the man. He changed his name to make it a point that 'I am no longer the same person.' From Saul, he became Paul and this Paul was the founder of Christianity. He was the first pope – a very strange pope!

I think there is not much difference between Paul and the Polack Pope – they are both living in a coma. But they have nothing to do with Jesus. I have a certain love for Jesus, although I cannot say he was an enlightened man – but very close. He was just with the wrong kind of people. Always choose your company very intelligently.

He finally came to his senses after the crucifixion. He did not die on the cross, he escaped to India. His grave is here in Kashmir. I have been to his grave. It is strange that no Christian takes note of that grave. If they take any interest in the grave it will show that Jesus died here, but they believe that after resurrection he simply went to paradise. If they mean it symbolically – Kashmir is known as the paradise of the earth – that's perfectly true. He *had* come to paradise, but he did not fly toward the sky.

He lived a long life – one hundred and twelve years. But he had learned the lesson: one crucifixion is enough. Here in this country, you cannot teach because everybody knows so much about spirituality. At the most, you can become a disciple. There is no possibility of anybody becoming a master or a prophet or a savior. Here everybody – nine hundred million people, even villagers – is a spiritual prophet. Everybody knows the scriptures like a parrot.

So coming to Kashmir with his small group of friends and fellow travelers, he simply remained silent, just working on those few people he had brought. The village is still in existence. He used to call himself 'the shepherd.' In Kashmiri the word for *shepherd* is *pahalgam.* The village is called Pahalgam, the village of the shepherd. And you can see by the noses of the people you find in Pahalgam that once they were Jews. In fact, the whole of Kashmir was once Jewish.

It was a tribe that Moses was taking to Jerusalem, to Israel, not knowing himself where Israel was. For forty years they wandered in the desert. The great prophet, Moses ... Almost seventy-five percent of his followers died in that forty-year tedious journey in the desert, and I don't think they ever found Israel. What they found was a helplessness. Finally Moses was too old and not willing to search – it was enough, he had searched enough. They settled on some land ... It was just to give a sense to his people. And they were no longer his people, they were the third generation. There was almost no relationship between Moses and the people he had brought there.

Those who had come out of Egypt with him had died long before. The young people were not very interested in his leadership, in listening to him. One tribe of the Jews had got lost in the desert. Just as an excuse, because he was feeling uneasy with his people ... They were new and young and they knew nothing about Moses or his miracles: that he had separated the ocean, that he had gone to see God and God had given him ten commandments – they had not seen all this, they came afterward.

Moses was not comfortable with them. So he said to them, 'You settle and I will go and look for the one tribe that got lost.' And that one tribe had reached Kashmir. In fact, Kashmir was a far better place than Israel. And when that last tribe found Kashmir, they really believed that this was the true holy place, so beautiful that there was no comparison in the whole world.

You will be surprised to know that Kashmir was Jewish, but Mohammedans forced all the Jews of Kashmir to be converted to Mohammedanism. But their faces, their noses, are so prominently declaring that they are not Mohammedans, they are not Hindus – they are Jews.

And a strange coincidence: Moses died in Kashmir and Jesus also died in Kashmir. Both graves are in Pahalgam, just near a forest, and the family that still looks after those two graves is Jewish. That family has been looking after those two graves for generation after generation. Those are the only two graves in India on which the inscription is in Hebrew.

But Christians will not take note of it. I used to talk to Stanley Jones, one of the very famous Christian missionaries. And he said,

'I can understand why you insist that I come with you, you want to show me. But we want to be clear with you, we don't want to see the grave of Jesus because that will destroy our whole idea that Jesus was directly called by God to heaven.'

People protect their superstitions and are not ready to encounter reality. And continuously for eighteen hundred years these popes have been protecting all kinds of Christian superstitions which don't correspond to reality. I am not against them, I am not against anybody in the world personally. But I am against all kinds of prejudices, all kinds of nonsense, all kinds of rotten ideologies that go on existing in the name of religion.

I simply want religion to be purified. I want there to be no religions in the world, but only religiousness, just a quality, not any organized church. No holy scripture, but the whole of life holy, and everybody coming to a consciousness which transforms his actions, his being into religious qualities – *sat-chit-anand*.

Everybody has to become the truth, the consciousness, and the bliss.

18

The Only Riches Are of the Heart

Osho,
You are running within melike silent water, merging meslowly into an inner smile! Thank you for being with us.

The path of a seeker is full of beautiful spaces and is also full of desert-like moments. It is full of joy, just as you see in the morning when the sun is rising and the birds start singing and the flowers smile all over the earth. But it is not always so. There are moments of immense darkness. One feels lost, one does not know where one is, whether the night is going to end or not.

It is something to be very deeply understood: the path is up and down, it is not always ecstatic. And it is good that it is not always ecstatic, otherwise you will be utterly tired from ecstasy. You cannot smile twenty-four hours a day, you need a little rest, too. Those moments when one feels dark, lost, are moments to relax. And those moments when one feels a joy, a smile, are the moments to rejoice. But one should not start choosing. Both are equally acceptable, both are equally inevitable.

You need to understand this equality of both moments – dark and negative; light and positive. And you are not asking for only the joyous moments. You are not asking for anything at all. You are simply rejoicing in whatever existence gives to you. Whatever the gift – maybe a dark night or a joyous morning, tears or smiles – it does not matter. Your gratefulness remains the same. Only such a seeker, whose gratefulness never wavers, whatever happens, is equally rejoiced. He is equally thankful for it.

It is a little difficult ... When things are going well, it is easy to be thankful. But real thankfulness is when things are not going well – then is the fire-test of your gratitude. And only through such moments does your gratitude become more and more solid, concentrated, centered. You start growing roots. It is very easy to feel thankful to God, to feel thankful to existence, when everything is good.

You are saying to me that you are thankful because I am with you. Your thankfulness should remain the same when I will not be with you. Only then is your thankfulness not situation-oriented, but centered in your being, not dependent on the outside, but springing from your inner being. It is yours only when no outer change can change it. For that you have to learn the art of choicelessness.

You are saying that I am running within you like silent water, merging you slowly into an inner smile. It is beautiful, but these are the moments for you to be reminded of the moments when the smile may not be there, when you may not hear the sound of the running water that is bringing the smile to you.

There are dark nights of the soul. But your real test – whether you are an authentic seeker or just a superficial curiosity-monger – is not the beautiful moment. The real test is the moment when everything seems to be lost, when everything seems to be against ... If you can still smile and be thankful to existence, then things will start changing for you. Slowly, slowly there will be smaller gaps of darkness and longer spaces of light. As your choicelessness deepens, the dark moments will disappear.

A day comes when there is no night any more. A day comes when it is always dawn and the birds are singing and the flowers are blossoming and you have a smile that is not an effort, hence you cannot be tired of it. It is simply there, just like the fragrance of the flowers. They are not tired of it. Or just like breathing – twenty-four hours a day, seventy years continuously – you are not tired of it. Only after a choiceless state of consciousness, does one come to the moment when one can remain orgasmically blissful every moment, each moment. And that is our target.

I have been working with thousands of people. And the trouble is that when things are going well, they are very thankful. When things are not going well and I go on making them aware that there will be times when things will not be going well – it is just how existence functions, how existence creates a dialectic between the opposites for your growth they become angry at me. Just as you are smiling and being thankful, they become revengeful, angry. And in both cases I am not involved at all.

When you are thankful, I am not involved; when you are angry and resentful, I am not involved. It is just you in both cases. This has to be deeply recognized: it is always you. You cannot throw the responsibility onto m . But if I accept your thankfulness, naturally you will tend to throw the responsibility of your resentment on me too.

So I always feel a little hesitant whenever I hear the words: 'Thank you, Osho.' Then I know there is danger. I am getting into trouble, because what will you do when the smile disappears and tears come to your eyes tears of sadness, of depression?

There are valleys and there are peaks. The path is long. When you are on the sunlit peaks, you shout with joy, thankful. But when you are in the dark, deep valleys, completely lost, you start being resentful. Remember: it is always your experience, don't project it onto me. It is better to be independent and take the responsibility. It will make you mature; and it will save me from the trouble of your resentments, your anger. I have no problem: you can be resentful, you can be angry, it is all the same to me.

Whether you are thankful or ungrateful, it is all the same to me. I want you to learn the art of choicelessness, so that it becomes the same for you, too. And the beauty of thankfulness, when there is nothing to be thankful for, is just a great miracle, magic, a moment of tremendous transformation. It needs great intelligence. I hope you will prove to have that intelligence. I trust in everybody that they have the right intelligence to understand the deepest mysteries of life.

One day a Polack walks into a store and asks for some egg-*ski*, some milk-*ski* and bread-*ski*. The shopkeeper looks at him and says, 'Are you Polish?'

'Yes,' replies the embarrassed Polack. 'How did you know?'

'Simple,' says the shopkeeper, 'you put *ski* on the end of all your words.'

The Polack walks out determined to improve his English. So for five years he goes to night school. When he is satisfied, he goes back to the market, walks into a store and with an impeccable English accent says, 'My good man, please give me a dozen eggs, a bottle of milk and a loaf of bread.'

The shopkeeper looks at him and says, 'Are you Polish?'

'My God!' exclaims the Polack. 'How the hell do you know that?'

'Simple,' says the shopkeeper. 'This is a hardware store.'

Osho,

I have listened thirty or forty times to the discourse on the inescapable. Each time I feel I'm grasping it, but it escapes me. This discourse is so huge that it is inescapable.

Osho, please elaborate on your discourse.

That which is the authentic, the truth, is always beyond the grasp of the mind. If you can grasp only this much – that it is beyond the grasp of the mind – you have done more than is ordinarily possible for a human being. The mind is a very small thing and existence is tremendously big.

Existence is so oceanic, so infinite, so eternal. Our minds are so small that it is no wonder that whenever you come close to the truth, you feel that your heart has fallen into a certain harmony. Your being has moved from its sleeping state into a certain awakening, but your mind remains in a very stunned and shocked state. The truth is beyond the mind, but not beyond the heart – the heart can grasp it. But this is the trouble: the heart cannot say anything about it. Yes, it can dance, it can sing, but it cannot use any language. Language is confined to the mind.

And as far as your being is concerned, which is deeper than the heart, it can have the full comprehension of the truth. But the very comprehension of the truth by your being makes it utterly silent. The very understanding makes your being filled with the feeling of the mysterious, the unknowable. The being cannot even do what the heart can do. It remains just as if it is no more. All has become silent, although the silence is very much alive. It is not the dead silence of a graveyard, it is the silence of the starry night – immensely alive.

But the deeper you go, the further you are from language. Even dance is a language, even gestures are a language, even your eyes – without saying anything – can say much. But as you go deeper and deeper, there is the world of *sat-chit-anand*, there is the truth and consciousness and bliss. Everything becomes utterly silent. The mind is left far, far behind. The mind cannot hear even faraway echoes of what is happening in the being. Yes, the mind can hear something of what is happening in the heart.

The heart is very close to the mind, although deeper. The mind can feel that a certain harmony is arising, a certain peace, a certain joy. It can understand the heart dancing with abandon, but the mind cannot express it in language. So it has a certain feeling from the heart, just a cool breeze passing through the mind. It can have a little taste – something sweet is happening somewhere deep, but how to say it?

I have told you the story, which is an ancient story, especially made for such a question...

Two beggars live in a forest, near a city. Naturally they are enemies, because they are in the same profession and in competition. One is blind the other is lame. And they are always quarreling about their clients. You don't know what beggars say about you. They have their clients, they have their territories.

I always used to give one rupee to a beggar whenever I went in or out of the railway station. And in those days I was traveling for almost twenty years continuously. One day I found that the old beggar was gone and a young man was standing there. I asked him, 'What happened to the old man?'

He said, 'I am his son-in-law.'

I said, 'You may be his son-in-law, but what happened to the old man?'

He said, 'He has given this territory to me in dowry. And he has moved to another place, to the bus stand.'

I said, 'I had no idea that I was being given in dowry to somebody.'

And he said, 'He has informed me about you, that you will give me one rupee. You are on my list.'

I said, 'People don't know that they are somebody's property, that they can be given in dowry.'

Beggars are continuously fighting. There is great struggle and competition. And those two beggars had been enemies for years. But one day the forest caught fire. The blind man was perfectly able to walk and run, but it was dangerous. He could not see whether he was going in the right direction – where there was no fire – or whether he was running through the fire toward more.

The lame man could not run on his own. The fire was spreading so fast and the winds were so strong, but he could see that there was still a possibility to get out. There were a few places where the fire had not reached yet. But soon it would be reaching there. Soon, they would be covered by fire from all over the place. They both forgot all their antagonism, competition. This was not the time to fight, this was a time to unite.

The blind man took the lame man on his shoulders and they became one personality. Now they had both eyes and they had legs. The lame man could see and direct where they had to run – and fast – and which directions had to be avoided. And the blind man was strong enough to run, carrying the lame man on his shoulders. They came out of the forest without being injured.

This ancient story is about your mind and your heart. Your heart can see, but cannot say. Your mind can say, but cannot see. If you are capable of bringing your heart and mind closer, your love and logic closer, your experience and expression closer, perhaps the mind can also say something significant. It may not be complete, it may not be an entire expression, but it may be an indication in the right direction. It may be a finger pointing to the moon. It may not be the moon, but it can indicate toward the moon.

You have been listening to one of my discourses on the inescapable, and you say, 'Each time I feel I have grasped it, but it escapes me.' The moment you feel 'I am grasping it' or 'I have grasped it,' that is the point where it escapes from your hands. There are things which you can grasp, but you cannot say 'I am grasping it.' Remain silent. Rejoice in the moment, but don't say anything.

It is almost like my open hand. I have the whole sky in my hand, but with my closed fist the sky has escaped. My closed fist is empty. The moment you say 'I have got it,' you have closed your fist. You *had* got it, but you should have remained silent, utterly silent. The moment you say 'I have got it, I am grasping it, this is it,' you have made it very small. It was too big, it cannot be confined to these small words. Your fist is too small and the sky is too big.

You can have the whole sky in your open hand; there is no problem. You can have the fragrance of all the flowers in the garden with the open hand, but if you close your fist there is nothing left – not even stale air. Fragrance cannot be grasped in your fist.

This is one thing which is fundamental for everyone to remember: when you feel that you are coming closer to something great, remember not to say anything – just rejoice in it. You are allowed to sing a song which has nothing to do with it; you are allowed to dance, enjoy – which has nothing to do with it. And your grasping will become deeper with your dance, with your song, with your music. Or you can simply sit silently. Deep down, you are experiencing. Something is singing and your whole being is feeling a new sweetness, a new liveliness, a new love radiating around you. But beware not to say 'I have got it.' The moment you say 'I have got it,' you have missed it. Immediately, you will find, 'It has escaped me.' Then you are in a vicious circle. Then you run after it, and the more you run the less is the possibility to understand it, to come closer to it.

It comes only when you are silent and relaxed. It comes only when you are not even looking for it. It just comes out of the blue, from nowhere – you don't hear its footsteps. But when it comes, rejoice. Rejoicing is the only way to keep it around you. The deeper you can rejoice, the deeper you can take it in with your breathing, with your heartbeats – but don't say a single word. Every word is a disturbance. It is a very shy experience. It does not allow itself to be exposed to the mind, to intellect, to reason, to logic. The moment you bring those in, it moves out through the back door.

One of the great mystics, Kabir, has the right symbol for it. He says it is like a shy, newly married girl. In the West, that girl has disappeared. But in the East, once in a while, you can find that shy, newlywed girl. With that girl Kabir symbolizes the experience of truth.

You have to be very sensitive and very alert, otherwise it will escape. It cannot expose itself to your logic: that is too harsh a world. It cannot expose itself to language: that is too primitive. Language has no grace; there is no possibility for the inescapable experience to be reduced to ordinary communication.

The moment you say 'I have got it' ... Why do you say it? If you have got it, enjoy it! Just old habits.

I have heard...

A drunkard entered into the pub. He could not believe his eyes. There were three men and a dog sitting around a table playing cards. He went around and around, again and again, watching.

'Is it really a dog or a man?' He was very drunk so he was suspicious, thinking, 'It may be that I am seeing something which is not the case.' Going around, again and again, he managed to figure it out, 'If I can see the three people as men, it is not possible that I see only the fourth man as a dog.'

Finally he said, 'My God, this dog seems to be very intelligent. Is he playing cards with you three?'

The owner of the dog said, 'Yes, he can play but he is not very intelligent.'

The drunkard said, 'What are you saying?'

He said, 'I am his owner, I know him. Whenever he gets a good hand he wags his tail. That's where he exposes himself. Then the whole thing goes wrong as that is the time when he should not wag his tail. He is a great player, but the tail ... Old habits. He becomes so joyful that he cannot stop. I have been telling him thousands of times, "You are a great player. You should not behave like a dog," but dogs are, after all, dogs!'

And that is the situation of the mind. The moment your heart feels something, the mind starts wagging its tail. It says 'I have got it.' And just because of the old habit something tremendously important is spoiled.

An Englishman, an Arab and a Frenchman are sitting at a sidewalk cafe in Casablanca, when a gorgeous oriental woman walks past them.

The Englishman drops his teacup and exclaims, 'By Jove!'

The Arab murmurs reverently, 'By Allah!'

The Frenchman smiles and breathes a soft 'By tomorrow night.'

Just different habits.

It is Monday morning in Washington and Ed Meese comes into the president's office looking very depressed.

'My God, Ed,' says Ronald Reagan. 'You look terrible. What happened?'

'Well, Mr. President, sir,' replies Meese, 'I had a terrible week. On Monday I crashed my car and had to pay ten thousand dollars to get it fixed. On Tuesday my daughter ran off to Pune. On Wednesday the stock market crashed. On Thursday I caught my wife in bed with the gardener. On Friday my son died, and on Saturday my house burned down.'

'Good Lord,' cries Reagan, 'what a terrible week. Was there nothing positive in it?'

'Oh yes,' replies Meese. 'On Sunday I got my AIDS test result.'

Osho,

Could you please speak of the mysteries of the heart?

That's what I have been saying: the mysteries of the heart cannot be spoken of. You can experience, and then there is no need for any explanation, for any expression. We are accustomed to figure out everything rationally. It is an old, long, perhaps a million-year-old habit.

We feel a little uneasy if we cannot figure out something completely rationally, logically. That which remains unexpressed haunts us. The whole of science is born out of it. It is the haunting of the unknown; it becomes almost a nightmare. It is perfectly good for science to be haunted by the unknown because the unknown can be made into the known.

Outside your being there are only two categories – the known and the unknown. What is known today was unknown yesterday, what is unknown today may become known tomorrow, so those two categories are not really different. It is only a question of time, inquiry, adventure. Everything that is objective can perhaps one day be reduced into the single category of the known.

But in the inner world, the world of the heart you are talking about, there is a third category – the unknowable. That's why science does not accept anything inside you. Science does not accept you at all because to accept you is to accept a mystery which is unknowable. And the scientific mind will become almost insane because the unknowable cannot be made known. That is simply the nature of it.

The mind wants everything to be known, just as Francis Bacon said – his was one of the most significant scientific minds – 'Knowledge is power.' The mind wants power, and the way to power is to know more and more and, finally, to know everything. The unknown is beyond the mind's power. You cannot dominate the unknown. How can you dominate it? You don't know about it. The whole territory is in darkness. You have first to bring the territory into light, within your control.

The mind is a politician and the whole of science is a by-product of the mind. And you can see the connection: finally what the mind creates goes into the hands of the politicians.

What Albert Einstein created reached the hands of President Truman. When he wrote the letter to the then American president, Roosevelt, saying 'I am working on splitting the atom,' he was welcomed immediately into America and given all the facilities. Now, Truman was the president. When he heard that Truman was going to drop those atom bombs that resulted from his researches ... He had created them only for an emergency, such as if the fascist countries were going to win and destroy the whole democratic world, then as a last resort atom bombs could be used and the whole situation changed.

Without Albert Einstein, Germany was hindered in its atomic research. But because Einstein was a Jew and Germany was killing Jews by the millions – although he was not going to be killed because he was too important for Adolf Hitler's victory and his idea of conquering the whole world – still, as a protest, he escaped from Germany and he wrote a letter to Roosevelt, a very famous letter. He was immediately welcomed, 'Come, and you can have all the facilities that you want to work on the atom.'

Truman decided to drop atom bombs on Hiroshima and Nagasaki without any reason: there was no urgency, there was no emergency. Germany had already fallen and Japan was going to fall within two weeks at the most. There was no way for Japan to stand alone without Germany. Japan's forces were already losing their morale and they knew perfectly well, 'If Germany is gone, how long can we carry on?'

All Truman's generals told him, 'It is absolutely absurd to drop the atom bombs, because within two weeks or even before that Japan is going to kneel down before us.'

Now, it is absolutely ugly to destroy two huge cities. And they had nothing to do with the war. Small children, old parents, wives – they had nothing to do with it. They were simply citizens living in those cities.

Albert Einstein wrote another letter, hoping that just as his first letter was welcomed, the second would also be welcomed. He was utterly disappointed. But I could have told him that he should not write the second letter, that nobody would even answer it.

It was not answered because he was saying, 'It is absolutely wrong, immoral, when a country is falling apart by itself ... I have not done all this research for such a situation. If Japan had been winning, I would have been the first to suggest that it was time to drop the bomb, but Germany is finished, Japan is almost finished. Dropping the atom bomb on an enemy who is losing ground every day is absolutely absurd and inhuman, and I protest against it. Please don't do it.' But nobody even answered, nobody even cared.

Einstein died in great sadness and depression. Once he was asked, 'If you were given another chance to be born, would you not like again to be a physicist? Much that you have been doing has been left incomplete. Obviously you would like to complete it.'

Einstein replied, 'Absolutely not. If I am given another chance, I would rather be a plumber than a physicist, because my whole life has been used by the politicians. I have been deceived.'

But the whole of science is in the same position. It is not a superficial phenomenon. The reasons are deeper – perhaps the scientists are not even aware. The mind is the politician and the whole of science is nothing but the search for power. And that's what politics is – a search for power in another direction, and one day finally they are going to meet.

One day the scientist is going to need the support of the politician because scientific instruments, labs, are becoming so complicated and so costly that no scientist will be able to afford them, as in the old days. Galileo could work in his own house with a small lab of his own – private. That is no longer possible. A nuclear plant has to be supported by a great nation with a huge amount of money, and thousands of scientists have to be supported. A single scientist cannot work ... Things have become so complicated that all scientific research has finally to be subordinated to the politicians. And once you are in their hands – just servants – they are going to use whatever you produce for their own purposes. You may not be producing them for destruction. That is not the point. You are producing under politicians, with their money, with their power. You are simply a servant. You are not going to decide what is going to be done with your discoveries, with your inventions.

The politicians have their own ends, but I can see a very deep connection. It is the same mind that moves in the direction of science, a search for power; reduce the unknown into the known, and the mind becomes powerful. The politician is also on the same search, the search for domination, power. And if science can support this, then the politician is willing to manage all the money, all the manpower, all the intelligence that is needed by science. But whatever it produces will be used for more power, for more domination, for a world-conquering, destructive process.

The heart has nothing to do with the known or the unknown. The heart is concerned with the unknowable. You can experience it, you can have all of it – the whole mystery of it, but don't ask for its demystification. That's what we are always asking: the mystery should be explained in a logical and rational way, so we can become powerful over it.

This is an ego trip. Knowledge is an ego trip. The heart is the world of love, not of logic, and the heart is not at all concerned with any ego trips. It knows nothing of the ego. It is very humble, very simple, very childlike. You are asking, 'Could you please speak of the mysteries of the heart?' I can manage, I am managing even this very moment for you to experience something of the mysterious, of the unknowable. It is surrounding you here. In this silence you can have a taste, you can enter the mystery of the heart, but slip down from the head. Don't ask for any explanation. Just be a little child who does not ask anything, who accepts everything.

Do you remember your childhood? It will help. Mostly we forget all about our real childhood. Do you remember the time when you were only two years old? You don't. People start remembering only from about four years old. That is the end of childhood. You have become part of the society. You have started learning its alphabet, its manners.

Parents feel very happy when a child starts being mannerly, starts talking with people the way grown-ups should talk. Parents feel immensely happy but they don't know what they have destroyed. They have destroyed a mysterious world – the world of fairies, the world of the wonderlands. The child was living in an innocence that they have completely erased.

That's why if you go backward trying to remember, you will be finally stuck somewhere around the age of four. Perhaps the women may be stuck at the age of three, because girls are one year ahead of boys. They mature sooner. They become civilized one year earlier. They behave better.

Experienced mothers have told me that even in their pregnant state, after the third or fourth month, they can feel whether it is a girl or a boy because the boy starts playing football. The girl remains quiet, relaxed, but the boy starts kicking here and there. That is going to be his lifelong thing. He is starting to rehearse before he comes out. Girls are quieter. Boys cannot even sit quietly for a few moments; they need continuous occupation, something has to be done. And this remains a lifelong thing.

Because the girls are more centered and more silent, they start learning social manners earlier than the boys. Boys have many other occupations – so many things have to be done, so they are always diverted. In schools, in colleges, in universities, they can't compete with the girls. Girls are always coming first in the class, are always getting the gold medals. It is very strange that all their gold medals are used only for finding a good husband. That means a rich husband – a doctor, an engineer, somebody with the possibility of being a professional success. But boys cannot compete with girls for the simple reason that their minds are diverted into so many directions that they cannot concentrate.

If you go backward you will be stuck either at the age of four or at the age of three. But you don't remember what happened in those three or four years because nothing logical happened, nothing rational happened, you did not ask for any explanation. You simply enjoyed the beautiful colors of the flowers, you enjoyed running after butterflies, you enjoyed collecting seashells, colored stones. And you were so immensely happy for no reason at all. Just because you had collected some seashells you thought, 'What can be more beautiful? What more could Alexander the Great brag about?' You had the whole world in your hands because you had collected a few wildflowers. You were enjoying very much, rejoicing, but you have forgotten all that authentic childhood.

The mystic has to learn to be a child again, and because you have been a child, the second childhood is not difficult. It is already there deep down in your being. It has to be rediscovered. I will not say 'discovered,' I would refer to it as 'rediscovery' as you have known it already. And once you enter that magic circle of your childhood, you will know the mysteries of the heart. But nobody can speak about them.

It is good that nobody can speak about them, otherwise you will never discover them yourself. You will remain with the explanations, with the ideologies. Hung up in the head, you won't enter the mysteries themselves. But now nature leaves no alternative: either you have to go into the heart yourself or you have to remain a superficial human being without any significance, without any grandeur.

Be a child again. That is the whole psychology of meditation.

Miss Goodbody, the pretty young school teacher, noticed that little Ernie had a gleam in his eye and his gaze followed her all around the room. He obviously had a crush on her, so she called him aside after school.

'Ernest,' she begins, 'your grades have been slipping lately and I notice that you are not paying attention in class. Is something distracting you?'

'Yes, Miss Goodbody,' says Ernie in a soft voice.

'By any chance,' she asks compassionately, 'is it me?'

Little Ernie nods and the teacher smiles. 'That's very sweet,' says Miss Goodbody, 'I'm very flattered. And to tell you the truth, I hope to have a husband one day who is as bright and cute as you.'

'Then why not me?' asks Ernie.

'Well,' says Miss Goodbody, 'I don't want a child.'

'Okay,' replies Ernie, 'I promise to be super-careful.'

Just start being a little more poetic, start loving more the things of the heart – music, painting, sculpture. Arrange your life not around the head but around the heart, in friendship, in love, in compassion. Rather than going after explanations, go after experiences, and you will be preparing the right path toward the heart.

One day, it explodes in tremendous luminosity and fills your whole being with a light of the beyond. And then you don't need any explanation. The experience itself is yours – what is the point of any explanation? Explanations are for those who are utterly poor as far as experience is concerned. I don't want my people to be poor. I want you to be as rich as possible – and the only riches are of the heart.

Once you are richer in the heart, a new dimension opens toward the being. You cannot bypass the heart. From the head there is no direct route to the being. First you have to come into the heart, and then only can you pass deeper into being. And from being, there is the ultimate quantum leap into the cosmic, into the ultimate, into the absolute. You disappear just like a dewdrop in an ocean.

Moishe is employed as a groom working in the Czar's stables. One day the crown prince comes rushing into the stable. 'Moishe,' he calls, 'get the finest carriage ready. The princess is coming home, I just received a telegram. The best harness with the bells and feathers.'

While he is getting everything ready, Moishe notices that one of the horses has an erection. 'Hey!' he says to the horse. 'Who had the telegram, you or the prince?'

Moishe must have been an innocent person. These innocent people are not counted at all by our so-called sophisticated society. We don't pay any respect to children. We don't pay any respect to those whose eyes are still filled with wonder. We have created a world just out of the head, denying everything else, even the existence of the heart.

Ask the physiologist and he will say there is no mystery in the heart – it is just a pump, no heart is there. It is simply a pumping station for the blood – what kind of mysteries are you asking about? A pumping station is a pumping station. The physiologist will not accept that you are feeling a deep love arising in your heart. He will laugh. He will say, 'In a pumping station? Love arising?' He will not accept that because of love you are having heartache – not possible. There may be some malfunctioning in the mechanism, but it can't be love.

Science cannot accept the existence of love. Neither can it accept the existence of your heart, nor the existence of your soul, nor the existence of any mysteries which are beyond logic. Maybe today they are beyond, but tomorrow they are going to be explained away.

I say unto you that science is a very incomplete approach to life. Our society is very lopsided because it has not taken note of the inner which is as big as the outer. There is a vast universe outside you and there is a universe similarly vast inside you. You are just standing between two infinities, two eternities. And because you are standing just in between these two wonderlands, you have the opportunity to enjoy both.

I am not against the outer. I am against the emphasis that only the outer exists and there is no inner. The inner is far more important because it is your very being. By not knowing it, not experiencing it, not going deeper into it, your life will remain empty, just a long, long, drag – boredom, depression. Nothing will flower in you, no songs will be heard within your being, no sunrises, no flowers, no stars. And all that was possible, you just never moved inward.

Moving inward is the path to the divine. Moving outward takes you toward objects. But you are not an object. You are a deep subjectivity and this subjectivity has to be explored. That is the ultimate mystery.

19

Creativity Comes out of No-mind

Osho,
Is there any difference between the state of no-mind and being present?

It is an intellectual question, nothing to do with your experience; because if you have experienced even a glimpse of no-mind, all questions including this will simply disappear. Questions belong to the territory of the mind. No-mind means absolute silence – no question, no answer, no thought at all. Hence we call it no-mind.

First you have to understand the mind because that's where you are, that's from where the question is arising. Unless you understand your space – the point from where you are raising the question – you will not be able, even intellectually, to comprehend some difference between no-mind and being present. There is no difference in experience, just two names for the same experience from two different aspects, two different angles.

No-mind is experienced within you. Nobody else can see it; it is purely subjective. With no-mind comes tremendous presence. When you are in the mind you are almost absent. The quantity of your presence or absence has to be measured by your consciousness. You have such a small layer of consciousness – that's your only presence. Otherwise, ninety percent you are absent.

But the man of no-mind is one hundred percent present. You can feel his presence from the outside. You cannot see his no-mind. The presence of his being is a radiation of a silent state within. That is beyond you, but if you are available, receptive, you can experience something of the tremendous presence of his being. In each of his gestures, in each of his looks, in each of his words, or even in his silence, you can be touched by his presence of being.

The presence of being comes into existence only when the person as such disappears. It is the melted state of the person – the presence – as if the flower has disappeared and only the fragrance has remained. You cannot catch hold of it, but you can be surrounded by it. Such people who have their being absolutely present – one hundred percent alert – are known in the world of language as having charisma. There is no other charisma. There is only one charisma and one charismatic aura and that aura comes from no-mind. But no-mind is the center within and the aura is the circumference of that mind, that no-mind.

When inside you everything becomes silent, you are no longer as you used to be – a person. Now you are just a fragrance, a presence. But your presence has deepened. It has become a solid pillar of light.

Anybody who is intelligent is bound to feel something new that he has never experienced before. So these are two viewpoints: one is the inner experience of no-mind, and the other is from outside. It is the by-product of no-mind, the presence of being. But first you have to understand the mind because that's where you are, and that's from where the journey has to start toward no-mind, culminating finally into a beautiful fragrance, awareness, a magic aura around you.

People have named it in different ways because people are different. Somebody will say 'It is a hypnotic force.' Somebody will say 'It is something like magnetism.' Somebody will say 'It is mesmerism.' Somebody will say 'It is charisma.' Somebody will say 'We don't know exactly what it is.' One thing is certain: it has a tremendous gravity, it pulls you toward itself. And if you are courageous, you can be drowned in it and you can be transformed in that drowning. It will be your death and your resurrection, both. As you are, you will die, as you should be, you will be born.

But the mind is a very dark place. To comprehend light from there is almost like a blind man trying to comprehend light.

A young English gentleman returns from a stay at a stately home.

'How was your weekend?' asks a friend.

'Well,' he replies, 'if the soup had been as warm as the wine, and the wine had been as old as the chicken, and the chicken had been as tender as the maid, and the maid had been as willing as the duchess, it would have been a perfect weekend.'

This is how the mind functions. If you look into it you will start laughing at your own mind. It is never in the present. It can't have presence because the basic quality is missing. It is *never* in the present. Either it is in the past, which is no more – just a memory, a faded memory, a faraway echo; perhaps a dream that you had sometime, but not more than that – signatures on water. You have not even completed your signature and it has disappeared. That's how the past goes on disappearing. You have not even lived it and it slips out of your hands. And then the mind goes on thinking about it.

So either the mind is past-oriented or it is future-oriented. Because it has missed the past, out of sheer necessity a projection arises about the future. The past is no longer in your hands, it is gone, and gone forever; there is no way to bring it back. All that you can do is to project into the future whatever you wanted to do, however you wanted to live ... Naturally, while you are thinking about the future, making it fuller than your yesterdays, you are missing the present moment. Your mind moves like a pendulum from the past to the future, from the future to the past. It never stops just in the middle, where reality is.

You are always real, but your mind is always unreal. You are always in the present, you cannot be anywhere else. But your mind is never here, it is all over the world. It will not be just at the point where you are. Except for that place, it can roam all over the world. It can go to the moon, it can go to Everest ... Everything is possible for it, whether it is memory or imagination, but the mind has no contact with the present. Your body is far more present, it is totally different from your mind.

And, very strangely, all the religions have condemned the body not the mind because they themselves were using the mind for the faraway future, farther away than ordinary people think about. You think about tomorrow or the day after tomorrow, or next year at the most. But all the religions were thinking about a future beyond death. Their heaven and their hell and their God are all so far away from the present moment. And remember: *you* will always be in the present moment.

And the distance between you and those imaginary spaces in the future will remain the same. It won't change. Because all the religions were using the mind as their foundation, they had to deny the body. It is very unfortunate, but nothing can be done about it. It has happened.

Your consciousness is exactly in the present, just like your body. So I am in favor of your body because it shares one thing in common with your being: your being is in the present, your body is also in the present. Only the mind is continuously moving here and there, never coming home.

There is a reason for it not to come home: in the present the mind has no function. What can the mind do in the present? The mind's capacities consist of memory, which is the past, or imagination, which is the future. That is the whole capacity of your mind. There is no place for the present moment. The mind will not know what to do. In the present you cannot remember, you cannot imagine; in the present you can be. But you can be only be in the present when the mind is no longer functioning.

Hence, my approach is totally different from all religions: I want you to respect your body because it is in the present. That will give you the clue – a direct route to your being because the being is also in the present. Just leave the mind aside. We are against the body, we are very condemnatory of the body, not knowing at all that this condemnation of the body is breaking the bridge to your being.

A man of authentic spirituality is deeply in love with his body because he knows his body shares many things with his being. The mind shares nothing, neither with the body nor with the being. It is an absolute stranger that has been forcibly put into you by the culture, the religion, the society. They are using the mind to enslave you.

And because you are *in* the mind you continuously go on asking about things of which you have no experience. You don't know what no-mind is, except a word. You don't know what presence of being is, except that you have heard about it. Just words won't do.

Move away from the mind, and when I say move away from the mind, I am saying move away from the inner chattering. That is the only disturbance that is preventing you from knowing yourself and this beautiful existence. Because your body is in the present, you are in the present, existence is in the present. They are all here now, only the mind is a strange phenomenon. You have been much manipulated by others. Your educational systems, your friends, your family – everybody is trying to make you a great mind. In other words, everybody is trying to pull you away from the present moment.

I am reminded of a great German philosopher, Immanuel Kant. He is a specimen of those people who are absolutely in the mind. He lived according to the mind so totally that people used to set their watches whenever they saw Immanuel Kant going to the university. Never ... It may rain, it may rain fire, it may rain cats and dogs, it may be utterly cold, snow falling – whatever the situation, Kant would reach the university at exactly the same time all the year round, even on holidays. Such a fixed, almost mechanical ... He would go on holiday at exactly the same time, remain in the university library which was specially kept open for him, because otherwise what would he do there the whole day? He was a very prominent, well-known philosopher. He would leave the university at exactly the same time every day.

One day it happened...

It had rained and there was a lot of mud on the way. One of his shoes got stuck in the mud. He did not stop to take the shoe out because that would have made him reach the university a few seconds late – that was impossible. He left the shoe there. He just arrived with one shoe. The students could not believe it. Somebody asked, 'What happened to the other shoe?'

He said, 'It got stuck in the mud, so I left it there, knowing perfectly well nobody is going to steal one shoe. When I return in the evening, then I will pick it up. But I could not be late.'

Once a woman proposed to him, 'I want to marry you' – a beautiful young woman. Perhaps no woman has ever received such an answer, before or after Immanuel Kant. Either you say yes or you say no.

Immanuel Kant said, 'I will have to do a great deal of research.' The woman asked, 'About what?'

He said, 'I will have to look in all the marriage manuals, all the books concerning marriage, and find out all the pros and cons – whether to marry or not to marry.'

The woman could not imagine that this kind of answer had ever been given to any woman before. Even no is acceptable, even yes – although you are getting into misery – is acceptable. But this kind of indifferent attitude toward the woman. He did not say a single sweet word to her; he did not say anything about her beauty. His whole concern was his mind. He had to convince his mind whether or not marriage is logically the right thing.

It took him three years. It was really a long search. Day and night he was working on it, and he had found three hundred reasons against marriage and three hundred reasons for marriage. So even after three years the problem was the same.

One friend suggested out of compassion, 'You've wasted three years on this stupid research. In three years you would have experienced all these six hundred, without any research. You should have just said yes to that woman. There was no need to do so much hard work. Three years would have given you all the pros and cons – existentially, experientially.'

But Kant said, 'I am in a fix. Both are equal, parallel, balanced. There is no way to choose.'

The friend suggested, 'By the pros you have forgotten one thing: whenever there is a chance, it is better to say yes and go through the experience. That is one thing more in favor of the pros. The cons cannot give you any experience, and only experience has any validity.'

He understood, it was intellectually right. He immediately went to the woman's house, knocked on her door. Her old father opened the door and said, 'Young man, you are too late. You took too long in your research. My girl is married and has two children.'

That was the last thing that was ever heard about his marriage. From then on no woman ever asked him, and he was not the kind of man to ask anybody. He remained unmarried.

The mind is very impotent in a way. It cannot give you any existential juice, any existential experience, and that is the only thing that matters. So please move away from mind. Don't ask about the difference, because there *is* no difference between no-mind and being present. No-mind is the inner subjective experience and being present is available for everybody. It is the circumference, and no-mind is the center. They are both together. Neither the circumference can be without the center nor the center can be without the circumference.

But the circumference can be experienced, and that's what has attracted millions of people to a man like Gautam Buddha or Chuang Tzu or Jesus or Moses. It was their integrity, their individuality, their solidity. In comparison to them, people felt hollow. They had immense presence. Other people looked just like shadows, without any souls.

George Gurdjieff started saying to his disciples, for the first time in the whole of history – he died in the year nineteen hundred and fifty ... He started saying a very strange thing, and although it is not right, he is not wrong. He started saying to people, 'You don't have souls.' What he meant was, 'You don't have any presence, your being is hollow. Inside you there is nothing but darkness, unconsciousness, absence. Everything is absent.' You have been told for centuries that you are born with a soul. It is absolutely wrong according to Gurdjieff. I know and *he* knows that what he is saying is not the truth, but it is a device. He is making you aware of your hollowness, of your emptiness, and he has chosen the best way to hit the nail on the head. He is saying, 'You don't have souls! Forget all the nonsense that tradition has been telling you. That was a deception, but you accepted the tradition: "We have souls already, there is no need to seek and search."'

He said, 'You will have to create the soul, you cannot have it just through birth. Through birth, you get only the body. Through your upbringing, you get your mind. And through a conscious effort to transcend into the beyond, you will achieve the soul.'

He said definitively that only a very few people have lived with souls. And without a soul, what are you? A cabbage, a cauliflower? I have heard there is some difference between cabbages and cauliflowers. The difference is that the cabbage is uneducated and the cauliflower has college degrees. But that does not make much difference – both are vegetables. Your life is a vegetation.

Of course I cannot agree with Gurdjieff as far as the truth is concerned. But I agree with him and his compassion; he did not bother about the truth. He bothered more about you. He wanted to make you aware that unless you do something, you are not going to create a soul. Soul is your own creation. But he went too far. I am not ready to deny you the soul, I only deny you the awareness of it. You are born with the soul as you are born with the body. The mind is a social product. You are not born with the mind. That's why a Mohammedan has a different mind and a Hindu has a different mind and a Christian has a different mind. You can see their differences of mind.

Since India's freedom, for forty years, Hindus have been fighting for only one thing, as if that is going to solve all human problems.

The greatest rich man of India, Jugal Kishore Birla – he is dead now – had been hearing about me. Finally, he could not resist the temptation and he invited me to his palatial house in New Delhi.

The man who had brought me the invitation – I was staying with him – was the MP from my constituency, and I could not say no to him. He was an old man, seventy-five years old. He was the only man other than Winston Churchill who had remained a member of parliament for sixty years continuously without any gap. He was called the Father of Parliament. He entered parliament when he was only fifteen. He belonged to one of the richest families himself, and he and Jugal Kishore Birla's family belonged to the same caste.

He persisted. I was reluctant. I said, 'What purpose is going to be served by my meeting that old man? I know about him ... Perhaps he does not know as well about me.'

But he insisted, 'He is not far away, and he has been very interested in you and he wants to talk to you.'

So I went, and what was the first thing he asked me? He said, 'I can give you a blank checkbook. You can use as much money as you want. All that has to be done is somehow to create a movement in the country so that cow slaughter is stopped.'

I said, 'What is going to happen if cow slaughter is stopped?' 'All problems of the world will be solved.'

Only a Hindu mind can think that by not killing cows all problems will be solved. This is such a stupid idea. But the Hindu has been so influenced for centuries, continuously conditioned that the cow is the mother – although they don't accept the bull as their father, which is a logical and rational approach.

I asked Jugal Kishore Birla, 'Do you accept the bull as your father?' He said, 'What are you talking about?' He became angry.

I said, 'Don't become angry. If the cow is your mother, then some bull is bound to be your father.'

He looked at the MP who had brought me and I said, 'You can keep your checkbook. Perhaps you will find some idiot who can do this work. I cannot say to anybody that the cow is my mother.'

He said to the MP, 'What is the matter? Is he not a Hindu?' Because a Hindu cannot think that anybody can deny that the cow is the mother.

I would have no objection if they were accepting all animals as mothers, as fathers, as brothers, as sisters, at least as faraway cousins. It would have been acceptable; it would have been a beautiful world if people accepted animals as their brothers and sisters. But just choosing the cow – that is the Hindu conditioning, that is the Hindu mind.

Every person gets a mind ready-made, and that mind is being forced into him by all methods and means. That is the only part that has not been given to you by existence. Existence has given you the body: love the body, rejoice in the body, let the body dance without any guilt and without any fear of these religions, and you will be coming closer to your being through the body.

Nobody has come closer to the being through the mind. The mind is the most arbitrary, artificial creation by the society to subdue the individual, to destroy his individuality, and to destroy the discovery of his own being.

You are born with the soul, but you are absolutely unaware of it – because of the mind. The mind never allows you to be in the present. That's the reason my insistence on meditation is so strong – because meditation simply means a method to get rid of the mind.

The moment the mind is not there, suddenly you are in a new space: so fresh, so beautiful, so blissful. That is your soul, that is your no-mind. And once you have entered that space, that space starts growing around you and creates a certain energy field. That becomes your presence of being.

Osho,

I suspected you of stealing my creativity, and in my unconsciousness made a secret bargain with you, 'Okay, take it. And in exchange give me love and meditation and bliss and myself.' You gave me glimpses, and then they too disappeared, and I was angry at you.

Beloved thief – I love calling you 'Beloved thief' – beloved thief, will you steal me?

Prem Pankaja, you are saying, 'I suspected you of stealing my creativity...' That's absolutely wrong. In the first place, what was your creativity – third- rate trashy novels? You know it perfectly well. You thought that was creativity?

I have not stolen your creativity. Just by being here you became aware what kind of rubbish you were writing. Yes, those novels were selling because there are people hungry for trash, just waiting for something third-class – they cannot comprehend anything better. I have not stolen your creativity because my whole purpose is to *give* you creativity. And if your old creativity is gone it is because you are now more understanding, more alert, more conscious, so you cannot go on creating that trash.

I have cleaned you of all rubbish. You had come to me with a mind full of bullshit. It has been a tremendous work to clean your mind. And you tell me that I have stolen your creativity? *Now* there is a possibility of your being creative. *Now* you can create something really beautiful, something that remains even when you are gone, which has a longer life than your life.

Even today the absurd stories of Chuang Tzu are as beautiful, as enchanting, as they would have been to his contemporaries. Twenty-five centuries have passed, but those stories of Chuang Tzu still retain the freshness of this morning's roses. And he wrote nothing but absurd stories – absurd for the simple reason that the whole humanity is absurd – to make you aware how absurd you are.

One morning he woke up very sad. That was very strange because he was a man who was continuously blissful, an enlightened being. His disciples said, 'This is a very strange experience. We never expected that you could ever be sad.'

He said, 'But something happened. I was also not expecting it, but it happened. Things go on happening without your expectations. And I am in such a dilemma.'

They said, 'Just tell us. Perhaps we can be of some use, of some help.'

He said, 'I will tell you, knowing that nobody can help me, neither you nor anybody else. But I will tell you, just to give you some idea of how much I am in a dilemma.

'Last night when I went to sleep, I knew perfectly well that I was Chuang Tzu. And in the night I had a dream that I had become a butterfly.'

All the disciples laughed. They said, 'You are too much. A dream is a dream, don't be bothered about it.'

Chuang Tzu said, 'You have not heard the whole story. Then in the morning when I woke up, I found that I am Chuang Tzu again.'

So they said, 'The problem is solved. What is the problem? It was just a dream, it has passed away. You are again Chuang Tzu.'

He said, 'You idiots, you don't understand the problem. The problem is: if Chuang Tzu can become a butterfly, then what is the guarantee that it is not now the butterfly who has become Chuang Tzu? And do you want me to be a butterfly? My problem is that a great doubt has arisen in me. I think perhaps the butterfly has gone to sleep now and is dreaming that she is Chuang Tzu. If Chuang Tzu can dream that he is a butterfly, what is wrong with vice versa? The butterfly can dream. And I have lost my identity. Who am I, I ask you?'

They were all silent. He had been telling absurd stories: now he has created an absurd situation. What to say to this man? And he was their master, so they could not be rude to him.

They said, 'We should go and meditate over it. What else can we do?'

Then his chief disciple, Lieh Tzu, came and all the disciples said, 'Perhaps you can do something. The master is very sad. He is sitting in his bed, not coming out.'

Lieh Tzu listened to everything, then went to the well, pulled out a bucket of water, carried in the bucket of water, and poured it on Chuang Tzu.

He said, 'You idiot, what are you doing?' And he jumped out of bed.

Lieh Tzu said, 'I am bringing you to your senses. Now tell me who you are, a butterfly or Chuang Tzu?'

Chuang Tzu laughed. He said, 'My son, if you had been here before, you could have saved me from so much sadness. The whole morning I was waiting for you, hoping that perhaps you would find some solution.'

Lieh Tzu said, 'Should I bring another bucket?'

Chuang Tzu said, 'No, this is enough. I have found my identity. The water was too cold and you have spoiled my bed too.'

Now the story is still fresh, it will never be old. It will always remain fresh, as if it has just happened. You can see the whole thing: Chuang Tzu jumping out of the bed saying, 'If you had been here before, you could have saved me from so much sadness.'

Creativity is a very rare phenomenon. For example, Kahlil Gibran wrote his first book, *The Prophet,* when he was only twenty-one years old. Then his whole life he tried to write something better than *The Prophet*, but he failed. There are at least thirty books written by a more mature, more experienced, more educated man, but even the last book he wrote before he died is nothing compared to *The Prophet.*

If you ask me, only *The Prophet* is the creative expression of his being. Everything else is just the mind trying to be creative. *The Prophet* came out of his being without any effort. He was so young, and he didn't think he was going to produce a masterpiece which would remain significant for centuries. After he produced it, the whole world responded with such great respect. It has been translated into all the languages; people find it holier than any Bible or any Koran or any Bhagavadgita.

But he himself got into trouble not knowing that *The Prophet* came out of no-mind. He was just playing; he had no idea that he could become a great writer. He was not writing for anybody. He was filled with insights and he was putting them on paper. His friends persuaded him, saying, 'This is a great work, you should publish it.' He was reluctant, hesitant, thinking, 'I was only twenty-one years old when I wrote this. People will laugh.'

But finally they succeeded in persuading him, and the book was published. After that he tried thirty other books along the same lines. But they looked like carbon copies, faraway echoes of *The Prophet* – but not that solidity, not that intuitiveness, not that beauty, not that grandeur. And it is not only with Kahlil Gibran; it is so with many creative people. Not all that they have produced is creative; it is production, composition. It may even be good, but it is not something that is going to be eternally fresh and young. Unless something remains eternally fresh and young, you have not created anything.

Michael Naimy has written one book, *The Book of Mirdad*, which in quality goes even higher than Kahlil Gibran's *The Prophet*. But Mikhail Naimy is again in the same trap. He must have thought that if he could write *The Book of Mirdad*, which should remain as long as man is on this planet, one of the greatest creations of man ... He struggled his whole life, but he could not surpass it. *The Book of Mirdad* had happened to him. Creativity is not something that you do, you simply allow the universal force to function through you. You become just a medium. You give your hands, your body, your heart, your being to existence and then existence sings a song and it becomes eternal, as eternal as existence itself. Only that is creativity. Other than that, I cannot conceive of anything creative.

I have not stolen your creativity, Pankaja; I *want* you to be creative! You have the possibility, the potentiality, but you are wasting your potential on absolutely meaningless novels. Yes, they were giving you money, they were being sold. But nobody will read your novels twice; once is enough, more than enough. Anybody who reads your novel will read it and then throw it out of the train window. It is of no use after that. It is just ordinary trash – and you know it.

But you don't know one thing: that you have the possibility of becoming a creator. I have taken away your so-called creativity to give you an authentic relationship with existence so something great can be born out of you. And that is the greatest bliss and benediction any man can experience: when existence uses you as a medium. That means existence has loved you enough, accepted you deeply – your worth, your value. Existence needed you.

And this is one of the things to be remembered: that the greatest need of man is to be needed. If nobody needs you, you will commit suicide. And if existence itself needs you, you will be raised to such heights that you have never dreamed of. I would like you to be a creator. And it is good that you are finished with your old so-called creativity.

You are saying, '...and in my unconsciousness made a secret bargain with you: "Okay, take it. And in exchange give me love and meditation and bliss and myself."' You are asking too much. I am an old Jew. For all your trash you have made a secret bargain with me to give you 'love, meditation, bliss, and myself'! There is no need to make a bargain with me. I am not a businessman. Once upon a time I was a Jew, but no more. You can have it all – love, meditation, bliss and yourself – for nothing. You don't have to pay for them, but you will have to work for them. You will have to work upon yourself. I am showering love, but you are protecting yourself with an open umbrella. Now if I take the umbrella you will say, 'You are stealing again.' And I don't want to interfere in your freedom. It is your umbrella and if you want to open it, it is your decision. But you can close it – it is not raining. Just keep it by your side.

You are from England ... These two places are strange: England and Bengal in India. No psychoanalyst has ever tried to figure out why these people are umbrella-fixated. They talk about father-fixation, mother-fixation – what about umbrella-fixation?

Again you are wrong, 'You gave me glimpses...' I have never given you any glimpses. Whenever you closed your umbrella you got them. And this is beautiful – first you think that I gave you glimpses, then naturally I know the second thing is going to happen, '...and then they too disappeared, and I was angry at you.' Now don't pull me unnecessarily into *your* mess! Just look at your umbrella. Whenever you close it, you have glimpses; whenever you open it, glimpses disappear. It has nothing to do with me. Just watch your mind.

Whenever your mind comes in, the glimpses disappear. You allow the mind in spite of me; whenever your mind is absent in spite of you, you have the glimpses. Don't throw the responsibility on me in any way. I can neither give you glimpses nor can I take them away. I never interfere in anybody's freedom. To me it is sacrilegious; your freedom is such a sacred thing to me. I want you to be dignified in your freedom.

These words that you write take you in the wrong direction. You start looking for me to give you something. You have everything you need. You just need to discover it within yourself. I can show you the way, I can show you the methods – that's what I am doing every day. Somehow – from some angle, from some aspect – perhaps you may discover how to find your treasure. It is *your* treasure; if you have lost it, it is your own blindness.

The mind is utterly blind. Put the mind aside and you will regain your insight. The Hindus in this country have called it the third eye. When you move beyond the mind, you have a strange experience – an eye opening inward. You start seeing your own splendor. You are as full of bliss, splendor, glory as any Gautam Buddha. Existence is very communist. It gives you the inner treasures equally. Differences arise because you discover the treasures slowly.

But the last thing you are saying is right. You are saying, 'Beloved thief – I love calling you "beloved thief" – beloved thief, will you steal me?' Perhaps only in this country! God has been given many names. The Sufis have given God one hundred names: ninety-nine can be pronounced, the hundredth can only be experienced, not pronounced. In India there are thousands of names given to God. The most beautiful is *hari*. And *hari* means 'the great thief.' The really courageous are the people who call God the great thief because he steals your heart!

So you can say it, although I have not stolen anything – I take away only that which does not belong to you, and I give you only that which you have got already. So my work is very simple! But if you love the word *thief* – it is an ancient name for God – you can use that name, whether I steal anything from you or not.

Sometimes I think of stealing your umbrella. What will I do with an umbrella? Thinking about it, I don't need it. I have never had an umbrella in my whole life. So once in a while I become attracted – why not have Pankaja's umbrella? That is the only experience I'm missing. But then it is unnecessary because I never go anywhere. If I keep the umbrella open inside my room, you will start thinking, 'Now he has really gone crazy.'

But it will be great if you can simply make a gift of your umbrella to me. In that way I cannot say no to you – I never say no to anyone. You will enjoy giving a gift, although I know the umbrella is very old. I will not even touch it, my doctors won't allow me. They go on insisting, 'You should not touch old rotten things.' They say, 'You are allergic, you should not touch such things.'

But still I will accept your umbrella, just so that you can get rid of it. I will throw it away; there is no other way. It cannot enter my house, but as a gift, just to help you to get rid of it ... And once you are vulnerable, open, and receptive, all my love is yours. Meditation will grow on its own accord with your trust.

And as far as the last thing is concerned, 'Will you steal me?' I have done that already; otherwise you would not have been here. The people who are with me are the people I have already stolen. I have to do strange things, steal people from different countries.

Every country is angry. The German government is angry that every German who goes to Pune simply disappears, never comes back. Now the Japanese are trying to compete with the Germans. Wives come and they forget all about their husbands. Husbands come and they write to me, 'I don't want to go back home, although I have a wife and children. What do you suggest?' What *can* I suggest? You have got a good opportunity to escape. Just be here. If your wife really hates you, she will come. It all depends on how much she hates you! She may even become a sannyasin, just to harass you.

Pankaja, you need not be worried about that. Pankaja goes back and forth. She goes to England and then within a few days she is back. I can understand her problems, but once you are *my* people, then you don't belong to any family, to any race, to any nation, to any religion. You belong to the whole universe.

Mrs. Grumblebum is always calling on the doctor for medicine for her aches and pains. One day the cures fail. She dies and is buried in the local cemetery.

Two weeks later, the doctor himself dies and is buried in the plot next to Mrs. Grumblebum. The mourners are just leaving the cemetery, when the doctor hears a tapping noise on the side of his coffin.

'Well, Mrs. Grumblebum,' he asks, 'what is it now?'

'Please, doctor,' she says, 'can you give me something for worms?'

Just old habits, although they have died. Pankaja, it is just old habit that you think you are separate from me and my people. Drop that old habit. That which you used to be is dead; there is now someone absolutely new.

Paddy gets a little high at the party and starts to make a play for the luscious babe playing the piano. But in his drunken fog he trips, and the piano cover closes on his fingers.

His wife, Maureen, goes over and picks him off the floor. 'Remind me to put a piece of ice on your black eye when we get home,' she says soothingly.

'But I haven't got a black eye,' says Paddy.

'I know,' replies Maureen, 'but you're not home yet.'

You are a long-time, old sannyasin, but you have never been totally here. And it happens to people who have been working with their mind and intellect. They cannot be in this silence, in this presence. They become fidgety, their mind starts dreaming about going here and going there. For years you have been repeating the same cycle. You cannot go away from me, you cannot go away from this silence. Wherever you go I am going to haunt you. So you go on coming back, but this split situation of going and coming disturbs your getting in touch with your being.

For a few days you try, and as you come closer to experiencing something, that is the moment when the mind makes trouble and starts dreaming of going somewhere. Always remember: the mind creates trouble only on the boundary line. It is an indication that this is the moment to remain in your meditation. Perhaps only one step more and you will be out of the fog of the drunken mind.

Before reaching the boundary line, you go away. So you have been coming and going for years. Many things that would have happened to you, you yourself have managed not to let them happen to you. It is enough time; I am not going to be here forever! I don't want you to repent when I am gone, because then you will think you have missed an opportunity – perhaps for many lives.

It will be easy to find another Gautam Buddha sometime in the future, because he is a traditional saint. It will be possible to find a Jesus Christ. It is almost certain you will find him someday because he was not enlightened; he has to come back to the earth. But you will not find me again, for two reasons. One, I am not going to come back to any body again and the second reason – you will never again find even a similar person. I have been so eccentric, crazy, so different from the traditional saint, that I don't think anybody else after me is going to dare to copy me. It is impossible.

You will repent. There is still time – your spring can come. There is still time for you to achieve your ultimate potential. But don't waste it in wavering. If you go on taking the plant from one place to another place to another place, it will never grow roots. You have to leave it in one place so that it can grow roots. Without roots there are no flowers. You are longing for the flowers, but you are not taking care of the roots.

20

Totally in the Present

Osho,

Thank you for letting us taste from your ocean of consciousness. Both Krishnamurti and Gurdjieff were talking about their waves of consciousness. Osho, are they the waves of your ocean?

J. Krishnamurti and George Gurdjieff are not just two waves in the ocean of consciousness. They are the very ocean of consciousness itself. The moment you become enlightened you are no longer an individual. You lose your ego, and with the ego you lose all your limits, all your boundaries. They are not waves of my ocean; the ocean belongs to no one. I am the same ocean as they are.

You are also the same ocean as I am. You just have to wake up and realize the fact that your imprisonment is your imagination, that your fetters are nothing but your thoughts, that your bondage is nothing but your own unconscious way of living. Otherwise you are as oceanic as any Gautam Buddha, as any Lao Tzu, as any Kabir, as anyone who has ever realized his ultimate, his *sat-chit-anand*.

We are not separate. We belong to one existence without any demarcation lines. All limitations are mind projections. The moment you are beyond the mind and you can see without the mind directly, you will be surprised that the trees and the stars and the oceans ... Nowhere is there any demarcation. The flowers of the trees are your flowers, the greatness of the stars is your greatness, and the smallness of the grass leaves is your smallness. The moment you start feeling this universalness, you have come home.

But remember always: do not put me above anybody else, just because I am your master. So don't say that I am the ocean and J. Krishnamurti and Gurdjieff are just waves. That is ugly. You may not be aware where these kinds of ideas continuously come from, and this is not only the case with you. Just today, Hasya was telling me about some Korean master, Su. He is going to come soon. He has disciples.

Lani has just come from Korea. In the Korean language, they have published more than thirty-five books of mine. Hundreds of people are interested in coming. They are not even aware where I am, whether I am still alive or some past master. Not only the so-called disciples go on praising their master as the highest. Even the so-called masters ... Certainly they are not masters, just so-called.

When Master Su's disciples asked him, 'What are the categories between you and Osho?' he said he belongs to the first category of enlightened people and Osho belongs to the third category of enlightened people.

Now such a man cannot be enlightened, to say nothing of first, second and third category: there are no categories in enlightenment. How can you be enlightened and still belong to a certain category? The category is a limitation. But the so-called masters will always put themselves higher than anybody else. The ego lingers on, whether you are in the world of matter, money, power, prestige or whether you are pretending to be a seeker, a searcher, a spiritual being. Even when you start declaring yourself as enlightened you are playing the same old game with new names. There is no difference at all.

I am waiting for Master Su to come. He is going to be in trouble! He does not know me. In the first-class enlightened category ... Why should a master who belongs to the first class come to a third-class enlightened man in the first place? This is strange! So let him come. He will have to stand in line for the first time in his life.

Once you are enlightened there are no categories. Enlightenment simply means going beyond all categories, all mind trips, all ego trips. It is simply becoming one with the universe.

The reason for people like Master Su is the simple pious ego, now acting in the name of spirituality. The game is old: one has to be at the top. But why do the disciples do this? The reason is the same. If I am the greatest master, then naturally – you are *my* disciple – you are the disciple of the greatest master. You are no ordinary disciple, you are not a disciple of a third-class enlightened man!

I have told you about one religious cult that exists only around the area of the Taj Mahal. They are called Radhaswamis. They were very much disturbed by the presence of the Taj Mahal. Now the Taj Mahal has nothing to do with their spirituality. But the disturbance began when their master died – they were determined to make his memorial better than the Taj Mahal.

The Taj Mahal is unique in the whole world, there is no other building that can be compared to it. It was made by a great emperor. It took nearly twenty years to build, and almost twenty thousand stonecutters, sculptors ... Master builders were gathered from faraway countries, the best from Iran, from Turkey, from Egypt, from Arabia. The emperor who was making it ruled over the whole empire of India and all the money was pouring into it.

Those twenty thousand people worked almost ... When they came they were young; by the time the Taj Mahal was completed, either they were old or dead. The second generation was working. Sometimes they had come old – they were famous so they were brought – so the third generation was working.

The emperor was making it as a memorial to his wife, Mumtaj, and on the other side of the river Jamuna, was also making his own memorial. When he died, he would be buried there. Emperors took care while they were alive to make their memorial too, because after they were dead nobody was going to bother to put so much money and effort into it.

But his whole treasure was finished with the wife's memorial. His own memorial has only the foundation stone. He could not complete it because he was dethroned by his own son and kept in jail, and the son immediately dropped the plan for the second memorial.

The Taj Mahal is made of white marble, all Italian marble. And the other memorial, just on the other side of the river – between them he was going to make a bridge – was going to be exactly the same as the Taj Mahal, but in black marble. He was creating a beautiful symmetry. The architect was going to be exactly the same, the building exactly the same, just the marble was going to be white on the wife's memorial and black on his own memorial.

Now these followers wanted to try to make something better than the Taj Mahal, because thousands of tourists were coming every day to see the Taj Mahal. Naturally they thought it was not only a question of prestige, it was also a question of business. It had been going on for almost one hundred years.

They have been able to make only the ground floor. Certainly they have made it far better than the Taj Mahal, but there seems to be no possibility that they will be able to complete it. They wanted to make it a three-story building, so it goes higher than the Taj Mahal, but all the money they could collect from their followers from all over India is finished. For one hundred years continuously, thousands of workers have been involved in making it. I have seen ... Their pillars are so beautiful, so creative and on the pillars they have made creepers in marble. The creepers have flowers of green marble, and on top of the creepers, roses made in rubies, emeralds, diamonds. They have certainly made it clear that if they complete it – even incomplete – it has gone beyond the Taj Mahal. They are immensely happy.

When I was speaking at Agra University they invited me to see their incomplete memorial. They have done a tremendously great job.

They took me inside. Inside they have a map drawn on the marble and on the map there are fourteen divisions. And they have put each enlightened person that they could think of in the division to which he belongs. There are not only three categories; according to them there are fourteen. Mohammed is in the third division, Jesus is in the fifth – so is Moses. In the sixth is Mahavira and Buddha. In the seventh, Kabir, Nanak, and in that way they went on. The names are engraved in the marble.

In the fourteenth there is only one man, their own master, who was not known outside Agra. All his following is centered in Agra. A few people have moved to different places, but basically, it is a one-city-oriented religion. They asked me what was my opinion about this map.

I said, 'Who has made this map?'

They said, 'It is in our holy scripture. Our master himself has made this.'

I said, 'Your master is right. He is in the fourteenth.'

They looked at me, because before me they had shown that map to many people. Everybody disagreed because their masters were put in the fifth category, somebody's master in the third category, somebody's master at the most in the seventh. After the seventh, the other six planes are empty. The fourteenth, the highest reach of consciousness, has been achieved by their master. Naturally no Hindu will agree, no Mohammedan will agree, no Jaina will agree, no Jew, no Christian, no Buddhist. Nobody is going to agree. I was the first man to agree with what they said.

They said, 'You are the only man who understands.'

I said, 'Certainly, because I am on the fifteenth and I know your master is trying, making every effort, to enter the fifteenth. I don't allow him! He tries hard, but I don't open the door. And as long as I am there on the fifteenth – and there is no sixteenth, so I cannot go anywhere else – your master has no chance.'

They said, 'Fifteenth? But in our scripture there are only fourteen.'

'I think that's natural. Your master knows about only fourteen because he has never entered the fifteenth.'

They were very shocked and angry. Their whole desire is that their master is accepted as the highest, then they are certainly the most significant people on the earth, following the greatest master. And the master was also on the same trip because in his own writing, which nobody reads except his own disciples – and they are not many, but they are very rich people...

They showed me their scripture. He has written with his own hand the names of Gautam Buddha and Jesus and Kabir on lower steps, and his own name he has written on the highest. That very stupidity shows that he is not even on the lowest, the first floor. He does not know anything about enlightenment. He may have been a learned scholar. That seems to be a possibility because he writes well. But he is writing everything as a parrot, repeating from old Indian scriptures. There is not a single statement which is original.

I asked them, 'Show me something that is original. A man who has reached the highest plane of consciousness must say something which nobody has said because nobody else has reached that plane. Show me something. Because all that is written in it has been said by people who are just on the third, the fourth, or the fifth. What is your master's own statement? What is his testimony?'

They could not find a single statement in their whole book which was not stolen. But this thing goes on and on.

The man who brought me to Pune for the first time, about thirty years ago, was a follower of Mahavira and he was also a follower of Mahatma Gandhi. He lived with Mahatma Gandhi in his ashram for years. His name was Rishabhdas Ranka. Many people of Pune must know him. Because Mahatma Gandhi was teaching continuously that all religions are the same, essentially the same – no religion is higher than the other, they are all equal – he also learned, like a parrot, to repeat it.

Then he wrote a book on Mahavira and Gautam Buddha, and he showed me the manuscript. I simply saw the title and I said to him, 'Just look at your title. I don't have to read your book – your title says everything.' In his title he wrote: *Bhagwan Mahavira* and *Mahatma Gautam Buddha. Bhagwan* is used for Mahavira, and for Gautam Buddha, just mahatma. There are so many mahatmas; mahatma is not something very special or unique.

I said, 'You are writing this book to show that Jainism and Buddhism are equal, and their message essentially is the same. And Gautam Buddha and Mahavira are equally enlightened.'

He said, 'Yes.'

I said, 'Then why this difference? Either put mahatma in front of both or put *bhagwan*.'

Now he was in a great dilemma. He could not write Mahatma Mahavira. The Jainas would kill him, they would expel him – he was a Jaina. Nobody, not a single Jaina in twenty-five centuries, has made such an insult – writing about Mahavira as just a mahatma. Mahatmas are available in this country for one rupee a dozen. They are so cheap, every village has its own mahatma. But he was not willing to write *bhagwan* before Gautam Buddha because no Jaina accepts Gautam Buddha as equal to Mahavira. He is enlightened, but not of the same height. Mahavira's enlightenment is complete; Buddha's enlightenment is incomplete – partial enlightenment, not total. And the same is the situation of the Buddhists. I have asked Buddhist monks. They are not ready to call...

One Buddhist monk was born an Englishman, but got converted when he was young. I don't know whether he is still alive or not, but he was a world-famous man, Sangharakshita. He lived in the Himalayas, in Kalimpong. He used to come to the university where I was teaching, and he became interested in me because he was always invited to the Philosophy Department. I used to raise questions and he was in difficulty trying to answer them. But he was a very nice person, he never became angry. On the contrary, if he could not answer me, he used to ask if I had some idea of what the answer could be.

I said, 'I never ask anything unless I know the answer.'

We became friends. He even started staying with me while he was in the city. I asked him, 'What do you think about Mahavira?' Mahavira and Buddha were contemporaries.

He said, 'About Mahavira? He was enlightened, but not so completely as Gautam Buddha.'

The same nonsense goes on around the world. But the reason the disciples are concerned or the so-called masters are concerned is the same. It is the ego that needs a certain kind of gratification.

As far as J. Krishnamurti and George Gurdjieff are concerned, they are both enlightened. Both have disappeared in the same ocean in which all enlightened people have always disappeared. And beyond enlightenment there is no distinction. There is no question, because the person is no more. When the dewdrop falls into the ocean, do you think there will be differences? When another dewdrop falls into the ocean, will it only partially fall into the ocean? Can a dewdrop partially fall into the ocean? Is it possible for any dewdrop to be different from any other dewdrop? They will all become the ocean.

I am a clear-cut, straightforward person. I don't want any nonsense to grow around me and I want the same to be true about you. When I say that every enlightened being disappears into the same universe – and there is no question of anybody being higher or lower – you have to learn it. It is the first time that anybody is telling his disciples to drop the ego which is hiding behind the idea of 'I have got the greatest master.'

It has nothing to do with the master, it has something to do with your own ego. Drop it. I am not the greatest master. In the world of masters there is no one who is great, and there is no one who is not great. All these categories are of the mind; they don't apply when the mind is no more. You are simply an utter silence, a pure presence with no person there.

It is the same experience, the same taste, the same sweetness, the same blissfulness, the same truth, the same consciousness, the same ecstasy.

> Osho,
> 'Living in the here and now, acting spontaneously,' will I find that my actions will still be guided by experience and responsibility?

I find it always difficult to answer questions which are only intellectual, which arise out of your fear, out of your reason, but not out of your experience, not out of your meditation. You are saying, 'Living in the here and now, acting spontaneously...' and the statement is in inverted commas. You must be quoting me. It is still not your experience. Just because I have been saying 'living in the here and now, acting spontaneously' is all that can be said about meditation – and if this is possible, everything else will settle down on its own accord – your mind starts spinning questions.

You are asking '...will I find that my actions will still be guided by experience and responsibility?' You don't know anything about spontaneity, you don't know anything about living here and now. Not only that, you don't know anything about responsibility and you don't know anything about experience. Your whole question is absolutely rootless, but I will try to answer it because I don't want to hurt you. You don't yet deserve it. Once you start deserving, then I don't hesitate. Then I hit you this way and that way and you rejoice in it. But when you are not ready, I try to be as polite as possible.

Now, you are saying '...guided by experience...' which means guided by the past. If you are here and now, how can you ask this question? It is a contradiction in terms. Guided by experience? Experience is certainly of the past. In other words you are saying, 'Being here and now, will I still be guided by the past?' Then you are not here and now. Then the past is more important than the here and now to guide you. Then you are afraid: perhaps if you act spontaneously, you may lose responsibility. You don't even understand the meaning of the word *responsibility*.

Society has been so cunning. It has destroyed our most beautiful words, given them distorted meanings. Ordinarily in your dictionaries *responsibility* means duty, doing things the way you are expected to do them by your parents, by your teachers, by your priests, by your politicians, by somebody else. Your responsibility is to fulfill the demands made upon you by your elders and your society. If you act accordingly, you are a responsible person; if you act on your own – individually – then you are an irresponsible person. And your fear is that in acting spontaneously, here and now, there is a danger you may start acting individually. What will happen to your responsibility?

The fact is that *responsibility*, the very word, has to be broken into two words. It means *response ability*. And response is possible only if you are spontaneous, here and now. Response means that your attention, your awareness, your consciousness, are totally here and now, in the present. So whatever happens, you respond with your whole being. It is not a question of being in tune with somebody else, some holy scripture, or some holy idiot. It simply means to be in tune with the present moment. This ability to respond is responsibility.

But without experience you will not be able to see the contradiction in your question. Yes, I say you will be able to act with absolute response- ability. But it will not be the responsibility that you have been taught and conditioned for. It will be a totally new phenomenon. It will be just like a mirror. If you stand in front of it, it responds, it reflects you. The moment you have gone out of its focus, it is again silent. It is not a photographic film that catches your reflection. It remains always clean and available. Whoever moves in front of it – it will respond with totality and reflect the reality. The consciousness which is in the present is just like a mirror. A situation comes...

There are times when you are in the present in spite of yourself. For example, if when walking on the path you suddenly come across a long snake, are you going to be guided by past experience? Are you going to be responsible? You will forget all that you have learned: all teachings, all scriptures, all teachers, parents. Suddenly you will find the here and now because this is not a time to think about what to do, what is right and what is wrong – you will simply jump out of the way. This will be responsibility, spontaneity.

Or your house is on fire and you are taking a shower, naked. Are you going to dress before you get out of the house? Put your tie right? Polish your shoes? Have a look in the mirror? See whether all the buttons are in the right holes? No, there is no time. The house is on fire. You have to jump out of your bathroom window. And you will jump even without a towel around you. You will simply jump naked out of the shower, through the window.

This is spontaneous. It is not guided because you have not been continuously experiencing your house catching fire. It has never happened before. So there is no past experience to guide you. Nobody – your father or your mother or your teacher – has ever told you that if you are under the shower naked, and the house catches fire, at least put the towel around yourself before you jump out of the window. Nobody has taught you. There is no book. I have looked into all the books about etiquette, not a single book gives any guidance. If you are waiting for guidance you will be stuck in the bathroom. You may search in your mind but you will not find any guidance at all.

If you think you cannot do anything without guidance, then you are finished. Then there is no more life for you, no more future. The window was open. You could have jumped. But it has to be a spontaneous action in the moment, here now. And I call it absolutely responsible, responsible to life, responsible to your own being. You are avoiding committing suicide.

But you have not lived a single moment here and now. And you have never acted spontaneously. Hence the fear is natural: if you act spontaneously, what about the guidance that you have been given? Do this, don't do that. What about all those ten commandments? What about all the religious and moral teachings?

When you are acting according to past experience and teachings and conditionings, you are not a real person. You are absolutely phony, because you are not looking at the real situation. You are searching for the right answer in the memory. And the memory has never come across such a situation. Every situation is so new that you cannot be guided by experience. If you are guided by experience, it is going to be wrong action and that is the whole misery of the world. Everybody is acting wrongly, trying to be right, trying to be in tune with past experience – this is the trouble. But this situation has never happened before. It is so new.

I was driving from Jabalpur to Nagpur. Just outside a small village the car broke down. I was hoping to reach the nearest government rest house, because it was time for my afternoon sleep. So I took out a blanket and went under a tree, and the three persons who were with me simply watched what I was doing. And I went to sleep.

They said, 'This is strange. We are looking embarrassed and stupid. We are sitting here and he has gone to sleep already. He does not bother that the car has broken down and something has to be done. And he was driving. We don't know how to drive, we don't know what has gone wrong.' They all came and shook me.

I said, 'Don't disturb me. Wake me at two! Car or no car, I have to have my sleep.'

They said, 'This is strange, where should we go now?'

I said, 'Go to hell, but don't disturb me!'

They said, 'This is strange, you were driving us.'

I said, 'Forget all about it. Now the car is not worth driving. Find some car. While I am asleep, do something!'

At two o'clock I woke up. All three were sitting by the side of the car, very sad-looking, hungry. I said, 'What are you doing?'

They said, 'What can we do? We are feeling very hungry and...' I said, 'The village is near, at least you could have gone there.'

They said, 'We could not leave the car, all our luggage and everything is in it.'

I said, 'Then at least one person could have gone, two could have remained here. Or two could have gone, one could have remained here.'

They said, 'Nobody trusts anybody.'

I said, 'This is strange. I went to sleep, I trusted you all, though I knew perfectly well with a broken-down car, where could you go?'

Then I stopped a car and I asked the man who was driving if he knew anything about cars to have a look at mine, because I have never looked under the hood.

I have never ... That is the work of Avesh or Anandadas, but I have never opened the hood. I don't know what is inside it. I don't know at all whether a ghost runs it or if there is an engine. I simply know how to drive. That too is illegal, because I cannot keep two things in mind. When I am driving, I am driving. Then as fast as the car can go, it goes. I cannot bother that the government thinks it should go only fifty-five miles per hour.

I think all these governments are a little unintelligent. If you don't want a car to go beyond fifty-five, then why are cars allowed to be produced which can go one hundred and forty miles per hour? Strange! It is such an absurd situation. If you allow cars to be produced that go one hundred and forty miles per hour, you are giving me permission. And I trust that if the car says one hundred and forty, it will go a hundred and forty.

So I told the driver just to have a look. And there was nothing wrong, just something small, and he fixed it within fifteen minutes.

Those three people said, 'This is strange. So many cars have passed, but the idea did not arise in our minds to stop a car and ask somebody to look at ours.'

I said, 'You must be waiting for experience to guide you.'

To me this was a new situation, my car had never broken down before. In fact I had never driven alone. Somebody was always driving ahead of me; sometimes two cars were driving, one behind me, one ahead of me, just to take care of my car. This was the first time that I had tried to go on my own.

Those two cars prevent me from being illegal. If my front car does not move at more than forty miles per hour, how can I? So they keep me within the limit. I wanted to try the car at its full speed and that was the reason why it broke down. Although they say it should go a hundred and forty nobody tries it. Nobody thinks that the roads are made for only fifty- five miles per hour. And in India, they are not made for even that much.

And the traffic is so crazy – many, many centuries all moving along in the traffic. A bullock cart, a camel, an elephant, you name it and you will find it in the traffic. And cows are resting in the middle of the road and because they are mother cows, you cannot disturb them. And father bulls are standing in the middle of the road and, being a nonviolent country, you cannot do anything against them. You cannot take them to the court or...

Life brings new situations every day. If you are waiting to be guided by past experience, you will miss the opportunity to act responsibly, to act spontaneously. To me the greatest morality is to act spontaneously. And you will always be right because your full awareness will be involved. More than that you cannot do. More than that existence cannot demand from you. And if you are focused totally in the present, what more can you do? You are bringing your whole energy and consciousness to solve the question, to get out of the situation. More than that is not possible. So whatever happens is right.

This whole idea of responsibility and being guided by experience is told to you by people who don't want you to be here and now. They go on giving you advice on how to act, what to do, but they don't know that life does not go according to their guidelines. Their guidance becomes misguidance in any real moment.

A rich old woman whose husband has just died decides to get married. But this time she wants to have some fun. So she advertises in the world press for a young, strong twenty-year-old virgin. She gets thousands of replies, all accompanied by a photograph, but she is particularly attracted to a huge, bronzed Australian from the outback.

She flies him to New York and they are married the next week.

On the wedding night, the old bride is fixing herself up in the bathroom when she hears strange noises coming from the bedroom. She opens the door to find the huge Australian moving all the furniture to the sides of the rom.

'What are you doing?' she cries.

'Well,' replies the man, 'if it is going to be anything like making love to a kangaroo, we are going to need all the space we can get!'

That man is guided by experience. He has known only how to love a kangaroo. If you bring a man from the outback of Australia, you are in for trouble. The poor fellow is simply guided by his past experience that the space seems to be too small. If it is going to be something like making love to a kangaroo, who is going to jump all over the place...

Don't be bothered by the past. What is past is past. You have to be in the present. This is the only way to be response-able; this is the only way to be adequate to the situation you are facing. Otherwise you will find yourself always inadequate.

A woman who loves rock and roll music goes to the local tattoo artist and says, 'I want a tattoo of Elvis Presley on the inside of my thigh. Can you do it?'

'Sure,' says the man.

When he has finished, the girl looks down and says in disgust, 'That does not look like Elvis. No way! I am not going to pay you for that.'

'Okay,' says the artist, 'let me try again on your other thigh.' When he has finished, the woman is furious. 'That does not look like Elvis either,' she exclaims.

'Wait a minute,' says the tattoo artist in desperation, 'I will go out and bring back a guy off the street. If he can identify the tattoos, will you pay me?'

The girl agrees, so he rushes out and finds a drunk staggering along the road. He drags him into the studio, points at the girl's spread thighs and asks the drunkard, 'Can you recognize these two tattoos?'

The drunk says, 'I don't know about the guys on the thighs, but that guy in the middle is definitely Mick Jagger.'

So you have to respond to the reality.

A wild, Irish wedding reception is brought to a premature end when Paddy grabs the microphone and announces, 'The party is over. We have run out of booze, there is no food left, and somebody has fucked the bride.'

As everyone is heading toward the doors discussing what had happened, another announcement is made.

'It is okay, folks, you can come back. We have found another case of Guinness, Maureen is making some sandwiches, and the guy who fucked the bride has apologized. So everything is okay, come back!'

You have to respond to every kind of situation in the world. Past guidance is not of much help. Every moment you will be coming across something new. The world is very inventive. That's why all so-called religious people who are guided by the past look so sad. They are always missing the train. They go on looking for guidance, but this is not the situation for which the guidance was given. It may have been right in a certain moment, in a certain situation, but it is nothing that can be eternally true.

Only one thing is eternally true, and that is your consciousness. If you can bring your consciousness to the present, you cannot go wrong. Whatever you do out of that consciousness is always going to be right, not according to any criterion, but just because it is coming out of a total awareness. Out of total awareness, nobody has ever done anything wrong.

According to me, right is what comes out of your spontaneity and out of your consciousness and out of your presence here and now. And what is not out of your spontaneity, consciousness and your being here and now is wrong. There is no other criterion than what I have just told you. All other criteria are dead. They may have been living at one time, but that time is past. Heraclitus is right, you cannot step in the same river twice. And he was stating something about life and existence.

Hence there cannot be any guidance. All guidance will create trouble for you. You have to be kept absolutely clean of all guidance, so that you can respond with total awareness to the present situation without any hesitation, without any thinking. Just out of your silent awareness arises the response and it is the most beautiful, the most honest, most authentic answer that could have come to anybody.

It is because humanity has always been forced to be guided by the past, that there is so much misery. If what I am saying is listened to by humanity, there will be great joy all over the earth, immense laughter, immense rejoicing, no repentance, no guilt, no confessions.

21

Seriousness Is a Sickness

Osho,
Is there laughter in the mysterious silence of sat-chit-anand? There must be, because you are such a laughter. Or is your laughter just for us?

The cosmos is full of laughter, but a laughter that is very silent, a laughter that you can feel but cannot hear; a laughter that spreads all over your being. You can feel the lightness and the benediction that it brings to you, but there is no way to hear it, and there is no way to compare it to the laughter we are aware of.

It was for this reason that none of the ancient awakened ones have talked about laughter. The danger was that you may think the laughter that you know is the laughter of the ultimate. The difference is very great. Our laughter is simply ripples on the surface of the lake. The cosmic laughter of *sat-chit-anand* is the whole lake, but without ripples – utterly silent and serene, still, just like a sweetness, joyfulness, very delicate, very subtle. The ancient awakened ones never mentioned it, just as they have never mentioned many other things out of a certain fear of misunderstanding.

They have not mentioned that there is an orgasmic joy in the experience of enlightenment. It is sheer fear that the moment they use the word *orgasmic* you will think about sexual orgasm. It is not sexual, it is nonsexual. But as far as the orgasmic experience of utter relaxedness, of absolute stoppage of time and mind is concerned, it is the same.

I have dared to walk on paths untrodden by the ancient awakened ones because my feeling is that the fear of misunderstanding should not prevent one from saying the truth. And if one is too afraid of being misunderstood, then there is nothing to say, because everything is going to be misunderstood. You talk about truth and it will be understood as a fact. You talk about consciousness, and people will think, of course, that they are conscious. Maybe it will be a bigger consciousness, but there is not going to be any qualitative change. There *is* going to be qualitative change.

In fact, at a certain point every quantitative change turns into a qualitative change. You heat water. Up to ninety-nine degrees it is water. The moment it reaches a hundred degrees a transformation happens. Water starts disappearing into vapor. This is a qualitative change. You can quench your thirst with the water, but not with the vapor. Water always goes downward, it moves toward the sea, which is the lowest level. Vapor goes upward: it creates the clouds. Their paths are different, their qualities are different. Water is visible, vapor soon becomes invisible. Or, from the other side, at a certain point water can become ice. The qualities are different. Water is continuously flowing, ice has lost that flow. It is static, it has become almost like a stone.

Quantity at a certain point brings a new quality. Out of fear of being misunderstood, many things have not been said to humanity. Not that they were not known to those who have come to the highest peak, but they have chosen to speak only of certain aspects. Even those certain aspects are misunderstood. And many they have left unsaid. They know that when you reach, you will experience.

I don't want to leave anything unsaid. I don't function out of fear at all. And I trust my people's intelligence more than any awakened person has ever trusted.

Mahavira never allowed his male and female sannyasins to be together, out of fear that they might fall back into their old habits. He arranged that the women sannyasins should remain separate from the men sannyasins. If you go into details you can see the fear. The women sannyasins had to always bow down to the male sannyasins, even if the male sannyasin was just one day old. He might have taken sannyas just one day before, but still a sixty-year-old woman sannyasin had to bow down to this young person although she had been a sannyasin for sixty years. The reason? The reason was that whenever a woman bows down to a man there is protection. She is paying so much respect to you that you cannot behave in any disrespectful way toward her. And according to Mahavira, even to think about sex is disrespectful.

But all these details have a hidden psychology of fear. All male sannyasins and women sannyasins had to move in a group of five; nobody was allowed to move alone. Why? Lions move alone because they are unafraid. What was the fear? Why should five men move together? So they could keep an eye on each other, watch that nobody fell below the discipline, that nobody did things which were not allowed.

Five women moving together will be alert, watch each other, see that nobody falls in love, nobody becomes very attached to someone. Mahavira put four against one. Their jealousy, their competitiveness, and their very nature of putting the other down kept them alert. But this is functioning out of fear.

And I know Mahavira was not afraid as far as he himself was concerned. He was afraid about his disciples. That means he was not as respectful to the disciples and their intelligence as he should have been. My feeling is that, if I am not respectful toward you and I cannot trust you, then no arrangement is going to help. And all these people in the past ... Although they thought of every detail, there were always loopholes. Sannyasins have been finding ways for perverted sex.

Gautam Buddha was even afraid to initiate women in his commune as sannyasins. He remained very stubborn. But that was out of a certain fear that if women entered the commune ... He did not believe in his own sannyasins. He knew that they would start falling back into their biological heritage.

Hence many things have not been said, and many disciplines have been created which ultimately turn into fetters – and all these people were trying to help you to attain ultimate freedom. But if you want freedom, then you have to start with freedom. If you start with bondage, you cannot end with freedom. Freedom has to be the first if you want freedom to be the last, because it is a growth. They fettered their people so tightly. In Buddhism there are thirty-three thousand rules of discipline. Now, you have put almost the whole Himalayas on the chests of your sannyasins. They are small things...

A sannyasin was going to preach in faraway places where Buddha couldn't go because he was too old. Before he left, Buddha said, 'Remember a few things. Don't talk to a woman.'

The young sannyasin must have been a man of tremendous courage. He said, 'Generally, you are right. There is no need for me to talk to any woman. But there is a possibility ... At least one percent you should keep open. Ninety-nine percent of the time I will not talk, but there may be a situation in which talking becomes absolutely necessary. If I am standing on a crossroad and I don't know where to go, where the village is, and a woman comes by, should I ask her or not? Or should I remain stuck on the crossroad? Or a woman falls into a ditch and I am passing by, should I ask her if I can help?'

Buddha was silent. Then he said, 'Okay, one percent is allowed, but remember this is only in emergency situations. But never touch a woman.'

The man again raised the same question. 'There may be a situation when I have to touch a woman. A woman falls on the road, maybe sunstroke, maybe epilepsy, maybe some kind of coma ... Do you want me not to touch her? There are emergency situations when it will be very uncompassionate not to touch the woman. And I think compassion is the foundation of your philosophy.'

Very reluctantly Buddha said, 'Okay, in emergency situations you can touch a woman. But remember one thing, whenever you are close to a woman, speaking to her or touching her, be very alert. Don't get back to your old habits, which are tremendously powerful as they belong to your whole past of millions of years.'

But that one percent emergency becomes the loophole. Who is going to decide what is an emergency and what is not? So all the rules, thirty- three thousand in all, have their loopholes. You cannot have a foolproof system. Human beings are human beings.

My approach is totally different. My approach is to bring men and women so close together that there is no need to keep arbitrary disciplines. Just their very closeness, slowly, slowly will make them drop their differences. Their closeness and understanding about each other will help them go beyond their biological heritage.

The farther away you put them, the stronger is the magnetic force. One is more attracted toward the unknown, the unachievable. If the woman is sitting far away, first she looks immensely beautiful, just a goddess who has descended to the earth. But neither can you smell her perspiration nor do you know that her teeth are false; you know nothing. From far away all grass looks greener.

My own understanding and approach are totally different from anyone who has lived before me. I want to bring the male and female sannyasins as close as possible, with no restrictions, with no repressions, with no inhibitions. Sooner or later they are going to be fed up. That is my hope. The whole arrangement here is to make you completely bored.

And every day somebody writes 'Sex has fallen away.' That's great if it falls away! Repressed sex is bound to create a psychological sickness within you. But when sex drops on its own accord, just like a dead leaf dropping from a tree, it does not leave any wound on the tree. When sex drops out of understanding, not with your effort but on its own accord and your unconscious is not carrying any repression, your whole being is purified.

So I am saying everything that has not been said. Laughter has been completely avoided because it seemed that it destroyed your seriousness. And all the masters of the past wanted you to be serious about your search. They misunderstood one thing: sincerity about the search and seriousness about the search are not the same thing. I want you to be sincere and authentic about your search – not only about your search but about everything, because you cannot be sincere only in one dimension. If you are sincere, then all dimensions of your life are sincere.

But seriousness has been misunderstood as sincerity. Seriousness is a sickness. A serious seeker is searching for truth with sadness, with a burden on his head. He is not interested in the pilgrimage. He is only interested in the end, the goal, the paradise, the heaven, or whatever name has been chosen by the master. My own understanding is: there is no heaven, there is no paradise, and there is no goal. Life is an eternal pilgrimage.

Making people serious is making them sick for eternity. They will lose all joy, they will shrink, all their juice will be gone. They will not see the beauty of the path, the trees and the mountains they will be passing through. Seriousness does not allow these things; seriousness condemns all this as mundane. To me, there is no division like mundane and sacred. It is one universe. There are not two universes.

Yes, you can look at the same universe in a mundane way, you can look at it in a sacred way. The distinction is not between two universes, the distinction is only in two outlooks. And my feeling is that the more joyous you are, the more full of juice, love, laughter, music, and dance, the more your journey will become a tremendously beautiful pilgrimage. And because there is no goal...

Life is eternal, hence there cannot be any goal. All ideas of goals are contradictory to the idea of eternal life. And if life is eternal, then you have to enjoy each moment as if you have reached the goal. Each moment is a goal in itself. Don't wait to rejoice until you have reached the goal. That kind of goal does not exist. Use every moment as if you have arrived. It is always as if you have arrived; you are always arriving.

I don't think existence wants you to be serious. I have not seen a serious tree. I have not seen a serious bird. I have not seen a serious sunrise. I have not seen a serious starry night. It seems they are all laughing in their own ways, dancing in their own ways. We may not understand it, but there is a subtle feeling that the whole of existence is a celebration. I teach you celebration. And laughter has certainly to be one of the major ingredients in this celebration.

You are asking, 'Is there laughter in the mysterious silence of *sat-chit- anand*?' Certainly! But a laughter which is very silent. A soundless sound; a ripple-less lake. Full of joy, but it is too great to be expressed. There is no seriousness in the ultimate experience of existence.

And the second thing you are asking is also true. 'There must be, because you are such a laughter. Or is your laughter just for us?' The laughter of the ultimate experience is silent. You can have a very delicate feeling, but it is not tangible, you cannot hear it. It is more like a whisper. So the second thing is also true, I am absolutely nonserious. I am laughter, but you cannot hear the laughter that I have achieved in my disappearance into the whole. I have to laugh for you the way you can understand it.

As far as I am concerned, there is no need for me to remain in the body even a single moment longer. I have done my homework. Whatever I am doing – talking to you, laughing with you, rejoicing with you – my silence, my words, are all dedicated to you, to provoke a certain synchronicity.

It is said Buddha never laughed. And you have seen Jesus – it is impossible that that face can laugh. Mahavira cannot laugh. There is only one man ... And because of his laughter, all the houses I have stayed in have been called Lao Tzu House. Lao Tzu is the only man who was born laughing. Every child is born crying, so that is absolutely unique about Lao Tzu.

There are many things in his life which are unique, but nothing to be compared with the fact that he was born laughing. Everybody was shocked. His mother and father could not believe it. Even a smile would have been too much, but he was laughing. And he remained a laughter all his life.

He chose Chuang Tzu as his disciple just because Chuang Tzu was continuously making everybody laugh. He was creating such absurd stories that nobody in the whole of the world's literature can be compared to him. The stories are so complicated and so absurd, you cannot figure out the meaning. But certainly they tickle you. There are points when you suddenly start laughing. Lao Tzu loved Chuang Tzu for the simple reason that he was an absolutely nonserious man.

Except these two enlightened ones, nobody has laughed. But because of their strangeness they have not been able to create a religion like Christianity or Hinduism or Mohammedanism. What they have created has remained an individual approach. They never created any organized church, a pope, a priest, an imam, a *shankaracharya*. Nobody has succeeded them. Once in a while some individual understands the significance. They have not even named their religion. It is simply called Tao. And Tao only means 'the path' – no goal. They understood exactly what I am saying: there is no goal, only the path.

Unless you learn to enjoy the journey itself, you will become more and more serious because the goal is not there. The farther you move on the path, the more shrunken and dead you will become. If you want to remain in tune with life, then remain always in celebration. Find in every moment, in every situation, a possibility of festivity– and I don't know a single situation in which you cannot find some way to celebrate.

I have even been teaching you to celebrate death. Somebody has become free of the body and you are crying. Feel ashamed!

Somebody is out of jail and you are weeping. You wanted the poor fellow to always remain in jail. Unless you know how to turn the worst into the best, you are not aware of the real essence of sannyas.

So certainly I am laughing for you, speaking for you, living for you, but it is not in any way making you obliged to me. It is just my joy. You need not even be thankful toward me. It is out of my own joy that I will continue to rejoice with you as long as existence goes on giving me a little more time to linger on this shore.

My time is up, that is certain. It has been up for almost thirty-five years. But existence is very understanding and very intelligent and very compassionate. It knows that I am not living for myself. And to take me away is not just taking *me* away, it is taking away millions of people's laughter, their joy, their possibility of flowering. Existence will not do it; it will allow me a longer holiday. Nor am I in a hurry to reach the other shore, because I know both the shores are the same. One is on this side of the river, the other is on the other side of the river. When you reach the other side you know it is the same shore, there is nothing different.

Existence certainly understands that my body or my mind are no longer a bondage to me. I am no longer confined to them. I am already free. There is no urgency for death to make me free. I will continue until I penetrate into the deepest core of your being. All that I have experienced I would love you also to experience. Hence I am not keeping anything secret.

A psychology professor is teaching a class and tells his students that he is going to conduct a survey about sex. He says to the class, 'If you have sex once a day, raise your hand.' About fifteen percent of the students raise their hands.

'Okay,' says the professor. 'If you have sex three times a week, raise your hand.' About forty percent raise their hands.

'Interesting,' says the professor. 'If you have sex once a week, raise your hand.' Another twenty percent do.

Then the professor asks, 'If you have sex once a month, raise your hand.' A few hands go up.

'And lastly,' says the professor, with a smile, 'does anyone have sex only once a year?'

A little guy in the back of the room starts waving his arms wildly, with a huge grin on his face.

'And what are you so happy about?' asks the professor.

The guy gets up, begins to dance and sing, 'Tonight is the night!'

The pope decides to visit America. When his plane arrives, a big crowd is there to meet him. As the pope steps off the plane, the crowd chants 'Elvis, Elvis, Elvis!'

He says to them, 'My children, thank you very much, but I am the pope, not Elvis.'

He is picked up in a long white limousine that has Elvis written on the side in big sparkling letters. As he steps into the limo he says, 'Bless you, but I am the pope, not Elvis!'

He is taken to the hotel where there is a huge crowd standing behind police barricades shouting 'Elvis! Elvis! Elvis!'

The pope says with growing irritation, 'Thank you my children, but I am the pope, not Elvis!'

At last he gets to his room and as he begins to unpack his bags, the door opens and in walk three beautiful women, all dressed only in their underwear.

The pope looks at them for a moment and then says, 'Okay girls. It's one for the money, two for the show, three to get ready and go man, go!'

Osho,

I am sure that no man has ever been loved so much by so many women. How does it feel to have the biggest harem in the world?

It feels really great! I can repeat what the pope said: 'Okay girls. It is one for the money, two for the show, three to get ready and go man, go!' It is true what you are saying. No man has ever been loved so much by so many women. But you don't know a secret: one woman is dangerous, so many women are not dangerous because they fight amongst themselves. I am completely at ease; they don't have time to fight with me. That is the beauty of having a great crowd of women. It is certainly the biggest harem.

And the second secret you have to understand: it is a love that is not of the ordinary kind. It is a love that has the same fragrance as prayer. It is a love that is the ultimate expression of trust. It does not have hate as its counterpart. It is love totally purified from any impact of its opposite. And moreover, listen to this small joke.

The women of the harem are sitting in a circle, casting dice on a thick Persian carpet. Slowly, the dice make their way round the circle to the hands of each excited player. All of a sudden, the cry goes up. 'It is Camelia tonight! Poor Camelia!'

With a deep sigh Camelia rises, and with dragging footsteps she goes out through the velvet curtains.

'I would hate to be that poor kid,' remarks Gloria. 'It's the third time this week she has had to wash the dishes.'

The women who love me, they have to wash dishes. They have to clean my clothes, they have to make my bed, they have to cook my food, they have to make my clothes. They have to do all kinds of things, take care of my garden, take care of my body. This is a totally different kind of harem. It is not the harem of the Arabian Nights.

Here, love is prayer, and because it is prayer, there is no jealousy. Otherwise, so many women, if they are in love in a biological sense, will create a chaos. They will start killing each other, just out of jealousy. But I know my people, jealousy does not touch them at all.

And this harem has a specialty: it is not only the women, it has men too. There has never been any harem where men were also in the same love, in the same trust, with the same heart dancing, rejoicing. But you are right, it is certainly something that has never happened before.

Although Mahavira initiated women, all his caretakers were male sannyasins, not a single woman. I see some hidden fear somewhere. Some repressed sexuality seems to be still lurking in the shadows, not very strong, but he has not forgotten his past completely. At least in his mind one thing is certain: women can drag him down.

The same was true with Gautam Buddha, although finally he had to concede. His own mother died after his birth, and his mother's sister never married – just to look after the child. This second mother, Mahamaya, in her old age came to ask for initiation. For almost twenty years he had refused to initiate hundreds of women, but he could not refuse Mahamaya. He was very much obliged to her as she had given him more than any real mother would give. All that he was, Mahamaya had contributed to. It was impossible to say no to her. So reluctantly he had to give her initiation into sannyas. But once one woman had entered, he could not prevent other women; then hundreds of other women entered.

But as far as personal staff was concerned, those who were taking care of his body, of his day, of his food, of every small detail, they were all men – not a single woman. Not even Mahamaya was allowed. I think it is something not worth appreciating. I love Gautam Buddha, but what can I do? I can see things which are not right. They are small things, nobody has noticed them. For twenty-five centuries nobody has criticized that women were not allowed. They could have cooked better. They would have looked after him better. They could have taken care of his health better.

Every woman is a born mother. Even a small girl has the qualities of a mother. The man can do the same things, but it doesn't come from his inner being. There are male nurses in hospitals – not yet in India, but in American jails I came across them. In my first jail there were five women nurses and one male nurse. That male nurse looked stupid.

In India, the word *nurse* has become feminine. We cannot conceive that a man is a nurse. He can be a doctor, but a nurse? It seems to be cuckoo.

I saw that man who was the nurse, because for one day each week he was there to take care of me – and I could see the difference. The women nurses were making me at home even in the jail. They were trying to bring the best clothes, they were changing my bedsheets and my pillow covers every day, which is usually done only once a month. They were changing everything every day.

They used to go to the market specially to bring fruit and vegetables, because I would not eat the jail food which was nonvegetarian. They would go to the market themselves and they would bring so much fruit and so many vegetables. I told them that I could not eat that much. But a woman is basically a mother.

They cleaned the whole place so that I would not suffer from any smell. They had come to know that I am allergic to smell. They were cleaning every day. And when they were cleaning they would remove me from that place, because while they were cleaning the dust might have disturbed me.

But when the male nurse was there, there was no question of making me feel at ease. On the contrary, the male nurse was torturing me. He would come to my cell and as he was interested in philosophy, he would start asking questions.

I said to him, 'Just don't harass me.'

But he would say, 'I may never see you again.'

Once it was two o'clock in the night and I said, 'It is enough! And now I will not be able to sleep at all, you have tortured me so much. And a nurse is not supposed to torture, you have to help me.'

He said, 'You don't think about me. I will never be able to see you again. So I will ask as many questions as have been in my mind.'

No female nurse ever asked a single question. It is a totally different world on the inside of a woman.

My effort is to create the same quality of love and trust in the men who have by chance joined my caravan. And those qualities are arising. If those qualities don't arise, you remain stuck in the head. If those qualities arise, then you can enter the heart. The woman is born with those qualities of the heart, the man is born with the qualities of the head.

A disciple has to be feminine. Whether he is male or female doesn't matter, because without reaching the heart there is no way toward being, and no way of disappearing into the universal life source, *sat-chit-anand.* One day, young Herschel tells Hymie, 'Dad, I have these urges all the time.' Hymie tells him to go and visit the rabbi.

'Rabbi,' says Herschel, 'even in the middle of the night I get an erection.'

'Pray harder,' advises the rabbi. Herschel goes home and a few days later approaches Hymie.

'Dad,' he says, 'I still keep getting these urges.'

'Go and see the rabbi again,' Hymie advises. The rabbi is out, so the rabbi's wife asks Herschel about his problem.

'I get these terrible strong urges,' explains Herschel.

'Oh, that's simple,' replies the rabbi's wife. She takes him into the bedroom and makes love to him.

When Herschel gets home, Hymie asks, 'What happened?'

'It was wonderful,' Herschel replies. 'The rabbi's wife has more sense between her legs than the rabbi has in his head.'

22

Movement Is Always Horizontal; Growth Is Vertical

Osho,
During the awareness walk in the Vipassana group today, I observed that my speed was slowing down and had stopped. There seemed to be no need for moving. To where, for what? There was simply no goal anymore.

Osho, would you talk about the secret of being in a body and what keeps it moving?

It is ambition, it is desire, it is hope in the future that keeps the body moving. The word for this ambition, desire, hope used by Gautam Buddha is *tanha*. It contains all these things.

You are always looking ahead for something to happen in your life; you have not lived yet. The past is empty; you know it has been a desert. The only way to move is to keep your eyes far away on some star. It is just your imagination, but it is enough to keep the body moving. If it has not happened up to now, there is no guarantee that it will not happen in the future. Tomorrow is always open, and it is the tomorrow that keeps the body moving and the mind moving – and not only in one life.

The Eastern understanding is far deeper than the Western understanding about the inner secrets. All the mystics born in the East may disagree on every other point, but on one point their agreement is absolute – the point of reincarnation. It is not only in one life that you go on moving because of some desire or many desires. You go on moving from one life to another life, from one womb to another womb, but the reason is the same: movement means you have something in the future to be achieved.

Your future is alluring you. You are fascinated by all the possibilities that can be yours. You are not at all finished, because the past was empty. The future can be fuller, richer, better. It is this hope that remains and never dies. Every day you will find it disappointed, every life you will find it disappointed. But still the future is there, always available, open, and giving you as many chances as you want.

It can happen in deep meditation that you come to a full stop, to a state of unmoving, just a feeling that there is no need to move, no need to go anywhere – because there is nowhere to go. You have been running after shadows for so many lives, yet everything has proved to be meaningless, and you never arrive at any goal.

In deep meditation the realization can come that there is no goal, and all movement is futile. If there is no goal, there is no need to move, since all movement is goal-oriented; they are together. If the goal disappears from your mind, you will find yourself slowing down, in your body, in your mind. A deep relaxation will start settling. It is one of the most beautiful experiences. Meditation is actually meant to bring you to this full stop, where for the first time you are no longer motivated by any desire, by any ambition, by any longing.

For the first time, the future has disappeared. It has never been in existence, it was only your imagination. The future is your projection of unfulfilled desires. The more unfulfilled you are, the bigger a future you have. The more unfulfilled your being is, the richer your dreams of the future will be. But it is just in your mind.

We divide time into three tenses: the past, the present, the future. But it is a wrong division. Time consists only of the present, and mind consists only of the past and future. You are mixing two things together. Meditation will help to give you the clarity to divide them exactly as they are.

The mind is memory of the past and the mind is imagination for the future. But time itself is, undividedly, only present. You never meet yesterdays, and you never meet tomorrows. What you actually encounter, always, is the present moment. The moment you realize this, you start settling within. All movement is outward, all movement is extrovert. No-movement is introvert, no-movement is going inward, just settling at the very center of your being – not even a ripple, no thought, no dream, no desire.

This is actually the state of meditation. The mind has gone with the movement; it was another name of movement. It kept you busy and occupied with the future, with the past, with everything except the present. It was very reluctant to come to the present. That's why people find it difficult to meditate.

The mind pulls them either toward the past or toward the future, where it is perfectly happy because only in the past or in the future can it live. The present is nothing but death for the mind. But death for the mind is the beginning of your authentic life. The mind keeps you living an unauthentic life. All your despair, all your agony, all your misery are the children of your mind. As movement stops, the mind stops. Suddenly you are here and now. For the first time you touch existence. For the first time you are awake. The dream of the mind, the sleep of the mind is no longer there.

In this awakening moment you find yourself – not the ego that you used to think is you, not the old personality that you always believed in and had remained identified with. That personality, that ego, were all part of the mind; with the mind, they have all disappeared. All that fog is no longer there – just a crystal clear clarity, a transparency, a silence, alive, full of peace and a subtle joy so deep that you have never known such a depth before. You could not have even conceived or dreamed of it.

This is not only your self, this is the universal self too. Because it is also the universal self, Gautam Buddha decided to call this experience *no-self*, simply to emphasize that you are no more. Existence is; you are gone. Now the whole has taken over. You are conscious, conscious for the first time in totality.

And new things start happening to you. They are just the opposite of what the mind was creating. Instead of agony, you have ecstasy; instead of misery, you have tremendous blissfulness; instead of despair, you are utterly at ease. Instead of feeling a meaninglessness, for the first time you see the significance and the beauty and the glory that has been bestowed upon you by existence. And without any effort on your part a tremendous urge arises to thank the whole, to be grateful, to dance in gratitude, to sing in gratitude.

To me, the only true prayer is that which comes out of gratitude, not addressed to any god, not addressed to get anything, but addressed to the whole of existence for all that it has already given you. It is so much; you suddenly see that you don't deserve all this. You have never earned anything of it: all this beauty, all these blessings, all this ecstasy. You cannot conceive that it is your earning. It is simply a gift from the beyond. You can only bow down to it – not to anybody in particular, just to the whole that surrounds you. As a fish is surrounded by the ocean, you are surrounded by the whole.

You are saying, 'During the awareness walk in the Vipassana group today, I observed that my speed was slowing down and had stopped. There seemed no need for moving. To where, for what? There was simply no goal anymore.' There is certainly no goal.

Existence is enough unto itself; only for those who are feeling empty is a goal needed. Once you know your fullness, you don't have space for any goal left within you. You are not only full, you are overflowing. So the question of going anywhere does not arise because wherever you are, you are in the whole; wherever you are, you are in the same ocean. Hence a tremendous transformation arises in you.

All your past lives ... Continuous movement, from one body to another body, from one life to another life, but the same desires, the same greed, the same anger, the same violence, the same competition, the same jealousy. The Eastern word for the world is *samsara* – *samsara* means the wheel. You go on moving on a wheel, the same wheel, which goes nowhere. You are just clinging to some spoke of the wheel. The wheel goes on moving and you think you are reaching somewhere. You are not reaching anywhere, but because you continuously *think* that you are reaching somewhere, you never look inward to find you are already there where you want to be.

The home that you are searching for is within you; the god that you have been seeking is within you. You are the greatest treasure of consciousness in this whole existence. The moment you realize your glory and splendor, you see yourself as an Everest high in the sky. You cannot conceive that anything more can be added to you. Your fulfillment is so complete that an absolute stop comes. This stop becomes the explosion of enlightenment, of awakening, of your buddha nature.

What has been happening to you is tremendously beautiful. Allow it to happen more and more; go deeper into this stopping; go further away from movement and you will be closer to yourself. Don't be again caught up in the net of the mind; it does not leave so soon. You may have a few glimpses, but it does not allow you to have more than small glimpses. Immediately it grabs you back, again a desire arises, again tomorrow becomes real, again the future becomes significant and the movement and the thought process – and the whole mind is back.

On an extended business trip overseas, the Englishman is asked whether he misses his wife.

'I don't miss her all that much,' he replies. 'One day a week I hire a local woman to come in and nag.'

The mind is your wife. Whether you are man or woman, it does not matter. The mind is your wife and a constant nag. It goes on nagging you, and you have become so accustomed to it that sometimes you even have to hire a woman to nag you; life seems to be so empty without somebody nagging you. The mind is continuously giving you new illusions, new hallucinations, new delusions; it is very inventive. It goes on creating new goals for you. If old goals are finished, if you have realized that there are no such goals, it will invent new goals.

That's how religious people have come to invent paradise, heaven, God – these are new goals. Old goals have been dropped, but the mind is very clever. It immediately comes from the back door with a new goal. It says: 'It is very good. Money is not the goal of life. And power is not the goal. Neither is respectability nor anything of this world. The real goal is God.'

God is a mind invention, just as money is a mind invention. Heaven is as much a mind invention as is respectability, name, fame – they are all mind projections. I emphasize again and again to you that there is no God. I have nothing against God; I cannot have because he does not exist. My emphasis is for a different reason – I am not an atheist. My emphasis is so that when in your meditation mind starts stopping, it cannot give you goals like God, paradise, heaven.

Those are the last tricks in its bag. I am removing them, for the simple reason that it is very easy to get rid of greed, but it is very difficult to see that heaven is nothing but your greed. It has come in with such a beautiful name, with such a great religious aroma around it, with such spirituality. Nobody thinks that God is your greed. Nobody has exactly said in the whole history of mankind that God is your greed, that God is nothing but the last effort of the mind to nag you again to move.

All that the mind wants is to go on moving. Don't stop, because when stopping, the mind starts trembling. To stop means digging a grave for the mind and, of course, nobody wants to die. Your mind has been with you so long, it wants to remain with you – an old friendship, a long companionship. In misery, in happiness, it has been with you. It has done everything that you wanted. It has played all kinds of roles. It has lied for you; it has always been a support for you. When life was continuously dark, it gave you glimpses of a faraway star: 'Don't be worried. If today it is dark, tomorrow it is not going to be dark. It is not going to be dark forever. One day, the sunrise is certain.'

This long, long friendship – and suddenly you stop. The mind tries in every way to push you, to nag you into some new project. Old projects are no longer working; it is a great salesman.

I have heard...

A man was complaining to a real estate agency: 'Where is that old fellow who sold me land?'

The owner of the agency asked, 'What is the problem?'

He said, 'What is the problem? I am going to shoot him. He has sold me land which is at least twelve feet below the road. In the rainy season it will become a lake. And I have purchased it to build a house for myself. My house will be drowned. Just tell me where that old fellow is!'

The owner said, 'Right now, he is not in the office. But when he comes back I will talk to him and if something has gone wrong, we will settle it. I will send him to your house.'

When the salesman came, the owner was very angry. 'This is too much. What have you done?'

He said, 'I told him everything. I told him that he will have the most magnificent house within the lake. Build the house and wait for the rains. And it is surrounded by such beautiful hills.'

The owner asked, 'Beautiful hills?'

He said, 'Yes, but they are thousands of miles away. They are very difficult to see. Only once in a while, when the sky is very clear, you can see them. And I have shown him.'

But the owner said, 'Something has to be done. He is very angry. He wants to shoot you.'

He said, 'Don't be worried. Just give me those two boats that we have been stuck with for many years and we have not been able to sell to anybody. They are getting completely rotten. Just give me those two boats.'

The owner said, 'What are you intending to do?'

He said, 'I am going to sell those two boats to that man who wants to shoot me.'

The owner said, 'If you want to try, good luck to you! Take those boats, but be careful. That man is really angry. I am not joking.'

After an hour the man came back and said, 'I have sold those two boats.

I again described the beauty of the lake and then I said "How secure your house will be. Nobody can reach it. And these beautiful boats ... You can just go in the boat to your house. And unless you want somebody else to come, nobody can come in. No beggars to torture you, no guests, no neighbors – just think of it. And on a beautiful lake, surrounded by hills and the hills reflected in a full-moon night." Then the man said, "Done. Give me the boats."'

The salesman said to the owner, 'Now, remember: don't give my address to that man, because this illusion that I have given to him is not going to last long. Soon he will come to his senses, because that place is really not worth anything. First to build a house there, and then the house will be half drowned. No electricity, no telephone, no neighbors, and the mountains are thousands of miles away; they don't reflect in the lake.

'That man is going to be angry and now he is stuck with those two boats. He does not know that they are not going to work, and he will not know until the rains come. He will be drowned in those boats; he will not reach his house. You know those boats perfectly well.'

But a salesman can manage to create an illusion. Just the description, and the mind is a great salesman. It goes on selling you new goals and you never think that all that it has ever sold you has failed. Nothing has ever succeeded. It is really a con man. It goes on creating, inventing new ideas, and because you are empty you are ready to be filled by any kind of rubbish. Your present is not a rejoicing; your past has just been tears; you get caught in future dreams very quickly.

Deepen your experiences. Let them happen more often. This is the whole purpose of all the meditations that are happening here – to bring you to a full stop. Then suddenly, the energy that was moving outward, starts settling inward.

When all your life forces have centered at the very roots of your being, you will start growing in a new direction. Now it will not be a movement, it will be a growth. Movement is always horizontal; growth is vertical. The tree grows vertically; you move horizontally. The world is horizontal; spirituality is vertical. Once your energies are all concentrated in the roots, there will be new sprouts, new foliage, new branches, and you have started moving upward, toward the stars.

This is not an old movement, it is a totally different phenomenon. The horizontal movement we know, when we say somebody is growing old. The vertical movement is when we say somebody is growing up. Just becoming old is not going to lead you anywhere except to death and a new life with the old desires again – the same circle. Once your life starts growing instead of moving, it takes a totally different dimension upward, against the gravitation of this world, toward the open sky. And only in this growth, one day your potentiality blossoms.

The day you see your flowers opening up and releasing their fragrance, you have come to know for the first time something that can be called spiritual. And it is not a goal. The trees are not growing toward some goal, they are growing toward their potential, which is intrinsic, which is hidden in them. They want to come to a point where what is hidden becomes available to the whole of existence. What is in the seed comes into the flower.

Enlightenment is your flowering.

Meditation will bring you to the point from where your existence takes a new dimension – the dimension of enlightenment. You can call it *sat-chit-anand.*

Osho,

Sitting close to you these last few mornings and looking into your eyes, I felt so much like a small child, full of innocence and excitement. Many times I wanted to wave my hand in the air wildly and shout, 'Hello, hello, hello, my most beloved.' Osho, can you talk about this blissful innocence that I am feeling and how it relates to meditation?

The innocence of a child has a similarity to the innocence of a sage. But it is not exactly the same. Because of the similarity, many mystics have used childhood as an example. You don't know anything about what happens in the innermost world of a sage. You need some examples of something you know about. So one thing has to be remembered: all those examples are not exactly what will happen in your ultimate state of realization, but they are certainly some indication.

The child is innocent, but his innocence is more ignorance than wisdom. You cannot call a child wise. His innocence is natural, but his ignorance is side by side with his innocence; they are almost together. The child's innocence is overshadowed by his ignorance.

The sage also has the same innocence, but there is no longer any overshadowing ignorance. His innocence is absolutely pure, unpolluted, and because his innocence is no longer associated with ignorance, it brings a transformation to the very quality of his innocence – it becomes wisdom.

The child is ignorant, the sage is wise, but the innocence has the same quality: just the association has changed. The child has the same innocence, but associated with ignorance; hence it has no value. The sage has the same innocence, but as it is no longer associated with ignorance, it has immense value; wisdom has blossomed. The child does not know, but he does not know that he does not know. The sage also does not know, but he knows it – and that makes a great difference.

Because the child does not know he is ignorant, he is bound to accumulate knowledgeability to cover up his ignorance. He wants to be knowledgeable like anybody else – as quickly as possible. The wise man is no longer ignorant, hence he does not need any knowledge. With ignorance, knowledge has also gone. It is just like when you are sick, you need medicine; when you are healthy again, the medicine is thrown away. Knowledge is a medicine for ignorance. But when there is no ignorance, what are you going to do with all your medicines? Give them to the Lions Club. These people go on accumulating all kinds of medicines.

The wise man is not knowledgeable. His wisdom has a totally different quality. He sees. He is a seer. He is not informed, he is transformed. He has come to a new stage of consciousness from where he can see far away.

P. D. Ouspensky uses this as an example. His master Gurdjieff also used to use the same example.

You are sitting under a tree. You can see the road on both sides to a certain extent and then it goes beyond your vision. You cannot see more than that. Somebody is sitting in the tree. His vision of the road will be far greater than yours. He will see miles on one side, miles on the other side. If, from the left side, a bullock cart comes along the road, he will see it. For you it is still in the future; for him it is in the present. For you it is in the future because you can't see it.

Soon the time will come when you see it – then it will become present for you. And the time will come when it will move away on the road toward the right and soon you will not see it anymore. It will become past. But to the man sitting in the tree, when it was future for you, for him it was present. When it was present for you, it was also present for him. When it became past to you, it was still present to him because he was seeing it from a higher viewpoint.

The man of wisdom is innocent, but on a far higher level. He is not childish. His innocence is out of maturity; his innocence is out of tremendous experience. The child is without any experience; the sage has passed through all kinds of experiences, good and bad, and he has transcended them. He has again become a child, but his childhood, the second childhood, is based on a very solid ground which cannot be taken away.

So what you have been feeling is beautiful, but remember: it is not the place to stop. It is the place to begin. It is beautiful to have a childlike innocence, but it is still far away from the authentic innocence of maturity.

Paddy climbs up a flag pole and begins shouting as loudly as he can. The cops arrest him and he is charged with disturbing the peace. Later he is sent to a psychiatric hospital for examination.

'How do you explain your behavior?' asks the head shrink.

'It is like this, doctor,' replies Paddy. 'If I didn't do something crazy once in a while I would go nuts.'

An innocent man is saying something immensely wise. He is saying, 'If I didn't go crazy once in a while I would go nuts.' It is a well-known, well-established fact that women go crazy once in a while – any excuse. And if there is no excuse, at least nature has provided them with the period. Then whatever they do is acceptable. Their craziness cannot be condemned; they have a rationalization. But even without the period they can go crazy at any moment; that saves them from going nuts. It is only men who go nuts, because they don't go crazy once in a while; they go on accumulating. Rather than going crazy in installments, they go wholesale.

Just look in the madhouses of the world. There are four times more men than women – it is not a small difference. Four times more men go mad. And what is the strategy of the woman so she avoids that much madness? She often goes crazy. So in installments – just a little bit of craziness today and a little bit tomorrow – she divides it up. All the time she remains sane, so there is no need for her to be in a madhouse.

Man has been told from his very childhood: 'You are not supposed to go crazy like women. You are not even supposed to weep and cry. Tears are not allowed to men. Even if somebody dies, you have to keep yourself together; you are not to behave like a woman.' Because of this nonsense teaching, four times more men than women are in madhouses.

I have made it absolutely compulsory that every morning you do Dynamic Meditation. That is nothing but giving you a chance every day of installment craziness, so the whole day you remain sane. It is enough for twenty-four hours. Then again comes another morning and you go crazy. None of my people are ever going to be mad. [*A loud laugh causes general laughter.*] You look! Sardarji is going crazy. But as he goes crazy once in a while, he is going to remain the sanest man.

After five days locked away in their hotel room, the honeymoon couple finally decides to go out for the evening. The husband calls the front desk to find out what is playing at the movies.

'Darling,' he calls out to his wife, 'do you want to see Oliver Twist?'

'Honey,' she calls back, 'if you show me one more trick with that thing, I'll scream.'

Two old cows are standing together in the pasture chewing the cud, when one of them looks up and says, 'Look, here comes that cross-eyed bull. We had better separate or he will miss us both.'

Different women have different reactions when their husbands kiss them in bed.

The French woman says, 'Ooh-la-la, Pierre, ooh-la-la, your kisses are ooh-la-la.'

The English woman says, 'Jolly well done! I say, Winston, your kisses are jolly well done.'

The Jewish woman says, 'You know, Sam, the ceiling needs painting.'

This is a crazy world. From your innocence, if it is childlike innocence, the ways depart in two directions. Either you will end up in this big madhouse that you call the world. Or if you move in a different direction and the path is available, you can end up with great wisdom. You can be a sage.

You just have to remember what is the difference between these two paths. The path that goes to the madhouse, the big madhouse you call the world, is very crowded. Avoid crowds. Be certain that where everybody is going is the wrong path. The ordinary logic says: 'That is the right path because everybody is on it; how can it be wrong?'

But I say unto you: find the path where nobody is going and there is every chance you will end up being wise. Your very first step alone is the right step toward ultimate realization. It is the cowards who go with the crowd – and I have never heard of cowards becoming enlightened. They can become Christian sheep, but they cannot become lions. And I would like my people to be lions.

Choose a path which leads you more and more deeply into aloneness. Choose a path which is not traditional, which is not orthodox. Choose a path which is basically revolutionary. Each step is a revolt against all that is past and old. That rotten crap is driving the whole world mad.

On this path you are no longer a Christian. You cannot be, because to be a Christian means to be part of a crowd. You are no longer a Hindu, because you are no longer part of a crowd, you are an individual. Only individuals have ever become awakened. Crowds never become enlightened. Only individuals, only people who have guts and courage to be alone are capable of stopping the movement of the mind and can settle into their inner innocence.

The deeper you go within yourself, the purer the sources of consciousness that you will find. When you reach the very center of your being, you have reached the center of the universe. Then wisdom blossoms; you become a sage. This is a rebirth, a resurrection. You die as the world wanted you to be and you find exactly what existence has been longing for you to be. Existence gives you all that you are asking, longing for.

The so-called mad world will only give you promises, but the goods are never delivered. People die in this world after a whole life of simple despair and anguish. If you want to live ecstatically and die ecstatically, you will have to choose the path of aloneness. And that is the path of meditation too, because your absolute aloneness is always inward.

Outside you will always meet with a crowd – on any path. You may have chosen a path that seems to be silent, no traffic, but ahead you don't know. On every path you will find some crowd. Somewhere a bigger crowd – Catholics; somewhere smaller crowds. But you will find them.

There is only one path that goes inward, where you will not find a single human being, where you will find only silence, peace. Then you will find yourself, and after that even *you* will not be there.

The aloneness becomes so thick and dense that you cannot be there, you cannot have an *I*, an ego, a sense of separation from existence. Your *I* is nothing but a sense of separation. When you find yourself one with existence, no knowledge is needed. In your innocence, you will know all that is great, all that is beautiful, all that is true. But it will not be a repetition from any scripture and it will not be anything borrowed. It will be truly yours, it will have your signature on it.

And this is one of the greatest blessings in life, to have some experience which is absolutely yours and not a carbon copy. Only that which is absolutely new – original, arising from the very source of your being – can give you satisfaction, fulfillment, contentment and a deep understanding of all the mysteries of life and existence.

It is good to start with innocence, but remember there are two kinds of innocence: one is of the child and the other is of the meditator. The meditator also becomes a child, but that is on such a different level, at such a great height – as if the child is in the valley and the enlightened man who has again become a child is on the sunlit peak. The distance is tremendous. But there is a certain similarity, a thread running from the child to the heart of the sage. The child cannot understand the sage, but the sage can understand the child. Always remember it as a fundamental rule: the lower cannot understand the higher, but the higher can always understand the lower.

If anything in your life can be compared with that high peak, it is your childhood. Try to rediscover it. Don't cover it with knowledge so that you can forget it. Remove all knowledge, so that you can rediscover your innocence. As you remove your knowledge, you will be removing your mind itself, because your mind is a collective name for your knowledge. It is not any entity – just as we call these trees around here 'the garden,' but the garden is only a collective name. If you go looking for the garden, you are not going to find it. You will always find individual trees, rosebushes, seasonal flowers, but you will not find the garden as such anywhere.

Remember, we get lost with collective names many times. We start thinking that those collective names are realities; they are not. Society does not exist. Organized religion does not exist; it only pretends. Christianity, Islam, Buddhism don't exist – all pretensions. What exists is the individual.

The mind does not exist, it is only a collective name for all your knowledge. Take out, by and by, all that you know and when all that you know has been taken away, you will not find any mind there, not even a container in which all that knowledge was contained. There *is* no container. Being purely innocent, centered in yourself, knowing that life is a mystery and there is nothing to know, that knowledge is by its very nature impossible, we are surrounded by the miraculous.

It is beautiful that we are surrounded by the miraculous because that makes life a continuous excitement, an ecstasy. You never tire of discovering new spaces within you. You are never bored because the deeper you move within yourself, there is always something new. The deeper you move within yourself, you are moving toward existence itself, because deep down you are rooted in existence. If a tree moves deep into its roots, it will find the earth, it will find the ocean. It is rooted in the earth, deriving water from the ocean.

If we move into our center ... You will be surprised to know that our center also has its roots in existence, though they are not visible roots. Our consciousness is just like air. It is not visible, but you can feel it. You can feel when the air is cool and you can feel when the air is hot. You can feel your consciousness in many ways: when it is pure, it is cool; when it is impure, it is hot. Impure with anger, impure with greed, impure with desires, impure with goals – then it is hot, then it is not at ease, then there is no peace inside. But when all these desires have left you, there is a tremendous coolness which goes on growing.

As you come closer to yourself, you are coming closer to the universe – and the greatest moment in your life is when you accept the mystery of existence as it is, without asking any question. Then you have understood one thing: existence is mysterious and is going to remain mysterious. There is no need of any knowledge. That means you have settled with the universe as mysterious and you have settled with yourself as innocent.

This is the second birth. In India we have called this state *dwij*, the second birth. And this is our search here.

Now, here is something to make your silence deeper.

Herman is an eternal optimist, and whatever happens to him, he always says, 'Well, it could have been worse.'

One day his neighbor, Amos, comes home and finds his wife in bed with a strange man. In a fit of rage, Amos shoots them dead, and is later arrested for murder.

While everyone is discussing the tragedy, Herman says, 'Well, it could have been worse.'

'How could it be worse?' says an angry neighbor. 'Two people are dead and a nice guy like Amos is going to prison for the rest of his life.'

'Well,' insists Herman, 'if Amos had come home on Thursday afternoon, *I'd* be dead!'

23

The World of Quality Not Quantity

Osho,
I love to cry and to feel this sweet pain of longing in my heart that has been visiting me for a while. It seems to be a treasure that is bringing me back after having been lost in the mind. I have experienced a stillness beyond this pain and tears; yet, sometimes it feels as if I would love to cry my way to God. Osho, is it possible to indulge too much in this sensation in my heart?

There are a thousand and one ways to reach to the ultimate. If your crying is out of joy, then your tears are more valuable than any laughter can be. It all depends on the quality. Tears can be of pain, tears can be of blissfulness, tears can be of silence, tears can be of gratitude. And when tears are of gratitude it is not suffering, it is rejoicing – just in your own style.

I don't deny any possibility of reaching to the divine. All possibilities are available – just choose the one that suits you best. Don't be concerned and don't compare with others; that brings complexity. Just watch yourself. If your tears are helping your growth, making you richer, making you more loving, making you more lively, if you feel tears are bringing your spring closer, these same tears will turn into flowers. So you have to be careful.

The criterion is simple: anything that gives you a feeling of fullness, overflowing; anything that gives you a sensation of your interiority, your subjectivity; anything that makes you aware of the immense mystery that you are and that the whole existence is, means you are on the right path. And everybody has to move on his own path.

There are no highways to the divine. Everybody has to move, not on ready-made pathways, but on the contrary, as you move you make your own path. And it is going to be only for you, especially for you. Nobody else will be able to walk on the same path. No two individuals are the same. Their uniqueness is such that their paths cannot be the same either. No two enlightened persons in the world have reached to the ultimate explosion in the same way.

This has created a great difficulty. You follow someone. Naturally he knows the way – he has reached – and he teaches you the way, forgetting completely that you are not him. Your path is going to be different. So the only authentic masters are those who don't give you details of the path, who don't give you a map to follow, a guidebook to carry with you. That guidebook may have been exactly the right thing for the master himself, but it is not going to be the right thing for you.

Although you would like the consolation of being definite, certain, guaranteed, these are wrong desires. These are the desires which create hindrances. The master can only give you a guarantee if you move on *his* path. He knows it, he has traveled on it. He knows the pitfalls; he can make you aware of mistakes which he committed. But this is going to be too cheap, and existence is not cheap at all. It is the costliest.

The problem for the authentic master is to give you not guidance, but only a longing, such a tremendous longing that it can make its own path. The master cannot give you the path, he can only create in you such a tremendous thirst that the thirst will create the path for you.

It is going to be different for everyone. Existence loves variety, and it is good that variety is acceptable to existence, otherwise life would have been utterly boring. Not only the ordinary life, but the extraordinary life of a seeker would also be boring. You would be like railway trains moving on fixed rails from one station to another, shunting from here and there.

No, you are not railway trains. You are far more like wild mountain rivers which go on changing their paths, which go on moving toward the ocean on their own intuitive indications. There is no guidebook, there is no map, there was never anything like that. But every river has reached the ocean, from all directions, from wherever it arises – it does not matter. In the deepest being of the river, one thing is certain: it is a river. It belongs to the ocean. However long the journey may be, however tedious the path, nobody can prevent it from reaching the ocean. It does not need any support, it simply starts moving on its own. It makes its way.

The same is true about enlightenment, the experience that brings you to your absolute flowering. You have to trust in yourself. The master can create the trust. The master can create the great love affair with the universe. The master can create a sweet pain of longing in your heart.

But the so-called ordinary teachers belonging to different religions don't create these things. They take them for granted, as if everybody is longing for God. The churches are full, the temples are full, the synagogues are full. There is a deception all around the earth that everybody is religious. But these same people who go to the churches, to the synagogues, to the temples, to the mosques, are the people who commit all kinds of crimes against humanity, against themselves. These are the same people who create wars and massacres and rapes. It is a very strange world. And every Sunday they are in the church.

So, on the one hand you can see everybody is religious and on the other hand, if you have a little deeper insight, you can see nobody is religious. Who has created this kind of situation? – the priests, the missionaries, the teachers who are more interested in putting you on a certain path, with a certain dogma and a certain discipline. *You* are not important to them. What is important to them is Christianity, Hinduism, Buddhism. But you should remember: thousands of years have passed and we have not been able to produce another Gautam Buddha, or another Jesus, or another Lao Tzu.

It is not that millions of people have not tried the same path, but the path that led Gautam Buddha to his highest consciousness does not lead anybody else anywhere, except to a certain phoniness, hypocrisy. I don't want any of you to be hypocrites. That is the ugliest thing that can happen to anyone. But how to protect you from being a hypocrite?

There is only one way: I should not give you any direct instructions about the path. On the contrary, I should give you so much thirst, so much longing, so much sweet pain in your heart, that the very longing starts finding its own path, making its own path. All of you will reach one day to the same height of consciousness, but from different directions, from different territories. It is beautiful that the whole of existence, wherever you are, has a way toward the highest consciousness.

Nothing is wrong about your tears. You are asking, 'Is it possible to indulge too much in this sensation in my heart?' No! You cannot indulge too much. There is no such thing as too much indulgence in love, too much indulgence in trust, too much indulgence in the search, too much indulgence in longing – there is no such thing.

You are always less than your potential. Your potential is tremendous. But remember: these tears, this sweet pain in itself are not the goal. It is just the beginning of a long journey, a beautiful journey. So don't stop at it. That is the only possibility of missing. Indulge as much as you can manage. And the more you can manage, the more you will be able to see that much more is still possible. There is no end to it. But don't make it your whole lifestyle, it is just a beginning. The seed is dissolving, and there *is* pain, and the new sprouts will be coming. But nowhere is there a stop. Just go on growing. You will pass through many different climates. Just keep the thread of longing alive and you cannot go astray.

The only fear is, I remind you again, that you may start enjoying this suffering. If it is not becoming a search, it will become a suffering. That's how masochists are created in the world. They start loving their suffering. Tears are beautiful, but just remaining at tears is dangerous. Who is going to reach the ocean? Your tears have to become oceans, you have to move onward. Your longing has to become deeper and deeper every day. Tears are a good beginning – and these same tears will bring you to greater joys than you have ever dreamed of.

Mendel Kravitz saves up for many years to buy a really fine tailor-made suit, his very first. But after he's been out in it for an hour, he notices that there are things wrong with it. He goes back to the tailor.

'The arms are too long,' says Mendel.

'No problem,' replies the tailor. 'Just hold your arms out further and bend at the elbows.'

'But the trouser legs are too long,' says Mendel.

'Right,' replies the tailor. 'No problem, just walk with your knees bent.'

'But the collar is too high, it's halfway up the back of my head!' says Mendel.

'Okay, just poke your head out further,' says the tailor.

So Mendel goes out into the world with his first tailor-made suit. As he's passing a couple in the street, the woman says, 'Look at that poor man! He must have had polio.'

'Yes,' her husband replies. 'But he must have a great tailor. His suit fits him perfectly.'

There are thousands of teachers like that tailor. They are not concerned with you, they are concerned with their suits. They will make you crippled. They will pull your hands this way and that, your legs this way and that, they will pull your neck. They will almost put you on a traction machine so you fit the suit. You are made for the suit, not the suit for you. That's what all the religions of the world are doing. They are not made for you, you are made for them. So you have to behave according to their principles, their criteria, their path. Otherwise you are wrong.

I say to you, you are not made for any creed, any dogma, any philosophy, any religion. You are just made for yourself. And you have to find your own way of living, your own way of seeing, your own way of silence, your own way to bliss.

Religion is absolutely an individual phenomenon. The greatest calamity that has happened is that all religions have become collective. And the moment a religion becomes organized, it is no longer a religion, it is just a kind of politics in the name of religion. It has no concern with people.

Joseph Stalin killed thirty million Russians after the revolution. Do you think Russia had thirty million capitalists? Even to find thirty capitalists in the pre-revolution Russia would have been very difficult. It was a poor country, one of the poorest. The revolution was made for the proletariat and then thirty million proletarians were massacred because they did not fit with Stalin's idea of revolution. You have to fit with somebody's idea, otherwise they immediately declare you a misfit. They condemn you.

As far as I am concerned, to be a misfit in your society is a great compliment. You are all misfits. I have been gathering all kinds of misfits. They fit with me perfectly well. The more far-out misfits they are, the closer they come to me, because I can see they are individuals. They have risked everything for their individuality, for their uniqueness. They have not allowed anybody to enslave them, any society, any religion, any political ideology. These are the real people, the very salt of the earth.

I want you all to be just yourself – not followers of anybody, including me, but only fellow travelers. You can exchange your experiences with each other, but you don't have to exchange your paths, because your path is just your path, exclusively yours. Nobody will ever pass on that path again, and nobody has ever passed on that path before – only you.

This is the beauty of existence: it gives space to everyone, each unique individual.

Osho,
Sometimes, while feeling inferior and lonely because of my handicapped body and wheelchair, I suddenly become aware that as long as I can feel this pain, I am very alive. In these moments, there is absolute joy inside me, so much gratitude for each and every thing.

Osho, is it really possible to grow even through suffering?

Prem Amido, I understand your situation and the problem, but you are facing your situation with great courage. I am happy with you. You *are* suffering because of a crippled body, but you are not the body. Nor are you crippled. Your consciousness is as free as anybody else's. Of course your path is going to be a little difficult. Your body is going to create continuous suffering for you.

But perhaps, if you are alert enough – and I can see you are – you can change suffering itself into a blessing in disguise. It is one of the most significant things to understand. Why have all religions insisted that their saints and sages should be very austere, ascetic, almost torturing themselves? They were not crippled like you, but they made themselves crippled in many ways.

In Alexandria, twelve hundred years ago, a Christian saint sat on an old pillar some thirty feet high. It was part of a ruin of a beautiful temple. He remained sitting on that pillar; he never came down. He never moved from that pillar until he was dead. You can understand his suffering. It was self-created. He had to sleep on that pillar, sitting – very dangerous, any moment he could have fallen. People used to bring food and he used to pull the food up with a rope. And he was defecating from the top of the pillar, pissing from the top of the pillar. He had no shelter from the sun, the rain, the cold – but he became very famous.

And this is not a unique case. Millions of saints of different religions have created a situation of suffering for themselves, either by fasting ... One Hindu mystic even took out his eyes, and eyes are the most sensitive part of your body. Eighty percent of your connection with existence is through the eyes. The other four senses between them have only twenty percent. To pull out your eyes with your own hands is to destroy eighty percent of your life. But he was very much respected.

What has happened to all these people? I have seen saints in India, standing for twelve years, fifteen years, not for a single moment sitting down or sleeping, just standing. They have a certain device on which they keep their hands, and by and by the upper part of their body shrinks and their legs become like elephants'. Now even if they want to bend them they cannot.

I have seen saints who have been living only on tea, no other food. Now, tea is not food, it is not nourishment. All these people were under the illusion that when you are living comfortably, without any pain, without any suffering, you may forget yourself, you may lose your awareness. They are using suffering as a means to awareness. I am not in support of it.

As far as you are concerned you are not creating the suffering. The suffering is there. You can use it to remain alert. And you are rightly observing that the pain keeps you feeling that you are still alive. I have seen you laughing. You cannot dance, but I have seen by the effort in your whole being that you want to dance. The body is preventing it; the body is not in the right position. You cannot do anything about it, but you can use this natural suffering to create a clearer awareness, more consciousness. And then suddenly you will feel even grateful to the suffering.

I am not saying that people have to create suffering, that is stupid. I am saying that if you find yourself in suffering, use that suffering for your inner growth. That is intelligence. And, in you

I see immense intelligence, and a consciousness which wants to celebrate. Even if your body is not cooperating with you, don't be worried. The body is going to die one day – everyone's body dies – but you are going to be eternally here. It is your consciousness that really matters.

It is perfectly good: you can grow even through suffering. One can grow from any place where one finds oneself. Growth is possible from infinite sources. Just go on enjoying even the pain because it keeps you alert to your being alive. Most of the people whose bodies are not crippled like your body, may, at the last count, be losers, not winners. They are so comfortable with their bodies that they remain identified with the body. You cannot identify with your body, it is too painful. You have to separate yourself from the body and this very separation will bring you witnessing, watching, alertness.

There may be many problems for you, but you can change every problem into a device – you have to. I have many sannyasins who are in the same position as you, in a wheelchair. But strangely enough – and I have watched all of them – they become immensely joyful, laughing, loving. The other day I had another question from you which I did not answer.

I felt your pain myself. You were saying that you would also like to love someone. I can understand – a natural instinct, and the instinct does not know that your body is crippled. And the people have become so body- oriented that they don't see inside the body a beautiful human being. They just look *at* the body. Naturally, no woman will feel attracted toward you; it hurts. It hurts me too, that's why I did not answer the question. I was waiting for you to ask some other question. Then I would talk about your first question too.

Take that too as part of your whole suffering. You are alone. Don't feel lonely. Just feel a deep aloneness and let that aloneness grow with your consciousness of suffering and pain. Accept that perhaps nobody is going to love you, but you yourself can love. You can love the trees, they are not so fussy. You can love the stars in the night. They will not object saying 'Amido, you don't have the right body.' You can love the whole universe. And perhaps in this place there may be some woman compassionate enough, meditative enough, who may be able to see your consciousness and will not bother about your body.

Anyway, women don't care much about the bodies of men. They are very conscious about their own bodies, but no woman is interested in the body of the man. In fact, when the man is making love to them, they close their eyes. They don't want to see all the gymnastics that the poor fellow is doing on top of them. They are praying to God, 'Finish it soon!' because a man making love does not have the same face, it becomes distorted. He is perspiring, huffing and puffing; love seems to be such an arduous thing, like going uphill. He himself knows it is stupid, but still the man wants the light to be on. He is interested in the woman's body.

Most men don't feel satisfied with a wife for the simple reason that she lies down almost dead, with closed eyes. She is just a victim, somehow waiting for this guy to finish. These people start going to the prostitutes. Prostitutes are phony, because they don't love those people, they love only their money. They moan and groan and they scream as if the man is doing great, making the woman so satisfied. This is all phony, this is all acting; this is the attraction of the prostitutes around the world for as long as man has been in existence. The prostitute is satisfying the customer. And the greatest satisfaction of the customer is to feel that he is man enough to satisfy a woman. And when he sees the woman moving from side to side, groaning, moaning, shouting 'Ooh-la-la' – all phony – he feels great!

But the wife does not behave in the same way because, in the first place, he is not her customer. It is not a business. Secondly, it is an everyday affair. In fact, every time a husband tries to make love to the woman, she makes excuses. Sometimes it is a period and sometimes it is a headache and sometimes she is too tired, and sometimes the cook has left. There are a thousand-and-one excuses. She simply wants to avoid the encounter. The woman is not interested in the man's body.

Now, because of the women's liberation movement, a few new things have come into existence for which history has no precedent: male prostitutes, and *Playgirl*, a pornographic magazine just to compete with all kinds of *Playboy*-type magazines. But I don't think it is natural to women: it is simply a reaction against men. Women are more interested in your loving qualities, more interested in your being, in your consciousness, in your friendliness.

Amido, it is possible – perhaps it is possible only in my place – that some compassionate woman may give you some experience of love. One has to transcend it, but I can understand your difficulty. You have not experienced it, so transcendence becomes absolutely impossible. But as far as you are concerned, don't hanker for it. Perhaps nature and existence do not want you to be in the same foolish game as all other human beings.

But biology is biology. A woman is needed to complete the man, otherwise both are incomplete. So you just wait in your wheelchair. And I know there are women of tremendous compassion who may come and take your wheelchair and you with it. Then don't make a fuss, because you don't have much choice. You can keep your eyes closed. Just a woman is enough; don't be romantic. Leave that for other fools.

Ronald Reagan has always had a complex about his small prick. One day he is taking a piss next to Ed Meese when he notices that Meese's prick is enormous.

'My God, Ed!' exclaims Reagan. '*That* is a fair-sized organ!'

'Well,' says Meese, 'it wasn't always this big. But every night I gave it three whacks against the bedpost and before I knew it, it started to grow.'

Reagan thinks this over very carefully and then decides to give it a try. When he goes up to bed that night, Nancy is already asleep. So he tiptoes over to the bed and whacks his prick against the bedpost three times. Nancy wakes up and murmurs, 'Ed, is that you?'

Osho,
For three days I have felt such a little space inside, such a little flame. And the only feeling I have is to protect this little flame. I feel she is so fragile, I just want to keep her, to caress her, and when I touch her, so many tears come. Osho, is it okay just to take care of her, to enjoy her presence just by myself, because it is hard to share her now. I am afraid to lose this space.

It happens to everybody when he discovers his inner life. It is a flame. In the beginning it is small, and the natural tendency of the mind is to protect it, not to share it. But whatever the natural tendency of the mind is, it not necessarily the logic of existence. If you don't share it, you will kill it. Only by sharing will it grow. You have to understand a totally different economics. One is the economics that if you share, your money will be less and less and less.

One day a man was stopped in his car by a beggar. He was in good spirits because he had won a huge amount of money in a lottery, just a few minutes before. He took a ten-dollar bill and gave it to the beggar. When he was giving it to the beggar he saw that the beggar's clothes, although old and rotten, must have been very costly in the beginning. His face also looked that of a cultured, sophisticated ... The way he spoke also gave the hint that he did not come from a poor family.

Naturally, the man in the car asked him, 'What happened? You don't seem to belong to the world of beggars, neither your clothes, nor your voice, nor your accent, nor your language, nor your face. Everything denies that you have been related to a poor beggar family. You seem to come from a very high-class one.'

The beggar laughed. He said, 'You are right. Once I used to be in better cars than the one you have. But I committed the same mistake that you are committing. I went on giving to people. Now you are giving ten dollars. I have not even asked for one dollar.

Before I could ask, you handed me ten dollars. If you go on in this way, soon you will be standing by my side.'

Ordinary economics wants you to be miserly because it is concerned with the quantitative world. If you give some quantity to somebody, you have that much less. But the world of consciousness is not the world of quantity: it is the world of quality. The more you give, the more you have. It follows just the opposite rule of ordinary economics.

But your mind knows only ordinary economics, so it is afraid that if you start sharing this small flame that has arisen in you – that is giving you so much peace and bliss and joy – because it is so small if shared, it will be gone, and you will be again in darkness. But it is not true. What is true: if you don't share it, it will be gone; if you share it, it will grow. Sharing is the principle tool of higher consciousness for growth. If you want this flame to become your whole life, a fire, a flame, then share. Don't be bothered about its smallness.

The seed is always small. But if the seed is afraid to dissolve into the soil, neither will a huge tree come into existence nor will thousands of flowers and fruit and millions of seeds – just out of one small seed. The scientists say just a single small seed can make the whole planet green. But it has to dissolve into the soil. If it protects itself, becomes defensive, remains closed, soon it will be a rotten seed. Then nothing will grow out of it.

Let your inner flame be a constant sharing so it is always fresh. And it will become more and more as you become less and less miserly. The more your compassion, the more your love, the more you give without any thought of getting anything in return, the more this flame will come to its full height. So don't get into this trap of the mind. The mind knows nothing about higher economics, higher mathematics, it knows only the much lower world of money, of things, and naturally its experience prevents it from sharing.

You are asking, 'Is it okay just to take care of it, to enjoy its presence just by myself?' No. It is not okay. It is exactly the wrong thing to do. Your fear is that it's hard to share it now. No, it is not hard. Howsoever small it is, it can be shared.

I have told you an ancient Sufi parable...

A dark night and it was raining hard; it must have been twelve o'clock. Some stranger knocked on the door of a poor man's hut. The hut was so small that only the husband and wife could sleep there, but the husband said to the wife, who was closer to the door, 'Open the door.'

The wife was reluctant. She said, 'But where are we going to arrange for him to sleep? We don't have any space here.'

But her husband, who was a Sufi mystic, said, 'Don't be worried. If there is enough for two to sleep, there is enough for three to sit and gossip. And the night is not very long, half is already past. But a man lost in the forest, in the darkness, and in so much rain ... Don't be ugly and don't listen to your small mind, just open the door.'

The door was opened, the man came in completely soaked by the rain. The Sufi gives him his only other robe and tells him, 'Forgive us; we only have a small hut. We are poor people, but our hearts are not poor. We cannot arrange for you to sleep, but we will all sit together. And I don't know much about the world because I live in this forest. For years I have not gone out. And you seem to be a man of the world, so you can tell us many things about what is going on in the world that we may not have heard. So let us enjoy the night.'

The stranger was very happy that at least he could get shelter. Otherwise he would have been lost in the forest where there were wild animals. And the rain was so heavy, he was shivering. But with closed doors, in changed clothes and a small space, he soon started feeling better and began to talk to the mystic. And the mystic was a great listener; he listened to his experiences in the world, what was happening in the world. And just then, another knock...

Now the stranger was sitting close to the door. The Sufi said to him, 'Please open the door.' The stranger was reluctant.

This is how the mind functions. Just half an hour before, he was in the same situation outside. He had forgotten all about it.

He said, 'What do you mean? Open the door? There is no space.'

The Sufi said, 'That's what my wife was saying when you were knocking. I know there is no space for sitting as we are sitting, but we will be sitting a little closer and the night is getting colder. Our being close will give us warmth. We don't have anything else to keep you warm. It is a good chance, don't miss it. Open the door.'

Naturally the stranger understood the point. He himself had been in the same position. So he opened the door. Another stranger who had lost his way, soaked by the rain ... The Sufi said to his wife, 'Give him your other dress, and ask forgiveness of the stranger because he will have to put on a woman's dress, but we don't have anything else. It doesn't matter, dresses are not male or female. They don't have sexual differences. Dresses are just dresses. And we will sit closer to each other.'

The man was feeling so cold that he was willing to put on the woman's dress. And now they were sitting very close together, touching each other, but they all felt better because now they were feeling much warmer. The Sufi told the second stranger, 'We were talking about the world, what is happening. If you have something to say – perhaps you have passed through different experiences than the first stranger – tell us. A very small part of the night remains. Soon the sun will rise, the rain will stop, and then you can find your way. And if you cannot find your way, I will come with you to the nearest village. From there you can move wherever you want.'

So the other man started telling his experiences. It was a beautiful night: the music of the rain, the silence of the forest, the closeness and the warmth, and strange stories. And just then came another knock, but a very strange knock. It did not seem to be that some man was knocking. But the Sufi said, 'Open the door. It is not a man, don't be worried; it is a donkey, a wild donkey. But he is very friendly to me and the rain is so heavy that he cannot tolerate it. So he has come.'

But now the new stranger, who was near the door, said, 'This is crazy. There is no space. We are already sitting so tightly, close to each other. Where is the donkey going to stand?'

The Sufi said, 'You are a man, you could have found some other place, but that poor donkey does not have that much intelligence. But he knows my love, he recognizes me. Don't be worried, we are sitting, now we will be standing. And we will keep the donkey in the middle so he also becomes warm. And the poor fellow, where can he go? Open the door!' The door had to be opened and the donkey walked in and now they were all standing around the donkey.

The stranger who came just before the donkey said, 'You seem to be a very strange fellow. You disturbed your wife's and your sleep, then you disturbed your sitting at ease when you allowed me in. Now you have disturbed even sitting. We have to stand the whole remaining part of the night.'

He said, 'No, I am not a strange man. I am just a human being who knows how to share. And this is a poor man's place. It may look small, but it has enough space.'

The question is not of the outer space, the question is of the inner space. There is no emperor's palace where there seems to be enough space – although it has so much space. The reality is that the palace has enough space, but the heart of the emperor has no space at all. And if you understand rightly, then what the Sufi is saying is that the real emperor is one who has the inner space and the capacity to share with others. A man may be a great emperor, but have almost nothing, no space inside him. He cannot share.

Don't fall into this trap. Something tremendously beautiful is happening to you. If you can learn the higher economics of sharing – and I say it with an absolute guarantee – the flame will grow bigger. It will soon be bigger than you. But if you want it to disappear, then protect it. It is almost like a candle. If you cover it with something to protect the flame because it is windy, the flame may disappear. If for protection you cover it with anything, you have killed the flame already. But if you keep it open, the flame is capable enough to move with the wind. It won't disappear so easily.

Your inner flame is eternal. It cannot die. But if you don't share, that means you don't deserve it. It will become smaller and smaller. And this is the trouble with the mind: you will become more and more afraid that it is becoming smaller, 'Now I have to protect more.' The more you protect, the more you are killing it. Sharing is the rule to protect it; not only to protect, but to help it grow.

Ronald Reagan goes into a bar in Washington looking for some action. He sees three women sitting together, a blonde, a brunette and a redhead.

To the blonde, he says, 'I'm the President; how much would it cost me to spend the night with you?'

'Two hundred bucks,' she says.

He asks the brunette the same question and she says, 'Three hundred bucks.'

Then he asks the redhead, and she says, 'Mr. President, if you can raise my skirt as high as my taxes, then get my panties as low as my wages, then get that thing of yours as hard as the times, and screw me the way you screw the public, believe me, Mr. President, it won't cost you a penny.'

24

Condensed into Two Words: Let Go

Osho,
The other day in discourse, your being, your beauty, struck me like a huge wave. I was again a child, looking with big eyes. It was like a window opening to something unknown, yet known.
Osho, would you like to speak on this experience? What is this amazement?

This amazement is pure love, a love unfettered by biological conditions. It is trust: a trust that has not been asked for, a trust that does not make you a slave, but gives you absolute freedom. This amazement is the whole secret that happens between the master and the disciple. Perhaps there is no other miracle in the world that can be compared to this. It is invisible, particularly to those who are unacquainted with anything like a master-disciple communion. It is omething from being to being.

It will be good to have this comparison. Sex is from body to body; ordinary so-called love is from heart to heart; trust is the highest form of love from being to being. As you go deeper, things go on becoming more and more amazing, more and more unbelievable, but more and more an experience so definitive that you cannot doubt it. It is a transfer, a transmission between the being of the master and the disciple.

Your description about it is very accurate: as if a window has opened. Suddenly where there was just darkness, a cool breeze comes and a window opens and the whole sky with all its stars becomes available to you. Certainly one is stunned. The mind stops, and because the mind stops, one feels as if one has become a child again.

You are also right in saying that it is something unknown, yet seems to be very much known. It is both. You have known it; it was your first experience when you were born and opened your eyes – your senses were immensely sensitive. Each day that has passed has been making them more and more insensitive. What people think of as the growth of a child is simply the death of the child.

The child knew something which even the old people don't know. But his knowing was so simple that he could not formulate it into words. He could not say anything about it. He saw the rose-flower in the garden and he saw the lush green trees, but he had no idea what green was and what a tree was and what a rose was, what a flower. He was seeing everything with better eyes than you have because your eyes are too much covered with dust.

Life is a continuous traveling in which your senses become tired, dust- covered, your mirror no longer reflects but distorts. And sometimes it stops even distorting, it is no longer a mirror. A thick layer of experiences covers it so totally that it becomes impossible for it to reflect anything.

The child's eyes are pure, clean; so are his ears and other senses. The first moment he opens to the world, he is filled with amazement and wonder. But there is no way for him to convey it. He has lived for nine months in a dark tunnel. No light penetrated there, no roses bloomed there. He was almost a part of his mother's body. He was not an individual. He was not even breathing by himself. It was the mother's breath that he was getting his oxygen from. He was being nourished by the mother. He had not even dreamed. He was not yet a separate entity. He was just like the hand of the mother or the leg of the mother, just part and parcel. His life was dependent on the mother's life, he was sharing it.

The moment of birth is a great trauma because the child naturally feels afraid, worried. He cannot think that it is going to be a birth into a bigger world, into a vast universe, that miracles are waiting for him. He can only conceive birth as a death. Just think about the child coming out of the mother's womb. He cannot conceive that he is going into authentic, individual existence, that he is moving into a vaster universe. For nine months he has known a certain life and he is being taken away from it. He cannot conceive life as something that is going to happen. He can conceive it only as a death compared to what has been happening for nine months. He is freaking completely. He does not want to come out.

That's why there is such a struggle and it takes the mother so much time. The child does not want to come out of the womb. He clings with absolute force. His life is being destroyed. He does not know what is happening, who is throwing him out of his home. It is the child who is creating all the pain for the mother because he is resisting coming out. But he has to come out. He cannot live forever in his mother's womb.

Except for one exceptional story, in the whole of history there is no incidence where somebody has lived longer than ten months, at the most, in the mother's womb. Just one man lived there for eighty-four years. His name was Lao Tzu. He is a strange man. You cannot predict what a man like Lao Tzu will do. For eighty-four years he lived in his mother's womb. When he was born he was already so old, his hair white, a long beard ... And the strangest thing was: he came out laughing. From the very start he behaved in a way that nobody has ever done, nobody has even tried. This story about Lao Tzu cannot be historical. You have to think about the mother carrying a child for eighty-four years. She would have been dead long before the child was born.

The scientific fact is that every human child is born incomplete. Many other animals are born complete. That's why they become immediately independent from the mother, from the father, and soon they have moved on their own way. They don't create a family.

A family is the need of the helpless child. A family is not created by man and woman, the family is created by the helplessness of the child. The child is not complete.

In fact a child needs at least four years in the mother's womb. But the mother cannot manage that long, a four-year-old child in the womb when even nine months is too much. It is just the infinite compassion and love of a woman that there are children in the world. If it were the other way round, that the man was going to become pregnant, you can take it for granted that no child would be born in the world. The man is so impatient. Nine months! Carrying such a load which goes on growing inside you. You cannot eat, you cannot drink, you are throwing up because there is no space inside you: the child is growing and taking all the space. It is only because of the patience of a woman that humanity exists.

But even the woman is not capable of more than nine months. Scientific understanding is that the child, *every* child, is a kind of abortion, even the natural birth. The child is born incomplete. That's why for four years at least he will need absolute support – and that is the minimum I am talking about. The actual fact is that a child often needs the support of the family for up to twenty-five years. Until he comes down from the university with a PhD he is dependent. He is still somehow part of the womb.

But the first moment of every child's birth is a tremendous experience for him. He is expecting to die. He is almost certain that it is going to happen. His life is being destroyed by unknown forces. Why is he being thrown out of his house? He has not known any other kind of life. The only life he knows is in the womb. He thinks he is going to die, but suddenly finds that instead of death, birth has happened. Instead of dying, for the first time he has become alive. The womb was only a preparation. It was not his life. It was just preparing him so that he could move into life.

The womb is just like a nursery where plants are prepared and then they move into gardens the moment they are strong enough to face the sun, the wind, the rain, and all kinds of problems and responsibilities of existence. The moment the experience of death turns into its opposite, the experience of life, the child feels his first amazement, which is never transcended unless he is born again in a spiritual sense.

The mother's womb was one preparation. The master's womb is another preparation. The energy field of the master is the womb. And you are being prepared to die to the past, to die to your personality that you have known as yourself and to enter into a new quality of life which you have not even dreamed of. So when you enter this new life, it brings great amazement. You cannot believe it. But you are right: in a way you know it, in a way you don't know it. You know it because your first birth had something similar in it. This is the same phenomenon on a higher level.

The master is your death and he is also your resurrection. Passing through the master you are going to enter a life which is eternal. No mother can give you an eternal life. She can give you only a mortal life, the life of the body which is going to die sooner or later. In fact it starts dying from the very first moment. It takes the body seventy, eighty or a hundred years to reach the grave, but it goes on moving toward the grave. Do you think that each birthday you are celebrating life? You are wrong. Each birthday you are celebrating death. Each birthday means one year has slipped by. You are more dead than you have been, and you are coming closer to the grave. The queue is becoming shorter and shorter.

The day my father died, I counted how many people are still in the queue in which I am standing. Two of my father's sisters had died, two of his brothers were alive, so they were the only two persons between me and the window. Just a few days ago one uncle died. Now there is only one uncle between me and the window. So I know how one gets closer and closer to the grave. Each moment you are moving without your knowing toward death.

The mother cannot give you a birth which is eternal. The mother herself knows nothing about the eternal. The master is another womb, another energy field, another preparation for a new life. The old is going to be ending any moment and if you don't get acquainted with the new, you have wasted your whole life in utter futility.

Once in a while you will be very close to the master but this is going to be a zigzag way. Sometimes you will be very close and then you will have that amazement of a new life dancing very close by. You can hear the music. You go on coming closer but then you go farther away. Your coming to the master is not a straight line without looking back.

There are a few people who have the guts not to look back, who never waver for a single moment, who don't go astray here and there, who go on coming closer and closer. Every step is toward the master's being. But not all are so fortunate, not all are so courageous. They come close and they see that it is going to be death – like the child who, in a certain unconscious way, would like to be free of this small space he has been imprisoned in for nine months, but is not conscious of it. He is coming closer to getting out of the womb, but then he steps back. Who knows? To go into the unknown may be worse than the known. It may be the very end of your existence.

But what happens to the child is very unconscious, dark. What happens to the disciple is not *that* unconscious because by becoming a disciple he is making every effort to become more and more alert. Once in a while he comes very close – when suddenly he sees through the master a glimpse of the new life. That is the amazement. That is the wonder. And that is going to be your guarantee that passing through the master is not going to be just a death. It is going to be the beginning of a new eternal life. Hence the joy. Hence the ecstasy.

It has been a beautiful experience. Now, don't move even a single inch backward. Much more is ahead. Just go on coming closer, be ready for a merger, for a melting, for disappearing as you are. Only then can you appear as you should be. That life knows no end. You have transcended death, you have reached the eternal source of life. This is the search.

And the master is certainly a window. You have to pass through him. Any master who tries to stop you somewhere, who wants you to cling to him, not to pass through him and go ahead is not authentic, is pseudo. Take a jump from the window into the infinite, the eternal, the ultimate. If he is not a window to jump into *sat-chit-anand* – into truth, into consciousness, into bliss – then he is not an authentic master. If he wants you to remain loyal to him, if he wants you only to believe in him, if he insists that you remain always a shadow of him, then he is your enemy, he is not your friend.

Most of the so-called masters in the past have been your enemies. That's why you are still shadows, you are still not authentic beings. They did not allow you to be. They enjoyed the game 'I have so many disciples,' which is a very pious game of ego. The ego is so subtle, it can catch hold of you in any place. It does not matter that you are trying to be spiritual, the ego can still manage to live within you.

I have heard about a master who used to live alone deep in the forest. One day a seeker came who was searching for a master. He had been to many masters, but had found nothing but ego trips in the name of spirituality. He had just left another master who was continuously bragging about how many disciples he had. He never forgot to tell any stranger who came to him how many disciples he had. The seeker, watching the whole scene that seemed to be a circus, felt it was not a place for spiritual growth because the man in the center was himself still not out of the games of children, the ego games.

So he went into the forest in search. Perhaps somewhere in the deeper forest he might find a master. And he found an old master, very silent, very serene and he felt that perhaps this was the right man. He told him, 'I have been searching. I have been to many masters, but I was not satisfied.'

The old man asked, 'What was the trouble? Why were you not satisfied?' H e said, 'They were all playing a political game, the politics of numbers. They were all comparing with each other who had more disciples, who had the king as a disciple, who had the prime minister as a disciple, who had the richest man as a disciple. It seemed they were more influenced by the king, by the prime minister, by the richest man than they were influencing those people.'

The old man said, 'Then you have found the right man. I don't have a single disciple. Now you need not go anywhere. I am the only one who has no disciples.'

Such are the ways, so subtle and so cunning ... Now he is enjoying the idea that he has no disciples, he is the only one.

But that young seeker said, 'Once you accept me as a disciple, you will not be able to claim what you are claiming now. I will not disturb your ego, I am going in search of an authentic master.'

The man said, 'But what more do you want? I am the only one who doesn't have any disciples!'

He said, 'That is the problem, they are all trying to prove this: that they are the only one – the only one who has ten thousand disciples, the only one who has twenty thousand disciples. You are the only one who has no disciples. But the idea that "I am the only one, unique," continues to haunt you. And that is preventing your own spiritual explosion.'

Such masters are bound to have a mutual conspiracy. They will pretend that they are the saviors, and they will enjoy the idea that they are not only saviors but the *only* savior. And the disciples who follow them will enjoy the ego that they are the disciples of the *only* real savior. All others are following fools, idiots, all kinds of stupid people. 'We are following the right person.' This is a mutual conspiracy. They are both fulfilling each other's egos.

I don't want you to be a shadow, I don't want you to believe in me; I don't want you in any way to be in a certain bondage or commitment. I want you simply to use me as a window so that you can go beyond. Beyond the window is the real, is the true, is the beautiful. You have used a very beautiful word, *window*. I am certainly nothing but a window. And if you can pass through me I will be, more than you can conceive, grateful to you because my only concern is that I should not become a bondage to you, I should not become an imprisonment, a slavery to anyone.

My love cannot allow any kind of bondage forced upon you, any belief, any discipline. I want you to be individuals in your own right, unique, growing to your own potential. At the most I can only be a window to the beyond, to the starry night. And it is something that you have known before on a small scale when you were born. Now you have to know it on a bigger scale, on a higher scale, so that you can be reborn.

These were exactly the words Jesus used to the professor who had come to see him in the middle of the night.

When everybody was asleep he came, very silently, and woke up Jesus. In the dark Jesus said, 'What do you want?'

He said, 'I have heard so much about you and once in a while in the crowd, standing behind the crowd, I have listened to you. I am a professor and I have been afraid to come to you because people think I know already. What is the need for me to go to a carpenter's son who is uneducated, who knows nothing? So I could not come in the daytime. But your words have such authority. They haunt me day and night. I have come in the night so nobody knows. I have a few questions to ask.'

Jesus said, 'Such a coward who doesn't even have the courage to meet me in front of others will not be able to understand what my answers are going to be. So first be reborn, and then come to me.'

What does he mean by 'be reborn'? He is saying, 'Drop all this rubbish knowledge, this personality, this respectability, this prestige of being a professor. Be reborn. Be a child again and then come to me, because only innocence can understand another innocence. Only a heart can understand another heart. Only a silent being can understand another silent being.'

Remember this experience, and much more is going to happen. But don't expect it, just let it happen on its own. Even your expectation can become a block. This happened spontaneously. Remember it: everything that is going to happen is only going to happen spontaneously and not according to your expectations. So just be here, enjoy this relaxed communion of seekers, this silence that is resounding in so many hearts, this music that joins everybody who is here with invisible threads.

Out of this rejoicing and singing and dancing, you will become more and more spontaneous and more and more available to me. You will be coming closer and closer to the window; the unknown will start becoming more and more familiar and cozy. The coldness of the unknown will disappear. And remember that the unknown is not enough. You have to move still further, you have to reach to the unknowable. Only then will you have entered into the mystery of existence. But it is going to happen. Just get ready.

I am not asking much for you to be ready. Every religion has been asking too much. In India there have been three religions who have asked so much from the disciples that one life was not enough. Many, many lives were needed for preparation. After many, many lives you may become enlightened. But I say unto you, you can become enlightened this very moment because my preparation is a totally new dimension. It is about being spontaneous, having a rejoicing heart, being in tune with love. It is more musical, harmonious; it is more relaxed.

My whole approach can be condensed into two words – let go.

Osho,
When Jesus ascended to heaven he went alone. When Mohammed ascended, he rode his horse. Will you drive?

The question you have asked is very complicated. It is not an easy question. First, I am not going the way Jesus and Mohammed went. My way is just the opposite. They have all been going to heaven. To be frank with you I am not interested in heaven! My whole interest is in hell because all the beautiful people are there: musicians, dancers, poets, painters, great creators in all dimensions. All the people who had some color to their being, people who had some juice are in hell, not in heaven.

In heaven you will find only dry bones. I cannot tolerate their company for a single moment. Just think of yourself surrounded by saints. It will be so suffocating. Heaven is no longer the place to go. If you want to meet Leo Tolstoy, Bertrand Russell and Albert Einstein, if you want to meet Gautam Buddha, Lao Tzu and Chuang Tzu, if you want to meet Dostoevsky, Chekhov and Turgenev, if you want to meet Van Gogh and Picasso, then hell is the place.

So the first thing, I am not going where Jesus went or where Mohammed ascended with his horse. I am not going that way. Whatever I have heard about that place does not appeal to me at all. For example, water is not available because the rivers are of milk and honey. I cannot take a bath in honey or milk. And it is such ancient milk that by this time it must have turned into curd, turned into butter, butter into ghee! It will be stinking. You cannot even get a coca-cola there. No cold drink, just that rotten honey and milk.

Just think! So ancient ... And all kinds of dirty saints are swimming in those rivers and doing all kinds of nasty things. India has produced more saints than any other country and you know what Indian saints will be doing, defecating around those rivers. An Indian is an Indian, he cannot change his habits, his civilization, his culture. Indians think that people who go to a toilet are dirty people. Why not go under the open sky, in the open air? Why go into small cabins? In my childhood I used to hear this. Most of the houses – almost ninety percent of the houses – in India don't have any attached bathroom or toilet. It is thought to be something against Indian culture.

Saints in particular: even if there is an attached bathroom and a modern toilet where they are staying, they cannot go in it because their religious scriptures don't allow them to defecate in water. The modern toilet has water in it, so they cannot use it. They have to find very dry land, only then can they defecate. With millions of saints in heaven for centuries, it must have become the dirtiest place possible. I am not interested at all.

You will be surprised that it is not only true about India. Just a hundred years ago there was a case in the Supreme Court of America. The Christian church brought a case against a man because he had brought all that was needed to make an attached bathroom with toilet from Europe. The Christians who brought the case to the Supreme Court said that God never created any house with an attached bathroom. That's true. God himself goes in the open! No scripture of any religion mentions that he has an attached bathroom. It was so obvious so the Christian church said: 'This man is going to spoil the whole morality of the country, the whole culture of the country. He should be prevented. You can have outhouses far away from your house but you cannot be allowed to have a toilet, a bathroom, inside the house. Are you mad or something?' And it is not a very old story, just a hundred years ago.

It was because of the intelligence of the Supreme Court of America that they gave the man permission. They said: 'There is nothing wrong in it. There is nothing against religion in it. God may not have created it, but we can see that this is perfectly clean.' But I don't think any modern technology has reached heaven.

All saints are against anything new, but everything that you are enjoying on the earth is new. It was not created in those six days when God created the world. I don't see any mention of shampoo or hair conditioner or soap. No mention of anything. It is all man-made. Whatever comforts you have, whatever luxuries you have, all are man-made. God left this world almost in chaos. In six days you cannot hope for much more.

My own tailor...

I was going on a journey for two to three months. I was not coming back, and I told him, 'I need my clothes ready by Saturday evening.'

He said, 'But that's only six days.'

He was a Christian, so I said, 'In six days God created the whole world and you cannot create two or three robes for me?'

But he was a very beautiful old man. That's how we had become friends and he had become my tailor. He said, 'Okay, I will, but have another look at the world! That will be the situation of your clothes too.'

I said, 'Then you take your time, because I don't want my clothes to be in the same situation as the world is, even today.'

He said, 'You are a sane man. I will try my best. But I am a poor tailor; even God could not manage.'

In the heaven of all religions there are beautiful women available for the saints as a reward. Strange reward! Their whole life they were told not to look at women: don't touch them, don't think of them. All the religions say woman is the cause of all your misery, all your sins. And then in the end, you end up with them as a reward! But those call girls in heaven have remained stuck at the age of sixteen. They have always been sixteen.

Here also women get stuck in many places. Sixteen, then for two, three years they are sixteen, but not more than that. Then at about twenty-six they will again get stuck. They hop. The age of thirty-five is the longest gap, because now it is more dangerous to go ahead. It has been calculated that at the age of thirty-five all intelligent women stop growing, at least for six years. In six years' time they will be thirty-six. This way it is very difficult to find out the actual age of a woman. But in heaven they are stuck at sixteen for millennia.

Now what kind of girls are these saints being given? They are not only secondhand or thirdhand ... How many saints have used the same girls? Most probably they are made of plastic, so that once in a while after dry cleaning the girl is again ready. Pump in the air and the girl is ready. I suspect it's plastic not without any reason – I never suspect anything without a reason – but because the scriptures say they don't perspire. Skin is bound to perspire. It is impossible for skin not to perspire, because it is the perspiration that keeps your temperature constant.

If you don't perspire when it is hot, your temperature will rise too high – and the span as far as temperature is concerned is not much. In years, your life span may be seventy or eighty, but as far as temperature is concerned, from ninety-eight to one hundred and ten – that is only twelve degrees – is the span. If on a hot summer day you don't perspire, the heat will push your temperature up to one hundred and five, and at one hundred and five you start becoming delirious. At one hundred and six or seven you start hallucinating. By a hundred and ten you are finished.

Perspiration keeps you constantly at ninety-eight degrees because the body goes on releasing water and the heat goes on evaporating the water. It is deceiving the heat. The heat gets involved in evaporating the perspiration and forgets to heat you up. The perspiration does not allow the heat to enter the body, it keeps it out.

You don't perspire when it is cold. Even if you try you cannot. When you are cold, you shiver. That is another way to keep the inner temperature again at ninety-eight degrees. By shivering you keep yourself hot, otherwise the cold will bring you down. On both ends there is a limit. Above, there is a possible range of at least twelve degrees. Below ninety-eight there is not even that much possibility – just two or three degrees and you shiver. You think that because you are shivering it is not good; you don't know it is saving your life. Your teeth will start chattering. That is keeping you warm.

But those girls in heaven ... If they are dead, either the saints just don't know exactly what they are doing, or perhaps after lifelong repression even corpses are enough.

I have heard about one drunkard. He was caught by the police in France because he was making love to a dead woman who had drowned and been brought by the waves to the shore. In the night the drunkard had staggered there and found a beautiful woman, so he made love to her.

He was caught, and in the morning was asked in the court, 'Why were you making love to that dead woman?'

He replied 'I had no idea that she was dead. I thought she was English!

You cannot punish me because of a misunderstanding.'

What are those saints doing there? I have never heard of any intelligent man going to heaven. Now, Mohammed going on his horse ... You think this looks intelligent? The poor horse will unnecessarily suffer with the saints. What does he know about saintliness? He will miss his girlfriend, and Mohammed will have no idea that the poor horse ... In heaven there is no provision for horses.

I am not going that way, that much is certain – and neither are you. From my window you will jump directly to hell! I have already fixed my window in the right direction. I want you to be in the best company. Every genius is there. As far as saints are concerned, most of them are retarded. At least in thirty-five years continuously roaming around this country, which produces nothing but poverty and saints, I have not come across a single saint who can be called intelligent.

I met one saint who even Mahatma Gandhi declared a great saint of modern India. Once he was a professor. His name was Professor Bhansali. Then he became a follower of Mahatma Gandhi and entered his ashram. It was not much of an ashram, just a miniature heaven. You could get some idea from Mahatma Gandhi's ashram of what is going to happen in heaven. Bhansali became a great saint because for six months continuously he was eating only cow dung and drinking only cow urine. And he became a great saint! Even Gandhi declared: 'I have seen saints, but Bhansali is superb.'

Now do you call this intelligence? When I saw Bhansali I told him, 'You are an absolute idiot!' He was very angry.

He said, 'Mahatma Gandhi used to call me a saint!'

I said, 'He was in the same category as you, but you surpassed him.'

If you want beautiful company, people of intelligence, genius, creativity, you will find them all in hell – all great scientists, all great technologists and they have already transformed hell completely. No new scripture is written, so nobody knows how things have changed. Hell is no longer the same. It has become the most beautiful place in existence because all the great people are there.

You are asking me if I am going to drive. From earth to hell the road is exactly as it was from Antelope to Rajneeshpuram. It is an American county road. I don't want to drive on it. Avesh and Anandadas are going to take my limousine and I am going to rest on the way. Avesh is needed because that road is long and no car has ever traveled on that road, so it's good to have a mechanic. And a perfect driver, Anandadas, is needed. Nobody knows how long the road is because there are neither milestones nor traffic. So they can take turns driving. And I always travel asleep. In trains and airplanes and cars, I always travel sleeping, because why bother unnecessarily? This is the right time to have a good sleep.

So I will be sleeping and it will be the first time anybody has gone to hell sleeping beautifully, restfully. People go toward hell in such fear, tension, paranoia. I am going there; many of my sannyasins are already there. Many I will send even before I go, just to prepare everybody that I am coming. We are going to create a real commune there. I think with God it will be very difficult. With the Devil I can manage. I can initiate him very easily into sannyas!

Nivedana, if you are thinking of going to heaven, drop that idea. You are coming with me. I never go alone: one car ahead, one car behind. In one of the cars, Nivedana will have a seat. He asked the question because, listening to me talking about Jesus and Mohammed and others, he must have thought that I am going to take the same route. No, Jesus and Mohammed are both repenting, but there is no exit from heaven. Once you enter, you enter for eternity. You cannot get out. That is one more difficulty. You cannot go as a tourist, just a three-week tour to see whether this is the place where you would like to stay for eternity.

I think he got into a misunderstanding because I have been using these names with deep love and respect, and with deep compassion because these poor fellows did not realize that where they were going was the wrong place. But once we are all in hell, we will try to create some back door in heaven from where we can pick up the right people who are in the wrong place. There are not many. Only very few people who are worth taking out have got into the wrong place.

Nancy and Ronald Reagan go out to a restaurant for dinner. The waiter approaches them and asks Nancy what she would like to eat.

'I would like to have a steak,' says Nancy.

'And would you like to have some wine with your meal?' asks the waiter.

'Yes,' she replies. 'A bottle of your finest.'

The waiter then asks, 'How about the vegetable?'

'Ah,' says Nancy, 'he will have the same as me.'

Identical twin brothers Hamish and Gordon lived in the same town. Hamish was married but Gordon was single and used to have an old rowboat. It happens that Hamish's wife dies on the same day as Gordon's boat sinks. The minister's wife meets Gordon in the street and, mistaking him for

Hamish, says, 'I am very sorry to hear about your great loss.'

'Ah,' says Gordon, 'I'm not sorry a bit. She was a rotten old thing from the start. Her bottom was all chewed up. The first time I got into her she made water faster than anything I have ever seen. She had a big crack and a big hole at the front which just got bigger every time I used her. Then the other day, four guys came around looking for a good time and they asked if they could rent her. Well, the crazy fools all tried to get into her at the same time, and she cracked right up the middle.'

The minister's wife collapsed.

Just misunderstanding, Nivedana. A few people have entered heaven without understanding the whole situation, and now they are repenting, but nobody has ever done anything to save them from heaven. These people used to think that they were going to save you. Now they are caught themselves in this situation, and nobody comes to their help.

I have plans. First let us settle down in hell, then we will try to take out a few really juicy people who are suffering, surrounded by saints. Saints are absolutely dead people who learned in their whole life only one thing: how not to live, how to be almost dead in this so alive existence. Their whole life's training will follow them in heaven too. They will continue with their long, sad faces, they will go on torturing themselves.

I can see Jesus feeling more pain and agony than he would ever have felt on the cross. Heaven is not the right place. Only wrong people, people who deny life, people who are against love, people who are against every celebration end up there.

People who love life, rejoice in life, love to dance and sing, for them hell is the right place. And you will find there all kinds of giants, all kinds of revolutionaries, all kinds of rebellious people. All those who did not agree with the world the way God has made it, who wanted to improve it, they all have gathered there in hell; these are not the people to sit silently. They have improved hell. They have changed the whole face. Beautiful restaurants, discotheques, and no discrimination between nations or religions or races or colors – sheer joy! And all those stories about hell fire are no longer true. They have used that fire for running railway trains, factories. Whatever you have heard about hell is no longer true at all. Everything has changed.

So you keep your suitcases ready. Only in hell are suitcases allowed, not in heaven. In heaven any kind of stupidity is allowed: Mohammed's going, sitting on his horse is allowed. But if you take a suitcase with you and toothpaste, you won't be allowed in.

In India, Jaina saints never use any mouthwash; they never clean their teeth; they never take a shower. That is part of their discipline. They stink so badly that when they used to come to see me, I had to tell them, although it looked very unmannerly, to sit as far away as possible. I am allergic to smells and this saintly smell was so bad, so foul, because they had not taken a bath for twenty or thirty years, they had never washed their mouths, they had never cleaned their teeth. You will have to meet some Jaina saint: it is an experience. Then you will never think of heaven because you will meet these people there.

These are smaller saints, but centuries ago even greater ones arrived. They ate standing on their heads and because they were allowed to eat only once a day, they would eat too much, so their bodies were thin. Only their bellies were big. They looked so ugly that I have thought many times that there should be an international competition for ugliness, just as there is a beauty competition. Then Jaina saints would come first, without any doubt.

They live naked. So there is no need for them to remove clothes, et cetera. They have removed them already. And just seeing them, one feels such pity that this calamity has happened to these people. Their faces show no life. All that is alive is their belly. Just looking at their belly rising up and down, you can see that they are still here. Otherwise nothing shows any sign of life. Everything is dead.

Nobody has given you the right description of heaven and hell. I am giving it to you. From now onward never think of heaven, always think of hell. And when we reach there we can change the signboard. It is so easy for us. We will have the craftsmen to do all kinds of things. Change the board to: 'The Real Heaven.' If the word *hell* hurts you, it is only a question of changing the board. And once the Devil becomes Swami Anand Devil ... I will tell Dhyan Yogi to keep his name and his *mala* ready.

The poor Devil has suffered badly at the hands of God. He has never done anything wrong. There is no description anywhere that he has done anything wrong. And still he has been appointed to take care of hell. But once we are there we will relieve him of his duty. We will take care. He has done enough; he needs retirement.

Nivedana, your question is really significant because it completes my theology.

25

Except Man, In Existence Nobody Plans

Osho,
I always hear you saying nice things about the women. Could you not stick up for the men once in a while?

It is a very difficult question. I could not sleep the whole night. I tried and tried hard to find something nice about men, but I have to admit to you there is nothing that can be said. You can see for yourself.

An interviewer for a ladies' magazine is questioning a famous British general about his sex life. 'Excuse me, sir,' she begins, 'but can you recall the last time you had relations with your wife?'

His upper lip stiffens for a moment and then he says, 'Yes, of course I can, it was nineteen forty-five.'

After a moment's silence the woman says, 'That was a long time ago.'

The general glances at his watch and says, 'Not so long really. It is only twenty-one forty now.'

Hymie Goldberg sends his eldest son to India on a cultural exchange, but is very upset when he comes back as a sannyasin.

Not knowing what else to do, he phones his old friend, Moishe Finkelstein, and tells him the sad news.

'Funny you should say that,' exclaims Moishe. '*My* son went to Pune and he too came back a sannyasin.' The two old friends decide to go to the rabbi for help.

When they have told the rabbi their unhappy tale, the rabbi scratches his head and replies, 'Funny you should say that. *My* son also went to Pune and *he* came back a sannyasin. We had better go to the synagogue and pray to God for advice.'

So the three old Jews go down to the synagogue and pray fervently for guidance. Suddenly there is a clap of thunder and a voice from above says, 'Funny you should say that. *My* son also went to Pune and became a sannyasin: Swami Jesus Christ.'

A man is a funny thing. If any of you find anything nice about men, please inform me. I accept my failure absolutely.

> Osho,
> Can one live without planning? Not counting the dreams about a hazy future, I see that a lot of my mind activity goes into planning – for next week, for next month.
>
> And when I try to act spontaneously I look like a weather vane that does not know which way the wind is blowing.

The problem of planning for the future is one thing; to start living in the future is another. The planning about the future is in the present and the more you are in the present, the better you can plan. The activity of planning is in the present. The problem with the mind is, it starts living in the future. It starts thinking of beautiful golden days that are coming. That is not planning; it is daydreaming.

I can understand planning, but remember, planning for the future is not equivalent to living in the future. Planning is a present-moment activity. And the more you are present, the more you have clarity and transparency so you can plan without any haziness or dreams lurking around you.

You are saying, '...I see that a lot of my mind activity goes into planning – for next week, for next month.' This is not being in the present. Being in the present there is no mind. The mind cannot exist in the present but when there is no mind there is clarity, absolute clarity. With this clarity you can see into the future; then something of immense importance will happen to you. But mind activity is simply living in the future: next week, next month, next year, next life.

In the name of planning, you are postponing living. You should *live*, not postpone. You should live the moment, and while you are living the moment – with the clarity that it gives to you – you can visualize. It is not mental activity. You can visualize a better moment that is coming to you. You have lived this moment, you know you can go even deeper, you know you can rejoice more; there is no limit to it. And when the next moment is coming you immediately go deeper into it, rejoicing more, more playful, more humorous.

You have only one moment at a time. So if you know how to live one moment, you can plan your whole life in that very living. You have tasted something of reality; next moment you can have a bigger chunk. But there is no need to plan for it because in planning you will forget to live.

Two things happen to the man who lives spontaneously: one, he never postpones; second, his future is lived through his present, through his experience of the present. Then planning is not a mind activity but an expansion of consciousness, an understanding of life that goes on deepening more and more every day. And the deeper you are, the more beautiful, more human, more fulfilled will be your actions.

You are also saying, 'And when I try to act spontaneously I look like a weather vane that does not know which way the wind is blowing.' There is no need to know. The man who is spontaneous just like the weather vane ... The weather vane never worries whether the wind is blowing south or north, east or west; wherever the wind is blowing the weather vane simply turns toward that side. It shows in what direction the wind is blowing. It has no resistance. It is absolutely free to move in any direction. It does not fight with the wind. It is absolutely spontaneous and neither lives in the past nor in the future. It simply represents the present.

You have chosen a very beautiful word, *weather vane*, for a spontaneous life. But what is the point of a weather vane knowing from where the wind is blowing? Your mind wants to know from where the wind is blowing because your mind has its own plans against existence. It wants the winds to blow toward the west and they are blowing toward the east. Then the mind is frustrated, angry and somehow, reluctantly, it manages to go toward the east. But by the time it does that – the wind has no idea of your mind or of fulfilling your expectations – the wind starts blowing toward the west and the mind again feels frustrated saying, 'This is a strange situation: when I want to go east, the wind blows west. When I agree "Okay, let us go to the west," the wind changes.'

These are the people who have made the proverb 'Man proposes and God disposes.' There is no God and nobody disposes. Your very proposition is wrong. Proposing anything from your side means you are not trusting existence. Just be a weather vane which slowly moves without any reluctance, without any resistance, wherever the wind is blowing. It enjoys all directions. The whole of life has to be enjoyed; existence in all its colors has to be enjoyed.

But the mind is one of the most stupid things that you are carrying within you. When it is morning, it is longing for the evening, when it is evening, it is longing for the morning. It is the root cause of all your misery and frustrations.

What is the need? I cannot understand why the weather vane should want to know which way the wind is blowing. Can you figure it out? Is there any need? Do these trees know from where the wind is blowing? Do the stars know? Except man nothing in this whole existence is reluctant to go with existence. That's why everything is happy, blissful. They don't have riches; what do these poor trees have? But they have spontaneity. When the wind blows they dance, when it does not blow they rest. Both are equally acceptable.

A tremendous trust exists between the earth, the sky, the wind, the sun. When the sun starts rising in the morning, the trees wake up – they don't need any alarm clock – and when the sun sets, they all start going to sleep. As the sun sets, the birds start coming back to their nests – it is time to rest. Nobody teaches them to go to bed early. Nobody teaches them ... In the morning as the sun is rising they all wake up, start singing, making sounds of joy, rejoicing, welcoming another day.

Life is so abundantly giving – again the sky, again the sun, the beauty of the morning, and the birds are so happy they cannot contain themselves. Their singing is not planned. When they had gone in the evening to their nests to rest, they had not planned 'Next morning, whatever happens, I am going to sing.' There is no need. When the morning comes, the singing will come on its own accord. It is a synchronicity, a deep communion with existence.

The flowers don't decide, they don't have a committee, they don't have files, they don't make any decision, any planning for the future. When the spring comes they will blossom, and when the fall comes, the trees will become naked, all their leaves will fall. There is no sadness anywhere; the trees are not full of tears because all their foliage is gone. No, they enjoy this too. Standing against the sky without any leaves, a tree has a beauty of its own. It has a beauty when the foliage comes, but that is a beauty of a different dimension.

Existence has all the colors and nobody is planning, except man. And nobody is in such a mess as man, because by your planning you are really trying to postpone living. There is no need to know which way the wind is blowing. Just go with it. It will never mislead you, because this whole existence is ours. Wherever we end up, it is our home. The wind cannot take you out of existence, but your mind takes you out of existence. Only your mind is capable of taking you into dreams which don't exist, which are unreal, illusory, and you get so caught in them that you forget that existence never misleads you – it cannot!

Only the spontaneous person is in tune with existence. And only the spontaneous person is always blissful because whatever happens, he immediately finds himself in tune with it. He has no desires of his own, no projections, no propositions of his own. He has simply accepted himself as part of the cosmos. Wherever the whole is going, he is also going, joyously, because the whole is certainly wiser than the part – and we are such small parts that all our planning makes us look stupid.

In this whole universe there is no planning at all. Everything is moving without any plan, every moment going deeper. Only man remains superficial: without living he goes on and on thinking to live sometime, but that time never comes.

Mrs. Rachel Saperstein has just sent the kids to school when the phone rings. 'Is your husband's name Amos Saperstein?' asks a voice.

'Yes it is,' she replies.

'This is the police,' says the voice. 'There has been an accident and we would like you to come and identify the body.'

Mrs. Saperstein arrives at the morgue, and an attendant shows her a body covered in a white sheet. He lifts the sheet. 'Was this your husband?' he asks.

Mrs. Saperstein's eyes widen. 'Oy, oy, oy!' she cries. 'How did you – yes, that's my husband – how did you ever get your sheets so white?'

Just a woman's mind! The husband is dead and she is worried about how you get your sheets so white!

The mind takes you away from reality every moment. Except the mind you don't have any other problem: neither sin nor past lives' evil acts, nor has God written your destiny on your forehead or in the lines of your hand or in the constellation of the stars. Your whole problem is very simple, if you understand that it is your mind constantly taking you away from existence. When I tell you to be spontaneous, I simply mean one thing, always one thing: don't be a mind because the mind can never be spontaneous. The mind is a mechanism of postponing. It will never allow you to live.

I have heard about a man who realized that he was alive only when he was dead. Then suddenly he realized, 'My God, seventy years I was alive, but I never lived.' And what can you do in your grave? You cannot even turn this side or that, they don't leave much space in the grave. You lie down flat for eternity.

My suggestion is: you can plan in your grave! You will have enough time and you can plan dreams as weird as you want. Right now while you are alive, live. When you are dead there is no problem – you can allow the mind to plan. In fact it will be a good companion in the grave: being so alone, the mind chattering will keep you entertained.

But while you are alive the mind has to be stopped from functioning on its own accord, stopped unless you want to use it. It has to be reduced to a servant. It has become the master. Spontaneity will bring it to its reality. It is just a mechanism. It was not meant to be your master. Your consciousness is your master.

Although people learning yoga stand on their heads, existence never meant you to stand on your head, otherwise it would have given you legs on your head like two horns. Or it might have made you a tripod – three legs, perfectly balanced – or legs with wheels, so you can go on moving on your head ... Existence certainly means you to be on your legs, not on your head.

But man is strange. The mind was given to you to be used as a servant, and as a servant it is beautiful and great. It is a biocomputer and nothing else. But you have made it your master and the master has been reduced to a dormant state. When the servants become masters, the most dangerous thing is that first they destroy the master.

It happened in a Mohammedan king's life...

He used to love his cook's food very much; he had one of the best cooks. One day the cook – because they had become very friendly

– was serving him food and chit-chatting. He said, 'Sometimes I wonder how it must feel to be a king.'

The king just jokingly said, 'Do you want to become a king? I can make you one for twenty-four hours.'

He said, 'It will be a great joy. I have always wondered how it feels to be the king of a great kingdom.'

So the king made the cook a king for twenty-four hours. And the first thing the cook did was to order the crucifixion of the king. For twenty-four hours he was the king, so the king was crucified. And the cook proved to be a real crook: he then remained forever the master.

Once a servant is in the position of a master, his first act will be to somehow repress the master to such a state that he cannot assert himself. That is his only fear. If the master comes back, he will have to descend from the throne. Your consciousness has been reduced into darkness, your light has been turned into darkness, your treasures have been hidden, your being has been disconnected. The mind has to do all these things just to remain in power.

A meditator tries to put things in their right place. The mind should be the servant and consciousness has to be brought back to the throne. And immediately you will have a spontaneous life. There is no other kind of life at all.

Osho,
Is it possible to become enlightened in a really easy and relaxed way, with not too much effort and lots of naps?

You are asking *me*, a man who has never done anything. Just through relaxation, without any effort and lots of naps ... Mostly I am asleep. I just get up to talk to you in the morning, then I go back to sleep; then I get up again in the evening to talk to you and go back to sleep. My total hours of sleep must be eighteen. Six hours

I am awake, two hours with you, one hour for my bath, for my food and the remaining time I am in absolute *samadhi*. And I don't even dream – so lazy. And you are asking *me* the question! This is my whole philosophy – you should not make any effort, you should relax and enlightenment comes. It comes when it finds you are really relaxed, no tension, no effort and immediately it showers on you like thousands of flowers.

But all the religions have been teaching just the opposite, that enlightenment is very arduous, it takes lifelong effort, perhaps many lives, and then too there is no certainty, no guarantee. You can lose the way even when you are only one step away from enlightenment. You don't know the way toward enlightenment, so there is every possibility of losing the way, of going astray. By chance a few people have stumbled upon enlightenment. It was just by accident.

Millions of people have been trying and finding nothing and they are not aware that their very search is making them too tense; their very effort is creating a state in which enlightenment cannot happen. Enlightenment can only happen when you are so silent, so relaxed, that you are almost not. Just a pure silence and immediately the explosion, the explosion of your luminous soul.

The people who have been very arduous simply destroyed their intelligence, or their body, and I don't think they attained enlightenment. The very few people who have attained enlightenment have attained in a relaxed state. Relaxation is the very soil in which the roses of enlightenment grow. So it is very good that you want to be relaxed, at ease, with no effort and lots of naps. This is the recipe. You will get enlightened. You can get enlightened today! Enlightenment is your innermost being.

But just because you are so engaged in effort – in seeking, in searching, doing this, doing that – you never reach your own self. In relaxation you are not going anywhere, you are not doing anything and the grass starts growing by itself. All that is needed is alertness, intelligence, consciousness, which are not efforts; witnessing, watching, which are not tensions. They are very joyful experiences. You don't get tired of them. You get very calm and quiet. Intelligence has not been known to be a part of your so-called saints. They destroyed it completely by their stupid efforts. And I say unto you, all efforts for enlightenment are stupid.

Enlightenment is your nature. It is just that you don't know it, otherwise you are enlightened already. As far as I am concerned you are all enlightened because I can see your luminous flame within. When I see you, I don't see your figure, I see your being, which is just a beautiful flame.

It is said that Gautam Buddha was surprised that the moment he became enlightened the whole of existence became enlightened. His own eyes changed, his own vision changed. He could look as deep into himself as he could into everyone, even animals and trees. He could see that they are all moving toward enlightenment. Everything needs to realize its own nature; without that life is not a joy, not a festivity.

Just be a little intelligent and enlightenment will happen on its own accord; you don't even have to think about it.

A woman walks into a bank and goes to the bank president's office. She walks straight up to his desk and says, 'I would like to make a ten thousand dollar bet.'

'I am sorry, madam,' replies the president, 'but this bank does not take bets.'

'I don't want to bet with the bank,' she says, 'I want to bet with you. I bet that by ten o'clock tomorrow your testicles will be square.'

'I think you are a fool,' says the president, 'but I will take the bet. Be here at ten tomorrow, and bring ten thousand dollars.'

At nine fifty-five, the woman walks in with a tall, stately looking gentleman. 'Who is this guy?' asks the president.

'He is my attorney,' replies the woman. 'He has come to see that everything is done right.'

'Okay,' says the president, and laughing he pulls down his pants.

The woman reaches over and feels if they are square. At that moment, the attorney collapses in a dead faint. 'What is up with him?' asks the president.

'Well,' replies the woman, 'I bet him fifty thousand dollars that by ten this morning I would have a bank president by the balls.'

Just be a little intelligent!

The manager, looking angry, strides over to Paddy's desk and taps him on the shoulder.

'Listen,' he says, 'do me and everyone a favor and stop whistling while you work.'

'Hey, man,' says Paddy, 'who is working?'

A cannibal chief treats himself to a Mediterranean cruise, and on the first night he sits down for dinner and asks for the wine list. He orders a bottle of French wine and consumes it immediately. Then the waiter approaches him and asks if he would like to see the menu.

'No thanks,' the chief replies. 'Just bring me the passenger list.'

A Catholic missionary is captured by cannibals and is surprised to find out that the chief has been to school in England and speaks perfect English.

'I can't understand it,' says the indignant priest. 'How could you have spent so much time in civilization and still eat people?'

'A-ha!' says the chief. 'Now I use a knife and fork.'

Just be a little intelligent. The world is not intelligent. It is functioning in a very unintelligent way and is creating all kinds of miseries for everyone, rather than helping them to be happier. Everybody is pulling on each other's legs, dragging them into deeper darkness, into deeper mud, into deeper trouble. It seems in this world everybody enjoys only one thing: creating misery for others. That's why such a cloud of darkness surrounds the earth. Otherwise there would have been a continuous festival of lights – and not ordinary lights, but the lights of your very being.

Why have the priests succeeded in convincing man that enlightenment is a very difficult, almost impossible, task? The reason is in your mind. Your mind is always interested in the difficult, in the impossible because that gives it a challenge, and the ego needs challenge to become bigger and bigger and bigger. The priests were successful in convincing you that enlightenment is very difficult, almost impossible.

In millions of people, only once in a while does a man become enlightened. Their idea was that you should not become enlightened. To prevent you from enlightenment they used a very clever device. They challenged your ego and you became interested in all kinds of rituals, in all kinds of austerities, self-torture. You made your own life as deep an anguish as possible. But people who have made their life a torture – masochists – cannot become enlightened. They go on becoming more and more endarkened. And people living in darkness start crawling like slaves very easily because they have lost all their intelligence, all their consciousness in their strange effort.

Have you seen a dog in winter just resting in the sun in the early morning? He sees his tail and immediately becomes interested. What is it? He jumps to catch the tail. But then he becomes crazy, because this seems very strange. As he jumps, the tail also jumps. Yet the distance between the dog and the tail remains the same. He goes round and round. I have watched: the more the tail jumps, the more determined he becomes; he uses all his willpower, tries this way and that way to catch hold of it. But the poor dog does not know that it is not possible to catch hold of it. It is already part of him. So when he jumps, it jumps.

Enlightenment is not difficult, not impossible. You don't have to do anything to get it. It is just your intrinsic nature, it is your very subjectivity. All that you have to do is for a moment relax totally, forget all doing, all effort, so that you are no longer occupied anywhere. This unoccupied consciousness suddenly becomes aware: 'I am it.'

Enlightenment is the easiest thing in the world, but the priests never wanted the whole world to become enlightened. Otherwise people would not be Christians, they would not be Catholics, they would not be Hindus, they would not be Mohammedans. They have to be kept unenlightened. They have to be kept blind to their own nature, and they have found a very clever way. They are not to do anything, they have just to give you the idea that it is a very difficult, impossible task.

Your ego became immediately interested. The ego is never interested in the obvious. It is never interested in that which you are. It is only interested in a faraway goal – the farther the goal, the greater the interest. But enlightenment is not a goal and it is not even an inch away from you – it is you!

The seeker is the sought. The observer is the observed. The knower is the known.

Once you understand that your very nature is enlightenment ... In fact, the Sanskrit word for religion is *dharma* which means nature, your very nature. It does not mean a church, it does not mean a theology, it simply means your nature. For example, what is the dharma of fire? – to be hot. And what is the dharma of water? – to flow downward. What is the nature of man? What is the dharma of man? – to become enlightened: to know one's godliness. If you can understand the effortless achievement of your nature ...

I'll call you intelligent only if you can understand this. If you cannot understand this, you are not intelligent, you are simply an egoist who is trying ... Just as some egoists are trying to be the richest man, a few other egoists are trying to be the most powerful, a few egoists are trying to become enlightened. But enlightenment is not possible for the ego: riches are possible, power is possible, prestige is possible, and they are difficult things, very difficult.

Henry Ford, one of the richest men of his time though he was born poor, was asked, 'What is your desire in the next life?'

He said, 'I don't want to be the richest man again. It has been a continuous self-torture my whole life. I have not been able to live.

I used to arrive at the factory early in the morning at seven o'clock, and the manual workers would arrive at eight o'clock, the clerks would arrive at nine o'clock and the manager would come at ten o'clock and leave at two o'clock. Everybody else would leave at five o'clock and I had to work late into the night, sometimes up to ten, sometimes up to twelve.

'I worked hard to become the richest man and I became the richest man. But what is the point? I could not enjoy anything. I worked harder than my laborers. They enjoyed life more. I had no holidays. Even on holidays I used to go to the factory to work out plans for the future.'

It is difficult, but you can become the richest man if you make enough effort. It is difficult, but you can reach the top of Everest if you make enough effort. But if you make any effort at all, enlightenment becomes impossible for you. If you bring your mind with all its tensions and worries to work out your enlightenment, you are moving in the wrong direction, away from enlightenment.

You need a total let-go, an utterly peaceful, tensionless, silent state of being. And suddenly: the explosion. You are all born enlightened whether you realize it or not.

Society does not want you to realize it. Religions don't want you to realize it. Politicians don't want you to realize it because it goes against every vested interest. They are living and sucking your blood because you are unenlightened. They are able to reduce the whole of humanity into stupid labels: Christian, Hindu, Mohammedan, as if you are things, commodities. They have labeled on your forehead who you are.

In India you will actually find brahmins with symbols on their foreheads. You can see the symbol and you can recognize to which class of brahmin this man belongs. These are means or commodities. They have their symbols marked on their foreheads. You may not have your symbol marked, but you know deep down it is engraved within your being that you are a Christian, that you are a Buddhist, that you are a Hindu.

If you all become enlightened, you will be simply light, a joy to yourself and to others, a blessing to yourself and to the whole of existence. You will be the ultimate freedom; nobody can exploit you, nobody can in any way enslave you. That is the problem: nobody wants you to become enlightened. Unless you see the point, you will go on playing into the hands of the vested interests, which are all parasites. Their only function is how to suck blood out of you.

If you want freedom, enlightenment is the only freedom. If you want individuality, enlightenment is the only individuality. If you want a life full of blessings, enlightenment is the only experience. And it is very easy, utterly easy; it's the one thing you don't have to do anything to get, because it is already there. You just have to relax and see it. Hence in India we have nothing parallel to Western philosophy. *Philosophy* means thinking about truth, love of knowledge. In India what we have is a totally different thing. We call it *darshan*. *Darshan* does not mean thinking, it means seeing.

Your truth has not to be thought about, it has to be seen. It is already there. You don't have to go anywhere to find it. You don't have to think about it, you have to stop thinking so that it can surface in your being. Unoccupied space is needed within you so that the light that is hidden can expand and fill your being. It not only fills your being, it starts radiating from your being. Your whole life becomes a beauty, a beauty that is not of the body, but a beauty that radiates from within – the beauty of your consciousness.

26

The Materialist and the Spiritualist

Osho,
Enjoying life seems to be the only thing I do, and I forget that I am a seeker. But when I think about it, a question arises: What am I seeking for?

Enjoying life is in itself a beautiful experience, but it is not enough. All the religions of the world have condemned it. Their condemnation has created a guilt feeling. So even though people are enjoying life, deep down they are feeling that they are doing something wrong, something they should not do. So their enjoyment remains halfhearted. They are in a deep split, a kind of schizophrenia. Part of them is pulling them away from the enjoyment and part of them is pulling them toward it. It becomes a very subtle tension.

But according to me, enjoying life in its totality and intensity is the very foundation of finding the higher and the ultimate significance of life. Enjoyment is blind, hence even if you are enjoying life, deep down a question remains: What is the significance of all this enjoyment? That's from where seeking arises: a desire to find the meaning. Is 'Eat, drink and be merry' all there is?

There have been two traditions in the world. One consists of those who are life-negative, life condemners, life poisoners. They have been in the majority, because most people love the negative. To condemn anything is very easy. To criticize anything is very easy. But to appreciate anything needs intelligence.

There is a beautiful story by Turgenev, *The Fool.*

A sage came to a village where the village idiot was condemned by everybody; the moment he opened his mouth people would start laughing, expecting him to say something stupid. The poor man came to the sage and told him about his misery, that he was the laughingstock of the whole village. As far as possible he kept completely quiet, but even his quietness was condemned: 'Look at that idiot. He thinks that we are all fools who are talking and he is something spiritual; being silent, meditative!'

'If I talk, I am condemned; if I don't talk, I am condemned. Show me the way to get out of this miserable state.'

The sage said, 'I will tell you the secret. And after one month I will be coming back; then you can tell me what happened in this month.'

The secret was very simple. The secret was: 'Do not say anything on your own account, but whenever somebody says something, immediately criticize. If somebody says 'Look, how beautiful is the full moon,' don't miss the opportunity. Immediately say 'What is beautiful in it? Prove what is beautiful in it. Do you know what beauty is?'

'It is very difficult to define it. Everybody knows that the full moon is beautiful. But perhaps you have never asked yourself "Do you know what beauty is?" And if you don't know what beauty is, how can you say anything is beautiful? The statement that something is beautiful implies that you know the definition of beauty. So immediately jump in and ask "What is the definition of beauty?"'

Not even the greatest philosophers who have been thinking all their lives about beauty and nothing else, like Croce who has written volumes upon beauty, end up with anything definable. The whole effort, hundreds of pages, and the conclusion is that it is indefinable.

'Just go on this way. If somebody says "That man is very virtuous," immediately ask "What is virtue? How do you know, on what grounds, what authority?"'

'Never make any statement of your own, so nobody can criticize you. And you go on criticizing everybody, don't miss a single opportunity, and ask for a definition.'

After one month the sage came back and the idiot fell at his feet and said, 'Your secret has done miracles. Now I am supposed to be the wisest man in my village. In just one month!'

To negate needs not much intelligence. To affirm needs tremendous intelligence. So there has been a majority tradition of condemners. That is the easiest way to prove yourself superior. They condemn everything, they condemn the whole world. There has been a small stream of affirmers also, but they are looked upon in a very derogatory way. These are the materialists. The majority thinks itself spiritualist. Yet there is a small stream which says: 'Eat, drink and be merry. This is all. There is nothing else to seek and search for.'

My situation is a little complex. I accept the materialist as far as he is saying eat, drink and be merry. But I deny that this is all there is. I accept the spiritualist's search for something higher, but I refute the spiritualist for his condemnation of life, enjoyment, the small joys of life. I am a materialist-spiritualist. Begin with this very earth and rise up to the sky, to the highest stars. This is one single universe. There are not two universes, one materialist and one spiritualist. Matter and spirit are continuously meeting with each other, dancing hand in hand.

You have to be a materialist to begin with. But don't stop there. That is only a beginning. The second thing that will make your journey complete is the search for significance. Otherwise every enjoyment is going to become boredom sooner or later. If you don't know the significance, if you don't know the eternal meaning of life, if you simply live superficially ... I am not saying it is evil, I am saying it is incomplete. It is getting lost in the very beginning; it is very superficial.

Life has depths beyond depths, and unless you reach to the very bottom and touch something eternal, you will not know the significance of existence, the splendor and the glory and the abundance of blessings. Your enjoyment will pay well for a long time. But then you will know that eat, drink and be merry was not enough. It was good enough, but not enough.

So I affirm materialism, I affirm spiritualism, because to me your body and your soul are not two separate existences. Matter and spirit are just two aspects of one energy. I accept the whole of life, body and soul, matter and spirit, this world and the beyond all together as one single organic whole.

To me the really holy man is one who accepts the whole without denying anything. The materialist denies the spirit. The spiritualist denies matter – both are in some way denying. Neither is a holy man. The holy man is one who accepts the whole without any denial. The whole orchestra of existence – different instruments, but they are all playing the same music, the same significance, the same glory.

You are saying, 'Enjoying life seems to be the only thing I do.' Nothing is wrong in it, it is a good beginning. But soon you will get fed up with it. How long can you enjoy the mundane things of existence? Just try to enjoy anything, then repeat it.

I have told you the story of Mulla Nasruddin. It is a Sufi story.

Mulla was appointed the adviser of the emperor. The first day he was sitting with the emperor at his dining table and the cook had made stuffed *bhindis*. The king liked them very much and Mulla Nasruddin said, 'Your liking is supported by all the wise people of the past. Those who know about vegetables say that *bhindi* is the ultimate in vegetables; it cures all diseases; it keeps you healthy, young; it gives you a longer life. It is very good that you like it.'

The cook heard everything. He thought, 'My God, I never thought that *bhindi* was such a miraculous thing.'

So, next day he prepared *bhindi* again, and Mulla Nasruddin praised it again. On the third day he again prepared *bhindi*. On the sixth day the king threw the plate away and shouted at the cook, 'Have you gone mad? I am bored with this *bhindi.* Can't you find any other vegetable? Have I to live my whole life eating *bhindi*?'

Mulla Nasruddin immediately said, 'There are many critics who say that *bhindi* is very dangerous to life, to youth. It brings all kinds of diseases. Old age comes sooner and death is a tremendously painful thing.'

The king said, 'Up to now you have been praising it. It is because of your praise that the poor cook has been cooking it every day. And now suddenly you have changed.'

Mulla said, 'Listen, I am your servant. I am not the servant of *bhindi*s. I don't know anything about *bhindi.* But if you like *bhindi,* I will appreciate it. You pay me, I am your servant. If you throw the plate of *bhindis* away, I will condemn them.'

Just look at your enjoyments. You fall in love with a woman or a man. How long does it remain? Before the honeymoon is over it is finished. Now you are wondering how to get out of it. Your enjoyments cannot give you a meaningful life, they are very superficial. I am not against them; that you have to remember. Once in a while *bhindi* is okay, but to think that it is everything is dangerous.

You are saying, '...and I forget that I am a seeker.' You will miss the opportunity. Enjoy life, but remain watchful. All that a seeker needs is a certain awareness that follows him like a shadow. Whatever you are doing, just remain alert.

The English word *sin* is very significant. Not in the way Christians interpret it, not according to the dictionaries – because they have been influenced by the religions – but according to its original roots. The word *sin* simply means forgetfulness. And that gives a totally new dimension to the word – a beauty. It is nothing for which you can be thrown into hell. It is something that you can influence. It is not concerned with any action in particular; it is concerned with your awareness.

To be aware is to be virtuous; to remain in unawareness is the only sin. You may be doing good things without awareness. But those good things are no longer good because they come out of darkness, unconsciousness, blindness. And as far as awareness is concerned, a man who is full of awareness, alert, cannot do anything wrong. It is intrinsically impossible.

Awareness brings so much clarity, so much perception, so much understanding that it is impossible to do anything that can be harmful to anyone. It is impossible to interfere with somebody's freedom or somebody's life. You can only be a blessing to existence, nothing else. So to forget that you are a seeker is dangerous. It is falling into sin. This is the only sin I accept as sin.

You are also saying, 'But when I think about it, a question arises: What am I seeking for?' The seeking is not *for* anything, the seeking is to know the seeker, who you are. There are two kinds of seeking: one is for money, for power, for prestige, for name, for fame, for anything outside you. That is not our seeking. That is not the seeking which can take you to higher states of consciousness and being. It is a totally different kind of seeking.

The first seeking goes forward, outward. It is objective. You are a seeker of the inner, of the subjective. Your search is for yourself. You don't know who you are. And not to know oneself is such an ignorance, such an indignity, such a self-insult, that no man who has a little understanding can forget about it.

Just a little intelligence and you will agree with Socrates and all those great people who have been telling you 'Know thyself, be thyself,' because without knowing yourself, you cannot be yourself. You will never come to a flowering. Your roses will remain unexpressed. Your fragrance will not be released to existence. Do you want to remain just a seed? Or do you want to grow with great green foliage and beautiful roses? Unless your roses dance in the sun, in the wind, in the rain, you have not known how much of life was hidden. It is almost like an iceberg. Only one part you see, nine times more is hidden underneath in the water. You know yourself only in a small way.

Because you know yourself only in a small way, you remain small. You can know yourself in a greater way. And the way that opens all the doors of your being, all the mysteries, all the secrets, will make you part of this vast universe. You will be as big as the ocean. There is no need to remain a dewdrop.

Rachel had lived a good life, marrying four times, and now she is standing before the Pearly Gates.

Father Abraham checks her file and says, 'I notice that you first married a banker, then an actor, then a rabbi and lastly an undertaker. What kind of system is that for a respectable Jewish woman?'

'A very good system,' replies Rachel. 'One for the money, two for the show, three to get ready and four to go!'

If this is going to be your only way of living, your style of life, your system, your philosophy, then enjoyment is enough. But not to know oneself is to deprive oneself of tremendous significance. Not to know oneself is to keep oneself away from the godliness of this cosmos. Not to know oneself is the ugliest thing that can happen to anyone.

Please remember, you are a seeker not for something, but for yourself.

> Osho,
> What is it that divides me?

Prem Pankaja ... Just a day ago I had answered her, 'Don't keep your umbrella open, because I go on showering on you and you go on protecting yourself.' So poor Pankaja has sent her umbrella to me. But this is not the umbrella I meant. What am I supposed to do with this umbrella? It was only a symbol, I never meant your real umbrella. This you can take back. You may need it.

When I say umbrella I mean all your defense measures. You are defending yourself. That's what keeps you divided. On the one hand you want to go whole-heartedly into the search for your own being, on the other hand you are afraid to go totally. You have other interests, other investments, and if you go totally into the search for your own being, you wonder what will happen to your other investments.

For example, she is a novelist. She is always afraid that if she goes deeper into meditation, her so-called creativity for writing third-class novels will disappear. That is certain. It *will* disappear because as your meditations deepen, you will not be able to write those trashy novels. That does not mean your creativity will disappear. Your creativity will be refined. Perhaps you will write something really great, something that becomes part of the great literature of the world.

Whatever you have written up to now is just like the daily newspaper. After one reading you just have to throw it away. You wait for it every morning so eagerly and after ten minutes it is useless. Not so is the case with Fyodor Dostoevsky's novels or Leo Tolstoy's or Maxim Gorky's. They will remain as long as man is on this planet. They will remain super- creations of human consciousness. Their beauty, their peaks, are such that you cannot finish them in one reading. You will have to read them again and again. And each time you read them, you will find new meanings, new depths, new significances. What keeps you divided is that you don't understand there are higher categories of creativity.

I am reminded of one of the great Indian painters, Avanendranath Tagore. He was a nephew of Rabindranath Tagore. Rabindranath became world famous because of the Nobel Prize. Avanendranath is not known so much because he was a painter, but India has never known such a painter. Each painting is unique. He had a student who became an even greater painter than Avanendranath. This disciple's name was Nandlal Bose.

And one day it happened ... Avanendranath and Rabindranath were of the same age, although Avanendranath was a nephew to Rabindranath. They were very friendly and they were discussing something, when just then Nandlal came to show his master something he had painted.

In Bengal, where these people happened to be, there is a certain class of painter. They are very poor people, but traditionally they paint only one thing and that is pictures of Krishna. In Bengal people love Krishna, and from generation to generation a certain class has been doing only one thing: painting beautiful paintings of Krishna. But they are poor people, and their paintings are sold very cheaply.

On this occasion, Nandlal had also made a picture of Krishna. Krishna's birthday was coming close and he wanted to show it to his master. Rabindranath, who was present, could not believe his eyes: Nandlal had done such a superb painting. He had seen thousands of paintings of Krishna, but he could not remember any painting that could be compared to it. Even Avanendranath had painted Krishna and his painting of Krishna was hanging on the wall of his sitting room. Rabindranath looked at both the paintings: Avanendranath's painting was not comparable to Nandlal Bose's. The disciple had defeated the master.

This was the first surprise. And the second thing that happened was even more surprising and shocking. Avanendranath took the painting, looked at it, threw it out of the door and told Nandlal, 'You idiot, you don't know how to paint. You should go and learn from those poor people.' The caste of the people who paint Krishna's pictures is called *patia* and in those days their pictures were sold at the most for four annas, which is one fourth of a rupee. To tell to Nandlal to go to the *patias* and learn how to paint Krishna was very humiliating.

Rabindranath had never seen Avanendranath so angry. Deep in his mind he thought that perhaps he was feeling jealous because Nandlal's painting was far superior to his own painting. Rabindranath himself was a great painter in his own right; he could judge perfectly well.

Nandlal touched the feet of Avanendranath and disappeared. For two years nothing was heard of him. Rabindranath told

Avanendranath many times, 'What you have done is absolutely absurd. You know perfectly well that he has defeated you.'

Avanendranath said, 'I know it. The moment I saw his painting, I immediately could see that one of my disciples is going to carry my tradition far ahead of me. But if I had accepted his painting, he would have stopped. I can see much more potential in him. I had to reject that great painting.'

After Nandlal had left, Avanendranath took the painting inside, cleaned it, removed his own painting from his sitting room wall and put Nandlal's painting there. There were tears in his eyes.

Rabindranath said, 'It is a strange drama. What is the need of all this?'

He said, 'You don't understand. I love Nandlal. I cannot accept that this is his whole potential. He has much more potential and I have to hit him hard to bring all his resources into flowering.'

After two years Nandlal came back. He looked just like those beggar painters of Bengal. He had lived amongst them, painted like them, learned their art; whatever the master said, he did. And finally he painted another painting of Krishna and he could see the difference. The first painting was great, but this was far greater. It was almost three-dimensional. It was as if Krishna was going to come out of the painting at any moment, it was so alive. He was full of gratitude toward his master who had insulted him.

This can happen only in the East. It is not possible in the West. The West does not know many dimensions of love. It is unaware. Avanendranath's behavior was out of love, out of great trust, and Nandlal understood it. He touched the feet of the master before he disappeared. For two years he moved all over Bengal, searching for any painter with whom he could sit and learn his art. And when he came back after two years, he brought this second painting. People could not believe he was the same man, he had become so thin. He could not earn much because he was living with poor people. And he was also selling his paintings at the same cost.

When Avanendranath looked at his painting, he ran to Rabindranath's house. They both lived in the same university that Rabindranath had founded in Shanti Niketan, the *House of Peace*. It is a university on its own, unique in the whole world, where beauty is God, where painting and music and dance are rated far higher than physics, chemistry or mathematics. These sciences are taught, but they are not thought to be the highest creations of man. They are lower, mundane. They can produce things, but they cannot create.

I am telling you this story, Pankaja, because you need not be afraid of losing your creativity. This is not the place where you are going to lose anything that is significant. Yes, you will lose many things which are false in you: your personality, your ego. But you will not lose anything that has any sincerity, that has any authenticity behind it. That is part of your real being. That will grow.

In this garden, your reality, your truth, your consciousness, your bliss are going to grow. Yes, many things will disappear which need to disappear and you are clinging to those things. That is creating a division. You are becoming more schizophrenic, more a split personality. You are half here and half not here, and I need you to be totally here.

A man was very embarrassed about his small prick. So one day he decided to go to the doctor for a new one.

'We have three sizes for you to choose from,' began the doctor. 'We have the regular six-inch model, then we have the super eight-inch classic, and last we have the ten-inch super deluxe.'

'Wow,' says the man. 'I will go for the ten-inch super deluxe.' So the doctor went into the next room and brought out the ten inches for the man to look at.

'Well, doc,' says the man, 'I love it. It is really great. But do you have it in white?'

People have artificial personalities. Everything seems to be artificial, synthetic. You cannot tell even whether the man sitting by your side is real or synthetic.

Just a few days ago in Japan ... Japan is the only country right now which is using robots instead of men in their factories. A robot can work for twenty-four hours without getting tired; it can work seven days a week without creating any trouble – no strikes or labor unions. Hundreds of robots, mechanical men, are working. And their work is more efficient than men's. Their productivity is immense. Where a hundred people were working, just one robot is enough. So they are very cheap.

A few weeks ago a strange thing happened which scientists have not been able to explain. If it goes on happening again and again, perhaps they will have to remove all the robots. In one factory, for no reason at all ... And it is not expected of robots because they are completely planned from the very beginning. They cannot do other than what they are built for. They have an inbuilt program that directs them. But without any inbuilt program, a few robots in one factory simply killed six men. All they have to do is to give a man a good hug and he is gone, because these are steel people. They look like human beings, but they are made of steel. As they were not programmed for it, how did they come to figure out that hugging was needed?

One of my sannyasins in New York runs a hugging therapy, where the whole work is to hug each other, and go on hugging till you get tired and fed up. Then you will never think of hugging anybody again in your life. He is a little crazy, but he finds crazy clients who pay him just to do this stupid act of hugging each other until they are tired and finished, and many feel that they have been helped immensely; they have been cured of their desire to hug. In New York everything is possible. But suddenly these robots learned the hugging therapy and they picked up poor human beings who were just passing by, hugged them and finished them.

The scientists who created those robots are simply shocked. It is a very difficult problem. If these people start doing things on their own, they can do anything. They can create havoc in society, they can run in the streets, they can stop cars. They can do anything. If they can hug, everything is possible. It is good they did not kiss. But they could do.

And the people who write science fiction have already written that in the twenty-first century men will be slowly, slowly replaced by mechanical men, by robots – because they will never die. There is no way for them to die for the simple reason that all their parts are replaceable. If a hand goes wrong, it can be replaced; if their heart no longer functions, it can be replaced. They can be plugged into the electricity or they can be fitted with a battery, and they will look just like you. They can be taught to speak any language. Everything can be inbuilt in their heads, in their computers.

What science fiction says has every possibility of happening. Then you will not know whether you are falling in love with a real man or a robot. You will know only when the robot suddenly runs out of battery power. Only then you will know: 'My God, this is a robot!' But call the technician and he will fix the battery and he will again be saying all sweet things to you, sweet nothings, 'I love you.'

He just has to be programmed. He can be programmed with good dialogues from all the films, and songs to sing; he can dance, he can sing. Just stay aware that his battery is intact. It is no longer science fiction. In Japan it is already happening. There is so much false in you that if you become aware of it, you will come to a great revelation.

Pankaja, this revelation is still missing in you. You are too much of a head and you have trained yourself as an intellectual. Your whole life structure is based on intellect. Here you have to come down from the head to the heart. Nor is the heart the full stop of the journey. From the heart you have to come even deeper to the being, and from the being to the universal, cosmic, eternal life. The head is the farthest point from your real life. But your whole training goes against your real life. That is dividing you.

You will have to choose. If you choose your head, you choose a miserable life, superficial, meaningless, anxiety-ridden. But if you choose to get out of the head, then be more meditative, be more feelingful, be more of the heart, be more sensitive.

Whenever I look at Pankaja, I feel a deep sympathy for her. She is completely enclosed in the head. She has forgotten the way to the heart. She is a woman, hence it is not very difficult to find the heart again; for a man it is a little more difficult. He is naturally head-oriented. The woman is heart-oriented. So what Pankaja is suffering from is headache; she has to come down to the heartache, which is another name for love. It has been the same situation for many years. It is time for you, Pankaja, to decide. Either forget me completely and be at ease with your head and your superficial life, or take the risk. Sannyas is nothing but risking the known for the unknown, risking the false for the real. But you don't know the real; you know only the false. And the trouble is, unless you drop the false you will not be able to see the real.

Hence a strange thing has been happening in the East of which the West is unaware, and that is a totally new dimension to love which we call trust, *shraddha*. If you can look into my eyes, trust me when I say you have a real self. Don't be worried about risking the false. Of course, it has to be only on the grounds of trust. I cannot do anything to make you see the real, unless you drop the false.

You can drop the false only if you trust my word or you trust my eyes or you trust my presence. It is not belief. Belief is always in a certain doctrine, philosophy. Trust is personal, intimate, the highest quality of love, what the Zen people call the great love affair.

If you feel that what I am saying is not just borrowed knowledge but my own experience, then take a jump. It is not a big jump. If you can manage to take a jump from the real to the false, just think: from the false to the real is a very small jump. You are only losing that which you don't have, and you are going to get that which is your reality.

Osho,
This morning I suddenly realized that there is nothing interesting in women. Is it true?

I was expecting at least a dozen Germans to get angry at me – just the Germans. I love Germans. The majority of my sannyasins are Germans. And even the German government is afraid of me, knowing perfectly well that I have a certain grip on the German youth. It is not without reason that they have passed a law in their parliament that I cannot enter Germany, though I have never asked to enter. Not only that, I cannot land my jet on any German airport for refueling. Such great fear and such a brave race!

But I was waiting, and I was absolutely right. Not a single person from any other country – and people from almost every country of the world are present here – but only Germans were very angry. I had said, 'I don't see anything nice in man.' This was certainly said to provoke the Germans, and they got caught. They are simple fellows in a way; they could not see the device.

Veet Prayas is a German. I have chosen two representatives from twelve letters. Prayas is asking, 'This morning I suddenly realized that there is nothing interesting in women.' This is his reaction.

Now I would like all the women in the ashram to boycott Prayas completely for seven days. Wherever any woman sees him, say to him, 'Ooh-la-la,' not more than that. And within seven days he will start seeing everyone as beautiful, even in the ugliest woman. It will take seven days; for other people it would not take that much time.

Seeing the situation, one of my doctors, Swami Devageet, did a great research, finding out what is nice in man. He became so influenced that finally he decided he wants to change his name from Swami Devageet to *Ma* Devageet. This is his research – now I don't know how to say it, whether to say he or she. At least in the beginning, I shall start with he, unless he declares that he has changed to Ma.

He is saying, 'I have researched deeply into the knotty problem of men's good points. It was not easy, but certain attributes have come to light. Men, it seems, are the best at:

putting out the garbage, f
rightening small children,
piddling on the toilet seat,
carrying suitcases,
putting hair in the bathroom sink,
making babies,
making spaghetti,
shouting at rickshaw drivers,
leaving dirty underwear in the bedroom,
snoring in bed,
fancying everybody's woman except their own,
grossing out people at breakfast time,
putting dirty footprints on the clean sheets,
falling asleep in the middle of lovemaking,
being unresponsive to any emotional situation,
providing the main topic for gossip,
giving women someone to henpeck,
paying the rent,
fixing things which are always worse afterward,
emptying the fridge at midnight,
breaking the best china,
leaving the bed unmade,
leaving the kitchen sink clogged with food.

But, most of all, men are the biggest pricks in the whole of humanity.'

The other sample that I have chosen, says:

Osho,
I want to defend my male race. Existence gave man the capacity to fight against existence, to swim against the stream, to be a doer, to say no. Hearing you and your therapists, I tried to drop this and this effort to drop only gave me misery. I don't believe existence made me a man in order to become female without ever blossoming into the full potential of my maleness, of my mind. Please comment.

Swami Antar Mario, Germany is the only land in the whole world which is called the fatherland. Every other land is called the motherland. I said I love the German people, except for a small inheritance that they have been carrying for centuries – a male chauvinist idea of themselves. It has created two world wars and it may create the third. It is not new that Mario is saying, 'I have to defend my male race.' This very idea of defending and the idea that he has to fight existence, he has to be a doer, he has to say no. Here, trying to drop effort, he has not been able to. He only became more miserable.

What kind of man are you, if you cannot drop effort? How are you going to defend the male race? Many women are dropping effort, and you cannot drop effort. You are defeated already. And why this fear of let- go, of going with the current? Why this fear of saying yes to existence? – just an ego trip.

It is one of the ugliest things in anyone, because it is the wall that prevents you from seeing beyond yourself. You are surrounded by a prison of your own and you cannot see beyond the walls, you don't know the sky, you don't know the stars, you don't know that this whole existence is in a tremendous let-go. Everything is effortlessly moving. The trees are growing. Do you think they are making any effort to grow? The stars are moving with tremendous speed. Do you think they are making any effort? You are breathing. Do you think it is something to do with your effort? Your heart is beating. Is it something to do with you and your doing? If it was dependent on your doing, in sleep you would forget to breathe, you would forget the heart, whether it is beating or not. And then no chance ... In the morning you would not even be able to remember that in the middle of the night you forgot to breathe. Once finished, finished. The whole of existence is in a tremendous let-go.

Adolf Hitler exploited the German race only because of this male chauvinistic mind. He himself was not a giant intellectual. He was a retarded schizophrenic, a psychologically sick person, but he impressed the whole German race with all kinds of stupid ideas. For example: Germany was not ruling over all the world because of the Jews. It is as absurd as to say that Germany is not ruling over all the world because of the bicycles. Unless we destroy bicycles, there is no chance for Germany to rule over the world. What have the poor Jews done? But he was convincing because he shouted loudly.

He organized big rallies which proved to people that they must be wrong, he must be right; he killed more people than anybody else in the whole history of man. But he is not responsible alone: every German is responsible. You supported him; you supported the very idea that you have to fight with existence to prove your manliness. You have to say no. But remember: a person who cannot say yes will always remain insane.

No belongs to death, *yes* belongs to life. Life is yes-saying. The deeper your yes, the deeper your surrender to existence, the greater is your bliss. Otherwise you become absolutely mechanical, like robots. And the very idea that you are special above any other race is simply nonsense. If Germany can drop this male chauvinistic attitude, can accept women as equal to men, not only will Germany be at ease and in peace, it will help the whole world to remain in peace. War can be dropped. Instead of war, more love, more friendliness, more joy can become our daily experience.

Helmut's new car has just been delivered. So he offers to give a lift to some of his friends who are going to a wedding. Unfortunately he has not even been told how to start the car, so after he has finished bluffing for a while, he confesses his ignorance.

The others are also German, not too smart either, but luckily at least Herman can read. He reads out from a button near the steering wheel: 'Push to start.' So they all get out to push.

A German traveling salesman has been on the road for weeks, when he sees a sign which reads: 'Mother Murphy's House of Pleasure, straight ahead.' He drives on a mile and the sign is repeated. This goes on every mile, until he reaches the last sign, which says: 'You are here! This is it! Mother Murphy's House of Pleasure!'

He is feeling pretty horny, so he pulls into the drive, where all he finds is a little wooden shack, but he decides to try it out.

He walks in and finds a little old lady sitting in a rocking chair. He apologizes and is beginning to leave, when she says, 'You are in the right place, sonny. This is Mother Murphy's. Just give me fifty bucks and go through that door over there.'

So he goes through the door and finds himself in the backyard, and the door locks behind him, so he can't get back in. He is really angry, and looking around, he sees a small sign in the next field, so he goes over to read it. It says: 'You have just been screwed by Mother Murphy.'

At least here, drop your German-ness; that is your disease. And it is not only about you. The Indians have to drop their Indian-ness; that is their disease. And the Italians have to drop their Italian-ness; that is their disease.

Nations are just man-made boundaries; races are stupid discriminations; religions are man-manufactured – and they are all dividing man against man. Sannyas is an effort to bring a new world into existence, where nobody is a German and nobody is an Indian and nobody is a Japanese; where nobody thinks that he is superior, where nobody thinks that women are inferior and slaves, where equality and equal opportunity to grow is simply accepted as natural.

I did not say that man has nothing to offer. He has much to offer. In fact all science, all technology is going to be man's offering to existence, but man has to remember that the works of the intellect and reason are not his highest creations. The higher creations come from the heart, in songs, in music, in poetry, in dances. Unless you can celebrate, what use is all scientific progress? And without a woman there is no celebration.

You put a hundred men together and they will all be serious. Just bring one woman in and immediately all their eyes start sparkling, they become interested. Life starts being juicy; something is going to happen. Man without woman is half, and woman without man is half. They are part of one whole.

I did not say anything in favor of men because men have done so much wrong to women that now it is better not to say anything about men's talents and genius. It is better to bring out the women's genius and talents. It is simply a compensation. I know there are a few things which only men can do, and there are a few things which only women can do. That makes life more beautiful and more attractive. Between these two polarities, life becomes a magnetic pull. Between these two polarities of man and woman, many mysteries happen. The whole romance of life, the whole poetry of life, is because of the polarity of man and woman. But man has ruled over women for millennia. He has been given every opportunity and chance and woman has been repressed continuously, has been crippled. She has not been allowed to compete shoulder to shoulder with man in life. That's why we don't know how many Gautam Buddhas on the women's side did not get the opportunity to blossom.

We don't know how many Albert Einsteins have simply been denied any possibility for growth.

It is a very strange thing that even dimensions like poetry, music, dance are dominated by men. The greatest dancers in the world have been men, not women. In fact, women should have been ahead of any male dancer. But one needs opportunity. One needs education, one needs training. If you bar the whole of womankind from education, training, discipline, you are making the whole society and the whole world poor, unnecessarily poor. My emphasis is to give respect to women – and equality is not against men. It is a world which belongs to you both and you both have to be together to make it as beautiful and as divine as possible.

Man alone – look at your question, Mario – has been creating only wars. In three thousand years, five thousand wars. Is life just to fight? Is life just to kill, massacre, rape? Your whole history is full of murder and you call those murderers your great men. Alexander the Great ... And you don't see that small murderers are being jailed, sentenced to death, but big murderers become your heroes. It is because the woman has been completely cut off from contributing anything to life; otherwise there would not have been so many wars.

No woman is interested in war, it is simply against the feminine nature. She is interested in love, she is interested in a beautiful house, she is interested in a beautiful garden around the house. She is interested in small things, but those small things make life worth living. She is not interested in creating atomic weapons, nuclear missiles. She cannot understand what man goes on doing. Is he insane or something?

Half of humanity is dying of starvation and the politicians who are all men and the generals who are all men go on piling up nuclear weapons. They have already more than they need – seven hundred times more than they need to destroy this whole world. All that is living on the earth – trees, birds, animals, human beings, anything that is living – we have already seven hundred times more than enough material to destroy it. And still they go on piling it up. Do you think this is sanity when half the human race is dying of starvation?

This is happening because man alone has been contributing to existence. He has not the compassion of a woman; he has only the hardness of a man. He does not allow the softness of woman to influence world affairs. We need a very balanced life, in which the man and the woman contribute equally. Life will be more peaceful, more lovable, more joyous. It will become a tremendous celebration.

And in that celebration, my hope is we will be able to go beyond the ordinary, mundane enjoyment into the cosmic bliss, into *sat-chit-anand* – into truth, into consciousness, into bliss.

27

Inner Beauty

Osho,
Your inner beauty I can only feel as far as I have discovered myself. But for ten years, whenever I see you entering the auditorium, there is this surprise about your unbelievable outer beauty too.

Osho, is the outer appearance always just a reflection of the inner?

The outer beauty comes from a different source than the inner. The outer beauty comes from your father and mother: their bodies create your body. But the inner beauty comes from your own growth of consciousness that you are carrying from many lives. In your individuality both are joined: the physical heritage from your father and mother and the spiritual heritage of your own past lives, its consciousness, its bliss, its joy. So it is not absolutely necessary that the outer will be a reflection of the inner, nor will vice versa be true, that the inner will correspond with the outer.

But sometimes it happens that you have so much inner beauty, so much inner light that they start radiating from your outer body. Your outer body may not be beautiful, but the light that comes from your sources, your innermost sources of eternal life, will make even a body which is not beautiful in the ordinary sense appear beautiful, radiant. But vice versa it is never true.

Your outer beauty is only skin-deep. It cannot affect your inner beauty. On the contrary, the outer beauty becomes a hindrance in search of the inner: you become too identified with the outer. Who is going to look for the inner sources? Most often it happens that the people who are outwardly very beautiful, are inwardly very ugly. Their outer beauty becomes a cover-up to hide themselves behind, and it is experienced by millions of people every day. You fall in love with a woman or a man because you can see only the outer. Just within a few days you start discovering his inner state; it doesn't correspond to his outer beauty. On the contrary, it is very ugly.

For example, Alexander the Great had a very beautiful body but he killed millions of people, just to fulfill his ego that he was the world conqueror. He met one man, Diogenes, when he was on his way to India, who lived naked, the only man in Greece who did, unique in a way. His beauty was tremendous, not just the outer, but he had so much inner radiance, so dazzling, that even Alexander had to stop his armies when he was close by in a forest near a river. He stopped the armies and went to see Diogenes alone; alone, because he did not want anybody to know that there exists a man who is far more beautiful than Alexander himself.

It was early morning and Diogenes was taking a sunbath, naked on the riverbank. Alexander could not believe that a beggar ... He had nothing, no possessions – even Buddha used to have a begging bowl, but that too Diogenes had thrown away. He was absolutely without any possessions, exactly as he was born, naked.

Alexander could not believe his eyes. He had never seen such a beautiful personality and he could see that this beauty was not just on the outer. Something infiltrated from the inner; a subtle radiation, a subtle aura surrounded him. All around him there was a fragrance, a silence.

If the inner becomes beautiful – which is in your hands – the outer will have to mold itself according to the inner. The outer is not essential, it will have to reflect the inner in some way. But the converse is not true at all. You can have plastic surgery, you can have a beautiful face, beautiful eyes, a beautiful nose; you can change your skin; you can change your shape. That is not going to change your being. Inside you will still remain greedy, full of lust, violence, anger, rage, jealousy, with a tremendous will to power. The plastic surgeon can do nothing about all these things. For that you will need a different kind of surgery.

It is happening here: you are on the table. As you become more and more meditative, peaceful, a deep at-onement with existence happens. You fall into the rhythm of the universe. The universe also has its own heartbeat. Your heartbeat, once it starts in rhythm with the universal heartbeat, will have transformed your being from that ugly stage of animality, into authentic humanity. And even the human is not the end. You can go on searching deeper and there is a place where you transcend humanity and something of the divine enters in you. Once the divine is there, it is almost like a light in a dark house. The windows will start showing the light; even the cracks in the wall or the roof or the doors will start showing the inner light.

The inner is tremendously powerful, the outer is very weak. The inner is eternal, the outer is very temporary. How many years do you remain young? And as youth fades away you start feeling that you are becoming ugly, unless your inner being is also growing with your age. Then even in your old age you will have a beauty that the youth may feel jealous of. Remember: from the inner the change to the outer happens, but I am not making it inevitable. Most often it happens, but sometimes the outer is in such a rotten state that even the inner radiation cannot change it.

There have been cases on record: one very great mystic of India whose name was Ashtavakra – I have spoken on him for almost half a year continuously. What he has written is tremendously important. Each sentence has so many dimensions to be explored, but the man himself was in a very difficult situation.

Ashtavakra – the name was given to him because he was almost like a camel. In eight places he was distorted in the body – one leg was longer, one arm was shorter, his back was bent ... In eight places he was distorted. That's how he was born, with a crippled, distorted body. But even in a crippled and distorted body the soul is as beautiful as in the most beautiful body. He became enlightened, but his body was too rigid to change with his inner change. His eyes started showing something of the beauty, but the whole body was in such a mess.

The story is...

The emperor of India in those days was Janak and he was very much interested in philosophical discussions. Each year he used to call a big conference of all the scholars, philosophers, theologians or whoever wanted to participate. It was a championship competition.

One very famous philosopher, Yagnavalkya, came a little late. The conference had started and he saw one thousand beautiful cows standing outside. Their horns were covered with gold and diamonds. This was going to be the prize for the champion. It was a hot day and the cows were perspiring.

He told his disciples, 'Take these cows. As far as winning the competition is concerned, I am certain. Why should the cows suffer here? Take them to our place.' They had their own place in the forest.

Even Janak could not prevent him, because he knew that Yagnavalkya had been the champion continuously for five years, and he would be the champion this time because there was nobody else who could defeat him. It is not right to take the reward before you have won, but his victory was so certain to everybody that nobody objected. So his disciples took away all the cows.

While Yagnavalkya was discussing, a very unknown scholar was also present at the conference. Ashtavakra was this unknown philosopher's son. His mother was waiting for her husband to come home. It was getting late and the meal was getting cold. So she sent Ashtavakra to bring his father home, knowing he could not win the competition. Why should he unnecessarily waste his time? He was a poor scholar and there were great scholars there. Ashtavakra went. There were at least one thousand people at the conference, the highly cultured and sophisticated scholars of the country.

As Ashtavakra entered, looking at his distorted body they all started laughing. But Ashtavakra was a man of tremendous integrity. As they started laughing, he laughed even louder. Because of his loud laugh they stopped. They could not believe that *he* was laughing.

Janak asked him, 'I can understand why they are laughing; it's because of your body, but I cannot understand why *you* are laughing. And you stopped all their laughing with your laughter.' A single man stopped one thousand people's laughter.

Ashtavakra said to Janak, 'I thought this conference was for scholars and philosophers, but these are all shoemakers. They can understand only the skin. They cannot see the inner, they can only see the outer.'

There was a great silence. What he was saying had a great truth in it. Janak dissolved the conference and said, 'Now I would like to inquire of Ashtavakra only. He has defeated you all just by his laughter and his statement "You can't see the inner, you can only see the outer; you are all shoemakers." Shoemakers work with the skin of different animals. I dissolve the conference and, Yagnavalkya, return those one thousand cows because you also laughed. And when Ashtavakra laughed, you also stopped.'

It was a very strange situation; it had never happened before. And then began the long inquiry of Janak, the emperor. He asked questions and Ashtavakra answered them. Each answer in itself carried so much meaning and significance. Because his body was in such a bad shape he could not get identified with it. Sometimes blessings come in such disguise. He could not go out, because wherever he went people would laugh, 'Look at that man! Have you seen anything uglier than this?'

So most of the time he was in the house, meditating, figuring out, 'Who am I? Certainly I am not this body, because I can be aware of this body, I can observe this body from within. Certainly that awareness has to be different from the body.'

Because of his crippled body he experienced enlightenment. The only barrier is identification with the body. But he could not identify, the body was so ugly. He never looked in a mirror; it would have been such a shock.

Yagnavalkya had to return those one thousand cows to Ashtavakra's house. He was young and he defeated one thousand old philosophers, well-versed in the ancient scriptures.

It is one of the strangest things in this country that on every book written by any prominent mystic there have been hundreds of commentaries, but nobody before me has commented on Ashtavakra. And he must be at least five thousand years old. For five thousand years nobody has bothered to look into his statements, which are so significant. But his inner enlightenment, his inner understanding, could not change his outer appearance. And yet for those who are going deeper into themselves, the outer does not matter. Even in Ashtavakra they would have seen tremendous beauty; it would not have been of the outer circumference, but of the center.

Most often the inner change changes the outer, if the outer is not too rigid. But the outer never changes the inner. You need to have eyes going deep into people's beings, which is possible only if you are going inward yourself. The deeper you go into yourself the deeper you can look into other people's beings. And then a totally new world opens its doors.

Flanagan is on his deathbed and Father Murphy has come to give him the last rites. 'Open your eyes,' says the priest. 'We have got to save your immortal soul.' Flanagan opens one eye, closes it and tries to doze off. He is having such a nice snooze.

'Come on now,' says Father Murphy. 'If you don't want to confess, at least answer me this: Do you renounce the Devil and all his works?'

'Well, I don't know,' says Flanagan, opening one eye again. 'At a time like this, it doesn't seem very smart to upset anyone.'

The inner comes out, you cannot hide it much. Now he is being very calculating. At the time of death, unnecessarily annoying anybody ... And who knows where you are going? It is better to keep silent.

A wealthy widower and his beautiful daughter are on a sea cruise. By chance the girl falls overboard, and Rubin Fingelbaum, aged seventy, splashes in afterward and rescues her. After the two are brought on board the ship, the widower throws his arms around Rubin.

'You saved my daughter's life,' he cries. 'I'm a rich man. I will give you anything! Ask for whatever you want.'

'Just answer me one question,' replies Rubin. 'Who pushed me?'

What is inside is bound to come outside. How can you hide it?

An old black preacher had used the letters BS, MS and PhD after his name for many years without ever having had anyone from his congregation ask what they meant. Finally, a nosy old woman questions him about it.

'Well, sister,' he answers. 'You know what BS stands for, don't you?'

'I sure do,' says the lady indignantly. 'Bull shit!'

'Right,' says the preacher. 'And MS just means more of the same, and PhD means piled high and deep.'

That's the inner side of most people: bull shit, BS; MS, more of the same; PhD, piled high and deep. No plastic surgeon can change it. But you are capable of changing it yourself. It is within your hands. Nobody can do anything about your inner being except you. You are the master of your inner world. As the inner world becomes silent, naturally your eyes become deeper, with an oceanic depth. As your inner being becomes cloudless, your face also becomes cloudless, just an open sky. As your inner being comes to discover the source of your life, the flame of your life, something of that flame starts radiating from every pore of your body.

This is the rule. Ashtavakra is an exception. Exceptions don't make the rule, they only prove the rule. But it has never happened vice versa before, and I don't think it can ever happen.

We are all trying to be beautiful on the outside: all kinds of make-up, all kinds of things are going on to make your outer beautiful.

I have heard...

A man was catching flies. Finally after two or three hours' effort he caught four flies. He told his wife, 'I have caught four flies: two are male, two are female.'

The wife said, 'My God, how did you figure out who is male and who is female?'

He said, 'Easy! Two were sitting for almost two hours on the mirror and two were reading the newspaper for two hours!'

We are so identified with the periphery of our being that we have forgotten that the periphery does not exist in itself. There must be a center inside. And the search for the center is the only religious search – not for God, not for heaven, not for any rewards for your virtues, not to avoid hell and punishment.

There is only one authentic religious search and that is to know your innermost being. It is the being of the whole universe. By entering your innermost temple you have entered the real temple. All other temples are false, man-manufactured; all other gods in those temples are false, they are man-manufactured.

Only one thing is not man-manufactured and that is your innermost dignity, your innermost grace. That grace starts flooding your outer being too. And that grace transforms not only the inner, but gives a new look to your outer being: an innocence, a serenity, a depth, a peace, a love, and these are all flowers blossoming around you. Then even your periphery becomes so beautiful, so musical, such a dance of rejoicing.

But you should start from the inner.

Osho,
What is civilization?

Civilization has not happened yet. It is a false idea that we are civilized people – civilized people and continuously preparing for war?

Even the animals don't eat, don't kill, their own species. It is only man who kills his own species – no lion will kill another lion, no dog will kill another dog. No lion will eat another lion. Man is the only one who can be a cannibal. There are still small groups around the world in isolated places who are cannibals. They are remnants of the past, but they are still there.

In Africa there is a small cannibal colony in the thick forest. There used to be three thousand at the beginning of this century, now there are only three hundred because when they cannot find anybody else, they have to eat somebody from their own group. They are getting reduced in numbers – they eat their own children, they eat their own parents. Once in a while they get a Christian missionary, but that is very rare.

Once they caught a very fat Christian missionary and they were immensely happy. There was dancing and celebration, a big pot on the fire was boiling and the Christian missionary asked, 'What is this celebration for? I have come here to give you a taste of Christianity.'

They said, 'You wait, soon we will have the first taste of Christianity.'

He asked, 'How are you going to have the first taste of Christianity if I don't give it to you?'

They said, 'Don't be worried, you will have to give it.'

The missionary said, 'I don't understand what you are talking about.'

They said, 'Look at that fire and the big pot. We will put you in the pot. When the water is hot enough, we will make a soup of you and that will be our first taste of Christianity!'

Once perhaps the whole of humanity was cannibal. In emergency situations one falls back. For example, when there was a famine in Bengal, people were found eating their own children. You cannot conceive it, but rather than die it seems to be logical and rational to eat your own children. Those who were not able to do such a thing sold their children, knowing perfectly well that the people who were purchasing their children would eat them. And with the money they purchased other people's children. This way they protected their conscience a little bit, but not much, because it was absolutely clear what was going to happen. In emergency situations man shows his real face; otherwise our civilization is only a mask.

In a civilized humanity a few things are absolutely necessary. One: there should be no possibility of war because it is life-destructive. And a civilized humanity will have the sensitivity not to destroy life in any form. George Bernard Shaw had around his house a beautiful garden where he had collected exotic roses from different countries, different colors, different fragrances. A friend had come to see him and he saw the roses. He could not believe that there were so many colors and so many different fragrances. When he went inside he said to Bernard Shaw, 'You have such beautiful flowers, but you don't put them in a pot inside your sitting room.'

Bernard Shaw said, 'I am a civilized man. I love children, but that does not mean I should cut off their heads and decorate my sitting room with them. I love roses, but that does not mean that I have to cut the living flower from its life source and put it here in my sitting room. That would be uncivilized behavior.'

Even to cut a flower is uncivilized behavior, what to say about people like Genghis Khan, who killed forty million people; Tamerlane, who killed thirty million people; Nadir Shah, he again killed forty million people, and statistics are not available about many others. There is no data available about Alexander the Great, Napoleon Bonaparte or Ivan the Terrible, but they must have killed more people than Genghis Khan, Tamerlane, Nadir Shah. Data *is* available on Joseph Stalin, Adolf Hitler, Benito Mussolini, and they were not very far away from our present time, just forty years ago. They killed millions of people for no reason at all. This destructiveness is a death-oriented ideology and it is so deeply rooted in our minds that it keeps us below the animals.

Man is not yet civilized. His civilization will begin by dropping war, by dropping nations. What is the need of nations if you are not going to fight? Nations are needed for wars. Why create these stupid lines on the map of the world? The world is one. There are no natural lines dividing nations. Then why do you go on with this? There is a deep desire to dominate and there are so many people in the world to dominate: they need many nations. Otherwise just a single government, a functional government for the whole world will be enough.

What is the need of so many laws if man is civilized? What is the need of so many courts, jails, so many legal advisers, if man is civilized? A civilized man will not commit murders, a civilized man will not rape women, but we keep this whole paraphernalia of courts, laws, constitutions, legal experts. For whom?

Man is still a criminal. These jails, these judges and these laws prevent nothing. Jails go on growing, judges go on increasing – more and more of them; more courts, more legal experts, thousands of colleges around the world producing legal experts every year. But even they cannot manage, for the criminals increase at a faster rate, and they don't have a college, they are not educated. Something is basically wrong, something is missing. What is missing?

I call it meditation. Only meditation can make humanity civilized, because meditation will release your creativity and take away your destructiveness. Meditation will bring your compassion and will take away your cruelty. Meditation will make you responsible to your own being and then you cannot be a criminal. To be a criminal needs great unconsciousness. Meditation destroys your unconsciousness, opens the doors of light and suddenly what you were doing in the darkness starts disappearing.

A civilization can be based only on meditation. The only people who have been civilized were people who were in touch with their own being: a Gautam Buddha, a Socrates, a Pythagoras, a Lao Tzu; these people are civilized. Only individuals once in a while have been found civilized, but the collective mass is still far below the standard of civilization.

It *has* to happen! Those who are with me, they have to create the foundation for a civilization, for a civilized humanity, by themselves becoming civilized.

It was the night before the wedding, and young Herschel Goldberg is having a drink with Moishe Finkelstein, his future father-in-law.

Soon the conversation turns to Ruthie, the bride-to-be.

'Well,' says Moishe, a little the worse for drink, 'are you going to be a man and do it tonight, or are you going to be a mouse and wait until tomorrow night?'

Before he can stop himself, Herschel blurts out, 'I guess I am a rat, sir – I did it last week.'

These are your civilized people.

On honeymoon, the young French bride is becoming exhausted by her ardent eighty-year-old husband. During a short lull, while he is shaving, she sneaks out and staggers into the hotel coffee shop downstairs.

'I don't get it,' says her friend, the waitress. 'Here you are, a teen-age bride with an ancient husband, and you look a wreck. What happened?'

'The old goat double-crossed me,' sobs the bride. 'He told me he had been saving up for sixty years, and I thought he was talking about money!'

Just look around, look at people's behavior and you will be surprised. This idea that we have become civilized is very dangerous. It is preventing us from being civilized, because once you accept that you are civilized there is no need to work for civilization. Once you accept you are healthy, there is no need to remove any sickness that you may be suffering from. The first thing to be recognized is that you are sick. Then only can something be done for your health. But if you deny sickness, which has been done for centuries by your so-called politicians...

They deny that we are uncivilized people, they say we are civilized people. And this camouflage prevents us from being civilized. We have completely accepted the idea and forgotten that we have to see whether it is true or not. It is certainly not true. Unless each man comes to the consciousness of a Gautam Buddha, there is no question of civilization.

After I left America, the US Attorney for Oregon gave a press conference in which he was asked, 'Why have you let Osho go and not jailed him?' And the US Attorney said, 'There are three reasons: one, our priority was to destroy his commune and we could not destroy it if we had not deported him.'

But why should they be interested in destroying the commune? The commune was not hurting anybody. It was the most civilized group of people in the whole world. Five thousand people living for five years together in a desert, with no rape, no madness, no stealing, no murder, no suicide. People were so happy and so joyous. Why was the US Attorney interested in destroying the commune? The fact is: the commune became a pain in their neck. They could see what is possible. No court, no laws, no army, no police and yet five thousand people are living peacefully, lovingly, understandingly. This was hurting the politicians of America, because soon people would start comparing: 'Why is it not happening all over America?' That was their number one priority – to destroy the commune.

'Second,' he said, 'we did not want Osho to become a martyr.' It implies that they had the intention to murder me, but they were afraid that murdering me would mean creating a new Christianity.

If the Jews had not crucified Jesus there would not have been any Christianity at all. That's why I never like to call it Christianity. I call it Crossianity. It has nothing to do with Jesus, it has everything to do with the cross. And you can see that cross hanging around the necks of all the missionaries and the bishops and the cardinals and the priests and the pope. The cross is the center. Anyway Christ was a Jew! And he always remained a Jew. He never even heard the word *Christian*. He died a Jew. But the cross created a great sympathy toward him. That was the fear: if they assassinate me, the danger is that sannyas will become a far more solid movement around the world.

But the desire was there, otherwise he would not have mentioned it. Whatever you say shows not what you are saying but what is hidden behind it. Mentioning 'We did not want Osho to become a martyr,' shows the desire that if it had been possible without making me a martyr, they would certainly have preferred to assassinate me. But he said, 'We will do everything to silence him.' And they did everything to silence me.

They influenced twenty-four countries not to allow me into their territories. The Indian government is under their pressure, making every effort ... They cannot do anything to me, but they can do one thing: they can ensure that no news media reaches me, that no seekers from outside India reach me. They are making all kinds of efforts to prevent people coming to me. Naturally I will be silenced. It will be equivalent to killing me without a cross.

The third thing is the most interesting thing he said. He said, 'Moreover, Osho has not committed any crime; we don't have any proof, we don't have any evidence.' This recognition by the US Attorney for Oregon – but still I was fined four hundred thousand dollars! They don't have any proof and they don't have any evidence, they don't think I have committed any crime. For what have I been fined? And they know perfectly well, I don't have a single dollar. I have not touched money for almost thirty-five years! Perhaps, because I don't have any possessions, they were hoping that I wasn't going to be able to pay almost half a million dollars. So naturally, if I could not pay them, they would have an excuse to put me in jail for at least twenty years, thirty years.

And you call this world a civilized world? For what reason did they deport me? They did not allow me even to stay a single night! I was ordered from the court directly to the airport; my jet was ready, its engine was kept running. 'Move out of America immediately.'

What was the problem? Why could I not stay at least for the night? The reason was they were afraid I might appeal to the higher court, I might go up to the Supreme Court. It was better to throw me out of America so I could not do that.

And this is a civilized world! America is very proud of its civilization. Absolutely innocent people are being tortured. Thirty million people in America are beggars. They are just on the street, with no food, no shelter, no clothes; they don't know from where they are going to get their food tomorrow. And exactly the same number – a strange coincidence – thirty million Americans are suffering from too much weight. They are looked after in the hospitals because they cannot be left alone in their houses. Devageet was right: in the middle of the night they empty the fridge.

Thirty million people are dying of overfeeding and thirty million people are dying without food. Is this civilization? Can't a simple understanding be there: 'Don't eat too much and what remains can save thirty million people?' Not eating too much is going to save the other thirty million who are dying of starvation. If they go on eating, sixty million people are dying unnecessarily.

You call this an intelligent world, a civilized world, a cultured world? No, I refuse to! A hundred times No! This world is not yet civilized. It needs civilization, certainly. But up to now no effort has been made to civilize it.

And strange things go on happening. I have been continuously receiving letters from sannyasins from all over the world that they want to come, but the moment they mention meditation – that they are going to India for meditation – the Indian embassies refuse them. They say 'India is not for meditation.' And for almost ten thousand years India has been the center of meditation, and pilgrims from all over the world have always moved toward India in search of meditation.

Now who are these idiots who are preventing people from coming to India because they want to learn meditation? They are allowing people who want to see the ruins of old forts, castles, caves. That's perfectly okay, you are a tourist. But if you are going to learn meditation, you are not to be allowed.

The fear is: if you are going to learn meditation, you will end up in Pune. Around the world this is the only effort being made on a large scale to make people civilized. But no politician wants people to be civilized. No country wants people to be civilized. They want a pretense, a hypocrisy, but not a deeper transformation.

We have to create that revolt around the world. It is not against anybody, it is against your false ideas, your false personality, your masks. You have to discover your original face, you have to discover your authenticity and you will create a small energy field. Whoever comes close to you will feel the flavor of civilization, of culture, of humanness. And if you go really deep into your being, you can radiate something which is the only argument and the only proof that the world is not dead, that it is alive, it is intelligent, it is divine.

All religions should disappear from the world. Religiousness alone is enough, and religiousness need not be organized. It is each individual's communion with the universe. There is no need for Christians or Hindus or Mohammedans. There is only need for religious people, seekers, lovers of meditation dropping all their masks, courageous enough to expose their original face to the world.

When the world has its original face, it will be a civilized world – not before that.

28

Meditation Is the Essential Awakening

Osho,

What is the transcendental?

The moment you start witnessing yourself, you will see three layers of existence within you. One is the outermost. Everybody can observe it: it is objective, it is material, it is your body. The second layer behind it is your mind, your thoughts, your dreams, your expectations. Only you can see them, nobody else can see them from outside. They are not objective. They are subjective, but they certainly are. They exist in their own way. You cannot deny their existence, certainly on a different wavelength – not as solid and physical as the body – but you can see them. They direct your life, they are your hopes, your projections, your expectations.

The first layer is called the objective and the second layer is called the subjective, but beyond both there is a witness which can watch both the body and the mind, the material and the nonmaterial. This witness, this consciousness, this awareness, is beyond both. It is neither material nor nonmaterial because it is beyond both. You cannot go beyond it. You cannot witness it. You have come to the very end of the rope, you have come to the very bottom of existence. This awareness is called the transcendental because it transcends the duality of body-mind. To be centered in it means you have come home. There is no way beyond it. Here the road ends.

Suddenly you find perfection in everything. Nothing is missing, nothing needs improvement, refinement; everything is as it should be, and this feeling, that everything is as it should be, brings tremendous gratitude. The perfection of existence fills you with the tremendous joy that you are a participant in a perfect existence, that you are an invited guest, that you are welcome here, that the whole existence needs you. If you were not here, it would miss you; some place would remain vacant. Nobody else can take your place. This gives you individuality and dignity and a great blissfulness. For the first time you are at ease with existence, with trees, with stars, with the ocean. The whole becomes your home. This is the transcendental.

It is called transcendental because it transcends all duality and brings you to a state of oneness. This is the ultimate outcome of a meditative consciousness.

Maharishi Mahesh Yogi calls his meditation Transcendental Meditation. That is an unnecessary repetition of words. *Meditation* is enough, or *transcendental* is enough; both mean the same. Meditation brings you to transcendence and every transcendence is nothing but the ultimate flowering of meditation. And what he calls Transcendental Meditation is neither transcendental nor meditation; it is just chanting a certain name. You can chant *your* name. It gives a certain relaxation.

The great English poet Tennyson, without being initiated by Maharishi Mahesh Yogi – there was no question of it because he existed a long time before Maharishi Mahesh Yogi was born – just found it by himself because he had to sleep in a room separate from his parents. They were rich people, they could provide each child with a separate room of his own. But he was so small and the nights were so dark. There was great fear – and particularly in England, which seems to be the most ghost- haunted country in the whole world.

It is strange, but nowhere in the world will you find so many ghost- haunted houses, so many people concerned about ghosts.

So naturally the little child, Tennyson, was very worried when it became dark and the lights were put out. Finding nothing else to hold on to, he discovered a trick. He would repeat his own name continuously: 'Tennyson, Tennyson, Tennyson, Tennyson,' just to avoid all kinds of ghosts who must have been around in the darkness, hiding in the nooks and corners of the room. He became so occupied with his own name that a certain curtain was created protecting him from all sides, so there was not even a small gap for any ghosts to enter.

He found – strangely, accidentally – what Maharishi Mahesh Yogi calls Transcendental Meditation. He became utterly silent, peaceful, and fell into deep relaxed sleep. And in the morning when he woke up, he would wake up with the same repetition – 'Tennyson, Tennyson' – that he had gone with into sleep.

This is something to be understood. Anything that you go to sleep with, the last thing that you remember before sleep falls over you, will be the first thing you remember when you wake up, even before opening your eyes. Psychologically of course you were not aware of it, but you repeated the same thing the whole night.

If Tennyson repeated his own name while he was falling asleep, slowly, slowly the sleep became deeper and the word *Tennyson* became farther and farther away like an echo, until finally he forgot all about Tennyson and fell into an unconscious state. But that word continued in the unconscious as an undercurrent. That's why in the morning, the first thing he remembered was his own name.

You can try it. Anything you fall asleep with will remain flowing within you and you will have to encounter it in the morning when you wake up. This means the whole night he was repeating consciously at first, then unconsciously, then again consciously, the same name. Naturally he could not dream. He could not think of anything else. His sleep became a very silent, deep, dreamless sleep – what Patanjali calls *sushupti*. Modern psychology is still not aware of it.

Patanjali, the man who first wrote the whole science of Yoga ... It happens very rarely that a single man creates a whole science. It is now five thousand years old, but in these five thousand years, nothing has been added to the science of Yoga. It remains exactly the same. And I don't think there is any possibility in the future either to make any improvement. A single genius completed the whole thing, not leaving anything out of it that could be added later on. Patanjali calls this state *sushupti*, dreamless sleep. It is a beautiful state, very healthy, very nourishing, very rejuvenating. But it is not meditation. It is just a kind of hypnotic sleep.

By repeating your own name continuously you create a certain kind of boredom. Obviously, if you repeat 'Tennyson, Tennyson,' how long can you remain interested? Soon you start feeling bored, and boredom is a very good state for bringing in sleep. Whenever you feel bored you start falling into sleep. The mind finds a way to get out of boredom by going to sleep. That's why in every church you will find almost everybody asleep, just having a good Sunday-morning sleep.

I have heard about a priest who was very famous and his congregation was very large. The reason for his congregation being so large was that there was no other preacher who was so boring. It was a strange reason. But he bored people to such an extent that even people who were suffering from insomnia fell asleep. The whole night, even with all their sleeping pills, they could not manage it, but the preacher was really a genius. His voice was so boring; what he was saying he had said so many times that people could hear it even in their sleep. He was also happy; with everybody asleep the whole church was silent.

He had only three sermons; there was no need to have more, three were enough. Nobody was awake so nobody knew which he was giving; nobody could repeat what they had heard. Everybody said that the man certainly cast a hypnotic spell.

Just one old man sitting in front of him, the richest man of the city, was a trouble. He snored. His snoring was not a trouble; the trouble was that because of his snoring, many people could not sleep. The preacher was very much disturbed that if it continued many people would stop coming. They came only to have a good morning sleep on Sunday. It was so rejuvenating, one hour's sleep, that it was enough to keep them relaxed, calm and quiet for the whole week. He had to find some way – and he found it.

The old man always used to come with one of his great-grand-children, just a small boy, but very alive. In fact, in the whole congregation only he was awake. The priest pulled the boy aside one day and said, 'Listen, I will give you a quarter of a dollar if you can keep your old man awake. Whenever you see he is snoring, just start nudging him. Wake him up. Don't let him sleep. And a quarter every week is certain.'

The boy said, 'Done.'

The next week the old man could not figure out what had happened to the boy. He always used to sit silently by his side. The moment he started snoring, the boy started waking him up.

Outside the church he asked, 'What is the matter with you? You did not let me sleep at all!'

He said, 'The priest is giving me a quarter to keep you awake.'

The old man said, 'Then you should have told me before. I will give you half a dollar to let me sleep!'

He said, 'Done.'

The next week the preacher watched. Again many times he gestured to the child, gave all indications, but the child simply sat there smiling, not even bothering about the priest.

The priest thought, 'What has happened? Has he forgotten completely?' When everybody was sleeping he even showed him a quarter. The child said no, just waved his hand. 'Strange...' After the meeting he got hold of the child and asked, 'What is the matter?'

He said, 'My old man is giving me half a dollar.'

The priest said, 'Half a dollar? I will give you one dollar, but don't let that old man sleep!'

He said, 'Done.'

But the priest thought, 'I cannot compete with that old man because he is very rich. I am a poor priest.' He said to the boy, 'Listen. I am a poor priest, I cannot give you more than that.'

He said, 'It all depends on the old man. If he says he is going to give me two dollars ... You are a man of understanding, business is business.'

And that's what happened. The old man said, 'Two dollars,' and the boy again stopped.

Finally the priest had to talk to the old man himself. 'Let us clarify the whole thing. I am not worried about your sleep. My problem is that because of your snoring many people cannot sleep and they are complaining. My congregation is the biggest in the city because they enjoy such a beautiful sleep. Anything boring is helpful.'

Now they have created many machines which simply create the noise of the ocean, the waves coming to the rocks, splashing, making their sound. You just have to plug into the mechanism and it gives you the continuous sound of the waves, and many people are helped by it. They fall asleep, it is so boring.

What Maharishi Mahesh Yogi is teaching people is a kind of dreamless sleep. It is not meditation. Meditation is awakening, not going to sleep. I have nothing against it, he just should not call it Transcendental Meditation. It is simply hypnotic sleep. He is using a wrong name and exploiting people because of the wrong name. People think it is meditation. This is sheer conmanship.

In the East, we have known for centuries that chanting is good for sleep, and sleep is good for health. So there is nothing wrong in it, just fifteen minutes or ten minutes in the morning and ten minutes in the evening. If you can do it, you will have better health, a better sense of well-being, so there is nothing wrong in it. But it is not meditation.

Meditation is just the opposite. It is awakening. It is becoming fully aware of your body, of your mind. And you have simply to be watchful. You don't have to repeat anything, because repetition means you have fallen into identifying with the thought process.

Chanting is also a thought process. Repeating a mantra or a name of God – Hindu, Mohammedan, Christian, it doesn't matter. You can simply count from one to a hundred and back again, from a hundred to ninety-nine, ninety-eight, ninety-seven, then go back. Go up, go down. Just climb the whole ladder up to a hundred and again come down. Four or five times you will be able to do it and then you will fall asleep. But the whole night you will have to do that, climbing up, coming down, climbing up, coming down. It may even be tiring, so that in the morning you may feel your back is hurting, something has gone wrong, you feel giddy. The first thing that you will find in the morning is that you are coming down or going up. The whole night it has continued. Don't choose such a thing.

It was perfectly good for Tennyson; he did it his whole life. In his autobiography he says: 'I don't know what the secret of it is. I simply stumbled on it out of fear. But I found it so peaceful, so relaxing, leading me into such deep sleep that I have used it my whole life. Whenever I have time, I repeat my own name, just sitting in the bus or in the railway train. There is nothing to do. I just close my eyes and go on repeating my name. And it is so peaceful and so silent.' But it is a silence which is of sleep, it is a peace which is of sleep.

You will not become aware at the very moment it is happening; you will become aware when you awake. You will see you have passed through a peaceful land. Only the remnants like a memory hang around you – some fragrance. But you have passed through the garden completely asleep. When you wake up, you find you must have passed through a garden because you can still smell the roses.

I entirely support what Maharishi Mahesh Yogi is doing. But I absolutely disagree with his using a name which simply exploits people who do not know what meditation is. He is giving something very cheap in the name of meditation. Meditation is always the essential awakening, witnessing, watchfulness, consciousness. It is never unconscious; it is never a deep sleep. It is a deep awakening. The moment you are alert, you can see the body, you can see your mind, and you can experience yourself. You cannot go beyond this *yourself*. You cannot go behind it or beyond it. It is your very being. You cannot jump out of it. It is not a dress that you can jump out of. It is you yourself. It is your very essence.

This essence is transcendental.

But all religions have created their own ideas about meditation. Except Gautam Buddha, no other religion has been able to find exactly the right meaning of meditation. Hence he remains a pillar of light to all those who are seeking, searching. All other religions have fallen into the trap of chanting, prayer, mantras, rituals. A single man in the whole of history stands alone like an Everest, denying everything except witnessing. That's what he means by *vipassana.*

It is the art of witnessing all your actions, physical or mental. As you watch them, they slow down. Your body becomes more at ease, tensionless; your mind becomes slowly, slowly thoughtless. And when the body is completely silent, and the mind is without any thought, your whole being is filled with a light that you have never known before. It is not the ordinary light that needs fuel. It is your very being radiating. From this moment onward, your journey will take a new turn. On each step, a new mystery will open its doors. You will be becoming more and more part of the miracles of existence.

Existence is a mystery. It is not something that you have to solve. It is not a problem, nor is it a puzzle; there is no solution to it. No philosophy can demystify it. You can experience it, you can enjoy it, you can dance it, you can live it, but you cannot know it.

The young mother is skeptically examining the new educational toy. 'Isn't it rather complicated for a young boy?' she asks the assistant.

'It is the very latest idea,' replies the girl. 'It is designed to adjust the child to living in today's world. Any way he tries to put it together is wrong.'

But this small anecdote is true about existence. Any way you want to explain it, your explanation is wrong. Those who know it do not try to explain it. They only describe its beauty, its truth, its glory, its blissfulness. They only give you some indications that may create a longing in you to find out what it is.

Once you enter it, you will forget all about finding out what it is. Enjoying it so much, who cares what it is? What are you going to do with your explanations? And anyway there is no explanation. The whole of existence is only an experience without any explanation. This is its transcendentalness. It transcends all understanding, all knowledge, all explanation, all philosophy. But you can experience it. You can become one with it. It is always ready to absorb you. Just as the ocean is ready to absorb any dewdrop.

Existence is always waiting and willing, welcoming. You just have to learn a little courage, just a little courage. One jump and you are gone forever into the mysterious. You yourself become a mystery. Every mystic is a mystery. He has become one with the ultimate mystery. Mysticism is not a religion because it has no theology, no philosophy, no doctrine, creed, cult. It explains nothing. It simply shows you the way to move into the unexplainable. It opens the door of the unknowable and pushes you in.

There is a beautiful story about the Great Wall of China. It must be a story because nobody has found the spot up to now. But it has been reported for almost three thousand years that there is a spot on the China Wall ... The wall is thousands of miles long and broad enough for a car to move along it. It is one of the miracles man has achieved. Millions of people died in making it. It took hundreds of years to build. They created almost a mountain against invaders.

It was reported again and again that there is a spot somewhere on the China Wall where, if you place a ladder and go up the wall ... Whoever has done that simply reaches the top of the wall, laughs loudly and jumps down the other side, where there is a deep ditch. The man is finished; you cannot even find pieces of him. But before jumping he laughs very loudly, perhaps the first belly laughter that he has ever laughed, with his whole body. It is the most mysterious point on the wall. Many have reported that they have seen people reaching the point where they laugh and jump. Nobody knows why they laugh.

Many people have tried, determined not to laugh whatever happens, and even if they laugh, not to jump. But whoever has gone to the point, even with absolute determination, suddenly forgets all determination, laughs loudly and jumps. Nobody has found any explanation yet of why it happens. And nobody comes back to tell you.

I don't think there is any such point on the China Wall, but perhaps it is a parable about mysticism. Something like that happens the moment you reach and the door opens. You have a good laugh and you jump.

But the mystery remains a mystery. And that is the beauty of the mystic: he does not try to demystify existence. He loves the mystery. The mystery has a certain romance about it, its unknowability is exciting. It is a great challenge, a great adventure for all those who have souls strong enough to go on such a pilgrimage.

Mysticism is transcendentalism.

Osho,
When the old road has come to its end and the new path is not seen yet...

When the past has no more meaning and the new dawn is still far away...

When everything looks old and futile and the new has not arisen yet...

When I know what I am not and I don't know who I am...

When there is no hope, not even for a new hope...

Osho, is this the dark night of the soul? Will I see the dawn?

Sarjano, it seems you have come to the point of the China Wall that we were looking for. Just have a good laugh and jump! The past is finished, there is no meaning in it. According to you, you have understood what is false, so there is no question of clinging to it; you don't have anything to lose. Why not have a good laugh and jump?

It never happens the way you are asking. You remain intellectual. You are saying the darkness has gone but the light has not come. Now what am I supposed to do? It can't happen in the very nature of things. The moment you understand the false as false, instantly you know what is real. These two things don't happen separately. There is not a gap of time, they happen together. Here you understand what is false, and immediately, instantly, you know what is real. How can you understand the false as false if you don't understand the real as real? Without the understanding of the real you cannot call anything false.

So your question may look very relevant – it is not. I will read it so you can see.

'When the old road has come to its end and the new path is not seen yet…' Then what are you seeing? That's just what I was saying, have a laugh and jump. The old road is finished and the new you cannot see. Certainly there must be a valley. Just say, 'Giddyap!' and take a jump! It does not need an answer, it needs a little courage. But I say to you, in the very nature of things it does not happen. 'When the old road ends…' That is where the new road begins. The end of the old is the beginning of the new. They are not two separate things; there is not a gap between the two.

If there had been a gap, then it would have been impossible to find the new, because you would need something to join the old to the new. What will you call it? Old or new? You will need something to make the join, a bridge, a road – what will you call it? If you call it old, then when you were saying the old is finished, it was not finished. If you call it new, you have already found it, you just move on. No, there is no gap ever. In existence there are not gaps; everything is continuous.

Do you know when your childhood ended and you became young? Can you remember the day, the date, the hour, the minute, the second? Everything is continuous. Do you know the day you will become old? Will you be able to mark it on the calendar? 'Today I am becoming old. Youth is finished. Now begins old age.' You never know. Things are continuous. Yes, one day you realize that you are now old, but it is not the moment when you become old. You don't become old in a single moment. It is a process. It goes very slowly, without making any noise.

You see that '...the old road has come to its end and the new path is not seen yet...' but I cannot concede that. If the old is seen as ending, that is the beginning of the new. Move on it. 'When the past has no more meaning and the new dawn is still far away...' It does not happen. You are asking a very intellectual question, but existence has no obligation to fit with your intellectual categories. Existence goes on its own way. You have to fit with it. If the past has no more meaning, you have become new. The dawn has come. The birds must have started singing, the flowers must be opening, the sun is rising.

Have you ever seen a gap between the night and the day? When the night ends, the day begins; when the day ends, the night begins – immediately. There is no gap at all. If there had been a gap, there would have been immense difficulty how to jump it. The day has ended, you are standing there and the night has not begun. Now how to jump? Where to go? Nature does not leave anything incomplete.

You say, 'When everything looks old and futile and the new has not arisen yet...' How then can it look old and futile? With what are you going to compare it? When you say everything looks meaningless, it implies that you have a certain understanding of meaning. You know what meaningfulness is. Only in comparison to meaning can you say that something looks meaningless. Only in comparison to life can something look like death. If you don't know anything about life, you cannot describe somebody as dead. These categories are combined. They are two sides of the same coin.

But you go on and on – 'When I know that I am not and I don't know who I am ... When there is no hope, not even for a new hope ... Is this the dark night of the soul? Will I see the dawn?' It is nothing so great as you are making it. The dark night of the soul is experienced only by very great mystics, Sarjano; it is not spaghetti! The dark night of the soul means you have come close to the dawn. The darker becomes the night, the closer is the dawn. The dark night of the soul is a moment of celebration because the dawn is not far away. If the dark night has come, then the dawn is implied in it. It is *bound* to come, in fact it *has* come. It is not separable from the dark night.

But you have a habit of complaining. This whole question is nothing but grumbling, complaining, that you have done everything that was needed. The old is finished, the false is dropped, the dark night of the soul has come, and nothing is happening. You remind me of Moses.

Moses is standing facing the Red Sea. Behind him, in the distance, clouds of dust from Pharaoh's army, hot in pursuit, arise. Suddenly with a mighty roar, the waters part, opening an escape route.

Moses looks ahead at the wet roadway and the cliffs of water on either side. He lifts his face to the sky and murmurs, 'Tell me something, God, how come I always have to go first?'

Such a great miracle is happening and he is not going to thank God. He complains about why it always happens that he has to go first.

If all that you are saying is really happening, be thankful. If the old has ended, you will see the new. If everything has become meaningless, you will find authentic meaning. If the dark night of the soul has arrived, dance, rejoice, the dawn is not very far away.

But always be grateful.

Prince Edward, the Queen of England's youngest son, meets one of Gaddafi's daughters at a party and they fall in love. Edward tells his mother that they want to be married, which puts the Queen into a dilemma. On one hand she is pleased because it will dispel all the rumors about Prince Edward's homosexuality, but on the other hand, to have any allegiance with Libya will annoy Ronald Reagan considerably. Her motherly instincts get the better of her and she consents to the marriage.

Still not trusting the girl's motives, the Queen instructs James Bond to spy on the young couple. The next morning Bond reports back to the Queen.

'What happened, Double-O-Seven?' she asks.

'Well,' says Bond, 'first she said to him "I offer you my honor," then he said to her "I honor your offer."'

'So what happened next?' asks the Queen excitedly.

'Well,' says Bond, 'after that it was *on* her, *off* her, *off* her, *on* her, all night long!'

What you need, Sarjano, is a good laugh and then just jump. If the old road has ended, jump. You will be on the new road. Certainly you cannot be on the old road. If everything has become meaningless that is a great freedom. It means the very effort of trying to find meaning in things is an exercise in utter futility. Life has significance but no meaning. Meaning is a mind trip. Significance is a great love affair of the heart.

You are not potentially a man of the head. You are potentially a man of the heart. But everything is topsy-turvy in you, upside down. You have not realized a simple fact about yourself: you are a man, not of logic, but of love. Drop all intellectual bullshit. Get deeper into your heart and you will be able to see the new light, the new path, the new dawn.

They are here, but your eyes are closed. The head is blind. Only the heart has eyes. It is strange that almost every culture of the world, every society, and every civilization that has up to now pretended to exist, they all say love is blind – without exception. But I want you to be absolutely clear about it: only love has eyes. Logic is blind.

But all these societies wanted you to be fixed in the head and forget all about the heart, because the heart is not much use in the marketplace. What is needed there is the head, what is needed there is cunningness, cleverness; what is needed there is reason. Love is not needed at all in the world that we have created. That's why it is ugly and miserable. Without love, man cannot get rid of misery, despair, anguish. He is bound to suffer. Only love is the savior, the redeemer.

Just get down from your ladder a little toward the heart. The heart is exactly in the middle between your head and your being. Once you are down in the heart, you will have a totally different vision of things. Then I can tell you: one step more, from the heart to the being, is a very relaxed, silent, peaceful journey with no hindrances. But from the head there is no direct way to the being.

Society has played a tremendously criminal trick on every human being. They have completely taken the heart away from you. This is the strategy so that you cannot reach your being. You can reach the being only via the heart. And the heart has been ignored by your education, by your religion, by everybody. It has been forced into darkness. So you are hung up in the head and you cannot go anywhere. You can only go on making questions, intellectual gymnastics, but it is all meaningless, futile.

Rather than questioning, you should start moving toward the heart. That is the true rebelliousness, love revolting against logic. And then from love to being is a very simple, very joyful way. It is a garden path full of roses.

Looking at your question, all that I can feel, Sarjano, is that you are not supposed to be an intellectual, a heady person. You are not. I have seen your tears and I have seen your laughter and I know that you are misplaced. It is within your hands to revive your heart, which has been repressed, and drop your head, which is not your destiny. It is nobody's destiny. The destiny is to realize the being and the being can be realized only via the heart.

Unless you know and learn the art of love, unless you are sensitive and creative, unless you forget all Aristotelian logic, you will never reach your being. And your being is the place where *sat-chit-anand* – truth, consciousness, bliss – are waiting for you. Just a small effort from the head to the heart, then there is no effort needed at all. Effortlessly you will slowly sink from your heart into your being.

This reminds me that all the Eastern mystics have been saying that no effort is needed to find yourself. From the very beginning they were all trained to be in the heart. The modern mind, particularly the Western mind, finds it difficult to understand that you can achieve something without effort. Some effort has to be made. The reason for this problem is that the modern man is head-oriented and the people who were talking about effortless let-go were heart-oriented. The situation has changed. That's why the modern man finds it difficult to understand the mystics of the East. There is a certain gap that has arisen. They were talking in the language of the heart, you are listening in the language of the head – and there is no communication between head and heart.

Moving from the head to the heart is the first step of any authentic meditation. But you don't have to take the second step; it happens on its own accord. There are only two steps. One you have to make – from the head to the heart – the other happens spontaneously, on its own accord. You simply relax and you will find yourself slipping deeper and deeper. One day, suddenly all is achieved. All that was missing has become available. The whole is yours. The whole mystery is yours.

> Osho,
> Being near you, I feel utterly at home, as if in the right soil. In the West, I worried: 'How to be near Osho sooner?' and often found it impossible to be meditative. Is it really possible to grow and flower in the harsh environment of the West?

It is certainly difficult to grow into meditation in the harsh environment of the West, but it is not impossible. It is certainly arduous because the whole surrounding is against meditation. Everything is mind-oriented and meditation is a state of no-mind. The whole of education, the culture, the society, the people, are all believers that there is nothing beyond the mind. The mind is their whole world. Meditation simply denies the mind and wants to go beyond it.

So I can understand, it is difficult. But even in the West you can find silent moments when society cannot interfere. In your own room, in the middle of the night, when everybody has fallen asleep, when the noises of city life have disappeared, you can find the East in your bedroom. When you have some time, weekends, holidays, you can move to some solitary place, you can go to a forest. Don't go where everybody else is going, just avoid those places. And you can always find ... The West is not as populated as the East. Here it is very difficult to find a place where people are not.

I have heard a story about the first astronaut.

When he landed on the moon, he found a few Indians sitting in a corner, smoking *beedies*. He asked, 'My God, how did you manage it? You don't have enough technology, particularly space technology, you don't have anything at all, how did you manage to reach, and not only one person, but a whole group?'

They said, 'It is very simple, there is no need of any technology. We just stood on each other's shoulders and went on standing. Finally we reached the moon.'

It is so crowded in the East, it is very difficult to find ... But the West is not so crowded, you can still find very silent, very peaceful places which have not been spoiled by the mind-oriented society. Trees don't get educated in your universities, nor have the mountains heard anything about the Vatican. Just take a small boat onto the ocean, and you are out of the West. You don't have to go far away, just on a river or the ocean. Just stop your boat there and the sunrise will be as fresh as it has ever been. West or East does not matter; the starry night above will be as young and as beautiful and as unpolluted as it has always been from eternity.

So you just have to be a little alert to find moments, spaces where you can relax, where you can meditate. I'm not telling you to meditate sitting in a London street. That is possible when you have known meditation and you have passed on that path many times, then it doesn't matter whether it is London or New York. Anywhere you can slip inside yourself. And your inner being does not belong to the East or to the West. It transcends all dualities.

But the problem is certainly there and the only way to solve it is – when you can manage it – come here, be here. Then forget the West completely and don't waste your time on anything else. Put your whole energy into meditation. Once you are centered in your being, once you know the inner path, then wherever you are, you can manage to go to the center without any difficulty. Even when you are dying, it will not make any difference. You may be sick, it will not make any difference.

A strange thing happened with one great English philosopher, C. E. M. Joad. He was always against George Gurdjieff. In modern times, Gurdjieff was the only man – very authentic – to take the message of inner crystallization from the East to the West. Many others have gone to the West. Most of them are hocus-pocus; they have gone to the West just to earn money. Now all over the West there are Indian monks, Japanese monks, Tibetan monks, but these are not authentic people. Their only desire is to exploit the gullibility of Western humanity.

Because the West has developed its mind to such an extent, you cannot defeat it intellectually. You cannot defeat it in wars. But it has forgotten its inner world completely, so completely that any idiot can exploit it, saying they will show the way. The West has become lopsided. The intellect has gone very far and the heart has remained very small, untrained, uneducated. So when somebody comes and brings a message about the heart, the West has no way to understand whether the man is phony or authentic.

As far as I know, nobody has made such a tremendous effort as George Gurdjieff to bring the Eastern methods of self-realization to the West. But even a man like C. E. M. Joad, a great philosopher, who has written many beautiful books on philosophy, laughed whenever George Gurdjieff's name was mentioned. 'That man is just a cheat, a fraud. There is nothing inside, no center. What crystallization? He is just using these words and cheating people.'

But C. E. M. Joad fell sick and death was coming close, and the doctor said, 'You are not going to live more than six weeks. So whatever you want to do, do!'

At that moment he realized, 'Perhaps there may be something inside. I have been denying it only intellectually, I don't really know. And I have been laughing at that man Gurdjieff, but my laughter was insensitive. I have not understood him at all, I have never gone to meet him while he was teaching in London.'

Finally he asked a friend, 'Can you bring George Gurdjieff to my place? At least I can ask his forgiveness for making a fool of him without understanding him or his message. I have been criticizing him without understanding him.'

Some friend brought Gurdjieff. Gurdjieff sat by the side of C. E. M. Joad's bed. Joad said, 'Please forgive me. I may not have another chance to see you again because my death is coming closer.'

Gurdjieff said, 'Forget about all that. It is death that has inspired you to call me. It is death that has made you waver about your whole lifelong stand that the mind is everything. But it is good! There is enough time. Six weeks will do. Even six minutes are enough. And a man of your caliber can even manage in six seconds. Just close your eyes – I am sitting here by your side – and watch your mind. Don't do anything else, simply watch.' When death is so close, one is ready to do anything. If death had not been so close, Joad would have argued that except the mind there is nobody who is going to watch, but there was no time to argue. It was better to experiment with what this man is saying – there can be no harm. He was amazed when he started watching the mind. He forgot about Gurdjieff, he forgot about his death, he forgot by and by all the thoughts, and there was an immense silence in the room surrounding him. It took almost three hours.

When Gurdjieff woke him up, he told him, 'I am immensely happy, watching your face changing deeper into silence, watching your eyes, that they have become unmoving.'

You can even see from the outside, from the eyelids, whether eyes are moving or not. If there are thoughts inside or dreams or anything, your eyes will be moving. If thoughts stop, dreams stop; if there is nothing on the screen of the mind, the eyes stop. So Gurdjieff was sitting there, watching, when Joad's eyes stopped moving and his body was almost relaxed – as if there was no fear of death – and his face started changing with his inner experience. As the witnessing grows, the face starts having a certain grace, a certain beauty.

Gurdjieff said, 'You have done it. Now these six weeks are enough. Continue. And you have twenty-four hours every day. While you are awake, lying down – you have been told to rest which is good – use this opportunity that has been provided by death and you will die a very crystallized being. You are intelligent enough to understand the situation: before death comes, you have to know something in you which is deathless.'

There were tears of gratitude in Joad's eyes. He didn't say a single word, but those tears said everything, his gratitude, his apology. Those six weeks were the most important in his life. His last statement to his friends was: 'I had never thought that it would finally be Gurdjieff who would help me on my new journey, who would help me to know something that is immortal and eternal.'

So wherever you are, just go on meditating. And it is just a question of a little intelligence to find a silent corner, a silent space. Once in a while move to the forest, to the ocean, to the mountains, and just meditate. The West cannot prevent you. If you cannot come here, then you have to find something there. But whenever you are here, devote your total time to meditation. All I would like you to do is to become so centered that you know the path very well. Become so acquainted with it that even in the crowd of any Western city you can manage to go inward. Nobody can prevent you.

One day, while decorating the bathroom, Hymie Goldberg repaints the toilet seat, but forgets to tell Becky about it. So when she uses the toilet, she gets stuck to it. She sits there screaming and crying until Hymie comes and unscrews the seat. He helps Becky to the bed and lies her face down.

Calling the family physician, Hymie does not tell him what has happened, but explains that there is no way that Becky can come to his office.

Reluctantly the doctor agrees to call by on his way home. When he arrives, Hymie shows him into the bedroom, where Becky gets up on her hands and knees to display her problem.

'Well, Doctor,' says Hymie, 'what do you think?'

Stroking his chin, the doctor replies, 'I think it is lovely, but why such a cheap frame?'

So whenever in the West, enjoy all kinds of stupidities that are going around. There are so many idiots in the West. Forty-three percent of people in America believe in flying saucers. Never before has there been such a great crowd of idiots in the world. Millions of people believe in crystals. It seems humanity is on the verge of absolute insanity. So enjoy. When you are in the West, enjoy all kinds of foolishnesses that are going around in the name of New Age.

While you are here, meditate, so that you can get in contact with yourself. That is the only religion there is. All else is simply exploitation of people who have lost grip of themselves, of life, who have forgotten how to approach their own being. And they have become vulnerable to exploitation by any kind of conmanship.

There are so many people doing all kinds of things that it seems soon there will be no possibility for any authentic religious movement. All these fake and fraudulent people are destroying the possibilities for any authentic movement. So while you are there, enjoy all the games that are being played in the name of spirituality. Here things are absolutely simple.

Except witnessing, I don't teach anything else. So just witness your mind and the meditation will be happening. And once you have got in tune with your being, you know the way, you know the how. Then it does not matter where you are. Alone or in the crowd, in the silences of the forest or in the noises of a marketplace, it is all the same. You can simply close your eyes and disappear inward.

29

Stillness, Calmness, and Serenity

Osho,
If, in a still and calm and silent moment, I whisper, 'Kill me now,' will you do it?

Anand Rakesh, I have every intention of killing you because without killing you, you can't have a new life. You will go on living the old, rotten personality which keeps you company and gives you a certain consolation. But the company is of misery and the consolation is only a hope; it never materializes. Just because it is old, you feel at ease with it. However dark and however painful, man has the greatest adaptability.

If he becomes accustomed to it, he can adjust in any situation; it only needs time.

You can see it happening in poor countries like India. About five hundred million people are starving, but they won't revolt, they won't start a revolution. They will starve and die, hoping for some god's messenger – avatar – some savior to save them. It is strange how blind man can be. So many saviors have come to the earth, so many messengers have come, but not a single one has been able to effect any change in human life. On the contrary, they have made it more miserable because they imposed unnatural systems of thought which go against your very potentiality. But the hope continues. It is the hope that keeps the starving person from revolting.

Secondly, this poverty, this hunger, have become so much part of his life, almost his lifestyle, that he does not conceive of any possibility of another kind of life. He will go on living as he has been living for centuries: in starvation, undernourishment, in slavery. It is simply unbelievable how man adapts to the old, to the acquainted, to the known and is afraid of the unknown. He may have nothing to lose, but still the fear of the unknown is very deep-rooted in man.

Perhaps it is from your very birth that the fear of the unknown settles in. And that is the bottom of your unconsciousness. Every child is born into an unknown world. He has to leave the known world of the mother's womb; reluctantly he leaves it. He makes as much effort to cling to it as possible. It is just by nature that he has to come out – it is impossible for him to remain there any longer. But he comes trembling, not knowing where he is going, what kind of existence, what kind of life. He is accustomed to the life of the womb. Hence the first thing that he experiences is the fear of the unknown. And that fear haunts him all his life.

You are asking me, Rakesh – but you may not have looked deeply into your question – 'If...' Remember, I don't like ifs and buts, so this is not a true thing that you are asking. You are simply supposing; it is hypothetical. *If* means the beginning of a hypothesis.

'If, in a still and calm and silent moment...' Do you know any still, calm, and silent moment? Is it your existential experience? If it were so, you would not start the question with if. But as far as I am concerned, if you are in a silent, calm and still moment, I will not wait for you to whisper, 'Kill me now'; I will kill you before that. I don't postpone anything and I don't wait for anything because the next moment is so uncertain.

And when you are calm and still and silent, from where will the question come? From a silent space when you are enjoying life in its real essence, when it is the most juicy experience, from where will the whisper 'Kill me now' come? In fact your stillness, your calmness and your silence have already killed you. And it is pointless to kill a man who is already killed. I am a lazy man, I don't make unnecessary efforts. Once killed, killed for ever.

But this very experience of death in silence is the beginning of a new life – very fresh, very young, just a green sprout, just the early morning cool breeze. It does not have the old connotations about death that your mind may be filled with: darkness, danger, angels of death surrounding you, pulling your soul out from your body while you cling to it. Death is a tremendously beautiful experience, perhaps the most significant moment in your whole life. It is the very climax, the crescendo, as if your whole life has become concentrated in a single moment. It is a known fact all over the world that sometimes when people are drowning, but don't die; they are saved. All these people have a strange experience, all over the world this similar experience. When a person is drowning, he knows he is dying. He has no idea that he will be saved. He comes up from the water one or two or three times at the most, just for a few seconds. But in those few seconds a strange thing happens: he starts seeing his whole life as a film, passing fast before him from the first day he can remember, up to the moment when he is drowning, as if the whole mind is exposing itself, all its memories.

It has been a great question mark for the scientists. How is it possible within two or three seconds to see your whole life which has taken you seventy years to live? But it happens. The film goes quickly. You see your whole life. If the man is saved, he will tell people that he saw his whole life.

This is about the ordinary man with a very small consciousness. When an enlightened man is dying he not only sees his whole life, he also sees death as the highest peak he has ever experienced. It is not an enemy, but a great friend, because it is not the end but the beginning of a greater life, of an eternal life.

So you need not even whisper; I don't literally have to kill you. Your silence, your calm, your stillness will do my work. I have to kill indirectly, otherwise it will be illegal and criminal. I don't touch you, I simply teach you something which is going to kill you. No court, no law can say that I kill you, can say anything against me. I was teaching you silence, meditation, I was teaching you to be joyous, I was teaching you stillness. No court, no law, no lawmakers have any idea that this is the situation in which one finally dies, as far as the old is concerned, and is reborn into a totally new vision with fresh eyes.

The whole world changes for you. It is no longer separate. It is not something you have to conquer, to fight, to prove your manliness. No! It is something so tremendously close to your heart; it surrounds you with such warmth and love that you simply allow a let-go. In that let-go is the crucifixion of the old and the resurrection of the new.

Ancient scriptures say 'The master is death.' They are right, but only half right. The master is also the resurrection. But as far as the disciple is concerned he has no idea about resurrection, he only sees death. And there is a very subtle psychology behind it, Rakesh.

You have not lived peacefully, you have not lived in stillness, you have not lived in silence; your life has been just vegetation. Naturally when you find stillness, calmness, and serenity, a desire deep within you arises that this is the right moment to disappear. You have never seen such a beautiful space. This is the space, not to pull back from, but to go deeper into – and disappear.

It all comes automatically. If you meditate to the very end, death will happen to you. It will happen at the very center of your being, and from there, just as a seed dies in the soil and a sprout arises out of the death of the seed, you will die. But something fresh, young, eternally fresh, green, will arise out of your death. On your death, roses of your enlightenment will blossom. The new life will be the life of light, the life of blessings, the life of love.

It has nothing to do with your old idea of death. You have to learn a new alphabet, a new language with new connotations. When you become a meditator, you cannot go on carrying the old associations with words that have been given to you by society, which is absolutely unconscious.

You don't need me to kill you. Although I am making every effort to kill you, I cannot kill you directly. And killing you directly is not going to help. It will be simply murder – of a vegetable! It is not a crime, in fact, because a vegetable-cutting knife would be enough. You are not yet ready to be killed. You are so fast asleep, so dormant, that it can be said you are absent.

First be present in this silence, which is still an *if* for you. Make it a reality. In this silence will arise your presence, and with that presence you will feel death as a welcome guest. It takes you out of the grip of the old and helps you to move into the cosmic existence. It is a blessing, but only for those who are conscious. For those who are unconscious it is a curse.

In the Upanishads there is a very beautiful story...

An old man, a very rich man, a super-high-caste brahmin, very learned in the scriptures, was distributing gifts to other, poorer, brahmins because he knew he was going to die soon. His small son, whose name is Nachiketa, looked at the things that he was distributing. They were all rotten junk.

People give these things as gifts. I have been watching gifts. They go on moving from one hand to another hand. Nobody uses them; they are so useless that the moment you get them you start looking for somebody to give them to.

He had thousands of cows – in those days in India cows were the symbol of richness. How many cows you had was your bank balance. But he had chosen the oldest cows which no longer gave milk.

In India an old cow is a burden. You cannot kill it because it is your mother. It does not give you milk, but you cannot let your mother starve. That is irreligious. You will not believe what Manu says in his scripture, which dominates Hindu society even today after five thousand years. It says: 'To kill a cow is almost equal to killing one hundred untouchables, the sudras.' The cow is so valuable that if you can kill one hundred sudras – the untouchables, the poor, the poorest of the earth – the crime will be the same. And you can be forgiven by God if you kill one hundred sudras, but you cannot be forgiven if you kill a single cow.

So he was giving old cows to other brahmins. As that boy was innocent he could not see the point. He asked his father, 'What are you doing? These people are already poor and starving and you are giving them old cows, which I know perfectly well don't give any milk. These poor brahmins cannot manage to find themselves two meals a day. How are they going to feed these cows?'

He was so persistent that the father became angry. He said, 'Be careful, I will give *you* away too!'

He said, 'To whom will you give me?'

In anger the father said, 'I will give you to death.'

So he waited while all the brahmins passed by. The ceremony of giving things was over and he asked his father, 'But death has not come and you were going to give me to death. I will have to go in search of death. In your anger, in a way you have already given me to death.'

The father knew... 'Where can he search for death?' He said, 'Okay, go and search. If you can find him I will give you...'

The story is very beautiful, although from this point on it becomes allegorical.

The little Nachiketa – one of the most beautiful names as far as seekers are concerned – goes on and on asking everybody where he can find Death. And finally he ends up at the house of Death.

But Death has gone to take a few people whose time has come. So he meets the wife. The wife, seeing a high-caste brahmin – and such an innocent child – asks him to come in.

He said, 'No, unless Death invites me, I will not come in. I will sit outside.' The wife brings food for him, something to drink.

He refuses. He says, 'I will fast until Death comes.' Three days pass and the wife is very concerned: the little boy has not eaten anything, has not drunk anything.

Finally Death comes and Nachiketa says, 'My father has given me to you.'

Death says, 'But you are too young. Your time has not come and your father has no right to give you. When your time comes I will come myself. You took such a long journey unnecessarily and then you have been fasting. Even I feel sad for you. What can I do for you? Just tell me – I will allow you three wishes. You can have all the money that you want, you can have a great kingdom if you want, if you have any desire for a beautiful woman, you can have her. Whatever you want, just tell me and I will do it.'

Nachiketa says, 'If I am a king, will you come or not?'

And Death says, 'You are asking strange questions. I will have to come one day finally, whatever you are, whether a king or a beggar.'

He says, 'Then there is no point in asking for a kingdom. And certainly death will be the same for the richest man. So there is no point in asking for money. Since you *are* going to come, I don't see any point in asking anything of the world. I will ask you only one question: When you come, am I going to die *really* or is it just a facade? Am I just going to change bodies like houses? You have to tell me the truth.'

Death is at a loss, because this is *his* secret. But the promise has been given, so Death says, 'It is very difficult for me to answer you, but I have to be truthful to such an innocent inquiry. I have never killed anyone. I have simply changed their old, rotten bodies, their old, rotten minds and given them new bodies. And there are a few who have lived so totally and so consciously that they don't need to come back into the world as a separate entity. They don't get another body again. To them I give the whole of existence to disappear into. They will be in this cosmos not as separate units, but as one with the whole.'

This is one of the most beautiful stories – very significant. The proverb I told you which says 'The master is death,' here shows the reverse: 'Death becomes the master.'

And Nachiketa says, 'Then there is no problem. I don't have to be afraid of you. You are just a fiction and nothing else. Those who are unconscious believe you are a reality; those who are conscious know that you are a fiction, just an appearance.'

> Osho,
> For over thirteen years now, you have been ignoring me. What I could never fully grasp is that what you ignored was my neediness, greed, and all kinds of garbage. For my part, though I have been physically close to you, I have managed in my ignorance and fear to keep a certain distance. Really I have been ignoring you.
>
> Osho, from the first day I knew I was yours. But I was, and still am, a coward and an idiot.

It is again Anand Rakesh. In the first question he was ready to die. But it was an 'if' question. Now he is far more real. Now he is exposing his thirteen-year-long, strange, insane behavior.

I don't ignore anybody, but this is part of the human mind's work: it projects everything onto somebody else. It ignores, but it projects on somebody else that it is *being* ignored. In fact somebody else becomes a mirror. You see your own face, but you think there is somebody in the mirror – small children do it. And everybody is a small child as far as spirituality is concerned.

It is worth watching: when small children start moving a little, just put a big mirror in front of them and they will be stunned. Seeing the other child, there will be a few moments of utter silence – mixed with fear – but then curiosity takes over. They try to touch the other child, and the other child also is touching them. They become clear that there is no danger, but where is the other child hiding? Behind the mirror? I have seen with my own eyes the child go behind the mirror to find where the other child is. He cannot conceive that it is just a reflection.

The master is a mirror: he only reflects you. But you go on projecting all kinds of things onto him. When you are in a good mood, he is a great master; when you are in a bad mood, he is just a fraud. Your conception about the master goes on changing every day. Sometimes he is so beautiful and sometimes he is just the incarnation of the Devil. Sometimes he is the Christ and sometimes the same person becomes the anti-Christ. But you never see the point: all these concepts and projections are yours. The master is only a mirror, a very clean mirror; it shows your reflections.

At least you have come to a situation where you can realize it; thirteen years have not been wasted. You say, 'Really I have been ignoring you.' Experiencing this, your life will take a new turn. Thirteen years you have been wandering zigzag, wanting my attention, but still keeping a distance. People go on doing that because they all have a split mind.

Physiologists have just discovered what the meditators have known for centuries: you don't have one mind, you have two minds. In your skull your mind is divided into two hemispheres, the right and the left – and they don't have any connection with each other. They are not on speaking terms with each other. They don't in fact know the other.

Strangely enough, there are a few things which only the left-side mind is capable of doing and there are other things which only the right-side mind is capable of doing. They need a great harmony so that they don't destroy each other's efforts. That's what goes on happening. What the right mind creates, the left mind destroys. They don't know each other. They don't have any idea that there is anybody else. One mind decides one thing, the other mind cancels it.

But in meditation a bridge happens. Other than by a meditative mind it has not been possible to create this bridge. The bridge happens on its own accord. As you become silent, calm and quiet, both minds start functioning together in harmony. Your life becomes integrated, you are out of the schizophrenic world.

This realization that you have been ignoring me is of great importance, Rakesh. From now on, you can start moving in the right direction. You say, 'From the first day I knew I was yours. But I was and still am a coward and an idiot.' These are great realizations.

Almost everyone is a coward, but hiding the fact so deeply that even *he* becomes unaware of it. Everybody thinks that he is a very brave man, but in fact to think of yourself as brave is nothing but a repressive technique of your cowardliness. This is a pose that you are putting on to cover your cowardliness. You can only become really brave when you know that death is a fiction. Before death becomes a fiction, it is absolutely natural that you will feel a certain cowardliness within you.

It is better not to cover it up. It is better to understand it because that is the way to get rid of it, to find ways that can make you aware that death is a fiction. Then you are no longer a coward. And the same is true about your being an idiot. The world is full of idiots. It is very difficult to find someone who is not, but everybody believes he is an intellectual giant. He may not say that to others, it wouldn't look right. He leaves it to others to understand; he knows himself that he is an intellectual giant, but because nobody recognizes his great intellect, he feels very offended.

I have come across many intellectuals who are feeling very offended that they don't have any recognition. I said, 'If you are certain of your intelligence, you don't need anybody's recognition. Do you need anybody's recognition that you have eyes? You've never thought about it. Only a blind man will think about it, "If somebody could recognize that I am not blind, it would be a great joy."'

Realizing that one is an idiot is simply realizing that one is unconscious. The word *idiot* is a little strong, just pure whiskey without water. You have to realize that your actual nature is simply unconscious. And out of your unconsciousness you go on doing things which prove to be idiotic.

The psychiatrist marries a very ugly woman. When asked by a friend about his reasons the shrink replies, 'I know that her face looks like the back end of a bus, that she has a terrible figure, that she is cross-eyed and stupid, but wow, what dreams she has!'

He has married her for her great dreams. The psychoanalysts are interested in dreams and nothing else. Even the people who are concerned with your psychological sanity are themselves sitting in the same boat you are in. There is not much difference.

Young Ruthie, the daughter of Hymie Goldberg, is watching her mother Becky as she tries on her new fur coat.

'Mum,' she says in disgust, 'do you realize how much a poor, dumb animal had to suffer, so you could have that coat?'

'Ruthie,' snaps Becky angrily, 'how dare you talk about your father like that.'

Out of our unconsciousness we are looking at things, seeing things, which are not there, hearing things which have not been said. Our whole life is a mess because we are not alert.

Becky Goldberg is watching the local news on the TV while Hymie is involved with a crossword puzzle.

'Darling,' she says, 'did you hear that? A man in New York has swapped his wife for a season ticket to the New York Yankees. Would you do a thing like that?'

'Hell, no,' replies Hymie, 'the season is half over.'

'Gentlemen,' announces the drunk at the registry office, 'I want to register this birth of twins.'

'Why do you say "gentlemen"?' inquires the official. 'Can't you see I am here all alone?'

'You are?' gasps the new father staggering back. 'Maybe I had better go back to the hospital and have another look.'

Perhaps he has seen twins where there was only one. He is seeing many gentlemen when there is only one.

If you can understand that you are unconscious, it is the beginning of becoming more conscious. Nobody can remain unconscious if he realizes it, because then he knows that all his life's misery and suffering is born out of this unconsciousness – there is no point in changing symptoms. Up to now you have been fighting with symptoms: how not to be miserable, how not to suffer, how not to be angry, how not to be jealous – these are all symptoms. You cannot fight with symptoms, you have to go to the roots.

The root is simply your unconsciousness, out of which all these poisonous things go on growing. Once you reach the root, then the only way is not to bother about anger or suffering or misery, but to put your whole attention and energy into making the unconscious conscious. In other words, what I call meditation is just an effort of transformation from unconsciousness to consciousness, from darkness to light.

A few years ago, when Ronald Reagan was still a third-rate movie actor, his little daughter was watching him in the shower. She pointed to his testicles and asked what they are.

'Those are my apples, dear,' replied Reagan. Quickly the child ran to her mother and told her what Reagan had said.

Nancy replied, 'That's nice, dear, but did he tell you about the dead branch they are hanging on?'

30

Love Needs No Responsibility

Osho,

What is the responsibility of love?

The mind creates questions. They may look very relevant and rational, but they are against experience, against existence. And because the whole world is communicating with each other only through the mind, nobody raises his voice against such basically wrong questions. For example, this question is fundamentally wrong. It is out of total misunderstanding.

Love knows no responsibility because love itself is responsibility. To separate love and responsibility is simply stupid. But all moral systems of the world separate them. Their idea of responsibility does not correspond with existence, only with their logic. And it has to be understood that logic is man-manufactured. It does not grow in the fields. It is not like the mountains and the stars and babies. It is simply a mind projection.

It has dominated humanity for centuries. It has destroyed many valuable possibilities, potentialities. It has closed many doors to the mysteries of life. It has made man almost blind to light, to consciousness, to bliss, to truth. But it has been such a long domination that it isn't easily apparent that it goes on committing mistakes against existence. I would like to dissect this question as minutely as possible. Only dissection of the question will make you aware that it does not need an answer.

Responsibility according to all moral codes is a kind of duty – and a duty is a burden. You have to do it in spite of yourself because you have been told to do it; it is a should. You feel guilty if you don't do it. You feel you are escaping from your responsibility. But if you do it, you feel enslaved, destroyed as an individual, your freedom destroyed. So on both counts, you are in trouble. Morality makes man psychologically sick. It gives you ideas which are going to make you uneasy whatever you do. Whether you follow them or not makes no difference.

You are told, 'This is your responsibility toward the nation.' Now, the nation is a fiction. There are no nations in the world as far as nature is concerned, existence is concerned. All your maps are just meaningless and a better humanity is going to burn all of them, because all the boundaries that discriminate against any part of humanity are ugly, insane.

I have told you a story...

When India was divided into two nations, India and Pakistan, a rumor was heard that there was a madhouse just on the boundary. Neither India nor Pakistan was interested in taking the madhouse. But something had to be done. It had to go somewhere. Finally, the chief superintendent of the madhouse called all the mad people and asked them, 'Do you want to go to India?'

They said, 'No, we are perfectly happy here.'

The superintendent said, 'You will be here. Don't be worried about that. Just tell me – do you want to go to India?'

They all looked at each other and they said, 'People think *we* are mad! Something has gone wrong with our superintendent. If we are going to be here then the question does not arise of going to India. Why should we go to India?'

The superintendent was in a difficulty how to explain to these insane people. He said, 'Then would you like to go to Pakistan?'

They said, 'No, not at all. We are perfectly happy here. Why should we go anywhere?'

He again tried to explain to them, saying, 'You will be here, whether you choose India or Pakistan. You are not going anywhere.'

Then they said, 'It seems to be very strange. If we are not going anywhere, then why should we even be asked about it? We are here.'

It was impossible to convince them that it is not a question of physically moving to India or Pakistan. It was a political question: 'Under which country, within which boundary do you want to remain?'

Finally it was decided by the officials that the madhouse should also be divided into two parts. One would be in India, one would be in Pakistan. They raised a huge wall, dividing the whole madhouse in two.

And I have heard that the mad people still climb up on the wall, talk to the people on the other side and say, 'We cannot figure it out. We are here, you are here, but you have gone to Pakistan and we have gone to India – just because they have raised this wall. And the strangest thing of all is that they think *we* are mad.'

It is a mad world. All boundaries are absolute nonsense. Anything that divides man from man is inhuman, uncivilized, uncultured. But nobody asks whether nations are a fiction, and because you never ask, you start believing in the reality of nations. Then questions of responsibility toward the nation arise. You even have to sacrifice your life for a nation which is a fiction. No such thing exists anywhere, no India, no Germany, no Japan, no America. It is a single planet, one humanity. But because of the fiction, people go on killing each other. Real people are killed for an unreal idea.

Responsibility toward the nation has been the cause of all wars. If all those people who had gone to war had refused – 'We are not going to kill anybody for a fiction and we are not going to be killed for a fiction' – there would have been no wars, no politicians. The world would have been a peaceful, beautiful place to live in. For centuries we have done nothing except fight, except kill. Our only profession seems to be war. Sometimes we fight, and sometimes we prepare for a future fight.

All the time we are engaged in a single profession – that of murderers – because we have been taught a stupid idea: responsibility toward your nation, responsibility toward your religion. All the religions have been teaching that your life is not more valuable than your religion. It is such a strange idea. All these things should be for man, not vice versa.

A religion exists to help man, not to destroy man. But all religions have been destroying man, none has been helping. They say: 'It is your responsibility. If your religion is in trouble or if your religion is trying to conquer bigger territories, to acquire more people, sacrifice is your responsibility.'

It reminds me of the primitive religions because it is a relic of those days. In the ancient book of the Hindus, Rig Veda, they sacrificed to a fictitious God. Nobody has seen him, nobody has any idea what you mean by the very word. There exists no proof, no evidence, no witness. But for that unreal, fictitious God, which is just a hypothesis, men were even sacrificed before a stone statue – a statue that you have made.

There is mention in Rig Veda of *narmedh yagna*. Sacrificing men to God was the greatest ritual. And the man who was ready to be sacrificed was thought to be a saint. Those who could not do such a thing were thought to be cowards, not fulfilling their responsibility. Dying for God – what can be more valuable than that?

After men, they started sacrificing animals. Today all the Hindus of this country continuously try to stop cow slaughter. But they are not aware that their forefathers in the Rig Veda were themselves killing cows as a sacrifice to God. And they were eating the meat of the cows; stone statues don't eat. You make an offering and then you can take it back as a divine gift. Everything is yours: you kill the cow, you offer it to a stone god, who cannot eat, and then you take it back and distribute it to all the worshippers. And those people are continuously trying to stop cow slaughter. They were killing horses, they were killing all kinds of animals. They are still killing.

In Kolkata, at one of the most famous temples of the mother goddess Kali, every day they still kill a few goats and then the goat meat is distributed as *prasad*, as God's gift to the worshippers. And this is a vegetarian country. A strange kind of vegetarianism! When they stopped sacrificing men ... It had been hammered more and more by people like Gautam Buddha and Vardhaman Mahavira that it was absolutely ugly and uncivilized, that eating man in the name of religion was just a strategy to hide their cannibalistic tendencies. Because it was criticized so much, finally they dropped killing men.

But something had to be found as a substitute. Even today, people who are using the substitute may not be aware what they are doing. They found a substitute in the coconut because it looks like the head of a man – two eyes, a little nose, a small beard, hair. In Hindi the head is called *khopri* and the coconut is called *khopra*, so there is not much difference. If you want to visit any temple, you will have to take coconuts. You don't know what you are doing! The statues were once bathed in human blood. Now, that has become difficult. Coconuts are being used, so the statues are colored red. Why red? Blood red.

In the name of God, which is a fiction, your responsibility was to sacrifice yourself. In the name of religion, there have been crusades: Mohammedans killing Christians, Christians killing Mohammedans, Mohammedans killing Hindus, Hindus burning Buddhists alive. And the greatest problem is that what you are doing to man is in the name of something that you cannot provide any existential proof for.

But responsibility ... Responsibility to your parents, responsibility to your wife, responsibility to your husband, responsibility to your children ... Perhaps you have never thought about it: if you love your children, there is no question of responsibility. Because you love, you do things, you enjoy doing them. Nobody can enjoy responsibility. It is too big a word, too heavy. If you are educating your children, is it responsibility or your love? If it is love, then there is no question of any burden; you are not doing something reluctantly, in spite of yourself, just because it has to be done.

But you are concerned about respectability, what others will say. You will be condemned, so you have to take care of your old parents – out of responsibility, not out of love.

Love is completely forgotten, because love needs a revolution in your consciousness. It is not as cheap as responsibility. Responsibility can be taught to you by the priests, by the teachers, but nobody can teach you love. You have to find love yourself, within your being, by raising your consciousness to higher levels. And when love comes, there is no question of responsibility. You do things because you enjoy doing them for the person you love. You are not obliging the person, you don't want anything in return, not even gratitude. On the contrary, you are grateful that the person has allowed you to do something for him. It was your joy, sheer joy.

Love knows nothing of responsibility. It does many things, it is very creative; it shares all that it has, but it is not a responsibility, remember. Responsibility is an ugly word in comparison to love. Love is natural, responsibility is created by the cunning priests, politicians who want to dominate you in the name of God, in the name of the nation, in the name of family, in the name of religion – any fiction will do.

But they don't talk about love. On the contrary, because they are unable to control love, they are all against love. A man of love acts out of his own heart, not according to any moral code. A man of love will not join the army because it is his responsibility to fight for his nation. A man of love will say there are no nations, so there is no question of any fight.

When I was a student at the university, it was made compulsory for every student to join army training, otherwise they would not be given their postgraduate certificates. It was my last year in the university. I went to the vice-chancellor and told him, 'It goes against my consciousness, it goes against my heart to learn anything destructive. And I refuse absolutely to join any training that you are providing for students. I don't care whether you give me the certificate or not.'

He immediately said, 'But don't you feel any responsibility for your nation?'

I said, 'Where is the nation? I have never come across it, except on the map.'

And I told him a story about two men sitting on the sea beach who suddenly began to beat each other. A crowd gathered and they were somehow separated. The police came, they were arrested and taken to the court.

The magistrate said, 'I know you both. You are known in the city as the best of friends. What happened?'

They both felt very ashamed and they looked at each other. One said, 'You tell him what happened,' and the other said, 'Better you tell it.'

The magistrate said, 'What can be such a secret that you are having so much difficulty in telling it?'

They said, 'It is not a secret. It is simply so shameful that we don't want to tell it, but if you insist, we will have to speak.

'We are great friends. We were just sitting on the beach, when this person – my friend – said that he was going to purchase a buffalo. I said, "Buffalo? But remember, she should not enter my field. I am going to purchase a farm and if she enters my farm ... I will not tolerate your buffalo simply because you are my friend. I will kill your buffalo."

'My friend said, "This is too much. Buffaloes are buffaloes. And I cannot follow my buffalo the whole day wherever she goes. She *will* go onto your farm and I will see then who kills my buffalo. I will kill anybody who kills my buffalo. I will not remember that you are my friend. You are my enemy if you kill my buffalo."'

Things came to such a head that the man who had made it clear that he would not tolerate the buffalo, drew a square on the sand with his finger and said, 'This is my farm. Now let us see where your buffalo is.' He does not have a farm yet, nor does the other man have any buffalo.

Both are *thinking* of purchasing.

The other asked, 'This is your farm?' and he ran his finger across 'the farm' saying, 'This is my buffalo. Now do what you want to do.'

And the fight started.

The magistrate said, 'This is too much. Neither does he have the farm, nor do you have a buffalo. You should at least have waited.'

They said, 'It was a hypothetical question, but we forgot that it was hypothetical. We became so excited. Please forgive us.'

We have all forgotten that many hypotheses are asking us to do things which we would never do in our senses, in our intelligence, in our consciousness.

You are asking, 'What is the responsibility of love?' You don't understand those words. You don't understand because you have not loved yet. That's the only reason that you don't understand. If you had loved, you would have experienced a responsibility arising out of it, with no sense of duty, with no sense of burden, but just a sheer joy, a dance, a song of the heart. You are doing something that is needed. You never think that you are obliged.

Love never obliges anybody. Love is always obliged that you allowed the heart to shower upon you its flowers, its joys, its songs. Love is obliged to you for your receptivity. Responsibility always thinks: 'I have done well and everybody should know it. And everybody should feel obliged. I have sacrificed so much for the freedom of the country. I have done so much in the war in defending the country. I am working so hard so that my children can be educated, can be well-nourished, and so that I can provide facilities for my grandparents or my parents.' But you find this a burden. You are crushed under it. It is not a joy, it is not blissfulness, it is not ecstasy.

My grandfather loved very much. He was old, very old, but he remained active to his very last breath. He loved nature almost too much. He lived on a faraway farm. Once in a while he would come to the city, but he never liked it. He always liked the wild world, where he lived.

Sometimes I went to see him and he always liked somebody to massage his feet. He was becoming so old and he was working so hard, so I would massage his feet. But I told him, 'Remember, I am not fulfilling any responsibility. I don't have any responsibility toward anyone in the world. I love you, and I will massage your feet but only up to the point where it is not troublesome to me. So when I stop, never ask me to do a little more. I will not. I am doing it out of my joy, not because you are my grandfather. I could have done the same to any beggar, any stranger, just out of love.'

He understood the point. He said, 'I never thought that responsibility and love are two things. But you are right. When I am working in the fields, I always feel I am doing it for my children and their children, as a duty. It is heavy on my heart. But I will try to change this attitude of responsibility. I may be too old to change – it has become a fixation in my mind – but I will try to change.'

I said to him, 'There is no need. If you feel it is becoming a burden on you, you have done enough. You rest. There is no need to continue working unless you enjoy the open sky and the green fields and love these trees and the birds. If you are doing it out of joy and you love your children and you want to do something for them, only then continue. Otherwise stop.' Although he was old, something synchronized between me and him.

That never happened with any other member of my family. We were great friends. I was the youngest in the family and he was the oldest, just two polarities. And everybody in the house laughed. 'What kind of friendship is this? You laugh together, you joke with each other, you play with each other, you run after each other. And he is so old and you are so young. And you don't communicate the same way with anybody else, nor does he communicate the same way with anybody else.'

I said, 'Something has happened between us. He loves me and I love him. Now it is no longer a question of any relationship; neither am I his grandchild nor is he my grandfather. We are just two friends: one is old, one is young.'

Once you taste love, you will drop the word *responsibility* completely. Hence your question 'What is the responsibility of love?' is simply irrelevant. Love needs no responsibility, and responsibility knows no love. I don't teach you any responsibility because I don't want you to be sacrificed in any fictitious name. I want you to live as naturally, existentially as possible. Don't live according to hypotheses. Don't live according to moral codes. Don't live according to Manu or Moses. Live according to your own heart and whatever you do will be right. Never ask anybody what is right. Only a man who has no heart asks that kind of question. Let your heart respond to your question. Your answer is not going to come by any scripture, any holy tradition.

I have heard...

When God made the world, he went to the Babylonians and asked them, 'Would you like to have a commandment?'

They said, 'First tell us what the commandment is.'

God said, 'Thou shall not commit adultery.'

The Babylonians replied, 'Then what shall we do? No, we don't want any such commandment.'

He went to the Egyptians with the same result. He went to other people – the same. They all asked, 'What is the commandment? Don't trick us into some trouble. First be completely clear: What is your commandment?'

Finally he went to Moses and asked, 'Would you like to have a commandment?'

Moses asked, 'How much?' God said, 'It is free.'

Moses said, 'Then I will have ten.'

Because of this Jewish mind, millions of Jews since that time have been living according to those ten commandments.

I was in Greece and one of my sannyasins, Amrito, told me that the Greek Orthodox Church is very old-fashioned, very traditional. It insists on every woman being a virgin until she gets married. She has been one of the most beautiful women herself. When she was young she was chosen to be the beauty queen of Greece and since then she has been a top model. She was telling me about this emphasis of the Greek church on virginity.

I asked her, 'But is it followed?'

She said, 'Don't ask such a question. You will not find a single virgin in the whole of Greece.'

I remember she told me that in a church a priest was hammering hard on the fact. 'If you are not a virgin, you will suffer eternal hell-fire. So if any woman here is a virgin, stand up.' Nobody stood up, everybody was looking down. He said, 'I give you another chance. Stand up! At least for God's sake, one or two women should stand up.' Finally, one woman with a small baby stood up. And the priest said, 'You think you are a virgin?'

She said, 'No, I am not a virgin. This baby is a virgin. But she cannot stand on her own. She is the only virgin in the whole congregation. She is only six months old, so I have to stand up.'

People have been forced into all kinds of nonsense, and they have been made to feel guilty if they don't follow the codes. If they follow them, they become unnatural. They start becoming miserable, they become unnecessarily tense. Because they are going against life, they lose all juice in life. Love is not a religious commandment. Love is your innermost longing, your very nature. Responsibility is imposed from outside and it is needed only by those who have not grown up in love. If you have grown up in love, you can throw away all responsibility. Love is enough unto itself.

Your question makes me feel sad that you have not yet experienced love. But this is the situation of the greater part of humanity. Forget all about responsibility, search deep in your being for the space which we call love. Once you have found that space within you, it expands. On its own, it starts growing. It goes spreading around you, radiating around you. It becomes your very aura, your very energy field, and whoever comes into that energy field is touched, deeply touched, by your joy, your celebrating realization, your love. But it is not a responsibility at all.

Little Ernie is playing with the girl next door. 'Let us play Adam and Eve,' he says. 'You tempt me to eat the apple and I will give in.'

Be Adam and Eve, as if you are the first people in the world. You don't have any past, you don't have any Moses and you don't have any Manu and you don't have any Confucius. There is no past.

Adam and Eve had a certain freedom which you don't have: they had no past, only an open future. You don't have any future because you are always looking at the past and the past is gone. You can see the dust a long way back on the road, but you cannot reach again to the same place. What is gone, is gone. And remember: existence has not given you eyes in your neck. If it was the intention of existence that you should look back, it would have given you eyes in the back of your head. What is the point of giving you eyes looking forward when you are not looking forward?

Responsibility is looking backward; love is looking forward. Be innocent like Adam and Eve, as if you have just arrived fresh and you don't have anything to do with the past. You have to find your own way; there is no guide, there is no holy scripture, there is no prophet, no savior. You are left alone to find your path. You will not find responsibility, you will find spontaneity. You will not find duty, you will find love.

If your life is nothing but pure love, you don't need any other spirituality. Love is the best name you can give to God because love is something which is not a hypothesis. It is your intrinsic reality – and it is the most precious thing in you.

A Jewish boy is courting a Catholic girl. 'I'm sorry I could not see you last night,' she says, 'but I had to go to confession.'

'I hope you don't tell the old priest all about the things we do when your parents are out,' says the boy.

'Sure, I do,' she says. 'But don't worry. I just slip Father Murphy ten bucks and he makes things okay for me.'

The next evening the Jewish boy arrives at the Catholic church to see the priest. 'Aha,' says Father Murphy. 'My son, I suppose you have come for confession.'

'No Father, not likely,' says the boy. 'I have come for my commission.'

In fact, all your religions are nothing but business. And the boy is right to ask for a commission!

Love is not a business and love is not a sin. Love is your greatest virtue. Love is your highest flowering. Sharing it is sheer joy. Don't call it *responsibility*. That word has become too heavy due to continuous use by those people whose vested interests are served by it. Love serves nobody. It gives you individuality and a tremendous sense of freedom. Love makes you courageous enough to assert your uniqueness in a world where the crowd respects only those who belong to the crowd.

The unique person does not belong to the crowd. He stands alone and aloof like a very tall tree reaching toward the stars. The small bushes, naturally, feel jealous. Hence every great man in the world is going to be condemned by the pygmies. They will find all kinds of excuses to condemn anyone who has something unique in him. Any individual who is not surrendering his freedom to the crowd is going to be condemned. I want you to be individuals, not respectable people. They are the ugliest people in the world. Those who are thought to be respectable are the most condemnable because they have sold their souls for their respectability. They have become slaves of a crowd which knows nothing of the higher things of life, the higher values of life.

Just be yourself, silent, peaceful, meditative, and love will arise in tidal waves and will go on coming to you from unknown sources which are hidden inside you. Those sources are as oceanic as any great ocean in the world. And you can share that love without humiliating anyone and without feeding your ego. These two things are done by responsibility; it feeds your ego, makes it stronger and humiliates the other person.

You may not be aware that whenever you do something because of responsibility, the other person can never forgive you. You have insulted him. But when you do something out of love, nobody feels any humiliation because love is humble; it cannot humiliate. Responsibility is not the quality of a humble person, it is the quality of the egoist who wants to make everybody obliged to him, who wants everybody to be a beggar and he the giver. He always wants to keep the upper hand. Nobody can forgive such a man. They may give him respect in the crowd, but behind his back they all feel utterly insulted – and they take revenge.

Love never humiliates; hence there is no question of revenge. It simply rejoices in giving: it gives and it forgets. It does not even remember to whom it has given, what it has given. It does not keep an account of all that it has shared. It goes on, moment to moment, singing its song to whoever is capable of understanding it. Whoever is capable of receiving it, will receive it. The person who does something out of love is not doing any social service, he is not a public servant. He is a man who knows how to celebrate. He is celebrating himself.

In the three hundred years of America, there have not been many men who can be compared to the great mystics of the world. Only one man, a poet, comes very close to the mystics – Walt Whitman. One of his beautiful poems is, *I Celebrate Myself.* America has not paid much attention to Walt Whitman, but he is the only one in the three hundred years of America's life who has reached the highest peak possible.

When he says 'I celebrate myself' he is saying everything about love. 'And if you can rejoice in my celebration, you are welcome. If you can be my guest, I invite you to celebrate.'

Love celebrates. It is not a responsibility at all.

Osho,
Why is it so hard to accept being a failure? I would rather sacrifice my well- being than admit that I have failed.

The question you have asked is the question of all those people who have been trained to be egoists, and unfortunately the whole of modern education, which is based on modern psychology, teaches everybody to be an egoist, strong, crystallized.

The idea is that you are being prepared by education for a world which is competitive. It is a constant battle. Everybody is your enemy because everybody is your competitor. And unless you have a very strong ego, you will not become a president, you will not become a prime minister, you will not succeed in becoming the richest man in the world. You will remain a nobody, left by the side of the road, and the whole caravan of competitors will move on ahead of you. You will be crushed under everybody. This fear has been created in every child from the very beginning: you have to be very strong, otherwise you will be crushed. Everybody is trying to be victorious in some way or other. Everybody is competing to get ahead, to become somebody special.

Your question has arisen because of this wrong teaching, this utterly inhuman teaching. You are a victim of a wrong world, of a wrong civilization, of a wrong educational system. You are asking, 'Why is it so hard to accept being a failure?' Because it hurts the ego; otherwise there is no problem.

I have told you about one incident that I have never forgotten and will never forget.

In India, there is one day every year devoted to the worship of snakes. On that day, all over India, there are wrestling competitions. For many years, my school used to be the champion of the whole district. This was due entirely to a single student who failed every year in matriculation. The school was happy about it because he was a good wrestler.

The principal and the teachers all said to him, 'Don't be worried. You can fail as much as you want, but every year you have to win the championship for the school. And when you are tired, we will give you some employment in the school. Don't be worried about your employment, although you are not even a matriculate. We will make some arrangements, we can make you a peon: you do not need to be a matriculate.'

He was very happy that a job was guaranteed and every year he was the hero. But the year I reached my matric class, that man unfortunately passed the examination. The whole school was sad and sorry. The principal called me and said, 'Now find somebody, for up to now we have always won.'

I said, 'It is a difficult thing to find a wrestler of his quality.' He was doing nothing but exercises the whole day, morning till evening. The school was providing him with as much milk as he needed, because every year he won the championship. 'It will be very difficult to find somebody, but I will try.'

In my class there was a man, a young man, not very strong and not in any way a wrestler, but a very beautiful person with a great sense of humor. I told him he would have to do this.

He said, 'I have never fought anybody. I have never been in any competition. I have never done any exercise. And the people who will be coming from other schools are trained.'

I said, 'Don't be worried. Somebody has at least to participate. At the most you can be a failure.'

He said, 'If that is all, then I am ready.' And what he did left an impact on everybody.

It was going to be decided in the semi-finals, and because my school was continuously the champion, every other school was afraid. They were still thinking that because of our man we would finally win. So they had brought a professional wrestler who was not a student. They could find no other way to defeat our man who had won continuously for ten years.

Naturally, they had to find some way. So they looked and found a wrestler who was not too old and they shaved him well and prepared him perfectly as if he were a student. But he was a trained wrestler and our candidate was not a wrestler at all. He asked me, 'What am I supposed to do?'

I said, 'Make it fun. Don't be worried.'

I had once seen a wrestler ... The village where I lived was famous throughout the area for wrestlers. There were so many gymnasiums in that small village and wrestlers from outside used to come to fight with the wrestlers of the village.

Once I had watched a wrestler and had become very friendly with him. His style was very new. First he would dance around. The other wrestler was standing in the middle, looking embarrassed, and he would dance. He had a very beautiful body. He would dance all over the place. His dance made the other man feel embarrassed and a little afraid also. 'If this man is dancing with such joy, there must be some strategy that will defeat me.' Then the wrestler would suddenly jump to the ground. He was not a very strong man, but he had a very beautiful body, a very proportionate body.

By his dancing he had made the other man so afraid by this time. It was so out of the ordinary – nobody danced. There was no real need to dance because most of the time he would anyway win.

I liked the man very much. He used to stay in a temple nearby, so I went to visit him. I said, 'This is very beautiful. This is how things should be. You have a great psychological insight.'

So I told the boy, 'You do the same. First you dance around. Make the other fellow feel completely embarrassed. And we are here, because the competition is going to happen in our school.

All the students, all the teachers will be there. We will clap when you dance. We will laugh and cheer you. So dance, and don't be worried about that man. Let him stand in the middle, embarrassed, worried, "What is going to happen, what is happening?"'

Nothing happened. He danced and we clapped and shouted and cheered, and that man looked near defeat. But the boy that I had chosen was no match for him. He was a wrestler and this boy had no idea. He danced, and then he simply jumped into the middle and fell flat on the ground.

In Indian wrestling, the person who falls to the ground with his back touching the ground and the other person sitting on his chest is thought to be defeated; the man sitting on his chest is the winner. So that boy without fighting simply fell in front of him and we all cheered him and the man could not think what to do.

The boy said, 'Sit on my chest. Sit down and be victorious!' The man could not bring himself to sit down on the chest of the boy who had fallen by himself. He looked all around and the boy was smiling.

The referee came over and said, 'What do you want to do with your opponent?'

The man said, 'I am simply puzzled. What kind of wrestling is going on? Sitting on this poor boy's chest looks so ugly. I have not fought, how can I be victorious? And he is telling me to sit down. He is almost ordering me.'

They were declared to be equal. We took the boy on our shoulders and we danced around. And the principal called to me, 'You managed at least to be equal. I had no hope that this was possible and when I saw that boy that you had chosen, I thought the trophy was gone. But you trained him well.'

I said, 'I only trained him for dancing. What he did was absolutely spontaneous. Seeing the situation he said "I am going to be defeated. What is the point of fighting unnecessarily and being harassed. Just lie down, rest."'

But he was a very humble person with a great sense of humor.

You feel unnecessarily worried that you cannot accept being a failure. You are saying, 'I would rather sacrifice my well-being than admit that I have failed.' The very idea of being competitive is egoistic. It is sick. There is nothing wrong in being a failure. Just be a total failure! Do everything that you can do, and if failure comes out of it, accept it with dignity. Somebody has to fail, somebody has to win. You should not be so attached to your own ego that you always have to win.

Once in a while, just for a change, failing is not bad. As much can be learned by failure as can be learned by victory. You can learn egolessness, you can learn humbleness, you can learn accepting whatever life brings to you. And all these things will give you maturity. Then who is bothered who is the winner and who is the failure? People are unnecessarily concerned that the whole world is watching. Nobody has time. Everybody is interested in his own competition.

After being elected as President of America, Ronald Reagan returns to the small town where he grew up. 'I suppose you folks here all know of the great honor that has been conferred on me?' he asks an old school friend.

'Yes,' comes the reply.

'And what do they all say about it?' Reagan asks.

'They don't say anything,' replies the man. 'They just laugh.'

Who cares? People simply laugh that this idiot has become the president. In fact, if you are a failure, you may have the sympathy of everybody. But if you are a winner, you won't get anybody's sympathy.

One should take life almost like a playground. One should learn gamesmanship. One should know that somebody has to be the winner and somebody has to be the loser. And if you are a humble man, you would rather be a failure than deprive somebody else of victory. Perhaps you have never thought about the possibility of enjoying failure because you have given somebody else the chance of enjoying victory. His victory depends on you. You could have deprived him of victory.

All that is needed is a deep awareness to think and to see that these are the only two possibilities. Fight with your total energy and intensity, but it is not necessary that you should be the winner. And when the other wins, rejoice in his victory too. It was a beautiful game. Don't feel defeated. Your failure is a defeat only if you have not put your whole energy into it. If you do, you can make your failure more valuable than victory itself.

You seem to be a very serious person. Take life as a game, enjoy every side of it: the failure, the victory, going astray or finding the right path, the darkness of the night and the beautiful dawn. Enjoy both sides, all the possibilities, and learn from every experience something that brings you more maturity. And learn to be a little less serious and a little more understanding. Have a little more sense of humor.

Just for you, a small story...

Three women die and arrive at the Pearly Gates, where they are met by Saint Peter. 'Did you avoid sex on the earth?' he asks the first lady.

'I absolutely avoided it,' she replies.

'Very good,' says Peter. 'Here is a golden key. It will open the doors of paradise.'

Then he turns to the second woman and asks, 'What about you?'

'Well,' she replies, 'about half and half.'

'Okay,' says Peter. 'Here is a silver key. It will open the doors of purgatory.'

Then he asks the third woman, 'What about you?'

'Me?' she replies. 'I did all the things you can imagine and also many things you can't imagine.'

'Great!' says Peter. 'Here is the key to my room. I'll be coming there in a minute.'

About Osho

Osho defies categorization. Mystic and scientist, a rebellious spirit whose sole interest is to alert humanity to the urgent need to discover a new way of living. To continue as before is to invite threats to our very survival on this unique and beautiful planet.

His thousands of talks cover everything from the individual quest for meaning to the most urgent social, political and environmental issues facing society today. Osho's books are not written but transcribed from audio and video recordings of his extemporaneous talks to international audiences. And he tells them, "Remember: whatever I am saying is not just for you...I am talking also for the future generations."

Osho has been described by *The Sunday Times* in London as one of the "1000 Makers of the 20th Century" and by American author Tom Robbins as "the most dangerous man since Jesus Christ." *Sunday Mid-Day* (Mumbai) has selected Osho as one of ten people – along with Gandhi, Nehru and Buddha – who have changed the destiny of India.

About his own work, Osho has said that he is helping to create the conditions for the birth of a new kind of human being. He often characterizes this new human being as "Zorba the Buddha" – capable both of enjoying the earthy pleasures of a Zorba the Greek and the silent serenity of a Gautama the Buddha.

Running like a thread through all aspects of Osho's talks and meditations is a vision that encompasses both the timeless wisdom of all ages past and the highest potential of today's (and tomorrow's) science and technology.

Osho is known for his revolutionary contribution to the science of inner transformation, with an approach to meditation that acknowledges the accelerated pace of contemporary life. His unique OSHO Active Meditations® are designed to first release the accumulated stresses of body and mind, so that it then becomes easier to experience a stillness and thought-free relaxation which can be taken into daily life.

Two autobiographical works by the author are available:

Autobiography of a Spiritually Incorrect Mystic, St. Martin's Press, New York (book and eBook)

Glimpses of a Golden Childhood, OSHO Media International, Pune, India (book and eBook)

OSHO International Meditation Resort

Each year the Meditation Resort welcomes thousands of people from more than 100 countries. The unique campus provides an opportunity for a direct personal experience of a new way of living – with more awareness, relaxation, celebration and creativity. A great variety of around-the-clock and around-the-year program options are available. Doing nothing and just relaxing is one of them!

All of the programs are based on Osho's vision of "Zorba the Buddha" – a qualitatively new kind of human being who is able *both* to participate creatively in everyday life *and* to relax into silence and meditation.

Location

Located 100 miles southeast of Mumbai in the thriving modern city of Pune, India, the OSHO International Meditation Resort is a holiday destination with a difference. The Meditation Resort is spread over 28 acres of spectacular gardens in a beautiful tree-lined residential area.

OSHO Meditations

A full daily schedule of meditations for every type of person includes both traditional and revolutionary methods, and particularly the OSHO Active Meditations®. The daily meditation program takes place in what must be the world's largest meditation hall, the OSHO Auditorium.

OSHO Multiversity

Individual sessions, courses and workshops cover everything from creative arts to holistic health, personal transformation, relationship and life transitions, transforming meditation into a lifestyle for life and work, esoteric sciences, and the Zen approach to sports and recreation. The secret of the OSHO Multiversity's success lies in the fact that all its programs are combined with meditation, supporting the understanding that as human beings we are far more than the sum of our parts.

Cuisine

A variety of different eating areas serve delicious Western, Asian and Indian vegetarian food – most of it organically grown especially for the Meditation Resort. Breads and cakes are baked in the resort's bakery.

Night life

There are many evening events to choose from – dancing being at the top of the list! Other activities include full-moon meditations beneath the stars, variety shows, music performances and "meditations for daily life."

Facilities

At the Meditation Resort you can buy all of your basic necessities and toiletries in the Galleria. In addition, the Multimedia Gallery sells a large range of OSHO media products. For those who enjoy shopping, Pune provides all the options, ranging from traditional and ethnic Indian products to all of the global brand-name stores.

Accommodation

You can choose to stay in the elegant rooms of the OSHO Guesthouse, or for longer stays on campus you can select one of the OSHO Living-In programs. Additionally there is a variety of nearby hotels and serviced apartments.

www.osho.com/meditationresort
www.osho.com/guesthouse
www.osho.com/livingin
Facebook: osho.international.meditation.resort

OSHO Books (English)

(OSHO books are available in Printed book and eBook formats, and most of them in audio format too. If a book is not available in one format, you can look up and buy it in another format.)

Early Talks

The Art of Living
Astrology
Breaking All Boundaries
Compassion and Revolution
Dimensions beyond the Known
The Eternal Quest
From Sex to Superconsciousness
The Great Challenge
Hidden Mysteries
I Am the Gate
The Independent Mind
Into the Void
Keys to a New Life
New Dimensions of Yoga
The Psychology of the Esoteric
Religion's Expiration Date
The Search for Peace
Woman and Rebellion
Work Is Love Made Visible

Meditation

And Now and Here
Body/Mind Balancing (Book & Audio)
Falling In Love with Darkness
In Search of the Miraculous
The Inner Journey
Just a Small Step
Meditation: The Art of Ecstasy
Meditation: The First and Last Freedom
The Path of Meditation
The Perfect Way
Silence: The Message of Your Being
Three Steps to Awakening

Buddha and Buddhist Masters

The Book of Wisdom
The Dhammapada: The Way of the Buddha (Vols 1-12)

The Diamond Sutra
The Discipline of Transcendence (Vols 1-4)
The Heart Sutra
The Great Secret
The Guest
The Path of Love
The Revolution

Indian Mystics

As if a Tree Starts Running (Yari))
The Beloved, Vols 1 & 2 (Baul Mystics)
Bliss:Living beyond Happiness and Misery (Shiva)
Die O Yogi Die (Gorakh)
Enlightenment: The Only Revolution (Ashtavakra)
Geeta Darshan Vol. 1 (Adhyaya 1-2)
Geeta Darshan, Vol.2 (Adhyaya 3)
Krishna: The Man and His Philosophy
The Last Morning Star (Daya)
Showering without Clouds (Sahajo)
The Song of Ecstasy (Adi Shankara)
The True Name (Vols 1&2) (Nanak)

Kabir

The Divine Melody
Ecstasy: The Forgotten Language
The Fabric of Life
The Fish in the Sea Is Not Thirsty

Western Mystics

The Art of Dying *(Hasidism)*
Come Follow to You, Vols 1-4 *(Jesus)*
Guida Spirituale (*Desiderata*)
The Hidden Harmony *(Heraclitus)*
I Say Unto You, Vols 1 & 2 *(Jesus)*
The Mustard Seed *(Jesus)*
The New Alchemy: To Turn You On (Mabel Collins)
Philosophia Perennis, Vols 1 & 2 (*Pythagoras*)
Reflections on Kahlil Gibran's *The Prophet*
Theologia Mystica *(Dionysius)*
The True Sage *(Hasidism)*
The Voice of Silence (Mabel Collins)
Zarathustra: A God That Can Dance (Nietzsche's *Thus Spake Zarathustra*)
Zarathustra: The Laughing Prophet (Nietzsche's *Thus Spake Zarathustra*)

Sufism

Just Like That

The Perfect Master, Vols 1 & 2
The Secret
Sufis: The People of the Path, Vols 1 & 2
Unio Mystica, Vols 1 & 2
Until You Die
The Wisdom of the Sands, Vols 1 & 2

Tantra

The Book of Secrets (Vigyan Bhairav Tantra)
The Tantra Experience (Saraha)
Tantra: The Supreme Understanding (Tilopa)
Tantric Transformation (Saraha)

The Upanishads

Behind a Thousand Names (Nirvana Upanishad)
Finger Pointing to the Moon (Adhyatma Upanishad)
Flight of the Alone to the Alone (Kaivalya Upanishad)
The Heartbeat of the Absolute (Ishavasya Upanishad)
I Am That (Isa Upanishad)
The Message beyond Words (Kathopanishad)
Philosophia Ultima (Mandukya Upanishad)
The Supreme Doctrine (Kenopanishad)
That Art Thou (Sarvasar Upanishad, Kaivalya Upanishad, Adhyatma Upanishad)
The Ultimate Alchemy, Vols 1 & 2 (Atma Pooja Upanishad)
Vedanta: Seven Steps to Samadhi (Akshaya Upanishad)
The Way beyond Any Way (Sarvasar Upanishad)

Tao

The Empty Boat (Chuang Tzu)
The Secret of Secrets (The Secret of Golden Flower)
Tao: The Golden Gate, Vols 1 & 2 (Ko Hsuan)
Tao: The Pathless Path, Vols 1 & 2 (Lieh Tzu)
Tao: The Three Treasures, Vols 1-4 (Lao Tzu)
When the Shoe Fits (Chuang Tzu)

Yoga (Patanjali)

Yoga: The Science of the Soul, Vols 1-10
- The Path of Yoga (Vol.1)
- The Heart of Yoga (Vol.2)
- Yoga: The Mystery beyond Mind (Vol.3)
- The Alchemy of Yoga (Vol.4)

- Yoga: A New Direction (Vol.5)
- Essence of Yoga (Vol.6)
- Yoga: The Science of Living (Vol.7)
- Secrets of Yoga (Vol.8)
- Yoga: The Path to Liberation (Vol.9)
- Yoga: The Supreme Science (Vol.10)

Zen and Zen Masters

Ah, This!
Ancient Music in the Pines
And the Flowers Showered…
And the Grass Grows By Itself…
A Bird on the Wing
Bodhidharma: The Greatest Zen Master
The Buddha: The Emptiness of the Heart
Christianity, the Deadliest Poison and Zen, the Antidote to All Poisons
Communism and Zen Fire, Zen Wind
Dang Dang Doko Dang
The First Principle
God Is Dead: Now Zen Is the Only Living Truth
The Great Zen Master Ta Hui
Hsin Hsin Ming: The Book of Nothing
I Celebrate Myself: God Is No Where, Life Is Now Here
Kyozan: A True Man of Zen
The Language of Existence
Live Zen
The Miracle
Nirvana: The Last Nightmare
No Mind: The Flowers of Eternity
No Water, No Moon
One Seed Makes the Whole Earth Green
The Original Man
Returning to the Source
The Search: Talks on the 10 Bulls of Zen
A Sudden Clash of Thunder
The Sun Rises in the Evening
Take it Easy
This. This. A Thousand Times This
This Very Body the Buddha
Turning In
The White Lotus
Yakusan: Straight to the Point of Enlightenment
The Zen Manifesto: Freedom from Oneself
Zen: The Diamond Thunderbolt
Zen: The Mystery and the Poetry of the Beyond
Zen: The Path of Paradox, Vols 1-3

Zen: The Quantum Leap from Mind to No-Mind
Zen: The Solitary Bird, Cuckoo of the Forest
Zen: The Special Transmission

Osho: On the Ancient Masters of Zen

Dogen: The Zen Master
Hyakujo: The Everest of Zen – With Basho's haikus
Isan: No Footprints in the Blue Sky
Joshu: The Lion's Roar
Ma Tzu: The Empty Mirror
Nansen: The Point of Departure
Rinzai: Master of the Irrational

Responses to Questions

Be Still and Know
Beyond Enlightenment (Talks in Bombay)
Beyond Psychology (Talks in Uruguay)
Come, Come, Yet Again Come
The Diamond Sword
From Bondage to Freedom
From Darkness to Light
From Death to Deathlessness
From Ignorance to Innocence
From Misery to Enlightenment
From Personality to Individuality
From the False to the Truth
From Unconsciousness to Consciousness
The Goose Is Out
The Great Pilgrimage: From Here to Here
The Invitation
Light on the Path (Talks in the Himalayas)
My Way: The Way of the White Clouds
Nowhere to Go but In
The Osho Upanishad (Talks in Bombay)
The Path of the Mystic (Talks in Uruguay)
The Razor's Edge
Sermons in Stones (Talks in Bombay)
Socrates Poisoned Again After 25 Centuries (Talks in Greece)
The Sword and the Lotus (Talks in the Himalayas)
Transmission of the Lamp (Talks in Uruguay)
Walk without Feet, Fly without Wings and Think without Mind
The Wild Geese and the Water
Yaa-Hoo! The Mystic Rose
Walking in Zen, Sitting in Zen
Zen: Zest, Zip, Zap and Zing

Osho's Vision for the World
The Golden Future
The Hidden Splendor
The New Dawn
The Rebel
The Rebellious Spirit

The Mantra Series
Hari Om Tat Sat
Om Mani Padme Hum
Om Shantih Shantih Shantih
Sat Chit Anand
Satyam Shivam Sundaram

Personal Glimpses
Books I Have Loved
Glimpses of a Golden Childhood
Notes of a Madman

Interviews with the World Press
The Man of Truth: A Majority of One

Meetings with Individuals
Above All Don't Wobble
Hammer on the Rock

Quotation Books
Gold Nuggets
More Gold Nuggets
Words From A Man of No Words

Letters and Writings
A Cup of Tea
Earthen Lamps
Flowers of Love
Life Is a Soap Bubble
Love Letters to Life
Seeds of Wisdom

For any information about OSHO Books, please contact:

OSHO Media International
17 Koregaon Park, Pune – 411001, MS, India
Phone: +91-20-66019999 Fax: +91-20-66019990
E-mail: distribution@osho.net
Website: http://www.osho.com

For More Information

The official website of OSHO International is www.OSHO.com

www.OSHO.com/AllAboutOSHO is a comprehensive portal to all things OSHO.

www.OSHO.com/AllAboutOSHO
www.OshoTimes.com
shop.OSHO.com
iOSHO.OSHO.com
YouTube: OSHO/OSHOinternational
Twitter: OSHO
Instagram: OSHOinternational
Facebook: OSHO.international
Facebook: OSHO.international.meditation.resort

ALSO IN THE MANTRA SERIES